THE BIOLOGICAL WEAPONS CONVENTION

This book is dedicated to a generation of scholars that supported the Biological Weapons Convention and worked tirelessly to prevent biological warfare becoming a reality. There is still much work to be done.

The Biological Weapons Convention
Convention
A Failed Revolution

JEZ LITTLEWOOD

ASHGATE

© Jez Littlewood 2005

All rights reserved. No part of this publication may be reproduced, stored in a retrieval system, or transmitted in any form or by any means, electronic, mechanical, photocopying, recording or otherwise without the prior permission of the publisher.

Jez Littlewood has asserted his right under the Copyright, Designs and Patents Act, 1988, to be identified as author of this work.

Published by
Ashgate Publishing Limited
Gower House
Croft Road
Aldershot
Hampshire GU11 3HR
England

Ashgate Publishing Company
Suite 420
101 Cherry Street
Burlington, VT 05401-4405
USA

Ashgate website: http://www.ashgate.com

British Library Cataloguing in Publication Data
Littlewood, Jez
   The Biological Weapons Convention : a failed revolution
   1. Convention on the Prohibition of the Development,
   Production and Stockpiling of Bacteriological (Biological)
   and Toxin Weapons and on their Destruction (1972)
   2.Biological arms control 3.Bioterrorism - Prevention
   4.Biological warfare (International law)
   I.Title
   327.1'745'09

Library of Congress Cataloging-in-Publication Data
Littlewood, Jez.
   The Biological Weapons Convention : a failed revolution / by Jez Littlewood.
     p. cm.
   Includes index.
   ISBN 0-7546-3854-5
 1. Convention on the Prohibition of the Development, Production, and Stockpiling of Bacteriological (Biological) and Toxin Weapons and on Their Destruction (1972) 2. Biological arms control. 3. Biological warfare (International law) I. Title.

   KZ5865.B56L58 2004
   341.7'35--dc22

                                                 2004019639

ISBN 0 7546 3854 5

Printed and bound by Athenaeum Press, Ltd.,
Gateshead, Tyne & Wear.

KC
1395
L4

Contents

List of Tables		*vi*
Acknowledgements		*vii*
List of Abbreviations		*ix*

Part I   The Biological Weapons Convention

Introduction		3
1	*Minimalism* and *Reform* in the Biological Weapons Convention	9
2	From VEREX to Ad Hoc Group	47

Part II   The Protocol Negotiations

3	Declarations	65
4	Visits and Clarification Procedures	89
5	Investigations	119
6	Export Controls	139
7	Peaceful Co-operation	163
8	The Organization	187

Part III   Failure and its Implications

9	The Protocol: Useful or Useless?	203
10	The Implications of Failure	223
Index		*245*

List of Tables

Table 1.1	Options and choices in 1991	31
Table 2.1	Measures identified and examined by VEREX	52
Table 3.1	Composite text declarations	68
Table 6.1	Export control models	150
Table 7.1	Statements related to Article X in Final Declarations 1980-1996	168
Table 7.2	Specific measures for Article X in Final Declarations 1980-1996	168
Table 7.3	Co-operation principles in the composite text	179
Table 7.4	Co-operation measures in the composite text	180
Table 9.1	Areas of strong differences in views	210
Table 10.1	From the individual to the international	235

Acknowledgements

A piece of research such as this would not have been brought into the public domain without the assistance of a great number of people and organizations. Principal among these is the Department of Peace Studies at the University of Bradford (UK), which provided me with a three-year PhD scholarship to do something on biological weapons. Without that funding this work could not have been begun. I remain extremely grateful for that financial and intellectual investment by the Department.

Within the Department, numerous people were of great assistance between 1997 and 2001. Particular mention must be made to the team of scholars involved in the *Project on the Strengthening of the Biological and Toxin Weapons Convention* who offered enormous amounts of help and assistance: Malcolm Dando, Graham Pearson, Paul Rogers, and Simon Whitby. Malcolm Dando supervised the research throughout my PhD and I could not have wished for a better mentor under which to serve my academic apprenticeship: I remain in Malcolm's debt. Particular reference must be made to the freedom he and the Department gave me to study and work in Geneva while ensuring this PhD was completed in the allotted timeframe. Many thanks.

Intrinsically linked to this is the thanks to be given to the BWC states parties and UN personnel who first took me on as an intern in 1998 and later bound me to the BWC through a number of short term contracts between 1999 and 2002. Ambassador Tibor Tóth of Hungary served as Chairman of the Ad Hoc Group and President of the Fifth Review Conference and gave me the opportunity to have a ringside seat at the BWC for a few years. As thanks for that I only hope I was able to make his work a little bit easier than it might otherwise have been and to have provided the Secretariat Ambassador Tóth put together with some added value. Silvana da Silva also deserves special mention for guiding me around the UN system with such skill and overseeing the work of the relatively young Secretariat team at crucial periods. Within the Secretariat two others are of particular mention. Carol Brown, who looked after all our documentation, took me under her wing and taught me how to get things done in the UN. Her presence in the Ad Hoc Group saved us many times over. Finally, Iris Hunger served the Ad Hoc Group from its seventh through to its twenty-fourth session (1997-2001). Iris organized its work with aplomb, made everyone's life in the Ad Hoc Group much easier, and her in-depth knowledge of BWC issues, the Ad Hoc Group, and her professionalism and contribution set the standard everyone else in the Secretariat had to attain. I am extremely grateful to have worked with such a model professional for what turned out to be four very demanding years.

Outside the Ad Hoc Group, Richard Lennane served as Secretary to the Fifth Review Conference and Secretariat members Jacqueline Simon and Piers Millett deserve special mention. Richard, for his solutions to so many problems and

viii   *The Biological Weapons Convention*

humour in the face of such adversity in 2001 and later in 2002; Piers for his technical knowledge and ingenious (if not always feasible) proposals to solve our problems; and Jacqueline for taking such a burden of work off my own shoulders from November 2001 while ensuring its 'get the job done' attitude would be maintained.

Many scholars and policy-makers have provided excellent advice and comment on my work throughout the last five years. I shall leave the policy-makers and diplomats as unsung here, but in the academic community the following offered support at critical moments of the Ad Hoc Group and PhD process, even if they didn't know it: Marie Chevrier, Mark Wheelis, Barbara Rosenberg, Daniel Feakes, Caitríona McLeish, Gurch Sanghera and Mike Bourne. Nicholas Sims deserves special mention because his own work on the BWC was such an inspiration and he offered many professional and personal assessments of the BWC's twists and turns which were invaluable. If this book can be as useful to someone as *The Diplomacy of Biological Disarmament* was to me then it will have been worth it. Finally, like everyone in the UK chemical and biological arms control community, I owe an enormous debt to Julian Perry Robinson. As the experts' expert on CBW issues, Julian offered advice on important issues and a much needed historical and broader context to my understanding. All I can offer is my thanks and the very highest respect.

At the Mountbatten Centre for International Studies, John Simpson, Darryl Howlett and Ian Kenyon provided excellent comments on the thinking behind this work and with Mark Smith and Tanya Ogilvie-White a much deeper understanding of the WMD treaty-regime process for which I am very grateful.

The University of Southampton and the UK Economic & Social Research Council provided funding for post-doctoral fellowships in calendar years 2002 and 2003 respectively, which provided me with the space and time to put this research aside and stand back from it before turning it into a book. I must also thank my publishers for their patience and advice in the delivery of this book.

Finally, to a person without whom I would never have pursued a degree, never mind an academic career: to Vikki Goddard I owe too much to mention so will let that brevity mask the depth of my admiration for her.

List of Abbreviations

ABM	Anti-Ballistic Missile Treaty
BL1 – BL4	Biosafety Level 1 – Biosafety Level 4
BWC	Biological Weapons Convention
CBMs	Confidence Building Measures
CCC	Consultation, Clarification, and Co-operation
CCD	Conference of the Committee on Disarmament
CD	Conference on Disarmament
CPI	Confidential Proprietary Information
CTBT	Comprehensive Test Ban Treaty
CTBTO	Comprehensive Test Ban Treaty Organization
CWC	Chemical Weapons Convention
ENDC	Eighteen-Nation Disarmament Committee
EU	European Union
FAO	Food and Agriculture Organization
G8	Group of 8
IAEA	International Atomic Energy Agency
INF	Intermediate Nuclear Forces Treaty
INFCIRC	Information Circular [of the IAEA]
NAM	Non-Aligned Movement
NATO	North Atlantic Treaty Organization
NGO	Non-Governmental Organization
NPT	Non-Proliferation Treaty
NSG	Nuclear Suppliers Group
NSI	National Security Information
OAS	Organization of American States
OCPFs	Other Chemical Production Facilities [under the CWC]
OIE	World Organization for Animal Health
OPBW	Organization for the Prohibition of Bacteriological (Biological) Weapons
OPCW	Organisation for the Prohibition of Chemical Weapons
PhRMA	Pharmaceutical and Research Manufacturers of America
START	Strategic Arms Reduction Treaty
UN	United Nations
UNMOVIC	United Nations Monitoring, Verification and Inspection Commission
UNSC	United Nations Security Council
UNSCOM	United Nations Special Commission
VEREX	Verification Experts Group
WHO	World Health Organization
WMD	Weapon(s) of Mass Destruction

PART I
THE BIOLOGICAL WEAPONS CONVENTION

Introduction

In 1995, when negotiations on an additional legally binding instrument to the Biological Weapons Convention (BWC) began, the future looked potentially dangerous with biological weapons and the spectre of bioterrorism creeping up the security agenda. The international community, however, appeared to be both aware and on top of the threat, and had agreed to do something about it at a number of levels. One of those levels – the multilateral one – included strengthening the BWC through an additional legally binding agreement; this was to become the BWC Protocol. The future no longer looks potentially dangerous; it is dangerous. The indiscriminate terrorism of 11 September 2001 and afterwards has altered perceptions. The anthrax letters in the US during Autumn 2001 and the ricin incidents of early 2004 represent biological attacks or crimes, if not quite bioterrorism as imagined by some commentators. Even suspected possession of chemical and biological weapons has been used as a *casus belli* in what may be the first counter-proliferation war of the twenty-first century. Prior to this turn of events, efforts to counter the biological weapons problem at the multilateral level, the Protocol negotiations, collapsed in August 2001. The post-Protocol strategy of the states parties to the BWC, agreed in November 2002, is interim in nature. Indeed its overall effectiveness depends on decisions in 2006.

Although that wider context does influence this book, the focus of this work is the Protocol negotiations themselves. The collapse of the negotiations generated greater interest in the media than their success could have hoped for. As a consequence, myth and reality became blurred. Three years on from the collapse of the negotiations competing conventional wisdoms suggest that either the Protocol was a signed and sealed agreement scuttled by the US at the last moment or a flawed undertaking doomed to fail from the very beginning. In neither example was this the case.

It is too soon to write a history of the negotiations because significant gaps in our information remain to be filled, but in the following chapters I examine the negotiations from their initiation to their collapse with the objective of allowing the intelligent reader to gain a picture of events. A full picture of the negotiations has not yet found its way into the public domain and thus this work will begin to fill that gap. However, 'full picture' is perhaps misleading because this is not an exhaustive study or assessment of all aspects of the Protocol. Important elements of the Protocol, such as the article on definitions of terms, are not covered. Neither is the book a line-by-line, negotiation primer. Space simply does not allow for such an account and, at least for most readers, it would soon become mundane and detached from the important broader perspective. The book does, however, address the central issues in the negotiations related to verification and compliance, non-proliferation, peaceful co-operation, and the formation of a new international organization.

4   *The Biological Weapons Convention*

Readers should also be aware – and constantly bear in mind – that this study represents first and foremost the view of the negotiations from Geneva, rather than the view from London, Washington, Moscow, Pretoria or Tehran. It is of course not an official view from Geneva, but my own personal assessment and interpretation of events based on my presence in Geneva between mid-1998 and the end of 2002. That proviso must be understood, but also added to, because the fact remains that no one ever has a 'full picture' because no one can ever know what is really in the minds of other negotiators and diplomats. And the diplomats themselves are at the mercy of their political masters in their respective capitals.

This work is perhaps best described, therefore, as a guide to the negotiations based on what is known to date. If the international community of diplomats, policy-makers and scholars are to learn the lessons of the BWC's 'failed revolution' then a greater amount of factually correct information must be placed in the public domain. No one can draw appropriate conclusions unless the facts are known. In that endeavour this book is only a useful starting point: it is not intended to be the final word on the Protocol. It aims simply to serve as guide to understanding why the negotiations were begun, what happened during them, and why they collapsed into such ignominious failure.

The structure of the book

This book is structured in three parts. In part one I deal with the pre-Protocol phase of the BWC and provide the background to the negotiations in order to explain how they originated and what they were supposed to deliver. In Chapter one the overall analytical context of this work, which is the notion of *minimalism* and *reform*, is established. I contend that there are two basic types of states parties in the BWC: *minimalist* and *reformist* states parties. *Minimalist* states parties generally support the BWC as a treaty but are reluctant to cede any decisions, power, or sovereignty to a supranational body. Their approach is state-centric and one based on state-primacy, and can best be understood in an international relations framework as being 'realist' in their approach. *Reformist* states parties are better understood as being in the 'liberal internationalist' framework and more particularly their approach can be understood as one rooted in co-operative security. They do not reject the primacy of the state, but recognise collective action is required to tackle a problem beyond their own resources or power to manage. In this respect, they have sought to endow greater power to the states parties collectively to use the BWC as a tool in international security. The two categories serve as a barometer for assessing events in the life of the BWC.

Chapter one assesses the evolution of the BWC from 1975, when it entered into force, through to the Third Review Conference in 1991. What becomes obvious in this period is the actual 'contest' between the two types of states parties. Individual states parties shift between *minimalism* and *reform* and the overall balance of power in terms of which bloc is ascendant, and able to ensure its objectives are met, may change, but the contest continues. Chapter two examines the outcome of the Third Review Conference, the Verification Experts (VEREX)

Introduction 5

group, and the ensuing Special Conference of 1994, which led to the establishment of the Ad Hoc Group. These chapters describe the *minimalism-reform* contest from 1975 through to 1994 and the gradual ascendancy of the *reformists* during this period. The main conclusion to draw from this is that a single state party tipped the balance of power in favour of the *reformists* in 1994. As such, that state party held in its hands the future of the BWC. Any reversal of that 1994 decision would tip the balance back to the *minimalists*. The balance of power in the BWC was therefore precarious and any analysis of the Protocol negotiations should always bear that in mind.

Part two of the book consists of Chapters three through to eight and is the substantive part of the text dealing with the Protocol negotiations. Here I examine the negotiations related to the key problems in the Protocol, in turn looking at the issue of declarations (Chapter three), visits and clarification procedures (Chapter four), investigations (Chapter five), export controls (Chapter six), peaceful co-operation (Chapter seven), and the establishment of an international organization to oversee implementation of the Protocol and the BWC (Chapter eight). Although the focus in these chapters is the negotiations themselves the context of *minimalism* and *reform* remain the basis of understanding. Through an examination of the final version of the draft Protocol, the so-called 'composite text', an assessment of the contentious issues is provided through references to how those problems were resolved, or not, between 1995 and 2001. In short, the on-going *minimalist-reformist* contest.

Part three of the book takes the reader through to the end of 2001 and the collapse of the negotiations on the Protocol. In Chapter nine we explore the different points of view on the strengths or weaknesses of the draft Protocol. In summary, an answer is sought to the key question of whether or not the Protocol was a useful or a useless tool in the fight against biological weapons. The emphasis is on the Protocol as a 'tool' and not as a 'solution' to the biological weapons problem. The important aspect is that most states parties always viewed the Protocol as one of many tools; the Protocol was not seen as a stand-alone agreement – indeed could not be given its link to the BWC – even though it was viewed by some as the central and most important tool to be made available to them in the future. Here, once more, the context of *minimalism* and *reform* provides a useful framework as the decision of a single state party does in fact tip the balance of power in the BWC back to the *minimalists*. In Chapter ten we draw out some of the implications of the failed revolution and the loss of over a decade's worth of effort. The purpose here is to focus in on what it may tell us about arms control, disarmament and non-proliferation in the twenty-first century.

Methodology and sources of information

Throughout this book I draw my own conclusions and outline my own interpretation of events, but where I ascribe a position to a particular state the evidence to draw that conclusion is already in the public domain. In places where it is not possible to decipher which state or group of states is responsible for a particular provision or phrase, I have used my own knowledge to try and deduce the most likely candidate(s), but do so openly. Thus, there is plenty of information that has yet to be comprehensively validated.

This may seem an odd approach given my presence in Geneva for all BWC meetings between July 1998 and December 2002. The reasons for this are twofold, one to do with the veracity of information available and what can actually be established as 'fact' in any negotiations and the second related to confidentiality. Not every state party's position is known or articulated in public. Some states parties are adept at disguising their position and allowing another state party to take the brunt of others' efforts, pressure and attempts to change that position, only to reveal objections after long negotiations appear to have resolved an issue. It is certainly true in these negotiations that a number of states parties were able to 'hide' behind the US position on key topics, as will be explored in later chapters. Events and changes in the negotiations also pass known positions by and the new position may not be stated formally. Thus, in this study the use of the official documentation, particularly the working papers, has its limits and can serve only as a guide to the general position of a state party, except in very specific instances.

That is why the use of secondary sources is important, but even this raises other problems in identifying a state's position on a particular issue. For the media, that information may come from on the record or off the record briefings, but must itself be interpreted and used on the understanding that a diplomat will not tell you something they do not want you to know. Loose talk does occur, but it is much safer to assume that there is always a reason for passing on information and it is not to be assumed that that reason is linked to 'truth' or 'facts' about the negotiations. For the non-governmental community of activists and pressure groups extensive use of the official documentation of the negotiations and, if available, some of the unofficial documentation, provides a deeper insight, particularly when combined with discussions with members of the diplomatic community.

For an academic, the above also apply, but problems begin with citing the source and permitting others to check and follow that source up wherever possible. It is a question of veracity. All those problems apply in this case, but there is the added burden of balancing confidentiality. The Ad Hoc Group first met in January 1995 and broke up in the dawn of 18 August 2001, and the Fifth Review Conference of the BWC convened in November-December 2001 and again in November 2002. I was present at all the official meetings of the Ad Hoc Group from July 1998 – that is from its eleventh session through to its twenty-fourth in August 2001 – and at both sessions of the Review Conference. As a member of the Secretariat I had a ringside seat at the BWC. Outside the plenary sessions of the meetings, which are open, all other aspects of the negotiations took place in private meetings, which are closed to all except delegations, the Secretariat and representatives of recognised bodies according to the rules of procedure. Those discussions are therefore confidential. However, a significant amount of information on the negotiations is already in the public domain, including much from diplomats themselves. It is in that sense why I offer the book as a 'guide' to the negotiations. Knowing the 'territory' of the Ad Hoc Group I am able to judge

Introduction 7

which sources provide useful assessments of developments in the negotiations. This, of course, does not mean that any source, reference or comment on a position of a state party in the negotiations published by anyone else that I fail to cite is incorrect. However, I do not lead the reader down false trails of ascribing positions to states parties which I know to be incorrect. Indeed I refute some claims I know to be incorrect and challenge those that are misleading. In addition, there were numerous bilateral, like-minded, caucus, private, and unacknowledged meetings and discussions, as well as deals arranged in corridors, to which I was not a part and have little or no knowledge: hence, the importance of recognising that no one ever has a full picture of the 'facts' or events in negotiations. Methodologically, I use the primary documentation of the meetings and the available secondary sources to reference the material. After August 2001 when the negotiations collapsed, too much hindsight and (re)interpretation of events and their meaning has skewed much of the analysis of the Ad Hoc Group and its work. All readers must therefore be cautious because revisionism has been rampant in assessments of the failure of the Ad Hoc Group. As we shall explore in Chapter nine, the Protocol was not as close to completion as some post-collapse assessments actually claim, not as strong as some of its proponents have intimated, and not as weak as many of its detractors have sought to portray.

Chapter 1

Minimalism and *Reform* in the Biological Weapons Convention

Introduction

Twenty years after the Biological Weapons Convention (BWC) entered into force (1975) its states parties convened in Geneva to begin the negotiation of an additional legal instrument; a Protocol. The BWC had been less than successful in achieving its objective of biological disarmament. At the time of its negotiation the US asserted that four states were pursuing biological weapons programmes, whereas by the end of the Cold War the US intimated it had suspicions about up to 10 states.[1] Such estimates are themselves subject to much discussion, but the numbers game does not mask the fact that the BWC has failed to achieve complete biological disarmament among its states parties. By the early 1990s, it was clear that certain states parties had failed to comply with their obligations not to develop, produce or stockpile biological or toxin weapons, hence the agreement to negotiate additional legal measures intended to strengthen the BWC. To paraphrase Beaton, more amiable peoples had in fact deceived themselves that they were safe from the use of disease as a weapon.[2]

The key deficiency with the Convention is the paucity of provisions to ensure compliance with the obligations undertaken under it; states parties essentially have to trust one another to implement the BWC honestly and effectively. The danger inherent in this approach was recognised during the negotiations by both states and non-governmental observers. Rectifying this weakness in the BWC has been central to the efforts to strengthen the Convention since 1975. Although work on the Protocol began in 1995 the negotiations represented a change in the direction and speed of a continual evolution of the Convention. That evolution began in 1980 and continues through to the present day, but is subject to periods of intense activity and periods of no activity. The decade between 1991 and 2001 was not so much an evolution as an attempted revolution. Rather than clarify the collective understanding and interpretation of the obligations contained in the BWC or agree politically binding measures which states parties were encouraged to undertake to enhance implementation of the Convention, its states parties attempted to develop a new, supplemental, legally-binding agreement which would have radically overhauled the implementation of the BWC. That revolution failed and at this juncture even the evolutionary process of strengthening the Convention has stalled. Thus, in considering the life of the BWC it is important to recognise that activity by states parties has been subject to peaks and troughs, very much dependent on the positions adopted by key states during the last twenty-five years.

In a study such as this on one particular period of the BWC's life it is necessary to understand how the particular period fits within the whole, if we are to draw meaningful conclusions or lessons from the events. The objective here is not to undertake a historical analysis of the operation of the Convention between 1975 and 2001. Rather, in order to assess the implications of the failure of the Ad Hoc Group it is necessary to understand whether or not that failure indicates something new, is a manifestation of something older, or part of a cyclical pattern.

The concept of *Minimalism* and *Reform*

The complexity of the biological weapons problem and the intricacies of the Protocol negotiations mean this task is far from easy. One method of providing such a picture is to place the development of the BWC into a conceptual framework. Through such a conceptual framework we can identify whether or not there is a pattern or underlying trend to the event(s). Existing work and analysis of the BWC indicates that its states parties have contesting views on its utility, implementation, strengths and weaknesses.[3] The BWC is not a treaty where all is well with its states parties and there has never been a period when that was the case; contrary to some observations a golden age for the BWC cannot be identified.[4] Like other major international treaties, provision exists for the Treaty's states parties to meet periodically to review the operation of the Convention. Under Article XII the BWC required a review conference to be convened no later than five years after its entry into force to assess implementation. That first review was held in 1980, with subsequent review conferences in 1986, 1991, 1996, and 2001-2002. The review conferences were the only meetings of states parties until 1986 and existing analysis of them indicates that divisions emerged in 1980 that continue to the present day. In short, a contest of ideas and competing policy proposals is evident.

It is from existing analysis which the conceptual framework for this study is derived, in particular the notion of 'reform'.[5] Nicholas Sims' analysis of the Second Review Conference introduced the notion of a 'reform party' in the BWC to explain the generic nature of the differences between the states parties and the various proposals put forward to strengthen the Convention. This observation encapsulates precisely the different approaches to the BWC among states parties.

Those who seek to improve implementation of the BWC and strengthen it via the development of additional mechanisms are the *reformists*. Those who seek to reduce the scope of any additional measures or reject the requirement for such measures favour the status quo, or minimal changes to it. It is this latter group which I identify as, and term, the *minimalists*. In effect, I have taken a key observation of Sims – the *reformist party* – and expanded it to include a counter party – the *minimalists* – and applied it to the life of the BWC as a whole. The framework is simple, but it does capture the essential essence of the tensions between states parties and aptly describes the contest of ideas.

The *minimalists* recognise that the BWC contains a number of flaws and that its implementation has been less than perfect, but they deem rectifying these flaws as too difficult a task, either because the necessary changes might undermine the BWC itself or because the necessary changes might require difficult political choices at the national level. The latter is the most important determinant of their policy. As such these states parties are reluctant to increase the powers or improve the mechanisms available to other states parties under the BWC at, potentially, their own expense. Their focus is state-centric and the retention of national sovereignty and restricting the power of supranational organizations or other states parties to impinge on their sovereignty is of paramount importance. In short, state primacy. In an international relations theoretical context these states parties would be termed Realists. As Mastanduno noted, '[t]here is no single or unified theory of realism, even though critics and proponents are sometimes tempted to treat it that way.'[6] The term 'realist' is therefore used only as a reference point because of the connotations and implications of using the realist tag and the amount of baggage the term carries with it. Moreover, this book is concerned with the actual negotiations themselves. It is about events related to those negotiations: collating evidence, rather than the application of empirical research in a theoretical framework. Hence, realism is a term deliberately eschewed. It is also because the logical counter to realists are idealists and such a term does not adequately describe the other states parties. Idealism is in short supply in the BWC and was long ago replaced by a necessary pragmatism. Those states parties which have in this context a realist bent are therefore described as the *minimalist* parties. That captures the tenor of their general approach to the BWC whereby many of them are willing to do something about its problems, but not too much, and at minimal cost to their sovereignty. As a term it also complements the second group of states parties, the *reformists*.

The *reformists* are basically strong supporters of the BWC but are critical of the implementation record of the Convention and maintain that its weaknesses should be rectified and addressed by remedial action at the national and international levels. Their approach is one rooted in co-operative security and multilateralism and in the international relations theoretical context they would best be described as Liberal-Internationalists. The *reformists* do not reject the role of the state but develop their policy on the basis that the biological weapons problem is beyond the ability of any state to resolve or adequately control. They support multilateral approaches as the preferred method of managing the biological weapons problem.[7] In that regard, they can be loosely described as regime-builders or institutionalists preferring to develop the principles, norms, mechanisms, rules, regulations, and decision-making processes which govern the prohibition on biological weapons.[8] They have sought to endow the Convention with mechanisms and procedures which grant greater powers to the states parties *collectively* as a means of managing their obligations and as a tool in international security. Again, because the objective of this work is empirical and not theoretical, the use of 'regime' is a reference point.[9] This work does not assess the evolution of the BWC within the context of regime theory, even though opponents and proponents of regime theory might find the empirical evidence useful in developing further theories on when and how regime-building succeeds or fails.[10]

What this translates into is a distinction between *minimalism* and *reform* as concepts and a categorisation of states parties into two types, *minimalist* or *reformist*, based on how they act within the BWC. Readers must distinguish here between the concept of *minimalism* and *reform* which I use as a framework for understanding the development of the BWC, and the identification of particular states parties at particular moments of time in relation to specific issues, as being *minimalists* or *reformists*.

The parameters of *minimalism* and *reform*, that is to say its limits, are not established by states parties *per se* but by the range and scope of proposals on a specific issue or range of issues at that particular time. It is about the scale of proposed changes and the spectrum of those changes. During the life of the BWC the parameters of *minimalism* and *reform* have changed at each Review Conference in 1980, 1986, and 1991, over the period 1991-2001, and since 2002. The parameters expand from 1980 through to 2001 and then begin to contract dramatically as the range of options narrows. For example, in 1980 at the First Review Conference the options available to states parties to strengthen the BWC ranged from doing nothing through to a formal amendment of the Convention. In 1991, the options available ranged from additional politically binding commitments through to the creation of a formal Secretariat and negotiation of a legally binding verification agreement. By 2002 the options ranged from doing nothing until 2006 (the Sixth Review Conference) through to agreement on a non-binding three-year work programme. Therefore, what constitutes *reform* in 1980 is not necessarily what constitutes *reform* in 1991 or 2002. I do not establish or identify criteria for judging *minimalism* or *reform*; it is a concept that is more amorphous and reliant on the general thrust of action at a particular period of time as a framework for understanding the evolution of the BWC.

A further factor is that *minimalism* and *reform* are not synonyms for negative or positive changes to the BWC; not all *reform* is necessarily beneficial to the Convention or would constitute progress. Likewise, not all *minimalism* is necessarily detrimental to the Convention or would constitute a step backwards. The adoption of definitions of terms and objective criteria is a good example here, particularly when we consider quantitative approaches to 'improving' implementation of the BWC. The Convention is constructed around what is known as the general-purpose criterion, contained in Article I:

Each State Party to this Convention undertakes never in any circumstances to develop, produce, stockpile, or otherwise acquire or retain:

(1) Microbial or other biological agents, or toxins, whatever their origin or method of production, or types and in quantities that have no justification for prophylactic, protective or other peaceful purposes;

(2) Weapons, equipment or means of delivery designed to use such agents or toxins for hostile purposes or in armed conflict.

The central point of the prohibition is that it covers everything at the same time as permitting legitimate activities, thereby capturing the essential dual-use nature of the agents, toxins, equipment and materials necessary for offensive or legitimate purposes. As Robinson notes, 'Botulinal toxin may be used for removing facial wrinkles but not for loading into bombs.'[11] The BWC does not, therefore, permit any quantity – great or small – of any pathogen or toxin to be an automatic justification for prophylactic, protective or other peaceful purposes. The presence of 0.1kg of *Bacillus anthracis* at a biodefence laboratory is very different to the presence of the same pathogen and the same quantity in a University laboratory, or in an individual's garage. What matters, as Article I of the BWC establishes, is whether or not the microbial or other biological agent or toxin is of a type and in a quantity that can be justified for prophylactic, protective or other peaceful purposes. Put simply, quantitative control mechanisms do not, of themselves, act as a suitable safeguard against biological weapons.

This work does not seek to categorise each and every state party as *reformist* or *minimalist* throughout the life of the Convention. This is not about the construction of archetypes to test a theoretical proposition. Rather it is concerned with providing a conceptual reference in a complex and dynamic negotiation process over a decade. A *reformist* is simply a state party that proposes, adopts or generally supports the available options at the *reform* end of the spectrum. Likewise, a *minimalist* is simply a state party that proposes, adopts or generally supports the available options at the *minimalism* end of the spectrum. There is, therefore, an inherent flux in the situation and a degree of imprecision in the two categories. The reasons for this are fivefold. First, very few states parties can be said to have been *reformists* or *minimalists* throughout the life of the BWC. Sweden, for example, has been consistently reform-minded but is an exception whereas the US has shifted through *minimalism, reform* and back to *minimalism*. Such an identification underlines the crudeness of these descriptors if applied to a particular state party *per se* because, as with the example of the US, it ignores the range of policies advocated for specific articles of the BWC and does not allow for a full understanding of the nuances in that policy. That is why the terms are used generically, because in seeking to ascribe all states parties to particular groups over time more is lost than is gained. Such an exercise would shift the framework from a concept to a caricature.

Second, such an exercise would become centred on justifying my allocation of each state into a particular group according to identified criteria, rather than one centred on encapsulating the thrust of events at specified times. International negotiations are dynamic. Compromise, changes in policy and positions and unexpected 'alliances' of states parties emerge during a negotiating process. Toward the end of any negotiations the options available to all states parties have usually been distilled into two or three competing positions. By this point in the negotiations most states parties are not 'happy' with the options available to them, but they can 'accept' or 'live with' the position they are supporting because while it may no longer reflect their ideal national preferences, it does represent something they consider to be in their national interest. Things change, and the

14   *The Biological Weapons Convention*

conceptual framework covering a decade of negotiations must be able to adapt to those changes and still serve a useful purpose.

Third, because of the reality of negotiations there is no absolute concept here, but shades of grey. If this was to be taken further we would end up with categories comprising at least *absolute minimalists, reform-minded minimalists, minimal-reformists* and *absolute reformists* which serves no useful purpose in this context.

Fourth, the *minimalists* and the *reformists* are not two competing groups of states parties. There are very few common positions held by alliances of states parties in this area that can be identified as *minimalist* or *reformist*. States parties do not organise themselves on *reform* or *minimal* platforms of action. They organise themselves in more traditional caucus groups (Western Group, Eastern European Group, Non-Aligned Group) or in regional groups such as the European Union, or in *ad hoc* coalitions on particular subjects. For example, on the issue of visits, which is discussed in detail in Chapter four, the European Union (EU) had a common position that has been identified as being *reformist* (as the EU was in most, but not all, areas). However, within the EU itself the favoured national positions on visit procedures or mechanisms were very different.

Over-categorisation would detract from the main purpose of this study, but that does not prevent the identification of individual states parties as holding *minimalist-reformist* positions on certain issues. Returning to the issue of visits, Germany was among the *reformists* in terms of its general approach to the Protocol, but was very sympathetic to the *minimalist* approach to the issue of visits vis-à-vis the purpose of such visits and the powers of the visiting team, but was *reformist* in terms of the scope of facilities to which visits would apply. Iran, in contrast, was *reformist* in its approach to peaceful co-operation and in its approach to strengthening Article III of the BWC (non-proliferation and export controls), while being *minimalist* in its approach to issues related to compliance and verification. Although states parties are not listed as being in one group or the other throughout this book it is possible to discern states parties advocating *minimalist* and *reformist* policies on certain issues.

Fifth, within these two broad camps there were a wide variety of opinions, as the example of Germany within the EU position illustrates. The key contests in the Protocol negotiations by 2001 were between the *minimalists* and *reformists*, but intra-party divisions were as important in determining what options were available by early 2001 as well as affecting the actual outcome of the negotiations as inter-party disputes.

The limitations of the conceptual framework must, therefore, be recognised. *Minimalism* and *Reform* are not absolute assertions, but reference points to assist in understanding the context of a proposal, a state party's position, and/or BWC history. Even with all those provisos in mind, *minimalism* and *reform* is a useful framework for understanding the Protocol negotiations. First, because it builds on a concept identified in the mid 1980s – reform – it is able to demonstrate a degree of continuity and the on-going contest of ideas between states parties to the BWC. In addition, it allows the reader to gain a useful understanding of the broader historical, political and security issues which affected the negotiations. Finally, it assists identification of the options available to states parties to strengthen the

Convention and both the general approach to the Protocol by a state party and a state party's specific approach to a particular issue through references to the options and proposals before the Ad Hoc Group. Overall it provides a useful continual reference point for those less well acquainted with the intricacies of biological disarmament to orientate themselves as this work guides the reader through the main issues in the Protocol negotiations and the life of the BWC to date.

Unfinished business from the original negotiations

Work on the actual negotiations of the BWC during the 1968-1971 period has shed considerable light on the important question of why the Convention is constructed the way it is: that is to say why does it prohibit certain things and not others; why does it lack meaningful verification provisions; and why does it contain a number of potentially contradictory obligations (non-proliferation and peaceful co-operation).[12] While a complete record of the original negotiations is still required such a detailed negotiating record is beyond the scope of this book. It is sufficient to note the observations on the final version of the BWC to gain an understanding of why the case for *reform* emerged and how certain states parties pressed that case from 1980 onwards.

The BWC was mooted by the UK in 1968, but negotiations on it between 1969 and early 1971 were disrupted by the key point of difference between the UK and its allies and other states in the Eighteen Nation Disarmament Committee (ENDC) and its successor, the Conference of the Committee on Disarmament (CCD).[13] Most states wished to negotiate a chemical and biological weapons convention, outlawing production, development and stockpiling of both types of weapons. Only the UK, the US and a few other allies were in favour of biological disarmament before chemical disarmament and their position was based on a policy which required chemical disarmament to be subject to verification, whereas biological disarmament would not be subject to the same standards of verification. The USSR initially favoured chemical and biological disarmament, but a reversal of policy in early 1971 permitted a superpower deal on the BWC to emerge and led the way to US-Soviet agreement on a draft BWC. However, during the period April-August 1971, 'US-Soviet bilaterals gutted the draft Convention of many (not all) of the strong points derived from the UK Working Paper' and 'the draft conventions of 1969 and 1970.'[14] Despite the range of options available for verification the Convention contained the weakest set of measures tabled during 1969-1971. In short the BWC was now:[15]

without an explicit ban on the *use* ... of the prohibited weapons; without an investigatory role for the UN Secretary-General; without a veto-free complaints procedure through the UN Security Council ... and without a single mention of research anywhere in the Convention. ... These features, had they been retained in the Convention, would have compensated somewhat for the absence of systematic verification provisions. [Emphasis in original]

Although chemical disarmament was not possible without verification, the necessity of verifying biological disarmament was evidently 'dispensable'[16] and '[i]t was a poor, gutted BWC that was finally transmitted to the UN General Assembly.'[17] So much had been lost that the US could not even secure a co-sponsor for the text it submitted in August, in conjunction with the identical text of the USSR, as the *fait accompli* of the Superpower deal on biological weapons.[18] Even the closest allies of the US were unable to support it in August 1971.

The weakness of the verification and compliance procedures contained in the BWC was underlined when France refused to join the Convention. In a statement to the First Committee of the United Nations in 1973 the French representative stated that verification, 'was a fundamental condition for our adherence'[19] and because, according to the view of France, the BWC lacked such provisions France would be unable to join the Treaty. The French position was not rhetorical; prior to entry into force of the Convention France adopted national legislation explicitly prohibiting within France the very actions proscribed by the BWC.

Equally critical of the Convention's compliance procedures was the former Swedish representative during the original negotiations. Myrdal noted that during the negotiations, '[r]equirements for verification and control had been abandoned.'[20] Furthermore, because 'no control measures were prescribed, there is in essence no assurance that it can be implemented.'[21] Myrdal advocated amendment of Article V of the Convention to rectify this deficiency 'in order to spell out the verification procedure.'[22]

The purpose of underlining the unhappiness of certain states both within and outside the BWC is to emphasise that all was not well with the Convention from the beginning.[23] Many felt it would be unable to imbue a high degree of confidence about biological disarmament and, since most of these states were advocates of arms control treaties, it was to be expected that they would attempt to strengthen or remould the BWC more to their liking. What they required was both an opportunity and a forum to pursue this objective. The forum for considering the overall operation of the Convention was the Review Conference under Article XII of the BWC. The opportunity was at the first such conference in 1980.

The First Review Conference 1980

The preparatory committee of the First Review Conference of the BWC met between 9-18 July 1979 and requested two reports be prepared for the Conference.[24] First, the UN secretariat was asked to prepare a background paper on the compliance of states parties with all their obligations. Second, the Depositary governments – the UK, US, and USSR – were requested to report on new scientific and technological developments relevant to the Convention. The report from the UN on compliance included observations on how the BWC was devised and it does offer a useful, but limited, starting point for explaining thinking on the issue of compliance. It notes that the UK draft convention of 1969 entrusted the UN Secretary-General to receive any complaint about alleged use of biological weapons, investigating such complaints and reporting on the results of that investigation to the Security Council (Article III:1). The 1971 draft of the USSR accorded this role to the Security Council only, a very important change because the UK proposal 'offered greater advantages to a complaining Party since it was designed to circumvent any delays in the investigation that might otherwise occur as a consequence of political deadlock in the Security Council.'[25] (The UK draft of August 1970 did entrust the Security Council under Article III:2 to investigate other breaches or allegations of non-compliance.)

The UK approach did not prevail and the USSR-US formulation bypassed the Secretary-General in favour of the Security Council, thus allowing them (together with China, France and the UK) to veto potential investigations of their own activities or those of their allies. This remained contentious in the BWC and in 1980 the principal cause of dispute among the states parties was the standard of the verification provisions. It is at this point where the *minimalist* and *reformist* parties can be clearly identified.

Those in the *reformist* camp believed that serious questions needed to be asked about the implementation and efficacy of the BWC. It included states such as Argentina, Australia, Brazil, Canada, Cyprus, Ghana, Nigeria, Sweden, Switzerland, Venezuela, and Yugoslavia.[26] Although no single proposal for change was submitted on behalf of these *reformist* states, or indeed commanded the support of all of them, they generally subscribed and were sympathetic to the view expressed by Nigeria, in that implementation of the BWC was 'on the whole satisfactory...[but] that did not mean that there was no need for the examination of strengthening procedures by closing loopholes and removing ambiguities.'[27] Sweden, however, was the driving force among the *reformists* having flagged its concerns about the verification provisions of the BWC in the pre-conference documentation. In its submission Sweden noted that:[28]

Verification of Articles I and II is not envisaged in the Convention. Therefore, violation can only be verified by chance or, possibly, by national means. The possibilities for clandestine violation on a smaller scale are substantial. Present trends of technological and scientific development within states – also states not party to the Convention – and organizations indicate that the potential for production of biological warfare agents is spreading globally.

This concern was compounded by the Swedish government's unhappiness with the procedures for dealing with concerns about non-compliance via the UN Security Council, which in its view resulted in a 'manifest inequality of obligations under the Convention.'[29] These complaint procedures had not been tested during the 1975-1980 period, but many of the *reformists* also sympathised with the view of the Canadian delegation when it pondered publicly whether or not the Convention could be relied upon as an effective mechanism to deal with possible violations, especially given scientific developments which pointed to greater ease of biological weapons development. In response to its own question the head of the Canadian delegation noted that he 'did not feel that it could.'[30]

Although it was clear that Sweden was unhappy with the verification provisions what Sweden was actually going to do about it was not made clear until it proposed to amend Article V of the BWC through the addition of a 'Consultative Committee', in effect separating the initial consultation and fact-finding element of potential or alleged non-compliance from the political consideration of the issue in the Security Council.[31] [32] This separation is exactly what the Netherlands pleaded for in the final stages of the original negotiations in 1971.[33]

Sweden's proposal acted as a catalyst insomuch that states opposed to the proposal found themselves in a counter-balancing group determined to head off and defeat the amendment. In reality this *minimalist* group contained a wide variety of views with many states parties recognising that something did in fact need to be done. The Soviet Union adopted a *minimalist* position supported by most of its Eastern bloc allies. In its view, as there had been no instances or issues of compliance brought to the attention of the Depositaries, 'there was no need to worry about problems which did not exist, for in the view of all concerned, the Convention was operating admirably.'[34] Other *minimalists* were less sanguine about the BWC than the USSR but had fewer concerns than Sweden. The UK, for example, objected to any amendment of the BWC because in its view an amendment would weaken, rather than strengthen, the Convention.[35] It was not what Sweden actually proposed – the Consultative Committee – but the process of amendment that created the problem. Under the Convention's Article XI an agreed amendment would only enter into force if it was agreed by a majority of the states parties and then it would only bind states parties which accepted the amendment. It would not enter into force for those that rejected the amendment; hence the effect would be to create competing legal obligations within the BWC.

Those seeking compromise coalesced around the UK which undertook the role of 'honest broker'[36] between the two extremes promulgated by Sweden – amendment – and the USSR – no action – with an approach intended to force a middle mass in favour of compromise. As Sims noted:[37]

The British ambassador laid stress on the concept of *clarification*. The significance of this was that it directed the conference's attention to the possibilities latent within Article Five. [Emphasis in original]

Intense negotiations between the UK, Sweden and the USSR in the final week of the conference produced the necessary compromise with the Final Declaration clarifying the provisions of Article V of the BWC and identifying procedures implicit within the Article that enabled any state party to use various international mechanisms to pursue concerns about implementation of the BWC's provisions. The procedures included, 'the right of any State Party subsequently to request that a consultative meeting open to all States Parties be convened at expert level'[38] to discuss and consider any problem brought before it. An element of clarity was therefore introduced into the text of the BWC vis-à-vis compliance procedures. The significance of this was that it pointed towards an accepted procedure to be followed in the event of non-compliance concerns being raised formally and followed up under the provisions of the BWC, either individually or collectively.

Despite the success of this compromise the Final Declaration made it clear that this was not the end of the matter because it noted the 'concerns and differing views on the adequacy of Article V, [and] believes that this question should be further considered at an appropriate time.'[39] Clarification of procedures for addressing non-compliance was only the first phase in strengthening the BWC for the *reformists*.

Events after the Final Declaration was agreed indicated that the concerns of the *reformists* about the efficacy of the BWC's verification provisions were very real. In its closing remarks the US referred to the outbreak of anthrax at Sverdlovsk in 1979 'which raised the question whether a lethal biological agent had been present in the Soviet Union in quantities inconsistent with the provisions of the Convention.'[40] The USSR countered that it:[41]

> had always scrupulously observed the Convention's provisions ... [and] [t]he incident in 1979 referred to by the United States delegation had in fact resulted from an epidemic caused by consumption of infected meat which had not been subjected to the normal inspection before sale, it in no way reflected on the Soviet Union's compliance with the Convention.

The Sverdlovsk outbreak led to intense speculation concerning whether or not it was a natural outbreak – the USSR contaminated meat theory – or an accidental release of anthrax from a factory reputed to be engaged in activities that contravened the BWC – the US allegation. The US and the USSR did indeed consult with one another over the Sverdlovsk issue, but it was in reality a 'dialogue of the deaf'[42] which resolved nothing. From a historical perspective the Sverdlovsk incident demonstrated the requirement for independent analysis and investigation of allegations of non-compliance and unusual outbreaks of disease. The very fears expressed by the Swedish delegation, that political considerations would stymie attempts to validate allegations, were realised in this case. No doubt part of the explanation for why the investigation provisions of the BWC were not invoked by the US, or any other state party for that matter, was the fact that the USSR would have vetoed any such investigation.[43]

It is therefore useful to see the First Review Conference as the opening salvo in the contest between the *minimalists* and the *reformists*. The success of the First Review Conference was that it kept those states parties which had concerns about its efficacy on board and demonstrated to those both inside and outside the BWC that effective action could be instigated to deal with their doubts about the compliance architecture. It also illustrated to the *reformists* that change was possible and further meetings held out the possibility of greater reform. However, events took a turn for the worse between 1980 and 1986.

The Second Review Conference 1986

By 1986 the tensions of the (renewed) Cold War and the allegations of non-compliance related to Sverdlovsk and 'Yellow Rain'[44] meant there was little doubt that the BWC was in a perilous state. Sims referred to the BWC as having 'suffered an alarming erosion of confidence'[45] while others considered the

20 *The Biological Weapons Convention*

Convention itself a 'nascent threat to international security',[46] or that the BWC was 'poorly done' and 'a new one would have to be more detailed and provide for a board of inquiry to deal with complaints.'[47] Others claimed 'that the BWC must be recognised as critically deficient and unfixable.'[48] A 'new one' – whatever that might mean – was out of the question and regardless of that view, no single interpretation of the strengths and weaknesses of the BWC detracted from its existence. The Convention certainly had weaknesses, but as Westing pointed out:[49]

> Let us not lose sight of the simple yet inescapable fact that any weaknesses, omissions, or loopholes in the ... Convention are not there through some oversight or through ineptness on the part of the drafters. Rather, they reflect exactly how far the parties wanted to go in restricting themselves. Improvement – that is, greater restrictiveness – in the treaty must therefore await greater enlightenment within the major governments, which in turn will depend to a large extent on more highly informed and aroused publics in major nations.

Did an environment of greater enlightenment exist in 1986? Early indications were that it did not. In a *Washington Times* article a government official stated that in the US the Reagan Administration 'think the treaty is irrelevant'.[50] That was only one view among the 101 states parties and as in 1980 a number of them voiced their doubts about the veracity of the verification and compliance mechanisms. Norway considered them 'inadequate' and that recent developments in the biological sciences had made the 'inadequacy all the more apparent.'[51] Finland believed that the procedures in the Convention did not 'fulfil the exacting standards'[52] being sought in the Chemical Weapons Convention, whereas China considered provisions for monitoring compliance and verification 'absent.'[53] Nigeria noted that certain articles 'were gravely deficient leaving dangerous loopholes'[54] and Australia voiced its opinion that the 'verification provisions had been increasingly recognised as inadequate by present day standards.'[55] As the Austrian delegation remarked:[56]

> There was a widespread feeling that the treaty regime needed to be strengthened in order to dissuade those who doubted its viability from engaging in the build-up of a biological weapons capability.

States parties had three options open to them. First, do nothing and hope that the norm against biological weapons would and could survive. Second, do nothing and accept that developments in biotechnology coupled with the weaknesses of the BWC would lead to biological weapon deterrence capabilities; tantamount to accepting abandonment of the Treaty. Third, seek to address the deficiencies of the Convention and restore some confidence in it. This would entail continuing the *reform* process of the First Review Conference.

Unlike 1980 amendment was not on the agenda. Switzerland spoke out against amendment and considered that in the political climate of 1986 amendment and revision of the BWC would weaken it even further.[57] Mexico also voiced its opposition to amendment and considered the best way to strengthen the Convention 'lay in informal measures taken by states parties by consensus or even

Minimalism *and* Reform *in the BWC*

unilaterally.'[58] The Netherlands proposed that confidence-building measures could be adopted in the short term and in the longer term 'more formal strengthening of the provisions relating to compliance procedures might be necessary.'[59] Sweden, once more at the forefront of *reform*, proposed a number of voluntary exchanges of information, but their rationale was not based solely on what was feasible in the political climate. Sweden had an incremental plan, perhaps shared by the Netherlands, for strengthening the BWC over time:[60]

> The inclusion of such voluntary measures in the Final Declaration would strengthen the Convention's authority and their application would help to build confidence among the States Parties. Their adoption would also make it possible to test what might become elements of a future more developed and systematic form of data exchange.

In other words, their adoption might lead to a formal declaration regime.

As in 1980 the USSR continued to espouse a positive view of the BWC stating that it 'offered an example of the successful solution of complicated security problems and bore testimony to the fact that real disarmament...was not an idealistic fancy.'[61] Its stance towards those unsatisfied with the BWC was, however, more magnanimous than in 1980. It expressed a willingness to look at ways to strengthen the Convention and then took the initiative and surprised the Conference with a proposal for a supplementary protocol to the BWC which would contain measures to strengthen compliance mechanisms.[62] What would actually be included in such a protocol was not elaborated, but it marked a clear departure from the previous Soviet position that changes or formal additions would undermine the BWC. Other states, including the US and the UK, considered the USSR proposal inopportune since in their view the verification requirements of the BWC and the future Chemical Weapons Convention (CWC) would need to be harmonized if either was to work.[63] As Sims put it:[64]

> Was the Soviet Union suddenly outbidding the reformist party? Was it calling the bluff of those who had been loudest in deploring the paucity of verification provisions in this particular treaty, and its consequent vulnerability to violation with impunity?

The post-conference response of a member of the US delegation castigated the Soviet proposal as 'an effort to postpone discussion of specific measures that might be taken to help the functioning of the agreement, with a hollow promise of unspecific verification improvements at some later date.'[65] The issue was, however, more subtle than this view suggested and more complex. As the general debate and specific comments in the Committee of the Whole made clear, confidence in the BWC was eroding fast.[66] Virtually all states recognised that something needed to be done at the Conference, but differences emerged over both the scope and the balance between the two approaches.[67]

> The danger ... was that rival proposals – *either* political commitments now, *or* legally binding obligations later – might cancel each other out, leaving only the disappointingly insubstantial lowest-common denominator [solution].' [Emphasis in original]

22 *The Biological Weapons Convention*

With radical proposals such as amendment not on the agenda and the USSR's do something later approach unacceptable, states parties adopted a dual strategy to redress some of the BWC's problems. As an immediate measure the Conference elaborated further their agreed interpretation of Article V thus continuing the progress of the First Review Conference. In 1980 states parties had agreed that problems with the BWC could be addressed through a consultative meeting convened under Article V. In 1986 the Final Declaration established the scope and powers of the consultative meeting, which the First Review Conference had not done. It was agreed that such a meeting could consider any problem related to the BWC, suggest ways and means to clarify any matter considered ambiguous or unresolved, and could initiate international procedures within the UN framework to facilitate a resolution to an issue. Furthermore, any state party or the consultative meeting itself could request specialised assistance in solving problems.[68] The language used masked the importance of the agreement, because it permitted any state party to at least initiate an investigation process through the specialised assistance provision of the consultative meeting without the threat of formal veto in the UN Security Council under Article VI of the BWC. While the consultative meeting might not have agreed to an investigation, indeed the state party subject to the complaint could reject such a process, the option was at least established and fact-finding was separated, in principle, from judgement.

The second track looked to the future and followed the path proposed by Sweden and other *reformists* through the adoption of informal exchanges of information; the so-called Confidence-Building Measures (CBMs).[69] The four agreed CBMs were intended to enhance confidence about implementation of the BWC and dealt with the following:[70]

- Exchange of data on research centres and laboratories dealing with biological materials that pose a high risk to individuals – the maximum containment laboratories;
- Exchange of information on outbreaks of infectious disease and/or toxins which deviated from the normal pattern of behaviour;
- Encouragement of publication of results of biological research; and
- Active promotion of contacts between scientists in research directly related to the BWC.

These four CBMs were couched in terms of strengthening both Article V and Article X of the BWC, which according to a former member of the Netherlands delegation bridged two different conceptual views. Western states wanted the measures to concentrate on information related to possible suspicious activities, whereas Socialist and NAM states opted for an approach whereby broad co-operation would engender and build confidence in itself.[71] Thus, the CBMs had two objectives: a very specific focus on potential areas of concern and exchanges of information which could go some way to allay such concerns; and to encourage wider dissemination of information and increase scientific co-operation to engender confidence from the bottom up.[72][73]

Merging the conceptual views was therefore a compromise and was by no means an easily reached one. The final remarks of the President recalled that during the actual three-week meeting, 'many delegations felt close to failure, but the numerous bilateral consultations and efforts by the middle-of-the-road delegations had put the conference back on the right track.'[74] In fact, much of the detail was agreed only at the experts' meeting in 1987 which had been charged with agreeing the modalities of the data exchanges. It marked, however, the beginning of a new approach to resolving some of the problems with the BWC through the innovative development of the latent possibilities. Hence, reform of the Convention was now built on both clarification of the language of the BWC itself and on the implementation of measures developed by the states parties after its entry into force. This was now a dynamic process.

As the President of the Conference was to remark, the conference had faced daunting challenges and to overcome them, 'it had to innovate; it had to go beyond what other review conferences had achieved; it had to strengthen an ailing treaty régime without the possibility of major surgery.'[75] The CBMs represented the innovative approach and offered hope for the future, but the substance was in the agreements related to the Consultative Committee and in the agreement to hold a Third Review Conference not later than 1991. In particular, the requirement for the states parties to review the politically-binding agreements of 1986 at the next review conference – including the efficacy of the CBMs – left open the possibility of additional changes. For the *reformists* it left open 'the possibility of creating legally-binding improvements to the Convention ... which could mean either the adoption of an additional protocol or a formal amendment to the Convention itself.'[76]

The US had a more circumspect view of the outcome of the Second Review Conference.[77]

> In retrospect, the United States believes that the course and final outcome of the Review Conference were generally positive. States parties came to Geneva prepared to take a hard look at the operation of the Convention. What they saw was not an image of an arms control agreement working according to plan, and to their credit, they reacted with a series of pragmatic steps which may help to promote a climate more conducive to compliance.

The cautious optimism of the US proved to be the more accurate assessment of the future, but that does not detract from the achievements of the Second Review Conference. It continued the process of incremental strengthening begun in 1980 and indicated a willingness to address the flaws in the BWC in a more systematic way. Few were under the illusion that the CBMs would resolve the problems in the BWC and many believed they should be expanded, but they did represent a positive move forward.[78]

Portents of other problems

Verification and compliance represented the priority concerns of key states parties.[79] However, the final document of the 1986 conference also contained

24 *The Biological Weapons Convention*

portents of problems. As in 1980, Article III and the topic of export controls was not contentious although Argentina, then a member of the Non-Aligned Movement (NAM), had proposed that the non-proliferation obligation 'should not be used to impose restrictions and/or limitations on the transfer ... of scientific knowledge, technology, equipment and materials to States Parties.'[80] The Final Declaration of the First Review Conference had noted that peaceful co-operation had not been hampered by the BWC, but no such statement made it into the Final Declaration of 1986 despite being proposed for inclusion by Hungary.[81] These changes indicated both the increasing concern about export controls and the ability of the NAM to shape the BWC to their own objectives and ensure their views were recorded in the Final Declaration.

In 1986 Article III did not result in substantive disagreements, but Article X on peaceful co-operation did. The report compiled by the Secretariat at the First Review Conference had referred to peaceful activities as being 'one of the central issues in the negotiations'[82] on account that, as the UK working paper had noted in its initial proposal, 'most of the microbiological agents that could be used in hostilities are also needed for peaceful purposes.'[83] To claim that peaceful co-operation was one of the central issues in the negotiations was highly misleading. True, the report noted that 'there was no objection in principle to the concept of peaceful application of biological and toxin agents'[84] but the ENDC and the CCD documentation shows very few calls for enhanced peaceful co-operation provisions in the BWC itself. The focus of the dispute in that period was disarmament and verification; not development. While a number of developing states had pushed for greater peaceful co-operation commitments in the latter half of 1971, they had been rebuffed.[85] However, like the *reformists* on verification, developing states were not going to ignore an opportunity to pursue their objectives while the review conferences provided a forum for airing concerns.

The 'somewhat opaquely drafted'[86] Article X of the Convention became a fractious obligation after 1975. At this stage it is sufficient to note that the context in which Article X was judged changed during the period between the Convention being opened for signature in 1972 and the First Review Conference in 1980. Nevertheless, in 1980 these states parties were not a powerful enough caucus to ensure their positions were adequately reflected. Hence, although the Final Declaration of the First Review Conference made a few references to Article X it was after 1980 that the issue became an increasingly contentious topic between the developed and the developing states parties. Even in 1986 it was not the issue of co-operation *per se* but the relative power of the NAM and the 'price' they extracted from the developed states parties which led to a re-interpretation of Article X that is important.

The power of the developing states could be seen in the CBM concept which was supposed to strengthen both Article V and Article X, as discussed above. Some Western delegations took the view that Article X was a problem.[87] That was one interpretation, but it contrasted with the understanding that had arisen around the Article from the states parties that were members of the NAM. They had taken the negative obligation – not to hamper – and reinterpreted it as a positive obligation to promote development.[88] A significant clash was avoided in 1986, but the portents were clear. Power in the BWC was now dissipating among a number of different groups; the developing and the developed states, the Western and Socialist Cold War blocs, and the *reformists* and *minimalists*. How these different groups interacted – and more importantly where they intersected – would be crucial to the future development of the Convention.

The Third Review Conference 1991

The Third Review Conference took place between 9-27 September 1991, but its tone and outcome were influenced by the significant changes in the international environment that had occurred since 1986. Unlike in 1980 and 1986 many states parties went into the conference with a high degree of optimism that something significant could be achieved. Indeed, by September 1991 there was a feeling that change was becoming inevitable in the BWC, due in part to the factors referred to by Westing; namely, greater enlightenment in the major governments and a more informed and highly aroused public.[89] The end of the Cold War; the activities of non-governmental organisations; developments in states parties' views; and, scientific and technical developments relevant to the Convention, all shaped perceptions about the options and choices open to states parties as they convened in September 1991. Of greater import, these factors converged in 1991 as they had not done in previous years. That does not mean the contest of ideas between the two camps was over or going to be concluded at the Third Review Conference. The Third Review Conference is significant because the options for strengthening the BWC were so wide ranging. In short, the parameters of *reform* were significantly expanded. Its outcome, though born of compromise, had a knock-on effect for the next decade and the effort begun as a result of the decisions taken at the Third Review Conference only ended with the 2002 decision at the Fifth Review Conference.

A changed international context

Without doubt states parties found themselves in a more propitious international climate in 1991 than they had been in 1986. The arms control environment was influenced by the completion of the Intermediate Nuclear Forces Treaty, the Final Declaration of the Paris Conference on chemical weapons, the Conventional Armed Forces Treaty in Europe, the UN Security Council resolutions on Iraq following its invasion of Kuwait and the ensuing ceasefire agreement(s), the completion of the START I Treaty, the signing of the Mendoza Agreement,[90] and the significant progress made towards completing the Chemical Weapons Convention. Collectively, these agreements demonstrated that complex, long-standing and technically and politically difficult arms control issues could be brought to a successful conclusion given political will and significant effort. Moreover, the UN Chapter VII action against Iraq and the subsequent requirement for the disarmament of Iraq indicated a new willingness to address the security

26   *The Biological Weapons Convention*

threats posed by certain weapons. Perhaps paradoxically, one of the positive effects of all these events was that they underlined the weaknesses of the BWC.

Such agreements did not guarantee significant progress would be made by the states parties to the BWC, but they did indicate to states parties – particularly those of a *reformist* bent – that major improvements could be achieved.

Non-governmental activities

The activities of non-governmental organizations (NGOs) in the run up to the Third Review Conference indicated a more highly aroused and informed public. In the period before the Third Review Conference non-governmental bodies proposed specific programmes of work to pursue in 1991.[91]

There were clear concerns about scientific and technical developments, particularly the threat posed by new or novel agents created through genetic engineering or biotechnology, chemical agents created biologically, and microbial or other agents and toxins harmful to humans, animals and plants.[92] In the area of non-proliferation the impact of the Gulf War (1990-91) and the threat posed by the Iraqi biological weapons programme were keenly felt. As such, prior to the conference it was correctly foretold that the non-proliferation obligation was 'likely to be more central' to discussions in 1991 than it had been in the 1980s.[93] Proposals for enhanced export controls and prohibiting any peaceful co-operation with non states parties were mooted even though the latter was tantamount to a *de facto* amendment to the BWC and, at best, a reinterpretation of the actual text of Article III.[94] Moreover, others recognised that the tensions between Article III and Article X, and the differing interpretations of their meaning, primacy, and scope were likely to make it difficult to 'strike the right balance' between these articles.[95]

The fulfilment of the 1980 request for an information exchange on national implementation measures taken to implement the BWC was also mooted.[96] National provisions were a focus of new attention, in part because of the implementing legislation required for many of the more recent arms control agreements, and in part because the 'lethargic attitude towards this international obligation' had been criticised in both the US and the wider world.[97]

Additional measures and mechanisms to bolster further the provisions of Article V also featured prominently in many proposals. These ranged from new and enhanced CBMs, including their extension and refinement to include declarations on all government and private facilities related to the Convention[98] and advance notice of 'open-air military training' in biodefence.[99] There were also calls for consultation procedures for clarifying the CBMs[100] as well as proposals to permit any state party to request the UN Secretary-General to conduct 'a timely fact-finding inquiry into compliance concerns'[101] which would cover more than use of biological weapons and thus go further than the existing powers granted to the Secretary-General. As an adjunct another proposal mooted that the conference should request the UN General Assembly to empower the Secretary-General to respond to such requests.[102] Efforts were also made to require adherence to the World Health Organization (WHO) guidelines on Laboratory Biosafety levels of containment in order to establish agreed international standards for containment.[103]

Organizational aspects of the BWC also loomed large in 1991, with proposals for some kind of intersessional body to oversee the BWC between its review conferences.[104] Such institutions were intended to replace 'the existing assortment of rules, norms and expectations' which had arisen *ad hoc* since entry into force.[105] In addition, states parties were encouraged to agree to review conferences being held at least every five years from 1991 onwards, thus avoiding the potential procedural difficulties which might result from a failure or dispute at a review conference in the future.[106]

Looking to the longer term, the Federation of American Scientists proposed a meeting of experts draft a protocol to the BWC on verification.[107] These proposals were, in effect, a preliminary outline of what eventually became the rolling text of the Protocol. Bolstering the norm against biological weapons through increased membership of the BWC also featured prominently. As such, 'increased diplomatic effort to encourage non-parties to join the treaty'[108] was widely supported by the NGO community. With the Gulf War proliferation of all types of weapons of mass destruction (WMD) in the Middle East was a particular concern, linked in part to the proposals for a Middle East Zone Free of WMD. A further aspect was the call for an end to past disputes on compliance and the resolution of outstanding issues in this area, notably the Sverdlovsk and the Yellow Rain allegations.[109]

Much of what was proposed was not necessarily new *per se*, since many proposals reflected what had been put forward by states parties at the preceding review conferences, or mooted at them, or built on the achievements and mechanisms in the more recent arms control agreements. However, the breadth of NGO-sponsored proposals indicates two important factors: first, there was not a paucity of ideas on how to strengthen the BWC, and second, there was a growing feeling that the time was now ripe for major change. Making significant progress, however, depended on the attitudes of states parties and how much effort they were willing to expend on the Convention.

Developments in states parties' views

All the issues discussed above, as well as scientific and technical developments discussed below, required states parties – or rather those truly interested in the BWC – to give consideration to what they might achieve at the 1991 meeting. The *reformists* adopted a proactive approach and attempted to break the mould of incremental and evolutionary strengthening of 1980 and 1986 with a leap forward. For the *minimalists*, while they were aware of the plans of some *reform-minded* states parties, they could afford to react to proposals rather than promote their own agenda. The *reformists* had to devise policy proposals, seek support for them, argue their case and gain sufficient support to push through adoption by all states parties. The *minimalists* simply had to sit tight and identify only a single concern as a means to frustrate or scupper any proposal.

Compliance with the BWC was still a major influencing factor for some states parties. By 1991 the UK and the US, as well as their allies, were more aware of the scale of Soviet deception and the magnitude of the Soviet offensive biological

28 *The Biological Weapons Convention*

weapons programme.[110] Soviet non-compliance was a stumbling block on any further progress because at the critical level what was the point of strengthening the BWC if the non-compliance of one of its depositaries was going to be ignored or any new mechanisms were unable to resolve the concerns of non-compliance? States parties could not afford to ignore non-compliance or pretend all was well with the BWC, even though some of them attempted to do so. Hence the US insistence, 'that the Soviets satisfy our serious concerns about their own compliance with the BWC before we proceed to discuss strengthening the Convention.'[111]

The contingent nature of US thinking, whereby non-compliance had to be addressed *before* strengthening the BWC could be discussed, might be understood in two ways. It drew attention to the key deficiencies with actual implementation of the Convention as it existed, which included non or selective acceptance of its prohibitions and obligations, and, in effect, insinuated that if a minimal agreement like the BWC was not complied with a more detailed agreement was not worth negotiating. Second, it established an obstacle which those in favour of further *reform* would have to overcome. The USSR had mooted proposals for a verification protocol in 1986 and repeated the proposal in 1990 in the Conference on Disarmament (CD)[112] and the US message to the USSR, and others, was quite simple: no *reform* without compliance. The alternative approach was greater pressure on the non-compliant through a stronger (reformed) BWC. Suspicions about the USSR's compliance meant its proposals for strengthening the BWC had to be treated with extreme caution, both in terms of the actual commitment of the USSR to the Convention and the extent to which such proposals were an attempt to deflect attention from non-compliance. However, in early 1991 the USSR claimed it was still working out its position for the Review Conference, but 'believed that both verification provisions and CBMs were needed.'[113]

The US and the USSR were not the only states parties thinking in detail about the September conference. In February 1991 the Netherlands convened a government seminar for 17 states parties, later described as a 'brainstorming session'[114] for future policy development. A Canadian government publication reported that:[115]

> The unstated assumption of all present was that opportunity exists to strengthen the BTWC from within – that is, not through the potentially divisive procedure of treaty amendments but through expanding provisions or adding, through agreed protocols or politically binding declarations, further commitments to transparency and confidence-building.

Canada's position did go further than this, however, since it also claimed it intended to seek agreement from states parties 'to convene a specially mandated conference, in 1993, to negotiate verification provisions for the Convention.'[116]

Austria set out its position in the CD on 14 March, noting it favoured elaborating general guidelines about national implementation of the Convention, 'stricter provisions' regarding the CBMs and that it could support 'a widening of the scope of such exchanges of information.' To address the question of

Minimalism *and* Reform *in the BWC*

verification some kind of intersessional committee and secretariat unit 'might seem useful' according to Austria.[117] At the Preparatory Committee of the Review Conference (8-12 April) it has been reported that the states parties 'basically agreed on forming a group of experts as an interim body, on increasing and improving the exchange of data, and on exchange of scientists.'[118] While this assessment is very close to what actually did happen, in the lead up to September and there was clearly much to play for.

The *reformist* zeal of France in 1991 encapsulated the scale of change from 1986. The French *Arms Control and Disarmament Plan* released on 31 May indicated that, *inter alia*, they would propose the addition of a verification protocol to the BWC in September.[119] However, the US attitude to verification was a significant obstacle to French and other states parties' plans. In an address to the US Air Force Academy, President Bush stated that the US supported 'implementation of existing BWC provisions and an improved mechanism for information exchange.'[120] This did not indicate a desire for far reaching *reform* in the US as the Assistant Director of ACDA stated.[121]

> I don't think that the United States feels it would be appropriate for the review conference to establish a mandate for a group to negotiate a verification Protocol. That is not appropriate from our point of view because we have not identified an effective way to verify the treaty.

In the UK it is also possible to detect a more reticent attitude. Parliament was informed of UK intentions, which were cautious but did indicate a medium term programme of work that was *reformist* in its outlook. Central to UK policy were 'proposals to improve and extend the regime of confidence building measures, to improve organizational arrangements by establishing a supportive body and to examine the feasibility of devising effective verification procedures.'[122] It was also suggested that the UK wanted to extend the CBMs to cover 'facilities working on the most dangerous organisms' and that a group of experts should examine the scope and possibility of inspecting declared and suspect facilities and investigation of suspicious incidents. However, an unnamed UK official was reported as stating that achieving these objectives 'will not be easy, and indeed [it] may not in the end be possible to devise an effective verification scheme.'[123] Whether or not this UK official was knowingly prescient is unclear.

Scientific and technological developments

The political drivers for change in the BWC arena were given greater weight by the submitted observations on scientific and technological developments relevant to the Convention and emerging scientific opinion that biological weapons were a resurgent threat to states.[124] Australia pointed to the many developments in the scientific field that had direct relevance to the BWC and, as a consequence 'many nations now have capabilities in the field of biotechnology ... that can, if misused, be applied to BW production.'[125] The UK held a similar view, noting that developments made BW production more feasible[126] and that in principle it may now be easier for an aggressor to acquire expertise and equipment suitable for the illicit production of BW.[127] The US echoed such concerns with a summary of many potential benefits to be accrued from biotechnology, but sounded a note of caution that the 'very same signs also give concern for the possibility of misuse of this biotechnology to subvert the Convention.'[128] Concerns about production technologies were shared by Australia, Switzerland, and Russia, the latter noting that creating hybrid toxins in large quantities did not present 'major technical difficulties'.[129] Toxins were of particular concern and underlined the scale of change between entry into force in 1975 and the situation sixteen years later. The US stated that production of potent toxins, which had previously only been available in minute quantities, was now possible in kilogramme quantities and therefore could be militarily significant.[130]

As a consequence legitimate scientific progress was eroding the distinction between production facilities and small laboratories. Sweden noted also that, 'the border between defensive and offensive research has become more indistinct and the time from research to industrial application is becoming shorter.'[131] Furthermore, the expansion of safety features meant that it was increasingly difficult to distinguish between permitted and prohibited activities. Finally, improvements in dissemination techniques for biological pesticides and spraying devices also posed risks because all were as applicable to BW agents as to microbial pesticides.[132] Put simply, 'confidence derived from the belief that certain technical problems would make biological weapons unattractive for the foreseeable future has eroded.'[133] That considered technically unfeasible in 1971 had become feasible in 1991 and politically evidence was mounting that non-compliance with the letter and spirit of the BWC had occurred among both states parties (Soviet Union) and signatories (Iraq).

Options at the Review Conference

The concrete proposals put forward by the states parties to address these, and other, problems are listed in the annex to the report of the Committee of the Whole. This annex provides a good indictor of the thrust of the states parties' vision(s) for the BWC and their main points of concern. Moreover, the absence of proposals – by particular states parties or particular states parties on specific issues – can be as an important indicator of the general debate and its tone, as those included. Taking all the proposals together it is possible to identify a set of measures, institutions and a programme of future work which was in fact quite radical, as set out in Table 1.1. At this stage the proposals from individual states parties had not been brought together into any package, but it is possible to identify the elements which eventually became important in the Protocol negotiations themselves and remain of significant interest today. Nevertheless, the snapshot is skewed because the proposals made in writing, and therefore recorded in the public domain, either reflect specific concerns of a state party or originate from those seeking to change the status quo. In that respect, the above measures are biased to the *reformist* agenda and ignore the fact that not every state party was as keen on enhancing and expanding the CBMs or adding to their responsibilities in other areas of the BWC.

Table 1.1   Options and choices in 1991

Measure	Proposed	Adopted
Detailed Consultative Meeting procedures	•	•
Requirement for timely consultations	•	•
Empower UN Secretary·General to investigate use of BW	•	
Recognise right to impose sanctions	•	
Recognise right to cease co-operation for non-compliance	•	
Explicit coverage of humans, animals & plants	•	•
Rectify omission of 'use'	•	
Recommend halt to open-air testing	•	•
Definitions, lists & thresholds for prohibited activities	•	
Establish licensing system for export controls & end-users	•	
International reporting system for exports	•	
Cease exports & co-operation with non-parties	•	
Apply controls only on non-parties	•	
Stress importance of national implementation measures	•	•
Recognise role of regional measures	•	•
CBM on 'nothing to declare'	•	•
CBM on BL4 facilities	•	•
CBM on BL3 & BL2 facilities	•	
CBM on infectious disease outbreaks	•	•
CBM on relevant publications	•	•
CBM on promotion of contacts between scientists	•	•
CBM on biodefence work	•	•
CBM on national legislation	•	•
CBM on past offensive / defensive activities	•	•
CBM on vaccine production	•	•
CBM on immunization programmes	•	
CBM on epidemiological surveillance	•	
CBM on open-air testing of agents/toxins	•	
Computerize CBM submission and analysis	•	
Reciprocal visits to biodefence facilities	•	
Establish a BWC Secretariat	•	
Agree on follow-up measures	•	•
Enhance peaceful co-operation	•	•

As noted, the US advocated dealing with compliance before strengthening the Convention and remained unconvinced about the utility of verification in the BWC. China, while recognising some improvements could be made to the modalities of the information exchange and that reporting legislation and other measures might be a useful addition, proposed that the Conference only encourage

32 *The Biological Weapons Convention*

all states parties to participate in the CBMs. Furthermore, in response to the possibility of new CBMs, the Chinese stated that:[134]

> In the interval between this Review Conference and the next, any State party may put forward new proposals on the further improvement of the exchange of information, which shall be transmitted by the Department for Disarmament Affairs ... to all States parties for study and, if necessary, can be submitted for deliberation at the First Committee of the United Nations.

This was not an endorsement of new CBMs, an intersessional committee or oversight body, or follow on meetings to establish more detailed verification provisions. China was by no means the only *minimalist*.

Choices made at the Review Conference

The range and scope of proposals made to strengthen the BWC indicate that the *reformist* camp was both growing and in favour of a break from the incremental nature of the strengthening process. Important in this was a recognition that the CBMs had 'not met the expectations of most States parties'[135] and that failure galvanised the *reformists* to attempt more radical changes. Nevertheless, although it is possible to detect 'strong support for the strengthening of the regime established by the Convention'[136] strengthening the regime encompasses many different viewpoints and is a sufficiently anodyne phrase to allow all to profess support for it.[137]

The opportunity to make significant improvements to the BWC in 1991 was squandered by the states parties. As Table 1.1 indicates the most radical and far reaching proposals did not gain support among the states parties. What the states parties could have created in 1991 was a stronger, but more flexible, BWC regime encompassing the following: declarations; consultation procedures (including possible on-site measures); improved investigation procedures; national implementation improvements; improved, and focussed, peaceful co-operation under Article X; improved non-proliferation commitments; the outlines of an agreed enforcement framework; and, a small organization to oversee implementation of the Convention. While the final achievements are far from modest – the Review Conference was by no means a failure – in 1991 with its propitious international political climate, widespread support for change, scientific and technical developments which increased the potential threat of biological weapons, and the number of proposals from states parties themselves, the outcome was a disappointment. Sims referred to the Third Review Conference as 'the most far-reaching missed opportunity.'[138]

The forthright approach to compliance with the BWC, the explicit recognition of animals and plants under the scope of Article I, and the recognition of the dangers posed by open-air release of the pathogens or toxins harmful to humans, animals or plants were important positive developments. In addition, the stress placed on measures to implement the non-proliferation obligation under Article III in the wake of Iraqi proliferation (even though most assistance had come from Western states) did signal a change in attitude to proliferation. A renewed emphasis on national implementation measures and the revisions and additions to the agreed mechanisms of the Consultative Committee were also a step forward.

Everything else in the BWC was subject to compromise. The CBMs were reviewed and expanded but their scope remained limited, not least in the area of vaccines where reporting was limited to vaccines for humans. Of greater concern was the fact that the procedures for submission and collation of the CBMs remained rudimentary. Analysis of the submitted information remained a national responsibility. The proposal to establish an interim secretariat for the Convention, which *inter alia* would have been able to rectify many of the deficiencies with the administration of the CBMs, was rejected and other supporting institutions proved unacceptable. The powers granted to the UN Secretary-General by the Security Council were recognised in the Final Declaration, but the emphasis in the text signalled a victory for those who supported the maintenance of the veto-power under Article VI on investigations of use.[139]

Most of this passed states parties and analysts by because the Third Review Conference is remembered for the establishment of the Ad Hoc Group of Verification Experts (VEREX). The decade of activity which flowed from the 1991 meeting masked the fact that the states parties failed to take a significant step forward at what was their best opportunity to date. Two different elements combined at the Third Review Conference to defeat the *reformist* agenda; the more important role the developing states had in shaping the BWC following the end of the Cold War, and US resistance to verification.

North-South disputes

North-South difficulties over Article X of the Convention and the application of the export controls mirrored debates in the Nuclear Non-Proliferation Treaty (NPT) and in the final stages of the negotiations of the CWC.[140] In the BWC the reinterpretation of the meaning of peaceful co-operation under Article X meant that, 'until the treaty regime yielded tangible benefits through the transfer of industrial technology its strengthening in other respects would be resisted.'[141] With the Cold War context removed additional leverage and bargaining power was presented to the developing states; their voice was more powerful. For a numerically important, if not always politically powerful, group of states parties strengthening the Convention went far beyond the measures envisaged by the Western states – which usually applied to Articles I, III, IV, V, and VI – to encompass technical co-operation and resource and technology transfer issues. For these states parties the contingent nature of their collective position – enhanced peaceful co-operation before strengthening of the BWC – allowed them to both reduce the scope of measures adopted in the Final Declaration, to scupper the establishment of any institutional arrangements[142] and to signal unambiguously that their concerns and their priorities must now be placed firmly on the agenda of the BWC. This was to become an important battleground in the 1990s.

34   *The Biological Weapons Convention*

The US position

By far the most damaging impact on the *reformist* agenda was, however, the 'obstructive role'[143] of the United States. While the NAM and its supporters were able to act as a bloc, the Western Group was unable to muster a common position on many key issues because of differences between the US and its allies. Fragmented, the positions of Western states parties could be played off against each other and in the area of verification a majority of states parties, including all but, 'the United States and a few non-western countries'[144] supported verification.

The US position vis-à-vis the verification question was based on the belief that the BWC was not verifiable using international means. However, this was not a new position, evidenced by comments made prior to the Second Review Conference and after the PrepCom in April 1991. The US had long standing concerns about the feasibility and utility of verification measures in the BWC and Washington opposed the negotiation of a formal verification Protocol on three grounds. First, biological production facilities could be dual-use and the lack of distinctive signatures between offensive biological weapons-related work and peaceful work made verification difficult. Second, a negotiated international verification agreement could not be intrusive enough to detect clandestine facilities and would, therefore, generate false confidence that states parties were in compliance with the Convention when in fact, in the view of the US, some of them were not. Third, a very intrusive inspection by a multinational team could expose both government and commercial facilities to foreign espionage and the US was particularly concerned about the loss of proprietary information, which could weaken the competitive edge of the US biotechnology and pharmaceutical industries.[145]

The position of the US on the BWC in 1991 was incongruent with its position on chemical weapons. While not disputing the significant technical differences between attempting to verify the CWC and the BWC, a study by the Office of Technology Assessment underlined that the question of verification was one of politics. The study noted correctly that the technical difficulties of verification in the BWC were real, but the principal issue for the US was a 'political debate over whether the burden of uncertainty associated with BWC verification would hamper more severely the verifier or the violator.'[146] This was not an unfamiliar position in another forum, the on-going CWC negotiations, but the requirement for effective verification under the CWC was altered by the Bush administration:[147]

No longer would the United States judge the acceptability of chemical arms control in terms of whether it was or was not verifiable. Instead it would seek a 'level of verification that gives us the confidence to go forward.' President Bush was thus signifying a new suppleness to the US negotiating position. The old criterion – that no agreement on chemicals could be worthwhile if compliance with it could not be assured – was to be superseded, replaced by an altogether different means of assessment. The judgement would now be a relative one: would the USA feel more confident in a world regulated by the particular chemical warfare arms control package on offer or in the world of the status quo?

As SIPRI's analysts went on to note, '[t]he importance of this change lay in its express recognition of what had been the case, that no international ban on chemical weapons could ever be fully verifiable.'[148] These political decisions by the US paved the way for finalising the CWC. In the BWC context however, there was no corresponding political decision to introduce 'suppleness' into the US position on biological verification. For the US the criterion remained effective verification and, as such, the BWC, according to the US, remained unverifiable.[149] One assessment of the US policy stated that:[150]

> In 1991-1992, with on-site verification conceivable – albeit unquestionably difficult – the Bush administration decided *in advance* that it could not work, that it could not produce a level of *absolute* confidence, and therefore opposed it entirely. [Emphasis in original]

The US preferred the status quo to the prospect of an improved BWC, whereas its Western Group allies accepted complete assurance via verification was unachievable. However, the latter believed that some verification mechanisms would provide them with greater confidence in the BWC. This debate split the Western Group:[151]

> In simple terms the argument was between those who considered that "some verification was better than none" and the United States which argued that "bad verification was worse than none."

The outcome was a compromise solution. The *reformists* were not easily pushed aside from their vision, even by the *minimalist* US and those who shared similar concerns such as China. It was decided that an Ad Hoc Group of Governmental Experts would be established 'to identify and examine potential verification measures from a scientific and technical standpoint'[152] – the so-called VEREX process. The kind of technical assessments of the utility of verification measures that had been on-going throughout the CWC negotiations would now be carried out on the biological weapons problem. The *reformists* did not, therefore, lose all hope that agreement on verification was beyond states parties; it would simply require a lot more work and more time to convince the *minimalists*.

Minimalism and *Reform* 1975-1991

Different views about the utility, strength and effectiveness of the BWC were aired from the time it entered into force. From the French refusal to join the Treaty and the observations of the former Swedish diplomat, Alva Myrdal, we gain a picture that indicates quite clearly that problems existed in the BWC. The official documentation of the First Review Conference includes a sufficient number of statements and observations from a sufficient number of states parties to underline that at least some states parties supported remedial action to rectify known deficiencies. While the axis of the East-West Cold War underpinned the different positions of states parties and the North-South development axis of conflict can be

36 *The Biological Weapons Convention*

identified, the catalyst for change did not originate from these axes. It was the *reformist-minimalist* contest of ideas that acted as the driver for change.

In 1980 the *reformists* had sufficient power to push through small but important changes to the consensus understandings about how the Convention could deal with an allegation of non-compliance or a request for clarification. The substantive success of this lay not in the measures themselves but the initiation of a process of reform. It was incremental, but it had without doubt begun.

In 1986 confidence in the BWC was eroding rapidly and action was necessary if the Convention was not to fall into complete disrepute. The President of the Conference was correct in noting that the Conference had been innovative in addressing the problems it faced and this innovation had originated with ideas put forward by the *reformists*. However, although the Conference was a success it did not address problems in a manner that provided, or sought to provide, immediate confidence. The allegations of non-compliance against the Soviet Union were increasing and no state, least of all the US, attempted to use the provisions of the Convention to address or clarify these allegations, beyond an initial attempt at bilateral consultation. Wider issues, such as concerns about the growth in biodefence programmes, were left unaddressed. States parties did not build upon the Final Declaration of the First Review Conference by ensuring that requests made in 1980, such as a United Nations conference on improving the implementation of Article X or the request to circulate national legislation, were followed up. And the CBMs looked to the future; only if implemented by all states parties on annual basis could they have provided greater transparency and helped to (re)build confidence that the significant majority were complying with their obligations. It was almost as if the states parties believed that as long as they did something and they promised to improve in the future, that would enable the Convention to withstand the present crisis. The most important aspect by 1986 was the shifting balance of power because although the *minimalists* remained in the ascendancy, 'the reform party [was] no longer crying in the wilderness.'[153]

By 1991 the convergence of factors brought about by scientific and technological developments, a more propitious international political climate, a more aroused public opinion, and a more enlightened approach among some states parties to the Convention (and in arms control agreements generally) indicated that it was time for significant change in the BWC. Sims' view that the Third Review Conference was 'the most far-reaching missed opportunity' will probably prove to be the most accurate assessment of its outcome. This is particularly true given the failure to agree on a Protocol. However, the tide of *reform* was in many ways unstoppable because expectations had risen so high and something had to give. *Minimalism*, nevertheless, still had its supporters and the combination of states parties which included the US and China, proved too great an obstacle for the *reformists*. In particular, a divided Western Group dictated a compromise solution.

At a certain level what the Third Review Conference lacked was real leadership. The US position of no *reform* before compliance ran counter to all of its closest allies, who envisaged *reform* of the BWC as a means to exert greater pressure on the non-compliant. With the US less willing than its allies to pursue biological disarmament through the BWC with sustained vigour those states parties which were less enamoured of intrusive verification measures in disarmament agreements, such as China, the USSR, India, Pakistan, and Iran, were therefore shielded by a US position which rejected verification as a means to strengthen the BWC. Intra-Western Group division let the reticent mask their real positions.

The implications of decisions and choices made in 1991 were significant. Although the Third Review Conference is remembered for the establishment of VEREX, and VEREX led to the Special Conference and that to the Ad Hoc Group, this linear progression created what proved to be a false impression of progress in the BWC. It masks what was lost at the 1991 Conference. Had the CBMs been expanded even more and a small secretariat created to oversee their implementation (as well as other existing commitments under the BWC), these developments together with the decision to examine verification may have effectively bought off the *reformists* in the 1992-1994 period. Such commitments would not have been overly ambitious, but neither would they have been insignificant. In effect, because the choices made in 1991 were so parsimonious given the wealth of options before the states parties the triumph of the *minimalists* served only to increase the demands of the *reformists*. The *reformists* left the Third Review Conference with the knowledge that change was being resisted in the most propitious of international climates. *Minimalism* was not imposed by the constraints of the Cold War: it was much more pervasive and from this point forward revolutionary change to the modalities of implementation of the BWC would, in the eyes of the *reformists*, be required to effect any meaningful progress.

Notes

1.   Milton Leitenberg, 'Biological Weapons Arms Control' *Contemporary Security Policy* 17:1 (April 1996) p.12.
2.   Leonard Beaton, 'The Reform of Power: A proposal for an international security system' (London, Chatto & Windus, 1972) p.197.
3.   Nicholas Sims has probably written more on the BWC itself than anyone else. In doing so he has provided the best work on much of the specifics and the evolution of the BWC as a whole and this chapter draws heavily from that extensive body of work. Useful starting points to understand the bigger picture of the BWC can be found in: Nicholas A. Sims, 'The Evolution of Biological Disarmament' *SIPRI Chemical & Biological Warfare Studies*, Number 19, (Oxford, Oxford University Press, 2001) and Nicholas A. Sims, 'The Diplomacy of Biological Disarmament: Vicissitudes of a Treaty in Force, 1975-1985' (New York, St. Martin's Press, 1988).
4.   Jez Littlewood, 'Strengthening the BWC: what is a realistic inter-Review Conference Strategy?' 18th workshop of the Pugwash Study Group on the Implementation of the Chemical and Biological Weapons Conventions: The Resumption of the Fifth Review Conference 2002 and Beyond Geneva, Switzerland, 9-10 November 2002. Nicholas A. Sims, 'Biological Disarmament Diplomacy in the Doldrums: Reflections After the BWC Fifth Review Conference' *Disarmament Diplomacy* Number 70 (April/May 2003), p.14. (Sims and I were referring to a claim made at a private meeting in London in January 2002.)
5.   I first came across this term in: Nicholas A. Sims, 'Biological and Toxin Weapons: Issues in the 1986 Review' *Faraday Discussion Paper* No 7, (London, The Council

for Arms Control, 1986). As a concept it is referred to more extensively in, Sims, 'The Diplomacy of Biological Disarmament' (1988) and Nicholas A. Sims, 'The Second Review Conference on the Biological Weapons Convention' Susan Wright (Editor) *Preventing a Biological Arms Race* (Cambridge Mass., The MIT Press, 1990) pp.267-288.

6. Michael Mastanduno, 'A realist view: three images of the coming international order.' T.V. Paul and John A. Hall (Editors) *International Order and the Future of World Politics* (Guildford, Cambridge University Press, 1999) p.19.

7. Abram Chayes and Antonia Handler Chayes, 'The New Sovereignty: Compliance with International Regulatory Agreements' (Cambridge, Mass., Harvard University Press, 1998). I take the term 'managing' directly from Chayes and Chayes, see pp. 109-11 for a summary of the 'managing compliance' strategy.

8. In this context 'regime' is understood, and used, in a generic sense based on the concept identified by Krasner that a regime differs from an institution, but acts and serves as a foci for converging expectations. In the context of the BWC the norm is of non-use and non-development, production and stockpiling of biological weapons and while the treaty has no international organization or designated implementing institution, states parties to it clearly share (or at least claim to share) the same expectation and legal undertaking. See Stephen D. Krasner, 'Structural causes and regime consequences: regimes as intervening variables' *International Organization* 36:2, (1982) pp.185-205.

9. It is also necessary to be aware of the different uses of 'regime' by the academic community – basically in line with Krasner's definition above – and the more generic use by the diplomatic community in line with a standard dictionary definition of a prevailing order or system.

10. I am grateful to an anonymous reviewer of earlier drafts of this work for pointing out this potential use of the empirical research.

11. Julian Perry Robinson, 'Some Lessons for the Biological Weapons Convention from Preparations to Implement the Chemical Weapons Convention' Oliver Thranert (editor) *Enhancing the Biological Weapons Convention* (Bonn, Dietz, 1996) p.97.

12. Jonathan B. Tucker, 'A Farewell to Germs' *International Security* 27:1 (Summer 2002) pp.107-148; Nicholas A. Sims, 'Four Decades of Missed Opportunities to Strengthen the BWC: 2001 Too?' *Disarmament Diplomacy* Number 58 (June 2001) pp.15-21; Susan Wright, 'Geopolitical Origins' Susan Wright (Editor) *Biological Warfare and Disarmament: New Problems/New Perspectives* (Lanham, Rowman & Littlefield Publishers, 2002) pp.313-342.

13. Even with the newer works on the negotiations listed above, the best starting point for understanding the context of the 1969-1971 negotiations remains the six volume SIPRI study on chemical and biological weapons. See in particular Jozef Goldblat, 'The Problem of Chemical and Biological Warfare' Volume IV *CB Disarmament Negotiations, 1920-1970* (Stockholm, Almqvist & Wiksells, 1971) pp.253-320. The details of the 1968 UK working paper can be found at pp.254-259, the discussions on the competing draft conventions pp.295-306, the analysis of the Soviet reversal of its position in 1971 pp. 314-320, and the competing revised UK draft BWC of 18 August 1970 (CCD/225/Rev.2), revised Socialist CBW draft of 23 October 1970 (UN General Assembly document A/8136), and the draft BWC of the Socialist states (Bulgaria, Byelorussia, Czechoslovakia, Hungary, Mongolia, Poland, Romania, Ukraine, and USSR) of 15 April 1971 in Appendix 1, 2, and 3 respectively, with the August 1971 version of the BWC in Appendix 4.

Minimalism *and* Reform *in the BWC*

14. Sims, 'Four Decades of Missed Opportunities to Strengthen the BWC: 2001 Too?' p.15.
15. Nicholas A. Sims, 'Reinforcing Biological Disarmament: issues in the 1991 Review' *Faraday Discussion Paper* No 16 The Council for Arms Control, (London, Brassey's, 1991) p.3.
16. Ibid.
17. Sims, 'Four Decades of Missed Opportunities to Strengthen the BWC: 2001 Too?' p.16.
18. Ibid.
19. ACDA, 'Statement by the French Representative (Rapin) to the First Committee of the General Assembly: Biological and Chemical Weapons, November 26, 1973' *Documents on Disarmament 1973* (Washington, U.S. Government Printing Office, 1973) p.830.
20. Alva Myrdal, 'The Game of Disarmament: How the United States and Russia run the Arms Race' (New York, Pantheon Books, 1976) p.273.
21. Ibid.
22. Ibid, p.275.
23. J. P. Perry Robinson, 'The impact of Pugwash on the Debates over Chemical and Biological Weapons' *The Annals of the New York Academy of Sciences* Volume 866, December 30, 1998, p.225.
24. United Nations, 'Report of the Preparatory Committee for the Review Conference on the Prohibition of the Development, Production and Stockpiling of Bacteriological (Biological) and Toxin Weapons and on Their Destruction' BWC/CONF.I/3
25. United Nations, 'Review Conference of the Parties to the Convention on the Prohibition of the Development, Production and Stockpiling of Bacteriological (Biological) and Toxin Weapons and on Their Destruction' BWC/CONF.1/4 (20 February 1980) Geneva p.11. (Hereinafter referred to as 'BWC 1RC' followed by document number, date and page reference(s) where appropriate.)
26. Unlike the Final Documents from the Third Review Conference (1991) onwards, the documentation of the First and Second Review Conferences included the 'summary records' of the discussions. See BWC 1RC, BWC/CONF.I/SR.1 (4 March 1980) to BWC/CONF.I/SR.12 (21 March 1980) for the actual discussions of the meetings.
27. BWC 1RC, BWC/CONF.I/SR.7 (11 March 1980) p.4.
28. BWC 1RC, BWC/CONF.I/4 (20 February 1980) p.24.
29. Ibid., p.25.
30. BWC 1RC, BWC/CONF.I/SR.8 (12 March 1980) p.8.
31. Sims, 'The Diplomacy of Biological Disarmament' p.174.
32. The most detailed account of the events of the First Review Conference can be found in, Sims, 'The Diplomacy of Biological Disarmament' pp.168-196.
33. ACDA, 'Statement by the Netherlands Representative (Bos) to the Conference of the Committee on Disarmament: Bacteriological Weapons, July 29, 1971' *Documents on Disarmament 1971* (Washington, U.S. Government Printing Office, 1971) p.451.
34. BWC 1RC, BWC/CONF.I/C/SR.3 (12 March 1980) p.7.
35. Sims, 'The Diplomacy of Biological Disarmament' p.184.
36. Ibid., p.181. (According to Sims the phrase 'honest broker' originates with Julian Perry Robinson.)
37. Ibid., p.185.

38.	BWC 1RC, BWC/CONF.I/10 (21 March 1980) pp.7-8.
39.	Ibid., p.8.
40.	BWC 1RC, BWC/CONF.I//SR.12 (21 March 1980) p.3.
41.	Ibid., p.5.
42.	Sims, 'Four Decades of Missed Opportunities to Strengthen the BWC: 2001 Too?' p.16.
43.	Matthew Meselson, Jeanne Guillemin, Martin Hugh-Jones, Alexander Langmuir, Ilona Papova, Alexis Shelokov, Olga Yampolskaya, 'The Sverdlovsk Anthrax Outbreak of 1979' *Science* (Volume 266) 18 November 1994, pp.1206. Jeanne Guillemin, 'Anthrax: The Investigation of a Deadly Outbreak' (Berkley and Los Angeles, University of California Press, 1999).
44.	For detailed discussions on the allegations see: Elisa D. Harris, 'Sverdlovsk and Yellow Rain: Two Cases of Soviet Noncompliance?' *International Security* 11:4 (Spring 1987) pp.41-95; Julian Robinson, Jeanne Guillemin, and Matthew Meselson, 'Yellow Rain in Southeast Asia: The Story Collapses' and Leonard Cole, 'Sverdlovsk, Yellow Rain, and Novel Soviet Bioweapons: Allegations and Responses' Susan Wright (Editor) *Preventing a Biological Arms Race* (Cambridge Mass., The MIT Press, 1990) pp.220-238 and pp.199-219 respectively. More recent works include Jeanne Guillemin, 'Anthrax: The Investigation of a Deadly Outbreak' (Berkley and Los Angeles, University of California Press, 1999), Michael D. Gordin, 'The Anthrax Solution: The Sverdlovsk Incident and the Resolution of a Biological Weapons Controversy' *Journal of the History of Biology* 30:3 (1997), and Jonathan B. Tucker, 'The "yellow Rain" Controversy: Lessons for Arms Control Compliance' *The Nonproliferation Review* 8:1 (Spring 2001) pp.25-42.
45.	Sims, 'The Second Review Conference on the Biological Weapons Convention' p.267.
46.	Mark C. Storella, 'Poisoning Arms Control: The Soviet Union and Chemical/Biological Weapons' IFPA Special Report, 1984, p.34.
47.	Joseph Finder, 'Biological Warfare, Genetic Engineering, and the Treaty That Failed' *The Washington Quarterly* (Spring 1986) p.13.
48.	Douglas J. Feith, 'Biological Weapons & the Limits of Arms Control' *The International Interest* (Winter 1986/87) p.39.
49.	Arthur H. Westing, 'The Threat of Biological Warfare' *Bioscience* 35:10 (November 1985) p.632.
50.	Iris S. Portny, 'U.S. to oppose efforts to change biological, toxin weapons treaty' *Washington Times* 9 June 1986.
51.	United Nations, 'Second Review Conference of the Parties to the Convention on the Prohibition of the Development, Production and Stockpiling of Bacteriological (Biological) and Toxin Weapons and on Their Destruction' Final Document Geneva 1986, BWC/CONF.II/SR.4 (17 September 1986) p.5. (Hereinafter referred to as 'BWC 2RC' followed by document number, date and page reference(s) as appropriate.)
52.	BWC 2RC, BWC/CONF.II/SR.5 (19 September 1986) p.5.
53.	Ibid., p.8.
54.	BWC 2RC, BWC/CONF.II/SR.7 (22 September 1986) p.16.
55.	BWC 2RC, BWC/CONF.II/SR.8 (22 September 1986) p.3.
56.	BWC 2RC, BWC/CONF.II/SR.5 (19 September 1986) p.7.
57.	BWC 2RC, BWC/CONF.II/SR.6 (18 September 1986) p.5.
58.	BWC 2RC, BWC/CONF.II/SR.7 (22 September 1986) p.11.

59.	BWC 2RC, BWC/CONF.II/SR.5 (19 September 1986) p.11.
60.	BWC 2RC, BWC/CONF.II/SR.7 (22 September 1986) p.3.
61.	BWC 2RC, BWC/CONF.II/SR.3 (18 September 1986) p.6.
62.	BWC 2RC, BWC/CONF.II/SR.7 (22 September 1986) pp.13-14.
63.	Jozef Goldblat and Thomas Bernauer, 'The Third Review of the Biological Weapons Convention: Issues and Proposals' UNIDIR Research Paper Number 9 (New York, United Nations, 1991) p.18.
64.	Sims, 'The Second Review Conference on the Biological Weapons Convention' p.270.
65.	Lynn M. Hansen, 'Arms control in Vitro' *Disarmament* X:1 (Winter 1986/87) p.62.
66.	BWC 2RC, BWC/CONF.II/9 (22 September 1986) pp.3-6.
67.	Sims, 'The Second Review Conference on the Biological Weapons Convention' p.270.
68.	BWC 2RC, BWC/CONF.II/13/II (30 September 1986) pp.5-6.
69.	Proposals for CBMs and/or the CBM process were put forward by Australia and New Zealand (on the CBM process), Finland (inoculation of armed forces), Australia, Canada, France, Japan, Netherlands, Spain, and the UK (maximum containment facilities) Australia, Canada, Federal Republic of Germany, Italy, Netherlands, Norway, Spain, and the US (information on activities related to protection against biological and toxin weapons), Australia, Canada, France, Federal Republic of Germany, Japan, Netherlands, New Zealand, Spain, Turkey, and the US (unusual outbreaks of disease), Ireland (general support for CBMs), Sweden (High containment laboratories, testing grounds for biological weapons pre-entry into force, and testing grounds used now for purposes not prohibited by the BWC, orientation of relevant research programmes, active promotion of contacts between scientists, and, unusual outbreaks of disease), and Pakistan,(research and other activities not prohibited by the BWC) can be found at: BWC 2RC, BWC/CONF.II/9 pp.17-23.
70.	BWC 2RC, BWC/CONF.II/13/II, p.6.
71.	Barend ter Haar, 'The Future of Biological Weapons' (New York, Praeger, 1991) p.72.
72.	Ibid.
73.	The idea of transparency and confidence-building through basic co-operation between scientists has remained a strongly supported element throughout the life of the BWC. As an example of the ideas mooted in 1986, see Sims, 'Biological and Toxin Weapons: Issues in the 1986 Review' pp.15-17.
74.	BWC 2RC, BWC/CONF.II/SR.10 (1 October 1986) p.6.
75.	Winfried Lang, 'Taking the Pulse of the Biological Weapons Régime' *Disarmament* X:1 (Winter 1986/87) p.48.
76.	Ibid., p.49.
77.	Hansen, 'Arms control in Vitro' p.64.
78.	Eric J. McFadden, 'The Second Review Conference of the Biological Weapons Convention: One Step Forward, Many More to Go' *Stanford Journal of International Law* 24:1 (1987) p.101.
79.	A good indication of thinking about the problems with the BWC can be found in Sims, 'Biological and Toxin Weapons: Issues in the 1986 Review' and McFadden, 'The Second Review Conference of the Biological Weapons Convention: One Step Forward, Many More to Go', both of which concentrate on compliance issues. In Sims' paper the references to Article X correctly identify the beginnings of a trend

to widen the scope of the Article pursued by the developing states at the expense of its original meaning.

80. BWC 2RC, BWC/CONF.II/13/II (1986) p.4 for the agreed version in the Final Declaration and BWC/CONF.II/9 p.16 for the version proposed by Argentina, which was slightly amended.

81. BWC 2RC, BWC/CONF.II/9, p.30 for the proposal by Hungary on behalf of a group of Socialist states.

82. BWC 1RC, BWC/CONF.I/4 (20 February 1980) p.1.

83. Ibid.

84. Ibid.

85. Sims, 'The Evolution of Biological Disarmament' p.128 (see footnote 28).

86. Sims, 'Biological and Toxin Weapons: Issues in the 1986 Review' p.15.

87. ter Haar, 'The Future of Biological Weapons' p.36.

88. Sims, 'The Evolution of Biological Disarmament' p.120.

89. Westing, 'The Threat of Biological Warfare' p.632.

90. Mendoza Agreement on the Prohibition of Chemical and Biological Weapons, between Chile, Argentina and Brazil, 5 September 1991.

91. The detailed studies which brought together many of the proposals made by NGOs included: Barbara Hatch Rosenberg and Gordon Burck, 'Verification of Compliance with the Biological Weapons Convention' pp.300-329, and for a wider perspective, Richard Falk and Susan Wright, 'Preventing a Biological Arms Race: New Initiatives' pp.330-351, Susan Wright (Editor) *Preventing a Biological Arms Race* (Cambridge, Mass., The MIT Press, 1990); S. J. Lundin (Editor), 'Views on Possible Verification Measures for the Biological Weapons Convention' *SIPRI Chemical & Biological Warfare Studies No. 12* (Oxford, Oxford University Press, 1991); Federation of American Scientists, 'Proposals for the Third Review Conference of the Biological Weapons Convention' *Arms Control* 12:2 (September 1991) pp.240-254; Jozef Goldblat and Thomas Bernauer, 'The Third Review Conference of the Biological Weapons Convention: Issues and Proposals' UNIDIR Research Paper No. 9 (New York, United Nations, 1991); and, Sims, 'Reinforcing Biological Disarmament: Issues in the 1991 Review'. For a commentary on aspects of the proposals see, Graham S. Pearson, 'Strengthening the BTWC Regime: A Defense View' *Chemical Weapons Convention Bulletin* Issue no. 12 (June 1991) pp.2-6.

92. Federation of American Scientists, 'Proposals for the Third Review Conference of the Biological Weapons Convention' p.241.

93. Sims, 'Reinforcing Biological Disarmament: Issues in the 1991 Review' p.18.

94. Federation of American Scientists, 'Proposals for the Third Review Conference of the Biological Weapons Convention' p.241.

95. Sims, 'Reinforcing Biological Disarmament: Issues in the 1991 Review' p.19.

96. Federation of American Scientists, 'Proposals for the Third Review Conference of the Biological Weapons Convention' p.241.

97. John Issacs, 'Legislative Needs' Susan Wright (Editor) *Preventing a Biological Arms Race* p.292.

98. Federation of American Scientists, 'Proposals for the Third Review Conference of the Biological Weapons Convention' p.241.

99. Ibid.

100. Matthew Meselson, Martin M. Kaplan, and Mark A. Mokulsky, 'Verification of Biological and Toxin Weapons Disarmament' *Science & Global Security* 2 1991, p.248.

101. Federation of American Scientists, 'Proposals for the Third Review Conference of the Biological Weapons Convention' p.241.
102. Ibid.
103. Ibid.
104. Ibid.
105. Sims, 'Reinforcing Biological Disarmament: Issues in the 1991 Review' p.19 & pp. 19-24 for detailed proposals on all aspects of these organisational bodies.
106. Federation of American Scientists, 'Proposals for the Third Review Conference of the Biological Weapons Convention' p.241.
107. Ibid.
108. Meselson *et al*, 'Verification of Biological and Toxin Weapons Disarmament' p.247; Sims, 'Reinforcing Biological Disarmament: Issues in the 1991 Review' p.16.
109. Ibid.
110. Michael Moodie, 'The Soviet Union, Russia, and the Biological and Toxin Weapons Convention' *The Nonproliferation Review* 8:1 (Spring 2001) pp.59-69.
111. Richard Clarke, Assistant Secretary of State for Politico-Military Affairs, Testimony to the Foreign Affairs Subcommittee on Arms Control (US House of Representatives) reported in 'News Chronology' 11 July 1990, *Chemical Weapons Convention Bulletin* Issue No. 9 (September 1990) p.14.
112. See comments by Serguei Batsanov, 'News Chronology' 16 August 1990, *Chemical Weapons Convention Bulletin* Issue No. 9 (September 1990) p.19.
113. The Arms Control Reporter, 19 February 1991, 701.B.70.
114. See 'News Chronology' 6-8 February 1991, *Chemical Weapons Convention Bulletin* Issue No. 12 (June 1991) p.8.
115. Ibid.
116. The Arms Control Reporter, 8 February 1991, 701.B.69.
117. The Arms Control Reporter, 14 March 1991, 701.B.71.
118. The Arms Control Reporter, 1 May 1991, 701.B.74.
119. See 'News Chronology' 3 June 1991, *Chemical Weapons Convention Bulletin* Issue No. 13 (September 1991) p.8, and The Arms Control Reporter, 31 May 1991, 701.B.75.
120. See 'News Chronology' 29 May 1991, *Chemical Weapons Convention Bulletin* Issue No. 12 (June 1991) p.22.
121. The Arms Control Reporter, 6 September 1991, 701.B.79.
122. See 'News Chronology' 25 July 1991, *Chemical Weapons Convention Bulletin* Issue No. 13 (September 1991) p.16.
123. The Arms Control Reporter, 17 July 1991, 701.B.77.
124. The responses of those delegations which submitted information on relevant scientific and technological developments can be found in: United Nations, 'Third Review Conference of the Parties to the Convention on the Prohibition of the Development, Production and Stockpiling of Bacteriological (Biological) and Toxin Weapons and on Their Destruction' Geneva, BWC/CONF.III/4 (26 August 1991) and BWC/CONF.III/4/Add.1 (10 September 1991). (Hereinafter documents of the Third Review Conference are referred to as 'BWC 3RC' followed by document number, date and page reference where appropriate.)
125. BWC 3RC, BWC/CONF.III/4 (26 August 1991) p.5.
126. Ibid., p.26.
127. Ibid., p.25.

128. Ibid., p.33.
129. BWC 3RC BWC/CONF.III/4/Add.1 (10 September 1991) p.9.
130. BWC 3RC, BWC/CONF.III/4 (26 August 1991) p.29.
131. Ibid., p.9.
132. Ibid., p.4.
133. Ibid., p.33.
134. BWC 3RC, 'Position of principle of the Chinese delegation on the Biological Weapons Convention and its third review conference [sic]' BWC/CONF.III/18 (20 September 1991) p.3.
135. BWC 3RC, BWC/CONF.III/4 (26 August 1991) p.52.
136. Ibid.
137. BWC 3RC, BWC/CONF.III/18 (20 September 1991).
138. Sims, 'Four Decades of Missed Opportunities to Strengthen the BWC: 2001 too?' p.17.
139. Given that the US and the UK had proposed inclusion of this text, France had embraced the reformist agenda with zeal and China rarely used its veto, the most likely block on this proposal was the USSR. China's extreme minimalist position cannot be ignored and China may have been responsible for the rejection of this text, however a personal deduction is that the most likely candidate was the USSR.
140. Thomas Bernauer, 'The Chemistry of Regime Formation' (Aldershot, Dartmouth, 1993) pp.40-42.
141. Nicholas Sims, 'Achievements and Failures at the Third Review Conference' *Chemical Weapons Convention Bulletin* Issues no. 14 (December 1991) p.2.
142. Ibid., p.4.
143. Ibid.
144. United States General Accounting Office, 'Arms Control U.S. and International Efforts to Ban Biological Weapons' Report to the Honorable Albert Gore Jr., U.S. Senate, (Washington, D.C., General Accounting Office, December 1992) GAO/NSIAD-93-113 p.16.
145. Statement of Ronald F. Lehman, Head of the United States Delegation, Biological and Toxin Weapons Convention, Third Review Conference, September 10 1991. (Also summarised in, U.S Congress, Office of Technology Assessment 'Technologies Underlying Weapons of Mass Destruction' OTA-BP-ISC-115 (Washington, DC: Government Printing Office, 1993) p.74.
146. U.S Congress, 'Technologies Underlying Weapons of Mass Destruction' p.75.
147. J. P. Perry Robinson, Thomas Stock and Ronald G. Sutherland, 'The Chemical Weapons Convention: the success of chemical disarmament negotiation' *SIPRI Yearbook 1993: World Armaments and Disarmament* (Oxford, Oxford University Press, 1993) p.715.
148. Ibid., p.716.
149. Marie Isabelle Chevrier, 'Verifying the Unverifiable: Lessons from the Biological Weapons Convention' *Politics and the Life Sciences* 9:1 (August 1990) pp.93-105. See particularly pp. 96-98 on the changing nature of verification in the US and the discourse used to justify or reject verification of certain agreements.
150. Milton Leitenberg, 'Biological Weapons Arms Control' PRAC paper number 16, Center for International and Security Studies at Maryland, (Maryland, University of Maryland 1996) p.62.

151. M. Moodie, 'Bolstering Compliance with the Biological Weapons Convention Prospects for the Special Conference' *Chemical Weapons Convention Bulletin* Issue number 25 (September 1994) p.2.
152. BWC 3RC, BWC/CONF.III/23 pp.15-16.
153. Sims, 'The Second Review Conference on the Biological Weapons Convention' p.283.

Chapter 2

From VEREX to Ad Hoc Group

Introduction

A comprehensive study of the meetings, process, discussions and conclusions of the Ad Hoc Group of Governmental Experts (VEREX) between 1992 and 1993 has yet to be undertaken. That omission is not rectified in this chapter. The fact that no detailed study of VEREX has appeared in the public domain tells us quite a lot about the context and the final content of the VEREX report. In context it reflects both how VEREX originated and what followed it. Until recently VEREX was viewed as simply another stepping stone on the way to a verifiable BWC. VEREX was born out of compromise to maintain momentum in 1991 and its tightly drawn mandate reflects these restrictions. In reality VEREX could both do much and do nothing.

One observer referred to the mandate as prescribing 'an elaborate exercise in futility'[1] but the VEREX exercise provided an acceptable balance for both *minimalists* and *reformists* who envisaged it as a means to an end. Without doubt states parties in both camps envisaged very different endpoints, but as a process and a substantive exercise it served the needs of all parties. In each meeting of VEREX the mandate was important because it was so explicit.[2] It was broad enough to permit an exploration of any measure, or at least a discussion of it, but sufficiently limiting to assuage the doubts of *minimalists* who did not want to be committed to any measure or series of measures identified by VEREX. The requirements for a consensus report, the circulation of that report, the necessity of further action to trigger a Special Conference to consider the report, and the fact that a Special Conference would have to decide on further action, if any, by consensus, established a sufficient number of safeguards for less ambitious states parties. Progress beyond VEREX would (and did) require significant political effort.

The final report of VEREX actually went as far as it possibly could to endorse the views of the *reformists* that additional measures would strengthen the BWC and that implementation of the Convention could be improved. Whether or not that constituted 'verification' depended on the definition of that term. Nevertheless, the outcome of VEREX began to tip the balance of power in favour of the *reformists*. In terms of specifics VEREX held four meeting during 1992 and 1993.[3] The first meeting identified possible verification measures, the second examined those measures in greater detail, the third evaluated the measures against specific criteria within the mandate, and the fourth drafted the final report.[4]

VEREX I and VEREX II

US objections to verification of the BWC continued after the Third Review Conference. In the candidate's forum for the 1992 Presidential election in *Arms Control Today* the different approaches of the US to chemical and biological weapons were nuanced by President G.H.W. Bush. Quite correctly President Bush stated that a total ban on chemical weapons had been a major priority of the Administration and that US leadership was making the ambitious goal achievable. However, the claim that the US had been 'equally vigorous in trying to strengthen the [BWC]' and that at the Third Review Conference the US had been successful in achieving agreement to 'make its measures more effective' was hyperbolic.[5] The approach and activities of the US in the CWC and in the BWC were not comparable in terms of effort or effect. A more accurate assessment of the policy of the US to the BWC was provided in the closing comment of President Bush in this forum: '[w]e continue to press the international community to do everything practicable to shore up this vital international standard.'[6] Shoring up the BWC was the US objective, not strengthening it by additional substantive measures. However, external events did impact on the US position and its attitude to VEREX, notably the completion of the CWC and the Trilateral Agreement between the US, Russia and the UK. Both underlined the importance of on-site activities in compliance assessments. As a result, '[t]he US position softened visibly'[7] between the first and second meetings.

As Dando noted, because of the initial US position 'the actions taken by the West Europeans and other usually allied countries became crucial for the eventual outcome of the VEREX meetings.'[8] With France supporting a verification protocol[9], the Netherlands having 'a clear objective of producing an inspection protocol'[10] and Germany looking to establish a regime of several elements[11] the *reformists* sought to press ahead. They were not, however, ignorant of US concerns, and in support of their case the *reformists* attempted 'to divide the verification problem into practically solvable sub-problems.'[12] This approach suited, and was most likely tailored to, the working methods of VEREX during its first year where states parties sought to identify and then examine the potential utility of certain measures for the BWC.[13] [14]

One of the first VEREX working papers offered by France is indicative of the *reformists* approach to the problem.[15] The French paper identified what could and what could not be done in terms of verification of the BWC, what lessons existing arms control treaties offered, as well as those inappropriate, and what the experience of the United Nations Special Commission (UNSCOM) added to the knowledge of states parties. The UK suggested that 'the aim of a BWC verification regime should ... be primarily aimed towards detection of BW programmes on a military scale.'[16] Germany followed a similar line of argument and was realistic about what could be achieved: 'answers which can be given will not be complete and final ... [it] never can be a 100%-regime.'[17]

The US took a different view, outlining what it considered and meant by 'effective verification' and which factors should be used to assess the verification measures, including their contribution to monitoring compliance, the degree of deterrent value offered to prevent treaty violations, and 'the degree to which the verification measures can detect violations *long before they pose a risk* to national and international security'[18] [my emphasis]. Although the US paper was useful it was also ambiguous because it gave the impression that the US was outlining criteria by which it would judge the verification measures VEREX identified, while including much that was subjective. Identification 'long before it poses a risk' is ambiguous. How 'long' is long: weeks, months, years? And, what distinguishes a 'risk' from a 'threat' in this instance? If assessors of compliance are attempting to establish or gauge the precision and usefulness of a particular measure, 'long before' and 'risk' offer an ambiguous framework under which to make that assessment. It is even more imprecise and politically slippery than 'imminent threat' vis-à-vis Iraqi WMD in 2002-2003.

Australia, like its European allies in the Western Group, took a more pragmatic stance recognising what could and could not be achieved.[19] India offered a quite promising 'preliminary position' through the identification of a multifaceted approach to verification, including declarations and investigations, while Iran proposed to use existing mechanisms and institutions such as the powers granted to the UN Secretary-General, the ability of the WHO to routinely monitor biological facilities (notwithstanding the debate over whether WHO possessed such abilities), an international assistance system, and peaceful co-operation.[20]

Verifying the BWC was a difficult task that was never ignored by the *reformists*. For the Europeans and their allies in the Western Group two factors became increasingly important: confidence and verifiability. First, they recognised that 100 per cent confidence in any BWC verification regime was unattainable. Second, they believed that the further along the process a state (or other actor) got to the weaponization aspect of biological agents, the more likely the chance of detection.[21] These were not nuances; rather this approach reflected a lesson learned in other disarmament agreements that 100 per cent confidence in any verification system was impossible, but that did not mean a verification system was unable to enhance confidence in compliance. No *reformist* expected to achieve total confidence in compliance from a strengthened BWC. What they sought was a system of agreed measures and mechanisms which would allow them to deal with compliance through the legal framework of action a Protocol would provide. Whether or not there was a willingness to pursue and enforce compliance is an entirely different question, but until a compliance architecture of agreed legally-binding mechanisms was put in place, such questions were moot.

In its report VEREX I contained a Chairman's paper which listed the measures identified during second week of the meeting. There were 21 such measures and once they had been identified it was time to begin the more contentious work of assessing the validity and utility of these measures at VEREX II.[22] To assist that process VEREX was supported by meetings outside the formal framework of the states parties. During 1992 meetings were held in Stockholm, Bonn and the UK on specific issues such as on-site inspections and other verification measures.[23] However, a factor that affected VEREX II (23 November-3 December 1992) was the election of a Democrat Administration and the prospect of it taking a more amenable position on BWC verification.

50   *The Biological Weapons Convention*

During VEREX II each measure was examined from a scientific and technical standpoint. Such examinations were brought together in a standard format which defined each measure, its characteristics and technologies, its capabilities, its limitations, its potential for interaction with other measures, and the list of documents introduced to VEREX on that topic.[24] By the end of VEREX II, with the 1993 deadline of reporting fixed in their minds and the policies of the new US Administration still to be worked out, states parties began to doubt they had allocated sufficient time to give the issue the attention it required. As a consequence, the VEREX II report noted that additional efforts would be required to prepare its future work. Flowing from that a broad range of intersessional activities were envisaged prior to the next meeting.[25]

In effect the first year of activity provided the *reformists* with some hope that they were making progress towards a verification regime. However, the US was still opposed to verification.[26] In addition, the scale of the task was beginning to become very clear to states parties not only from the work of VEREX but also the difficulties UNSCOM was having in ascertaining the facts about the Iraqi BW programme, and the obstacles encountered by the US and the UK under the Trilateral Agreement with Russia. The VEREX group may have been tasked with assessing the scientific and technical aspects of verifying the BWC, but the politics of verification was never far from the minds of either *reformists* or *minimalists*.

VEREX III and VEREX IV

By VEREX III the CWC was open for signature. It was now time for diplomats to turn their attention to other areas of the arms control debate. In reality this meant the Comprehensive Test Ban Treaty and preparations for the Review and Extension Conference of the NPT, but it also included the BWC. The Netherlands summed up the view of many European states with a statement in the CD while VEREX III was in session: '[t]horough verification of the [BWC] would close another loophole in the broader regime for weapons of mass destruction. It would thus add to the security of us all.' [27]

Not all states parties held that view, even allowing for differences over what constituted 'thorough' or 'effective' verification. A UK government statement outlined a less ambitious position: '[e]ven though no verification regime in this difficult area could guarantee detection of non-compliance, it is likely that worthwhile deterrence could be achieved by a web of measures restricting potential violaters' room for manoeuvre.'[28] Critically, however, the anticipated new direction provided by President Clinton was not forthcoming. Four months into an Administration elected for its emphasis on domestic political issues this was not too much of a surprise. Waiting for the Clinton Administration to provide leadership and act as a catalyst for change, however, became a familiar event in the 1990s. Thus, despite the new Administration the US did not seem to be any more positively disposed towards BWC verification than it had been previously;[29] but, privately there were indications of a further shift in the US position.[30]

Another familiar pattern in the 1990s emerged at this juncture. With the prospect of a new US position more favourable to verification other problems began to emerge in public. States parties that had been able to disguise the depth of their opposition to the *reformist* agenda necessarily had to expose their positions. India, for example, 'characterized all but six of the 21 measures – including inspections, remote sensing and continuous monitoring – as technically unsound, prohibitively costly or unacceptably intrusive.'[31] This was a move away from the promising Indian position of 1992 and implied an intrusive CWC-type verification regime for the BWC was unacceptable to India. Political issues were also beginning to creep into the discussions in a much more open manner. The NAM made an unequivocal statement that VEREX had 'concentrated on accommodating the interests of the developed countries' and that in their view any measures identified to strengthen the BWC 'should be the least intrusive as possible.'[32] These actions were a shot across the bows of the *reformist* camp, confirming that even if US resistance to verification could be overcome the objections of others to intrusive verification would have to be addressed head on. The lines of contest had been identified and 'most delegations had made up their minds.'[33]. The consensus requirement for a report meant that on the eve of the final meeting of VEREX the balance of power in the BWC still lay with the *minimalists* who could prevent progress if they so decided.

The fourth meeting of VEREX was reported to be the 'most difficult'[34] and states parties undertook the drafting of a report for circulation among all other (non-attending) states parties to the Convention. The VEREX report identified 21 potential measures to assess compliance with the BWC's disarmament obligations, as per Table 2.1.[35] In its conclusion the report stated, *inter alia*:[36]

> The findings of the identification, examination and evaluation of the 21 potential verification measures against the agreed mandate criteria indicated that capabilities and limitations existed for each measure in varying degrees, although reliance could not be placed on any single measure by itself to determine [non-compliance].

Moreover, the consensus view of the states parties was that, 'potential verification measures as identified and evaluated could be useful to varying degrees in enhancing confidence, through increased transparency, that States Parties were fulfilling their obligations under the BWC.'[37] The report was by no means conclusive and identified both where further consideration and technical and financial implications of certain measures required additional examination. However, the critical outcome of VEREX was the consensus finding that some measures would – not could or might – contribute to strengthening the Convention:[38]

> Based on the examination and evaluation of the measures described ... against the criteria given in the mandate, the Group considered, from the scientific and technical standpoint, that some of the potential verification measures would contribute to strengthening the effectiveness and improve the implementation of the Convention, also recognizing that appropriate and effective verification could reinforce the Convention.

52　　　*The Biological Weapons Convention*

This finding left open many practical and political questions, but by identifying and recognising that certain measures *would* strengthen the BWC the states parties committed themselves to a follow-up process.

Table 2.1　Measures identified and examined by VEREX

Category	Sub-Category	Measure
Off-Site Measures	Information Monitoring	(1) Surveillance of Publications
		(2) Surveillance of Legislation
		(3) Data on Transfers
		(4) Multilateral information sharing
	Data Exchange	(5) Declarations
		(6) Notifications
	Remote Sensing	(7) Surveillance by satellite
		(8) Surveillance by aircraft
		(9) Ground-based surveillance
	Inspections	(10) Sampling and identification
		(11) Observation
		(12) Auditing
On-Site Measures	Exchange visits	(13) International arrangements
	Inspections	(14) Interviewing
		(15) Visual inspection
		(16) Identification of key equipment
		(17) Auditing
		(18) Sampling and Identification
		(19) Medical examination
	Continuous monitoring	(20) By instruments
		(21) By personnel

Government analysts who had been close to the CWC negotiations noted that 'VEREX concluded that the verification of the BWC *was* feasible, at least from a scientific and technical viewpoint.'[39] [My emphasis] To be fair, these analysts represented a state party, Australia, in favour of a verification regime for the BWC, but from a scientific and technical perspective the BWC could certainly be strengthened through the addition of measures and procedures which would permit a number of different verification activities. States parties could not, after recognising that the BWC needed further strengthening and identifying the measures by which they could achieve that objective, leave their work unfinished. The use of 'would' effectively bound them to further action.

This is not to say that consensus had broken out at the final meeting of VEREX or all were agreed that future action should be undertaken. There were strong indications that a final report hung in the balance. By its nature the consensus report reflected a range of different views and was influenced by both the discussions during VEREX and the different ideas about what should happen after

From VEREX to Ad Hoc Group 53

VEREX. The US 'withheld a complete endorsement of its conclusions'[40] and issues about the costs of verification, the potential intrusiveness of inspections, and the threat some believed on-site measures posed to confidential proprietary information nearly scuppered the final report. The US was also concerned that complete endorsement of the report would both commit it to a follow on mechanism which had not taken shape and imply the BWC could be effectively verified.[41] As a result, it was 'far from clear that the US ... reached a new consensus supporting far-reaching change.'[42] Nevertheless, the US position was critically important, as Dando reported:[43]

> If the USA has not basically changed its position, other countries may also find opportunity to obstruct. China and India, among others, are clearly not yet enthusiastic supporters of the VEREX conclusions. ... A less benign interpretation would suggest that such states might be using concerns over the confidentiality of information as a cover for preventing intrusive inspection systems that they object to for reasons of national security.

China and India sought to avoid intrusive verification 'and seemed determined to block VEREX from reaching an agreement by consensus.'[44] Although the NAM was keen to have its view recorded and determined to influence the debate, many of its states were also proponents of arms control and verification. As an actor the NAM was *minimalist* in many respects (as opposed to the Western Group which failed to act as a group on most occasions), but a significant proportion of the non-aligned states were supporters of the *reformist* agenda. With many of the NAM determined to reach consensus and 'a favourable assessment' of the report, the efforts of India and China at blocking progress were prevented, not least by the Latin American states parties.[45] Iran, also, was a problem state party in the final stages of the meeting insisting that export controls be condemned; an effort 'which met fierce resistance' from the Western Group and the Chair of VEREX.[46]

The combination of US support and NAM *reformists* pursuing their own agenda led to what was considered a favourable final report. According to one assessment, '[t]he generally positive and constructive tone of these conclusions stands in striking contrast to the reports of discord that could be heard in the earlier phases of the VEREX process.'[47] The positions of many key states parties were reported as follows:[48]

> experts from Australia, Canada, France, Germany, the Netherlands and the UK might well have supported stronger language in the conclusions. The Brazilian and Cuban experts, too, worked for a strong report. The Chinese and Indian experts ... like their US counterparts, cautioned against the use of language that might lend support to intrusive measures of verification. Iranian concerns about impacts on technology transfer processes found some expression. Russian and East European contributions were not assertive.

Although attempts to prevent further progress were defeated this in no way reflected a comprehensive *reformist* victory. The splits among the states parties were clear and they explain why the VEREX report was, as Leitenberg put it, 'not particularly a blaze of enthusiasm'[49] for verification. Through its identification of measures which, according to all states parties, 'would contribute to strengthening

54 *The Biological Weapons Convention*

the effectiveness and improve the implementation of the Convention' VEREX went as far as it possibly could. The key question was now political because a Special Conference was required to decide on any further action.

The Special Conference, 1994

The politics of most of the states parties that would determine the future direction of the BWC were now readily identifiable: the US, Russia, China, India, and Iran on the *minimalist* side of the debate and the European states, Australia, New Zealand, and Canada, for the *reformists*. Others had yet to be convinced or to reveal their position openly and while it is disparaging to all other states parties to assert they were secondary players in determining the future of the BWC, the significance of many states parties, including those in the Western Group, was the extent to which they could forge the agenda, be the driving force for change, and carry other states parties with them; particularly the US. With the US on board the *reformists* could win the contest; without the US, the combination of China, India, Iran, Russia and the US would thwart the *reformists*. This combination of states parties was of critical importance. They did not hold a common position. In fact, they deliberately distanced themselves from each other and their power rested on withholding support. If they all withheld support for a particular course of action it added up to an insurmountable obstacle to the *reformists*. The other identifiable issue here is the ability of India, Iran, and to an extent China, to use the NAM as political cover for their *minimalist* outlook. If the majority in the NAM pursued their *reformist* preferences the *minimalists* among them were exposed and became vulnerable to political pressure. If NAM solidarity was deemed more important then the *minimalists* among them held sway and the *reformist* states parties in all caucus groups could be thwarted.

For the *reformists* the increase in their number during 1992-1993, the ability to draw on support from Western, Eastern and NAM states parties, and the positive outcome of the VEREX exercise reinforced their political will to continue to push for change. The balance of power in the BWC was tipped decisively in favour of the *reformists* late in 1993 and during 1994 when the US administration softened its approach and moved from the *minimalist* camp to align with its Western Group colleagues and other *reformists*. On 10 November 1993 US Undersecretary of State Lynn Davis stated to the House Committee on Foreign Affairs that, 'we are parting company with the previous Administration and promoting new measures designed to increase transparency of activities and facilities that could have biological weapons applications, thereby increasing confidence in compliance with the Convention.'[50]

This change of position left China, India, and Iran exposed and open to criticism if they continued to block progress in the BWC. However, the step-by-step nature of further action built into the VEREX mandate meant China, India, Iran and other *minimalists* could focus on the political, rather than technical, issues related to strengthening the BWC. These were bought openly into play once more in 1994, as Dando noted.[51]

The fact that government experts have reached a positive conclusion on the possibility of verifying the [BWC] from a scientific and technical standpoint does not mean that this multilateral process has had a successful outcome. Great difficulties could lie ahead over the next few years.

Under the mandate the final report of VEREX was to be circulated to all states parties to the Convention. If, following such a circulation, a majority requested a Special Conference to consider the report in greater detail such a conference would be convened by the Depositaries. By 13 December 1993 53 states parties had requested or expressed an interest in a Special Conference.[52] Zimbabwe added its voice on 16 February 1994, thereby providing the required majority necessary for the Depositaries to act.[53]

Prior to the Special Conference the Netherlands and Australia mooted the possibility of negotiating the additional agreement under the CD in Geneva, but at the Preparatory Committee (11-15 April) the indications were against this route.[54] It was also clear that a follow on process would not be reached through easy agreement. The US still had reservations[55] and in the UN Disarmament Commission Iran stated that the NAM had concerns about verification of the BWC, claiming that the NAM:[56]

will not go along with an intrusive verification system … [without] real guarantees and commitment for the removal of all restrictions as well as transfers of material and related technology by the producing countries before considering a new verification system.

In simple terms export controls and the Australia Group were put on the agenda and in the sights of hard-line NAM states parties. In the run up to the Special Conference, however, it was not all bad news; the US position was further clarified and the goal of 'a legally binding protocol specifying a set of mutually reinforcing off-site and on-site measures' was established. Australia, Canada, Finland, Germany (for the EU), Sweden, and Switzerland, shared similar objectives.[57] The *reformist* caucus was looking increasingly powerful and such power was reflected in the official documents of the Special Conference.[58]

The European Union and its allies drew attention to the poor implementation record of the BWC. In their view, '[e]xperience had shown that measures that were not legally-binding were insufficient … [and] [m]ore binding obligations were necessary, like the ones stipulated in other recent conventions in the field of disarmament and arms control.'[59] Second, linked to this, '[t]he VEREX results had convinced the European Union that verification of the Convention was possible.'[60] Finland associated itself with the EU statement.[61] Sweden followed a similar line noting not only by its historical discontent with the BWC's provisions but that the facts demonstrated that politically-binding measures, particularly the CBM results 'were not encouraging'[62] and that the VEREX debate had shown it 'was possible to elaborate a verification regime.'[63] Switzerland and Australia concluded respectively that proliferation concerns and scientific developments meant 'measures to strengthen the Convention were important and urgent'[64] and that 'the issue of verification was the key to the future health of the Convention.'[65] Canada

56   *The Biological Weapons Convention*

shared these sentiments.[66] Those in the *reformist* camp updated, but essentially repeated, positions from 1986 and 1991. The decisive factor was the US position, which was articulated as one which 'fully supported the preparation of a protocol containing a regime to strengthen [the BWC].'[67] The actual discourse used by the US was significant both in 1994 and for the future because the objective and purpose of the Protocol to the US was not verification.[68]

> The measures set forth in the protocol should help strengthen the Convention by establishing an official benchmark for identifying discrepancies or ambiguities pertaining to facilities or activities and for seeking clarification, providing a mechanism for pursuing specific activities of concern and allowing for direct diplomatic engagement to resolve compliance concerns.

The envisaged legally-binding protocol would not *verify* whether states parties were complying with the BWC; rather the new agreement would strengthen the Convention. For the other *reformists* this distinction did not matter a great deal in 1994, not least because no *reformist* state party believed the BWC could be verified with absolute confidence. For most *reformists* it was about degrees of confidence and having an agreed legal framework, benchmarks, and concomitant mechanisms in place to pursue legitimate concerns about implementation of the BWC. This was exactly what the US was now advocating.

The US may have altered its position and joined the *reformists*, but other states parties had not and remained in the *minimalist* camp. China was much more circumspect, arguing that '[c]onfidence-building measures had proven to be a sure way of strengthening the effectiveness of the Convention...[and that] the VEREX group's study had shown that the technical means for verification of biological weapons were still inadequate.'[69] This position was clearly at variance with that of other states parties who considered – and were on record as considering – the CBMs a failure ('not encouraging' in diplomatic parlance) and that the technical means of verification were adequate. China was by no means the only reluctant state party. Indonesia urged caution, the avoidance of artificial deadlines, and a recognition that 'the application of sophisticated technology in verifying the BWC should avoid hampering ... national sovereignty as recognised by international law.'[70] India underlined the need for a number of issues to be 'fully examined'[71], which was a code for buying more time. Iran went further, outlining its view that 'providing a verification system for the BWC had proved far more demanding than originally anticipated' and that regional security concerns – viz. Israel – the question of peaceful co-operation, the legal status of any future Protocol, and the 'ambitious and unnecessary' idea of an independent organization to oversee the Protocol and the BWC all needed to be considered.[72] According to Leitenberg, 'several nations – Iran above all – wanted to see nothing further take place'[73] in 1994, an assessment which would fit with Iran's statement to the Disarmament Commission and the emphasis placed on CBMs, expressions of the need for caution and necessity for further and full examination of the range of options described by China and India.

China, Iran, and India would not risk being openly branded as unsupportive of arms control and disarmament measures.[74] These states did, however, maintain significant leverage by virtue of their status in the NAM and through that caucus their numbers. In addition, consensus was required on how to proceed with strengthening the BWC and this provided a strong bargaining position. As Sims had noted at the 1991 Review Conference, the developing states were unlikely to agree to a partial strengthening of the BWC through improvements only to the compliance architecture. In their view all obligations under the BWC required improved implementation; and that included Article X.[75] Furthermore, a number of developing states were not satisfied with the non-proliferation provisions of Article XI of the CWC and they were determined to prevent a similar situation arising in any new instrument of the BWC. This led to disagreements about the scope of any new measures to strengthen the Convention, particularly whether scientific co-operation had to be improved.

These disputes were reflected in the Chairman's rolling text of the final declaration and its revised version[76] whereby the initial mandate of the Ad Hoc Group was rejected because it lacked specific mention of peaceful co-operation and the non-proliferation concerns of the NAM. The influence of China, Iran and India can be clearly seen, because the final mandate follows closely the language used in their trilateral working paper.[77] The necessary compromise was contained in the agreed mandate of the new Ad Hoc Group. States parties decided to:[78]

establish an Ad Hoc Group, open to all States Parties. The objective of this Ad Hoc Group shall be to consider appropriate measures, including possible verification measures, and draft proposals to strengthen the Convention, to be included, as appropriate, in a legally binding instrument, to be submitted for the consideration of the States Parties. In this context, the Ad Hoc Group shall, inter alia consider:

- Definitions of terms and objective criteria, such as lists of bacteriological (biological) agents and toxins, their threshold quantities, as well as equipment and types of activities, where relevant for specific measures designed to strengthen the Convention;

- The incorporation of existing and further enhanced confidence building and transparency measures, as appropriate, into the regime;

- A system of measures to promote compliance with the Convention, including, as appropriate, measures identified, examined and evaluated in the VEREX Report. Such measures should apply to all relevant facilities and activities, be reliable, cost effective, non-discriminatory and as non-intrusive as possible, consistent with the effective implementation of the system and should not lead to abuse;

- Specific measures designed to ensure effective and full implementation of Article X, which also avoid any restrictions incompatible with the obligations undertaken under the Convention, noting that the provisions of the Convention should not be used to impose restrictions and/or limitations on the transfer for purposes consistent with the objectives and provisions of the Convention of scientific knowledge, technology, equipment and materials.

58   *The Biological Weapons Convention*

Measures should be formulated and implemented in a manner designed to protect sensitive commercial proprietary information and legitimate national security needs.

Measures shall be formulated and implemented in a manner designed to avoid any negative impact on scientific research, international cooperation and industrial development.

Despite the length of the mandate the key component of it was quite simple: 'draft proposals to strengthen the Convention, to be included, as appropriate, in a legally binding instrument.' Note, however, the language used and the manner in which the mandate was constructed: verification measures were possible, but not a requirement; the measures could be in a legally-binding instrument, *if appropriate*, but other types of instrument and other types of agreement were not ruled out if a legally-binding agreement was deemed inappropriate for such measures; and, it was all for the consideration of states parties at a future date and was not immediately binding on them. Furthermore, the Ad Hoc Group was required *to consider* definitions, CBMs, compliance measures, peaceful co-operation – the identified aspects – but it was not required *to agree* any such measures related to them, whether singularly, or in combination, or in a legally-binding instrument. None of these issues *had* to be in a legally-binding instrument.[79] Such distinctions were not extraneous to the agreement on the mandate because the mandate was a very carefully crafted compromise. Yet, as the Ad Hoc Group embarked upon its task the precision and the nuances were left behind. In practice, the interpretation and the understanding was that the new legally-binding instrument would contain measures which addressed all these elements. That was the required compromise deal if the Convention was going to be strengthened.

Minimalism and *Reform* 1992-1994

The compromise born out of the 1991 Conference reflected both the increasing power of the *reformists* to move the agenda forward and the resilience of the *minimalists* to hold back the push for reform. Even when giving ground to the *reformists*, as in the creation of VEREX, the *minimalists* were able to establish a series of further obstacles down the line. The *reformists* had to commit themselves to a process and to stay committed to it if they were to succeed. There was no automaticity and apathy – so prevalent under agreed treaties – served the *minimalists*.

VEREX went as far as it could possibly go in endorsing verification. With all the provisos and explanations in the final report the critical element of it hinged on the use of the word 'would'. It was true, as the report's conclusion outlined, that of the 21 measures identified in the first week of VEREX some had greater capabilities and utility than others; some had significant limitations; technical and scientific shortcomings existed; some were not capable by themselves of differentiating between compliance and non-compliance; the mandate of VEREX did make it difficult to assess the feasibility and effectiveness of the identified measures; that concerns about the protection of national security and commercial proprietary information existed; that the evaluation of some measures was not exhaustive; that measures in combination with each other would probably produce better results; and, that no single measure could differentiate conclusively between permitted and prohibited activities. All states parties, however, considered that some of the measures would contribute to strengthening of the BWC. Everyone knew there was a problem with the BWC – otherwise VEREX would never have been established – and now everyone agreed that a number of measures had been identified which would begin to alleviate some of those problems. VEREX committed the states parties to further action.

Critical to further action was the attitude of one particular state party; the US. This was particularly true in the run up to the Special Conference. Through its change of policy which moved away from insistence on its singular interpretation of 'effective verification' to strengthening the BWC, the Clinton Administration effectively followed the line of the previous Bush Administration vis-à-vis the CWC. To paraphrase Robinson *et al*, the importance of the change in position lay in its express recognition of what had been the case, that no international ban on biological weapons could ever be fully verifiable. The US joined the *reformist* camp and in doing so tipped the balance of power in their favour. The *reformist* tide became unstoppable at this juncture and the remaining *minimalists* were exposed and vulnerable to the increased pressure.

Although the US had changed its position, the balance of power was still precarious and the BWC was not the major arms control issue on the agenda. Extension of the NPT in 1995 and the negotiations on the CTBT were the main areas of attention. As a result even with agreement to negotiate legally-binding measures a 'key issue was to find time for meetings.'[80] The Ad Hoc Group secured a procedural meeting (3 days) and two further meetings in 1995, each of two weeks. It also secured four weeks in 1996, when its strongest proponents had initially expected it to submit a Protocol to the Fourth Review Conference. The allocation of only eight weeks negotiating time 'was interpreted by some delegations as indicating a lack of priority and evidence that the BWC needs greater political support.'[81] [82] As it turned out, that was a correct interpretation. The balance of power may have shifted, but time, apathy, changing political situations, and attrition were the allies of the *minimalists* now. As 1995 dawned the states parties convened in Geneva twenty years after the entry into force of the BWC for an ultimately decisive contest between its *reformists* and *minimalists*.

Notes

1. Barbara Hatch Rosenberg, 'Progress Toward Verification of the Biological Weapons Convention' J. B. Poole and R. Guthrie (Editors) *Verification 1993* (London, Brassey's (UK), 1993) p.189.
2. United Nations, 'Ad Hoc Group of Governmental Experts to Identify and Examine Potential Verification Measures from a Scientific and Technical Standpoint',

BWC/CONF.III/VEREX/9 Geneva 1993, pp. 1-2. (Hereinafter referred to as 'VEREX' followed by document number (and date where appropriate).)

3. VEREX meetings were as follows: VEREX I 30 March-10 April 1992; VEREX II 23 November-4 December 1992; VEREX III 24 May-4 June 1993; and VEREX IV 13-24 September 1993.

4. Tibor Tóth, Erhard Geissler and Thomas Stock, 'Verification of the BWC' Erhard Geissler and John P. Woodall (Editors) *Control of Dual-Threat Agents: The Vaccines for Peace Programme* SIPRI Chemical and Biological Warfare Studies Number 15 (Oxford, Oxford University Press, 1994), pp.67-76.

5. 'George Bush and Arms Control: The Questions in 1992' *Arms Control Today* 22:3 (April 1992) p.5.

6. Ibid.

7. Rosenberg, 'Progress Toward Verification of the Biological Weapons Convention' p.190.

8. Malcolm Dando, 'Biological Warfare in the 21st Century' (London, Brassey's (UK), 1994) p.164.

9. Ibid.

10. Ibid.

11. Ibid., p.165.

12. Ibid.

13. VEREX, BWC/CONF.III/VEREX/9 Geneva 1993, pp. 3-6.

14. For the detailed proposals and positions of states parties during VEREX reference should be made to the working papers of VEREX. Some of the VEREX documents are available online at the Biological and Toxin Weapons Convention website http://www.opbw.org/

15. VEREX, 'France, Group of Experts on the Verification of the Biological Weapons Convention' BWC/CONF.III/VEREX/WP.2 (30 March 1992).

16. VEREX, United Kingdom, 'Verification of the BWC: Possible Directions' BWC/CONF.III/VEREX/WP.1 (30 March 1992) p.3.

17. VEREX, Germany, 'Options for the Verification of the BWC' BWC/CONF.III/VEREX/WP.4 (31 March 1992) p.2.

18. VEREX, United States, 'Verification Measures: Goals and Purposes' BWC/CONF.III/VEREX/WP.8 (1 April 1992) p.1.

19. VEREX, Australia, 'The Biological Weapons Convention: A Possible Verification Regime' BWC/CONF.III/VEREX/WP.10 (1 April 1992).

20. VEREX, India, 'A Preliminary approach to the verification regime for the Biological Weapons Convention' BWC/CONF.III/VEREX/WP.29 (9 April 1992), and VEREX, Islamic Republic of Iran, 'Elements of Biological Weapons Monitoring Systems' BWC/CONF.III/VEREX/WP.25 (7 April 1992).

21. Dando, 'Biological Warfare in the 21st Century' pp.165-166.

22. VEREX, 'ANNEX I, VEREX I Summary' in BWC/CONF.III/VEREX/9 p.37.

23. News Chronology, *Chemical Weapons Convention Bulletin* Issue number 18, 26-29 October 1992, p.20.

24. VEREX, 'ANNEX II, VEREX 2 Summary' in BWC/CONF.III/VEREX/9 pp.52-122.

25. News Chronology, *Chemical Weapons Convention Bulletin* Issue number 19, 4 December 1992, pp.11-12.

26. The Arms Control Reporter, 3 December 1992, 701.B.104-701.B.105.

27. News Chronology, *Chemical Weapons Convention Bulletin* Issue number 21, 3 June 1993, p.15.
28. Ibid., 5 July 1993, p.22.
29. Ibid., 4 June 1993, p.15.
30. The Arms Control Reporter, 24 May-6 June 1993, 701.B.116.
31. News Chronology, *Chemical Weapons Convention Bulletin* Issue number 21, 3 June 1993, p.15.
32. VEREX, BWC/CONF.III/VEREX/WP.150, 'Statement of the Non-Aligned and Other Developing Countries Before the Meeting of the Ad Hoc Group.'
33. Barbara Hatch Rosenberg, 'A regime to Monitor Compliance with the Biological Weapons Convention Moves Closer' J.B. Poole and R. Guthrie (Editors) *Verification 1994* (London, Brassey's (UK) 1994) p.129.
34. Tibor Tóth *et al*, 'Verification of the BWC' p.69.
35. VEREX, BWC/CONF.III/VEREX/9.
36. Ibid., p.7.
37. Ibid., p.9.
38. Ibid.
39. Annabelle Duncan and Robert J. Matthews, 'Development of a Verification Protocol for the Biological and Toxin Weapons Convention' J. B. Poole and R. Guthrie (Editors) *Verification 1996* (Boulder, Westview Press, 1996) p.156.
40. The Arms Control Reporter, 13-24 September 1993, 701.B.118.
41. Ibid.
42. Dando, 'Biological Warfare in the 21st Century' p.178.
43. Ibid., p.179.
44. The Arms Control Reporter, 13-24 September 1994, 701.B.118.
45. The Arms Control Reporter, 13-24 September 1994, 701.B.119.
46. The Arms Control Reporter, 13-24 September 1994, 701.B.118.
47. News Chronology, *The Chemical Weapons Convention Bulletin* Issue number 22 (December 1993) 24 September 1992, p.17.
48. Ibid.
49. Milton Leitenberg, 'Biological Weapons Arms Control' PRAC paper number 16, Center for International and Security Studies at Maryland (Maryland, University of Maryland, 1996) p.67.
50. The Arms Control Reporter, 10 November 1993, 701.B.120.
51. Dando, 'Biological Warfare in the 21st Century' p.178.
52. The Arms Control Reporter, 13 December 1993, 701.B.121.
53. News Chronology, *Chemical Weapons Convention Bulletin* Issue number 24 (June 1994) 16 February, p.15.
54. The Arms Control Reporter, 27 January 1994, 701.B.123.
55. The Arms Control Reporter, 11-15 April 1994, 701.B.128.
56. The Arms Control Reporter, 19 April 1994, 701.B.129.
57. The Arms Control Reporter, 9 August 1994, 701.B.130.
58. United Nations, 'Special Conference of the Parties to the Convention on the Prohibition of the Development, Production and Stockpiling of Bacteriological (Biological) and Toxin Weapons and on Their Destruction' Geneva, 1994. For information on the positions and statements of delegations see the summary records, pp.73-125. (Hereinafter referred to as 'BWC SPCONF' (followed by document number).)
59. BWC SPCONF, BWC/SPCONF/1 Part IV, p. 86 (from summary record number 2).

60. Ibid., p.87.
61. Ibid., pp.87-88.
62. Ibid., p.90.
63. Ibid.
64. Ibid., p.96.
65. Ibid., p.91.
66. Ibid., pp.99-100.
67. Ibid., p.88.
68. Ibid., p.89.
69. Ibid., p.104.
70. Ibid., p.110.
71. Ibid.
72. Ibid., pp.111-112.
73. Leitenberg, 'Biological Weapons Arms Control' p.67.
74. The Special Conference documentation and the secondary sources on the events of September 1994 make it clear that India, Iran and China were the principal obstacles to consensus and demanded significant concessions. See for example, 'China's View on Follow-up Mechanism for Strengthening the BWC' (Working Paper 13), BWC/SPCONF/1 Part III, p.42, 'China, India, Iran (Islamic republic of)' (Working Paper 15) BWC/SPCONF/1 Part III, pp.44-45.
75. Nicholas Sims, 'Achievements and Failures at the Third Review Conference' *Chemical Weapons Convention Bulletin* Issue number 14 (December 1991) p.2
76. BWC SPCONF, BWC/SPCONF/1 Part III, pp.65-70.
77. BWC SPCONF, BWC/SPCONF/1 'China, India, Iran (Islamic republic of)' (Working Paper 15) pp.44-45.
78. Ibid., Part II, Final Declaration, p.9.
79. Onno Kervers, 'Strengthening Compliance with the Biological Weapons Convention: The Protocol Negotiations' *Journal of Conflict and Security Law* 7:2 2002 p.282.
80. Annabelle Duncan and Robert J. Matthews, 'Development of a Verification Protocol for the Biological and Toxin Weapons Convention' p.156.
81. Ibid.
82. The Arms Control Reporter, 19-30 September 1994, 701.B.132.

PART II
THE PROTOCOL NEGOTIATIONS

Chapter 3

Declarations

Introduction

This first chapter in the main section of the book examines the declarations included in the draft Protocol and their role in the compliance architecture established to strengthen the Convention. As in the preceding section the conceptual framework is provided by *minimalism* and *reform*. Using the declaration requirements contained in the composite text the rationale for the inclusion of each declaration and how the composite text sought to balance the objectives of both *minimalists* and *reformists* is analysed. We then go on to identify those declarations and notifications which were not included in the composite text, but were proposed in the rolling text.

Providing information on activities and facilities relevant to the Convention was not contested for two reasons. First, supplying information to an international organization on relevant activities was central to both the NPT and the CWC. Under the safeguards system administered by the IAEA declarations were required on peaceful nuclear activities, whereas under the CWC declarations were the foundation of the verification system of the OPCW. Second, states parties had recognised the usefulness of supplying relevant information in 1986 with the development of the CBMs, which were revised and expanded in 1991.

The critical question is which of the two competing visions – *minimalism* or *reform* – gained the ascendant position? Even among the most reluctant *minimalist* states parties there was an acceptance of formalising certain CBMs and *minimalism* can therefore be understood as an approach that would have made relevant existing CBMs mandatory. The baseline for the draft Protocol can therefore be set as mandatory declaration requirements for: (1) maximum biological containment facilities; (2) biodefence research and development programmes; (3) information on legislation and regulations taken to implement the Convention; (4) vaccine production facilities licensed for the production of human vaccines; (5) reporting of outbreaks of infectious disease; and, (6) information on past offensive and defensive biological weapons programmes. These declarations would cover six of the existing eight CBMs (ignoring the 'Nothing to declare' CBM). Notwithstanding the fact that some of these CBMs were themselves contested or unpopular, for example reporting on outbreaks of disease, the inclusion or exclusion of any of these six CBMs as mandatory declarations in the Protocol would provide an indication of the *minimalist-reformist* contest and which camp gained the upper hand in the final version of the draft Protocol.

Among the *reform* party the inclusion of relevant existing CBMs plus those proposals made by *reformists* in 1986, 1991 or the intervening period, and/or measures brought in from other agreements, for example from the IAEA safeguards or CWC, appeared to be a reasonable expectation. As a baseline *reformist* vision declarations based on the CBMs and, in addition, the following activities could be expected: (1) work with certain agents and toxins, based on the assumption of an agreed list of pathogens deemed to be of greatest concern and because both the IAEA and the CWC envisaged declarations of information based on work with certain types of material or chemicals; (2) genetic modification of biological agents and toxins, because of concerns expressed by states parties at successive review conferences about the potential threat of genetic modification of agents and toxins;[1] (3) animal, as well as human, vaccine production facilities, on the basis that such facilities contained similar relevant equipment for the production of biological agents and toxins; (4) military, civil or industrial facilities with the capability to produce biological weapons, in order to improve information on production capabilities; (5) aerobiological activities, on account of aerosol dissemination of agents and toxins being the most effective method of delivering a biological or toxin weapon; (6) information on laboratories or facilities with certain containment or biosafety levels; (7) information on agents and toxins, materials and equipment subject to national controls and/or export licensing requirements in order to provide information relevant to strengthening Article III of the Convention.[2]

Neither of the above represent a complete list of the activities, facilities or capabilities that might be relevant to the BWC, but they do represent that already accepted as relevant by the states parties – the CBMs – or that proposed as relevant by at least some states parties. In that sense it is important to understand the states parties had been considering which facilities and activities were most relevant to the BWC for nine years (from 1986) and had recently completed VEREX. As a consequence, there were no major surprises in terms of the types of activity or facility on the agenda for mandatory declarations. The inclusion or omission of some or all of the above declarations would not, by itself, decide the contest between the *reformists* or *minimalists*, but the final declarations would provide a good indication of the actual scope of the future Protocol and how far states parties were willing to increase transparency about their activities.

The role of declarations

There is a wealth of literature on the actual purpose and function of declarations in arms control agreements and it is instructive that both IAEA safeguards and the CWC are based on the submission of information to the organization by its states parties; i.e. declarations. Guthrie referred to declarations as 'the starting point for most verification regimes'[3] and identified three functions: first, to provide a baseline of information that may be checked and from which discrepancies might be identified; second, to create confidence in explanations for the legitimate possession of materials and to reduce misunderstandings; and, third, to make

Declarations 67

cheating difficult because declarable activity at undeclared facilities would become conspicuous.[4] During VEREX declarations were defined as, '[m]andatory, periodic reporting on a regular basis of information considered to be of relevance for verification of the BWC'[5] and VEREX identified them as the most useful measure to the verification architecture.[6] As Pearson noted, 'there is a very wide international agreement that declarations have a central role to play'[7] in any strengthened BWC. However, the provision of information (declarations) is not a panacea to disarmament or dual-use problems. The utility of declarations is dependent on the accuracy of the information provided within them. As such, in both VEREX and the Ad Hoc Group, states parties recognised that they were not a stand-alone measure; simply one measure to be used with others in combination.

Throughout the negotiations the debate was less a question of declarations *per se*, rather, what equipment, work, or activity required a declaration? That is to say, what would *trigger* a declaration? This latter issue revolved around a more focussed debate on declaration triggers. As indicated in the *minimalist* vision above, the obvious starting point for consideration of what might have been declared was the CBMs since they were existing politically binding declarations. However, the exchange of information under the CBMs indicated that certain CBMs had greater significance than others in devising a legally binding compliance architecture. For example, while the CBM related to the promotion of contacts between scientists illustrated one approach to enhancing confidence in the Convention, it was considerably less important than information on containment, biodefence, and vaccine production facilities in terms of compliance. During the course of the negotiations it is worth noting that many of the proposed declaration triggers were in a recognisable form from the first version of the rolling text (1997). In addition, seven of the declarations were recognisable from the CBMs. Both factors illustrate the nine years of activity in this area, but four years later, in early 2001, of the agreed declarations in the last version of the rolling text – those without square brackets – all but one were based on the CBMs; the exception being the declaration of work with listed agents or toxins. This suggests quite strongly that agreement was most likely if the outcome of the negotiations was evolutionary, building on agreements from previous review conferences and taking the CBMs one stage further; a *minimalist* outcome.

The composite text

The last version of the rolling text contained twelve declarations. Of these, two were categorized as initial declarations, ten were categorised as annual declarations and there were, in addition, three notifications, as outlined in Table 3.1. In contrast, the composite text contained provisions requiring two initial declarations and six annual declarations, with no notifications. This should not be construed as a simple reduction in the number of declarations because within the composite text certain declarations contained provisions for more than one type of facility or activity and, as a result, some of the rolling text declaration requirements previously listed under separate headings were incorporated into more generic

68 *The Biological Weapons Convention*

headings. While there was logic in grouping together, for example, all production facilities, the formulation used shifted also delegations' attention from long-standing points of difference over headings and types of facilities. Avoiding headings which by inclusion or deletion underlined which delegations had and had not achieved their preferred objective(s) served a useful psychological purpose and meant everyone would have to examine the text in some detail. As indicated, most of the declarations contained in the rolling text found their way in some shape or form into the composite text.

Table 3.1 Composite text declarations

Rolling text	Composite text	Comment
Initial (Offensive)	Initial (Offensive)	
Initial (Defensive)	Initial (Defensive)	
Current Biodefence	Current Biodefence	
Vaccine Production		*see Production facilities #12*
Maximum containment	Maximum containment	
High containment	High containment	
Plant pathogen containment	Plant pathogen containment	
Work with listed agents	Work with listed agents	
Other production facilities	Production facilities	*see Production facilities #13 & #14*
Other facilities		*Aspects of this were shifted to Work with listed agents*
Transfers		*Not included*
Article X implementation		*Shifted to Article 14*
National legislation		*Notification amended to a CBM, Article 15*
Outbreaks of disease		*Notification amended to a CBM, Article 15*
Thresholds		*Notification not included, see Article 3, section C*

Initial declarations

Initial declarations served as a baseline of information for historical reference and additional transparency under the new regime. A number of states parties had made initial declarations through the existing CBMs. However, there were two reasons for requiring the same, or more extensive, information under the Protocol. First, the information was now mandatory. States parties which had not returned information on their past offensive and defensive activities would be required to do so. Second, the format for the initial declarations in the Protocol required much more information than that submitted under the CBMs. Moreover, while the principal objective was not to subject such declarations to detailed scrutiny, under the Protocol there were more ways to seek clarification of issues and ambiguities in these initial declarations.

The initial declarations dealt with past offensive and past defensive work. While at least one delegation favoured a combined past offensive/defensive declaration, indicated by the inclusion of alternative combined and separate offensive and defensive declarations, other delegations had expressed support for separate initial declarations. In the composite text two initial declarations were required; one on offensive biological and toxin programmes prior to the entry into force of the Convention (not the Protocol as CRP.8 stated), and one related to national biological defence programmes ten years prior to entry into force of the Protocol for the state party. However, the actual submission of information was on a single form (Appendix A) which was in two parts, hence an element of the combined approach was in fact retained.

One of the contentious questions in the negotiations was the date from which the declaration must be made. Options included 17 June 1925, 1 January 1946, and 26 March 1975, covering respectively the Geneva Protocol, the period after the end of the Second World War, and entry into force of the Convention. The cut-off of 1925 was favoured by those states parties which wished to gain a fuller understanding of past activities or require certain states to acknowledge officially their biological warfare activities. Thus, China was known to favour a cut-off date of 1925 in order to capture Japan's offensive biological weapons programme.[8] Had this date been chosen providing detailed information on activities that far back might have been a problem, and one compromise mooted during the negotiations themselves was 1937, which would still fulfil China's objective of requiring Japan to declare formally its former offensive programme.[9] Others, such as France, were known to have favoured 1975[10] or perhaps a date prior to that.[11] South Africa proposed 1946[12] as did Germany and Sweden.[13] In its favour 1946 was the date under the CBMs and that under the declarations required under Article III of the CWC.[14] Those with former offensive programmes understandably favoured information being required from 1975 because that would allow them to draw a line under their own past, but since most of them had already submitted information under the CBMs the 1975 option was most likely a bargaining chip rather than a substantive issue, particularly for Western states such as the UK and the US. Only Japan, which still fails to acknowledge the depth of its offensive biological warfare activities in the 1930s and 1940s, had a substantive problem with any date prior to 1946, although others objected to it and were extremely dubious about their own abilities to provide accurate records going back that far.

In true diplomatic style the composite text used a date to which all had previously agreed under the existing CBMs; 1 January 1946. However, the information required under the declaration on offensive biological weapons programme was a narrative statement for the period spanning 1946 and up to entry into force of the Convention. This allowed Russia to continue its obfuscation with respect to the Soviet Union's offensive biological weapons programme between 1972 and 1992. Thus, the value of an unambiguous account of past biological warfare activity was lost.[15] For the declaration on past defensive activities, the initial declaration was limited to the period ten years prior to entry into force of the Protocol, on the basis that the CBMs had required much of this information and a separate annual biodefence declaration requirement would provide additional transparency.

From a historical perspective the initial declarations could be considered a disappointment since they were unlikely to reveal much more information than that known pre-Protocol.[16] However, the initial declaration on offensive programmes certainly required more detail than that requested under the politically-binding CBM on past offensive activities (CBM 'F') and, on balance, the initial declarations were of secondary interest. It was more important to achieve a robust contemporary declaration requirement than historical accuracy. An intrusive retrospective declaration system was not worth the price of weakened annual declarations.

Annual declarations

Information provided in annual declarations served as the baseline from which an assessment of compliance with the Convention was formed. In the composite text six annual declarations were listed, based on the four agreed declarations and two of the five contested declarations contained in the rolling text. A detailed consideration of the annual declaration requirements would need to examine both the actual declaration trigger and the information required under the declaration according to the relevant appendix to the Protocol. Given the focus on the overall compliance architecture and the *minimalist-reformist* debate, the following analysis is based on the declaration requirements and not the information provided through the declaration formats.

Defensive biological and toxin programmes and/or activities Considered as one of the most important declarations, the annual declaration on 'National biological defence programme(s) and/or activities against bacteriological (biological) and toxin weapons conducted during the previous year'[17] was devised, at the basic level, as a significant compromise to the US. There were two competing approaches to this declaration. One approach was to declare everything under a state party's biodefence programme. This would include not only scientific work in government laboratories, but the scientific and technical work outside laboratories and that contracted to private industry and universities. It would also include non-scientific work, for example that on threat assessment or literature reviews. Many of the NAM, as well as China, favoured this option: the mandatory declaration of all facilities involved in defensive biological programmes. The rationale was that such facilities and activities were the most likely place for conducting and concealing offensive activity under the guise of legitimate activity. The thin line between prohibited and permitted activities meant, according to this view, that all such activities should be declared.[18] Another approach was founded on the argument that not all activities taking place within a biodefence programme were relevant to the Protocol. This approach favoured some kind of cut-off formula which targeted the most relevant facilities and activities for declaration. The US was the main proponent of this approach arguing that non-scientific work, such as literature reviews of publicly acknowledged capabilities and activities, was of no relevance to compliance issues and should not be declared. Proponents of this approach were also concerned that a requirement to declare all activities would have a major impact on research in this area conducted by any organization outside the government, such as in universities and industry.[19]

The US won out. In the composite text the biodefence declaration required a summary of the general objectives of the biodefence programme and a summary of research and development conducted on ten activities: prophylaxis; pathogenicity; virulence; diagnostic techniques; detection; aerobiology; medical treatment; toxinology; physical protection and decontamination; and, aerobiological testing and evaluation. Facilities were divided into three categories. All facilities which conducted research and development on four of the above elements – pathogenicity, virulence, aerobiology, or toxinology – were to be declared if 15 or more technical and scientific person years or 15 or more technical or scientific personnel were undertaking such research and development as part of the national biodefence programme. In the event that fewer than 10 facilities were declared, a state party was to declare the largest facilities which represented 80% of the national biodefence programme. If a state party had no facilities to be declared under these criteria, it was to provide a *list* of all facilities where two or more technical and scientific person years or two or more technical and scientific personnel were engaged in research and development involving experimental work on the 10 areas identified in the summary programme. If three or more facilities were listed under this criterion, the largest facility would be declared and the remainder listed, in accordance with the appropriate appendix. Listed facilities were not subject to randomly-selected transparency visits; declared facilities were subject to such visits.

The composite text followed the basic model proposed by the US throughout the negotiations[20] in relation to the high number of personnel that triggered the declaration. The European Union was known to have favoured a much lower number and Germany and Sweden had proposed a figure of five personnel/person years as the cut-off during the negotiations,[21] a figure also mooted by South Africa.[22] Significant compromises were made to the US, including by the US' closest allies, on this declaration.

Despite the differences and difficulties during the negotiations on this declaration, its existence was never in doubt because biodefence programmes were recognised as one of the main areas of concern. Nevertheless, the cut-off of 15 person years/personnel was high and a state party with a large biodefence programme, in effect defined as one with more than 10 facilities meeting the 15 person year/personnel criteria, would not have to declare any facility where fewer than 15 personnel were conducting any research and development activities related to the biodefence programme. That was as a significant loophole in the Protocol given that the information provided in the CBMs illustrated that the US and the Russian Federation had biodefence programmes of an order of magnitude greater than any other state party.[23] Even so, it was a difficult issue and non-governmental organizations also had different approaches to this declaration. The Federation of American Scientists proposed *all* facilities directly participating in a biodefence program should be listed, regardless of the fraction of their activities, time, budget, and staff involved (although the use of 'listed' was most likely a nuance).[24] Others supported the targeted cut-off formula given the real potential burden of having to declare everything.[25] Under the composite text states parties with the largest biodefence programmes provided, overall, less transparency than other states parties. Dando identified the concerns of both some states parties and non-governmental organisations when he pointed out that, 'a State Party with a very large programme could carry out innocuous work at 10 facilities having 15 persons involved and then not be subject to monitoring of what it did elsewhere.'[26] Although Dando went on to note correctly that the required summary of the overall programme would indicate the existence of and work at other facilities, and that clarification and consultation procedures could be used to address any issues, the note of caution about this declaration was warranted.

Leaving aside the question of equality of treatment, what is of greater concern is that one state party, Russia, inherited a biodefence infrastructure still largely unseen by, and unknown to, other states parties. The Trilateral Process had not succeeded in gaining access to all military facilities in Russia and concerns about the actual status of the Russian biological weapons programme still existed.[27] This biodefence declaration offered less transparency than was necessary or desirable. Neither can the issues raised by investigative journalists and non-governmental organisations about the scope of activities in the US biodefence programme be ignored.[28] The biodefence declaration was less stringent than required: in fact the biodefence declaration was weak.

Maximum biological containment Biological containment was recognised as an area of relevance to the Convention, but different approaches emerged on which containment facilities were most relevant to the BWC. While the inclusion of the maximum biological containment facilities was never in doubt the question over high biological containment facilities and the inclusion of plant pathogen containment facilities was subject to much debate during the negotiations. Since maximum biological containment facilities were already declarable under the annual CBMs, their inclusion in the Protocol was not a contentious issue and the composite text required the declaration of each facility designated as maximum biological containment annually. This would result in considerable transparency, given the importance of Biosafety Level 4 laboratories to work on the most dangerous pathogens.[29] In addition, early analysis suggested this declaration might result in catching those facilities of significant interest not already captured under the biodefence declaration.[30]

High biological containment In early sessions of the Ad Hoc Group high containment referred to both Biosafety Level 3 (BL3) and Biosafety Level 4 (BL4) facilities, in accordance with the WHO classification of biosafety level.[31] The Ad Hoc Group split BL4 and BL3 containment facilities into maximum and high biological containment respectively. High Biological Containment referred to

Declarations 73

those facilities with containment levels at BL3 and the Ad Hoc Group faced many difficulties with this declaration trigger. One of the major problems was that there was no agreed international standard from which to agree a definition for BL3. Although the WHO Laboratory Biosafety manual defined BL3 based on physical characteristics the manual did not contain mandatory requirements. It served only as a guideline and its recommendations were not necessarily reflected in national practice. Defining maximum biological containment presented a similar problem, but whereas the inclusion of BL4 laboratories was not contested, the inclusion of BL3 laboratories was. The upshot was that political issues compounded practical problems with this declaration. At the practical level South Africa noted that:[32]

> the utilization of the WHO Classification BL3 in the future Protocol will cause uncertainty and misinterpretation of a trigger which may lead to either unnecessary declarations of facilities or the not declaring of facilities that should be declared.

This observation led South Africa to champion the use of the term *high biological containment* rather than the use of WHO terminology. Furthermore, because the WHO guidelines were not mandatory requirements, South Africa argued that the physical characteristics it listed could not be used as the basis of a definition for the facilities to be declared because there would be confusion over whether all, or only some, of the physical characteristics would be required for the definition of a laboratory as high biological containment. Therefore, it proposed that laboratories be designated as high biological containment if they undertook work on pathogens which posed a high risk to human and/or animal health and the physical characteristics of the laboratory included specific attributes, such as negative air pressure and access control.[33]

The concern of the Western states with such a declaration was that it would capture a significant number of facilities that, in their view, were of little practical relevance to the Convention. The UK claimed that a stand alone high biological containment trigger would result in a declaration of hundreds of facilities within the UK, many of which were in hospitals.[34] The Netherlands considered that the declaration was not effective on its own, but might be combined with other declaration triggers, such as work with listed agents.[35] Either way, the balance of declarations would have been very heavy for Western states because of the requirement for some industry to operate at BL3 'to conform to domestic health and safety regulations.'[36] In short, high biological containment might not, by itself, necessarily indicate the presence of work, materials or equipment of greatest relevance to the Convention. Western states also pointed to past programmes that suggested offensive biological weapons activities had not been tied to containment levels.[37] All these elements meant that the Western Group considered the high biological containment declaration unacceptable and impractical.[38]

In contrast, China remained a staunch proponent of a separate trigger for high biological containment facilities, although it also rejected the use of that term and steadfastly stuck to categorization as BL3.[39] The purported rationale for the Chinese approach was that state-led offensive biological weapons activities were more likely to occur in facilities with containment levels of BL3 or higher. China

74 *The Biological Weapons Convention*

was well aware the heavy declaration burden a stand alone BL3 trigger would result in for industrialised states, but maintained the trigger was appropriate. According to Wilson, because 'the majority of resources are in the West, China postulates the most likely risk of illicit biological warfare proliferation comes from the West.'[40]

The differences over the inclusion of this declaration trigger were never resolved in the rolling text and the composite text attempted to satisfy both those in favour of a separate high biological containment declaration and those against it. It did so by requiring the declaration of each facility designated as high biological containment (as defined in Article 2) where the working area was under a continuous system of high biological containment that exceeded $100m^2$ *and* the activities conducted related to the production of vaccines, production of micro-organisms and toxins, and genetic modification work with listed agents and toxins. These activities were an exact reproduction of the declaration requirements under paragraphs 11 (b), 11 (c), 12, 13, 14, and 15 of Article 4 of the composite text. Thus, while China achieved its objective of a separate high biological containment trigger it would not require the declaration of any additional facilities because the facilities were already triggered for declaration under other declaration requirements.

Had the negotiations continued there can be little doubt that China would have sought changes to this declaration. Among both the industrialised states and the analysts from Western non-governmental organizations, however, there was no support for declaring all BL3 facilities. More than any other declaration this one indicated that political considerations play as important a role as practical scientific and technical considerations in disarmament negotiations.

Plant pathogen containment South Africa proposed that all facilities designated as plant pathogen containment facilities, in accordance with the appropriate definition, be declared to complement other facilities triggered by containment requirements. This would ensure the Protocol covered plant pathogens in a more systematic manner. The stated rationale was that facilities, 'producing plant inoculants and biocontrol agents can very easily be used for the production of biological weapons against plants and should therefore be declared.'[41] In contrast to this assessment the UK concluded that a declaration for plant pathogen containment was, 'neither practical nor useful as a focus of information.'[42] The view of the UK was that no universal standard of containment existed and such containment was simple to install and inexpensive with 'the resulting facilities [not being] particularly remarkable.'[43]

Other delegations were also unconvinced by the South African proposal and the declaration remained contested throughout the life of the rolling text. In the composite text a similar approach to that for high biological containment was taken, whereby all plant pathogen containment facilities were to be declared where the working area was under a continuous system of plant pathogen containment and exceeded $100m^2$. South Africa achieved its objective and given that anti-plant biological weapons programmes had existed in the past and that recent assessments of the potential problem had resulted in calls for the BWC to strengthen its

Declarations 75

provisions with respect to anti-crop biological warfare prohibitions[44] [45] the South African insistence on this provision could have proved to be a useful addition in strengthening the Convention.

Work with listed agents and/or toxins In Annex A of the Protocol 26 human and zoonotic pathogens, eight plant pathogens, six animal pathogens and 11 toxins of significant relevance to the Convention were identified. The list was illustrative rather than definitive: meaning there was no exclusion of unlisted biological agents or toxins from the prohibitions of the BWC.[46] Flowing from the inclusion of such a list was a logic that the Organization and states parties needed to know which facilities were working with the listed agents and toxins. The work with listed agents and/or toxins declaration was designed to capture such facilities and, as with the declarations for biodefence, maximum biological containment, and vaccine production facilities, the inclusion of this declaration trigger was never in any real doubt.

Nevertheless, there were problems with the development of this declaration requirement. Not least the proposal that only work with listed agents and/or toxins under high biological containment be declared, which according to the European Union 'entirely negated' the intrinsic objective of this declaration requirement. In their view the declaration was to ensure laboratories having certain capabilities of particular relevance to the Convention were declared.[47] In the composite text any facility working with listed agents and/or toxins, where such work involved production above a certain threshold, or genetic modification, or intentional aerosolization of such agents and/or toxins, was required to be declared.

In terms of production the quantitative threshold balanced alternatives contained in the rolling text for lower or higher thresholds. Many of the states parties preferred to avoid the declaration of facilities conducting routine and small scale research work with such agents, whereas others, including China, considered research work significant, despite the fact that research is not explicitly covered by the BWC. All states parties agreed on the exclusion of routine work from the declaration trigger.[48] The European Union compromise on this declaration trigger agreed to a reduction in the production thresholds in order to 'ensure [the] declaration of facilities carrying out work with an agent on such a scale that there is a strong argument for transparency under the Protocol because of the inherent scientific and technological potential of such a laboratory.'[49] This was to avoid thresholds being set so low as to catch routine work.

For genetic modification, the rolling text contained different proposals relating to increased pathogenicity or virulence and ease of production, or changes to the antigenicity or immunogenicity, antibiotic resistance, stability, or disease causing properties of the pathogen. Both formulations were captured in the composite text which required a declaration of work involving genetic modification of a listed agent and/or toxin when it involved the insertion of a nucleic acid sequence, or intentional modification of the nucleic acid sequence, of such an agent and/or toxin, when *the purpose* was to create a novel or genetically modified agent, organism or toxin or to enhance the production of a toxin or its toxic sub-units. A declaration was also required when the work was for *the purpose* of creating a novel or genetically modified organism with increased disease causing or toxic properties characteristic of an agent/toxin listed in the Protocol, or to enhance production of a toxin or its toxic sub-units.

The formulations raised an interesting question through the use of the language, 'for the purpose of creating' which was, and arguably is, subjective and open to some interpretation. While clearly linked to the general-purpose criterion which underpins the BWC, and therefore correct and justifiable, as an example would the laboratory which inadvertently developed the Mousepox strain in Australia at the beginning of 2001[50] be subject to a declaration when the result of that work was not the actual purpose of it? While the answer depended on what other activities the facility was involved in, it offered a potential loophole for the determined non-compliant state party: develop a legitimate, but not declarable, purpose as cover for the proscribed work, because purpose hinged on intent which might be either explained away or used to create ambiguity, absent other declarable activities.

Intentional aerosolization of any agent and/or toxin listed in Annex A was also required to be declared when the work was undertaken in or by an explosive aerosol test chamber, or any other aerosol test chamber with an internal volume greater than $5m^3$, or when such work was conducted in the open-air (unless it was for routine vaccination or agricultural applications), or when aerosolised particles were applied to the respiratory tract of 101 or more single species of rodent or 6 or more mammalian species (including non-human primates) per year. The composite text merged the different proposals under the rolling text, but omitted work conducted in smaller dynamic or static aerosol test chambers. The omission of these smaller aerosol test chambers was a compromise by the European Union, among others, who considered any intentional aerosolization work relevant regardless of the type of chamber used, and regardless of the size of the chamber.[51] A compromise by the EU indicates a Western Group split on this particular issue, which itself leads to a deduction that the US must have had strong views on this particular aspect of the declaration. The logic of including only explosive test chambers has not been elaborated in the open literature, but the 'or' formulation did mean the scope of the declaration was quite broad. A possible rationale is that dissemination of biological agents and/or toxins in a weapon development phase is most likely via explosive test chambers; hence, those chambers were of greatest relevance to the Convention. Explosive test chambers certainly offered experienced inspectors the opportunity to confirm non-compliance and US and UK nationals had extensive experience with these chambers from the Trilateral Process.[52]

Other proposals contained in the rolling text included the requirement for a declaration of listed agents if research and development work was conducted under high biological containment or when culture collections of listed agents and/or toxins were contained in maximum or high biological containment installations. In the European Union's working paper on this declaration, the rationale for declaring only work under high biological containment was rejected because of the different approaches in each state party and the fact that not all listed agents were either of risk group 3 or risk group 4 (requiring high or maximum biological containment respectively).[53] Examples were provided, including *Bacillus anthracis*, which in early 2001 was defined as risk group 2 in the United States but considered as risk group 3 in the European Union.[54] Neither provision made it into the composite text.

Production facilities As intimated, the composite text contained a generic declaration title for production facilities that encompassed vaccine production, production of micro-organisms and diagnostic reagents, and production of biocontrol agents, as well as requiring a listing of facilities involved in the production of microbially produced substances. In effect, this encompassed the different proposals under the rolling text headings of vaccine production, other production, and other facilities to a greater or lesser extent.

Vaccine production facilities Vaccine production facilities were added to the CBMs in 1991 on the basis that such facilities worked with agents and toxins of relevance to the Convention and they had the capability to produce a significant quantity of pathogens and toxins. In the Protocol vaccine production facilities included both human and animal vaccines, whereas the CBM required only human vaccine production facilities to be declared. During the Third Review Conference it had been proposed that animal vaccine production be included in the CBM declaration. However, this was rejected due to the concerns of a number of delegations about their ability to implement the measure.[55] Inclusion of animal pathogens was an important addition given the potential scope of anti-animal biological weapons in the future and the fact that animal vaccine production facilities contained similar equipment and technical expertise as those for human vaccine production facilities, thus, in principle, being of similar relevance.[56] There was not, however, universal support for the declaration from industry or non-governmental organisations, some of which questioned whether this declaration would capture any facilities not already covered by the scope of the other declarations and the broad production facilities declaration itself.

One significant question during the negotiations was whether or not the declaration applied only to facilities working with and producing vaccines for pathogens contained on the agents and toxins list, or to all vaccine production facilities. An early UK paper noted that, '[l]imiting vaccine production declaration to vaccines for listed agents could ... result in the non-declaration of many vaccine facilities with the potential to produce pathogens and toxins on a considerable scale.'[57] This view prevailed and the declaration applied to all vaccine production facilities.

Other production facilities This declaration requirement was once a separate declaration trigger, but the composite text contained a few important variations from the rolling text. Primarily, the composite text was broader in scope by virtue of the omission of the clauses relating to production being in either primary production containment or high biological containment and the deletion of the exclusion clauses related to the manufacture of soaps, detergents, cosmetics, fertilizers, pharmaceuticals or food and beverages for animals. The rationale for the declaration in the rolling text was to capture facilities that 'possess the appropriate scale and expertise to be relevant under the Convention in view of their capability to produce microorganisms in significant quantities.'[58]

The danger was that this trigger would be too broad and thus capture too many facilities of little or no relevance. Various options had been considered for combining this proposed declaration with others, for example with containment or work with listed agents, and China wanted to restrict the declaration to facilities operating at BL3 levels of containment.[59] Given that evidence suggested offensive activity was not necessarily linked to containment levels, the Chinese proposal would have left relevant production capabilities outside the future regime.[60]

In the composite text production was not limited to listed agents. The production and recovery of any micro-organisms or microbially produced diagnostic reagent for public sale was to be declared if any of the identified equipment or materials were used in such production.[61] Production of food or beverages for humans or as waste or by-product was excluded from the declaration requirement, although production of food for animals was not, which the European Union had considered a necessary exclusion.[62] A further possible exclusion not contained in the composite text was production for the purposes of fuel. A second requirement for declaration was the production and recovery of any biocontrol agent or any plant inoculant using certain equipment and materials.[63]

Facilities meeting the above criteria would be declared and thus subject to randomly-selected transparency visits. This still left a number of facilities which some states parties deemed relevant and others deemed irrelevant. In order to appease both views the final requirement was for a *list* of all facilities not already declared which produced for public sale microbially produced substances – whether or not chemically modified – using identified materials or equipment.[64] Substances produced for human food and beverages as well as those produced as waste or by-product were exempt from the listing. For the first five years of the life of the Protocol facilities listed under this criterion would not be subject to randomly-selected transparency visits, but the First Review Conference of the Protocol was mandated to consider whether or not such facilities should be subjected to these visits, based on the experience of implementation and the fulfilment of the objectives of the Protocol. Furthermore, the declaration clarification procedures available to states parties did not apply to these listed facilities. However, the Consultation, Clarification and Co-operation procedures under Article 8 of the composite text did apply, because the latter covered 'any matter which may cause concern about possible non-compliance with the obligations of this Protocol or the Convention.'[65] Listed facilities were therefore not entirely exempt from any possible scrutiny.

This meant that certain facilities would, in effect, be subjected to a CBM-type regime; at best, notwithstanding the possibility of an investigation or clarification procedure, these facilities would only be subject to the panoply of measures within the Protocol five years after its entry into force. Such a system of gradual phase in of measures was supported by some non-government actors,[66] but had not been subject to detailed discussion within the Ad Hoc Group. The measure was therefore an attempt to reduce the burden on states parties and civil industry during the first few years of the Protocol's existence. However, it signalled to both industry and states parties that such facilities were of interest to the future Organization. The envisaged delay was an attempt to seek an acceptable compromise among states parties; those who objected to the declaration of such facilities could note the non-declaration requirement, whereas those who supported the declaration of such facilities could hold out for future strengthening of the Protocol five years after entry into force. The argument was simply put on hold.

Declarations omitted from the composite text

The composite text omitted three declarations contained in the rolling text: other facilities; transfers; and, scientific co-operation. The declaration for *Other Facilities* captured production sites working with biological agents and toxins that contained equipment for aerosol testing and dissemination and conducted genetic modification to agents and toxins.[67] Very little was in fact omitted because elements of this proposed declaration were incorporated into the more generic production facilities declaration.

A proposed declaration on *Transfers* was part of the package of measures to improve implementation of Article III of the Convention, supported by the NAM, whereby any transfer of an agent, toxin or equipment listed in Annex A of the Protocol would have been declared annually.[68] As identified in chapter six, this omission was a political consideration rather than one based on the utility of the declaration in strengthening the Convention. The implicit threat such a declaration (supposedly) posed to the continued existence of the Australia Group was sufficient to ensure it had no support in the Western Group, but it is important to note that it is only a vaguely implicit threat and not an explicit one that stands up to any detailed scrutiny.

The final declaration was that related to the implementation of Article X of the Convention and was part of the overall package to enhance scientific and technical co-operation. Its deletion was not significant because when first proposed at the eighth session of the Ad Hoc Group it was contained in both Article III and Article VII of the rolling text.[69] In the composite text the declaration requirement was retained in Article 14 on *Scientific and Technological Exchange for Peaceful Purposes and Technical Cooperation*. Thus, its omission was from this particular article rather than the Protocol itself, although as outlined in chapter seven, the shift from one article to another does imply a different status of the declaration.

Notifications

In the VEREX report notifications were defined as a sub-set of declarations which addressed new or unforeseen information and their role was to pre-empt compliance concerns.[70] This understanding was not carried over to the Ad Hoc Group where notifications were broader in scope. Three notifications, all contested, were proposed in the rolling text; national legislation and regulations, outbreaks of disease, and thresholds. Two of the notifications, national legislation and outbreaks of disease, originated from the CBMs, whereas the proposed notification on thresholds was linked to the first element of the mandate of the Ad Hoc Group: objective criteria.

In 1991 the Third Review Conference expanded the CBM requirements to include information on national legislation and regulations enacted to implement the BWC. Although the final scope of the CBM was narrower than that originally proposed by the UK[71] its objective remained the same; to provide details on how states parties implemented the Convention. Discussions in the Ad Hoc Group went a step further and expanded the envisaged declaration to include how access to buildings which handled pathogens and toxins was controlled and how access to areas where an outbreak of infectious disease was regulated. At one level this incorporated the growing concerns about access by non-state entities – be they terrorists or criminals – and at another level reflected the depth of regulations required to actually implement the BWC. This was not a new initiative and should have been uncontroversial.[72]

Certain parties, however, objected to the proposal when it was made in the Ad Hoc Group. In part this was due to the differences in approach to Article IV of the BWC and national implementation. Many of the NAM considered how the BWC was implemented at the national level an issue of sovereignty. They rejected efforts to outline any kind of blueprint of what states parties should do at the national level. The US, however, was a strong supporter of this declaration. Compromise became inevitable when the element was continually downgraded, first from an initial declaration to a notification and second when the US proposed a deal on declarations. Early in 2000 the US noted its opposition to the declarations for *High biological containment* and *Other facilities* involving aerosol chambers and other genetic modification work, but reiterated its support for the declaration on *National legislation and regulations* and the notification of *Outbreak of disease*. In an effort to streamline the rolling text the US invited delegations to consider the deletion of all four, thus denying the national legislation declaration of one of its main supporters.[73] This suggested deal was never taken up. In ignoring this attempt to strike a deal and begin trading on contested elements of the Protocol with the US other states parties (particularly the EU and the other members of the Western Group) were remiss. At the suggestion of South Africa, the original proposal was later included in the composite text as a confidence-building measure under Article 15.[74]

The second notification, reporting outbreaks of disease, was introduced as a CBM in 1986. Thinking in the West was that a requirement to report unusual outbreaks of disease would assist transparency among states parties. The Soviet Union had offered less than overwhelming support for this CBM in 1986 and in 1991 attempted to have it deleted.[75] All states were supposed to report disease outbreaks to the WHO, the World Organization for Animal Health (OIE) and the United Nations Food and Agriculture Organization (FAO). However, although such reporting was often sporadic, the utility of requiring the reporting of disease outbreaks to the BWC Organization was always questioned. If WHO and other organizations could not be guaranteed information on diseases, the BWC Organization had little hope of receiving such information in practice.

Nonetheless, as in the CBMs, states parties which supported the inclusion of this measure sought information on unusual outbreaks of disease and identified a number of factors to define what this actually meant in practice. Countering this approach, the NAM issued a working paper which noted their concerns about outbreaks of disease being used as a precursor for an investigation request, given that most disease outbreaks occurred in the South. Unambiguously, they did not support such a declaration requirement.[76] Furthermore, the proposed declaration requirement was not supported in the later stages of the negotiations by a number of NGOs[77] and its utility in strengthening the Convention was increasingly questioned. In a victory for the NAM the composite text contained provisions for reporting investigations on outbreaks of disease as a CBM under Article 15.[78]

The notification on thresholds was proposed by Ukraine.[79] Thresholds were a difficult question throughout the life of the negotiations, as was the identification of other objective criteria such as definitions and other quantitative approaches to resolving verification problems. The concept of threshold quantities was based on the establishment of an identified amount of an agent or toxin which would be considered as being for legitimate purposes and therefore permitted under the BWC. Thus, for example, Russia had proposed during VEREX that anything below 5kg of 'biological material' was permitted for protective purposes under Article I of the BWC.[80] The Western Group was steadfastly against such ideas, because it undermined the general-purpose criterion, and no formal meetings addressed the topic after 1998. Private meetings did, however, explore a number of possibilities for developing quantitative criteria to strengthen the BWC. In the composite text a notification requirement was incorporated in Article 3 as a transparency measure on thresholds for agents and toxins. It was not entirely without some value, but it was viewed by many as being superfluous and its inclusion was almost exclusively for political reasons for Russia and Ukraine.

Minimalism or *Reform*

As a concept declarations were not contentious and it was accepted that they formed the basic building block of the compliance architecture intended to strengthen the Convention. Analysis of the rolling text illustrates that *minimalist* and *reformist* preferences for the scope of declarations were established during the early phase of the negotiations. Indicative of this is the fact that few new declaration requirements were proposed after the second version of the rolling text was released. Nevertheless, it is also clear that delegations failed to convince each other about the utility of certain declarations. Although a reasonable minimum to be expected was the existing CBMs, only in one case could states parties agree on specific proposals beyond such a *minimalist* interpretation. There was, however, a narrowing of differences and compromise became evident in the final sessions of the Ad Hoc Group, which indicated that the final package of declarations would go beyond the *minimalist* vision.

A number of declarations in the composite text were highly contested. In particular, the scope of the declaration on biodefence, that on high biological

82 *The Biological Weapons Convention*

containment and the declaration of production facilities. In addition, industry was not supportive of the declaration requirements contained in the composite text.[81] Whether or not these differences would have led to a narrowing of the scope of the declarations in the endgame is a moot point, but two areas of concern stand out. First, the biodefence declaration contained a loophole for those states parties – Russia and US – with a significant biodefence programme. The US supported a limited biodefence declaration and in practice acceptance by the US was essential if the Protocol was to have any chance of being adopted. Conscious of this reality others had to accept a weak biodefence declaration as a compromise. Notwithstanding the concerns this created of itself, such a weak biodefence trigger would, potentially, serve the continued obfuscation by Russia vis-à-vis the offensive and defensive biological weapons infrastructure it inherited from the Soviet Union. That had to be a cause for concern in the future.

A second concern was the deletion of the declaration on transfers. Delegations which had supported this declaration had not helped their cause by elaborating or clarifying what it would actually encompass and what would be required under such a declaration. The failure to clarify or develop the proposal was either poor negotiation strategy or a sign that its sponsors were not that serious about the issue. However, it is also important to note that opposition to the declaration was political. The Western Group never supported the declaration because of its implicit threat to the existence of the Australia Group. As such, the omission of this declaration meant that there was no international paper trail to trace agents, materials and equipment from source to destination.[82] The lack of such information was a weakness in the Protocol and indicated that states parties were not as willing to agree to intrusive measures as they had been under the CWC. In the CWC there was at least an obligation to report transfers of scheduled chemicals. The Protocol contained no such requirement, although some states considered it an appropriate way to strengthen the Convention.[83] It has not escaped notice that such a measure is the basis of biosecurity; a concept that has become increasingly important since 11 September 2001.

Against these two identified weaknesses is it possible to say whether the *minimalist* or *reformist* vision won out in Article 4 of the Protocol? The scope of the declarations went further than the *minimalism* of relevant CBMs but not as far as the *reform* party had advocated in the past. Overall the declarations were closer to the *reformist* vision and, on that basis, the indication was that *reformists* were actually succeeding in moving states parties away from an evolutionary and incremental approach to strengthening the BWC. However, the compromises were significant and much was still contested by July 2001.

Notes

1.   See for example the papers submitted on new scientific and technological developments of relevance to the Convention submitted at the Third Review Conference,. BWC 3RC, BWC/CONF.III/4 (26 August 1991) and BWC/CONF.III/4/Add.1 (10 September 1991).

2. United Nations, 'Ad Hoc Group of the States Parties to the Convention on the Prohibition of the Development, Production and Stockpiling of Bacteriological (Biological) and Toxin Weapons and on Their Destruction' BWC/AD HOC GROUP/17 Declarations Working Paper submitted by the Friend of the Chair on Compliance Measures (13 July 1995). (Hereinafter referred to as 'BWC AHG' followed by document number, title of document and date (where appropriate).)
An indication of the possible declaration requirements above and beyond those contained in the CBMs was provided at the second session of the Ad Hoc Group by the Friend of the Chair paper on declarations which noted, inter alia, the following declarations were under consideration: military microbiological programmes/facilities; high containment facilities, including BL4 and BL3; work with listed pathogens and toxins; aerobiology/aerosol dissemination; production microbiology; genetic manipulation; and, others including equipment and transfers.

3. Richard Guthrie, 'Technological Aspects of Verification: Declarations, Managed Access and Confidential Proprietary Information' Malcolm R. Dando, Graham S. Pearson and Tibor Tóth (Editors) *Verification of the Biological and Toxin Weapons Convention* (Dordrecht, Kluwer Academic Publishers, 2000) p.153.

4. Ibid.

5. VEREX, BWC/CONF.III/VEREX/9 pp 166-173 for a summary of the discussion on declarations and their interaction with other verification measures. See also BWC AHG, BWC/AD HOC GROUP/28 Annex III/I p.6 for a re-run of this debate in the early stages of the Ad Hoc Group.

6. VEREX, BWC/CONF.III/VEREX/9 p.12.

7. Graham S. Pearson, 'Discriminating Triggers for Mandatory Declarations' Bradford Briefing Paper #3 (Bradford, University of Bradford, 1997) p.3.

8. Jenni Rissanen, 'Hurdles Cleared, Obstacles Remaining: The Ad Hoc Group Prepares for the Final Challenge' *Disarmament Diplomacy* Issue Number 56 (April 2001) p.20.

9. Malcolm Dando, 'Preventing Biological Warfare: The Failure of American Leadership' (Basingstoke, Palgrave, 2002) p.149.

10. Rissanen, 'Hurdles Cleared, Obstacles Remaining: The Ad Hoc Group Prepares for the Final Challenge' p.20.

11. France, for example, had proposed an initial declaration going back 20 years prior to accession to the Convention during the Third Review Conference; see BWC 3RC, BWC/CONF.III/23 p.102.

12. BWC AHG, BWC/AD HOC GROUP/WP.300 'Working paper submitted by South Africa: Proposed Text for Article III – Declarations' (24 August 1998) p.2.

13. BWC AHG, BWC/AD HOC GROUP/WP.390 'Working paper submitted by Germany and Sweden' (12 July 1999) p.1.

14. In diplomacy it is often easier to reach agreement if there is a precedent in another or similar agreement. It is harder to resist something if you have accepted it elsewhere. Thus the CWC offered a useful reference point, not least because so many states wished to emulate the CWC. Under the CWC there were a number of different declaration requirements. For example, that related to abandoned chemical weapons included the period after 1 January 1925 and before 1 January 1977, and those dumped at sea before 1 January 1985. With respect to chemical weapons production facilities and chemical weapons on its territory the date was established as 1 January 1946.

15. David C. Kelly, 'The Trilateral Agreement: lessons for biological weapons verification' Trevor Findlay and Oliver Meier (editors) *Verification Yearbook 2002* (Nottingham, Russell Press Ltd, 2002) p.104.

16. That of course does not discount the fact that the initial declarations under the CWC in 1997 resulted in two more states parties declaring offensive chemical weapons programmes than had been anticipated by the majority; two more states have since declared programmes. Thus new information may come to light as a result of the 1946 deadline.

17. BWC AHG, BWC/AD HOC GROUP/CRP.8 (Technically corrected version) (30 May 2001) Article 4, paragraphs 6-7 pp.18-19.

18. Rissanen, 'Hurdles Cleared, Obstacles Remaining: The Ad Hoc Group Prepares for the Final Challenge' p.20.

19. Oliver Thränert. 'The Compliance Protocol and the Three Depositary Powers' Susan Wright (Editor) *Biological Warfare and Disarmament: new problems/new perspectives* (Oxford, Rowman & Littlefield Publishers, 2002) pp.351-352.

20. BWC AHG, BWC/AD HOC GROUP/WP.378 'Working paper submitted by the United States of America – Article III – D. Declarations – I. Submission of Declarations' (29 June 1999).

21. BWC AHG, BWC/AD HOC GROUP/WP.340 'Working paper submitted by Germany and Sweden – Proposed Language for Article III – Declarations' (7 January 1999).

22. BWC AHG, BWC/AD HOC GROUP/WP.325 'Working paper submitted by South Africa – Proposal for Declaration of Current Defensive Programmes' (30 November 1998).

23. Marie Isabelle Chevrier and Iris Hunger, 'Confidence-Building Measures for the BTWC: Performance and Potential' *The Nonproliferation Review* 7:3 (Fall-Winter 2000) pp.24-42.

24. Anonymous, 'Declaration Triggers: Critique of the Rolling Text' Federation of American Scientists Working Group on BW Verification (September 1998) p.1.

25. Graham S Pearson, Nicholas A Sims, Malcolm R Dando & Ian R Kenyon, 'The BTWC Protocol: Proposed Complete Text for an Integrated Regime' Evaluation Paper No 19, (Bradford, University of Bradford, 2000). p.38 (see footnote 53).

26. Dando, 'Preventing Biological Warfare: The Failure of American Leadership' p.150.

27. Kelly, 'The Trilateral Agreement: lessons for biological weapons verification' pp. 93-109.

28. Judith Miller, Stephen Engelberg, William Broad, 'Germs: The Ultimate Weapon' (London, Simon & Schuster, 2001) pp.287-314.

29. Raymond A. Zilinskas, 'Verification of the Biological Weapons Convention' Erhard Geissler (Editor) *Biological and Toxin Weapons Today* (Oxford, Oxford University Press, 1986) pp.82-107.

30. BWC AHG, BWC/AD HOC GROUP/31, 'Procedural Report of the Ad Hoc Group of the States parties to the Convention on the Prohibition of the Development, Production and Stockpiling of Bacteriological (Biological) and Toxin Weapons and on Their Destruction' (26 July 1996) p.11.

31. The second edition of the 1983 'Laboratory Biosafety Manual' of the World Health Organization (Geneva 2003) is available, as interim guidelines, at: http://www.who.int/csr/resources/publications/biosafety/Labbiosafety.pdf During the Ad Hoc Group delegations were referring to the 1983 edition. Infective micro-organisms are classified by WHO in certain 'Risk Groups' with risk group 1 posing

no or only a low risk to individual or community health, risk group 2 a moderate level of risk, risk group 3 a high risk (i.e. causing serious human or animal disease) and risk group 4 a high individual and community risk whereby such a pathogen would cause 'serious human or animal disease and that can be readily transmitted from one individual to another, directly or indirectly. Effective treatment and preventive measures are not usually available.' (See page 1 of the interim guidelines). Risk group 1 relates to the biosafety level 1 in terms of practices and equipment in the laboratory, risk group 2 to BL2, risk group 3 to BL3 and risk group 4 to BL4. States draw up their own national or regional classification of micro-organisms and the laboratory biosafety guidelines are not mandatory; they are guidelines not requirements.

32. BWC AHG, BWC/AD HOC GROUP/WP.242, 'Working paper submitted by South Africa, The Use of Containment in Declarations' (15 December 1997) p.2.

33. Ibid.

34. BWC AHG, BWC/AD HOC GROUP/WP.81, 'Survey of Microbiological Facilities in the UK Working paper submitted by the United Kingdom of Great Britain and Northern Ireland' (23 July 1996) p.2.

35. BWC AHG, BWC/AD HOC GROUP/WP.10, 'Discussion paper of the Netherlands, The Relevance and Effectiveness of (Combinations of) Criteria for Declaration' (28 November 1995) p.3.

36. Henrietta Wilson, 'Strengthening the BWC: Issues for the Ad Hoc Group' *Disarmament Diplomacy* Issue Number 42 (December 1999) p.32.

37. Graham S. Pearson, 'Improving the Biological Weapons Convention: The Role of Lists and Declarations' Oliver Thränert (Editor) *Enhancing the Biological Weapons Convention* (Bonn, Verlag J. H. W. Dietz, 1996) p.125.

38. Wilson, 'Strengthening the BWC: Issues for the Ad Hoc Group' p.32. See also, in addition to the above working papers of the Ad Hoc Group the following documents: BWC/AD HOC GROUP/WP.3 'The Role of Containment in Facility Declarations under the BTWC Working paper submitted by the United Kingdom of Great Britain and Northern Ireland' (27 November 1995), BWC/AD HOC GROUP/WP.9 'France/Germany Discussion Paper Declarations in a BTWC-Verification Protocol' (28 November 1995), and BWC/AD HOC GROUP/WP.12 'Friend of the Chair on Compliance Measures Declarations' (29 November 1995).

39. Wilson, 'Strengthening the BWC: Issues for the Ad Hoc Group' p.31.

40. Ibid.

41. BWC AHG, BWC/AD HOC GROUP/WP.242, 'Plant Inoculant, and Biocontrol Agent Production facilities with plant quarantine capabilities as a trigger for Declarations, Working paper by South Africa' (14 July 1997) p.1.

42. BWC AHG, BWC/AD HOC GROUP/WP.3 p.2.

43. Ibid.

44. Simon Whitby, 'Biological Warfare against crops' (Basingstoke, Palgrave, 2002); Paul Rogers, Simon Whitby and Malcolm Dando, 'Biological Warfare against Crops' *Scientific American* 280:6 (June 1999) pp.62-67.

45. Paul Rogers, 'Characteristics of Natural Outbreaks of Crop Diseases' Malcolm Dando, Graham Pearson and Bohumir Kriz (Editors) *Scientific and Technical Means of Distinguishing Between Natural and Other Outbreaks of Disease* (Dordrecht, Kluwer Academic Publishers, 2001) p.60.

46. BWC AHG, BWC/AD HOC GROUP/CRP.8 (Technically Corrected Version) 30 May 2001, Article 3, p.13.

47. BWC AHG, BWC/AD HOC GROUP/WP.421, 'Working paper submitted by France on behalf of the European Union, Declaration Trigger for Work With Listed Agents and/or Toxins' (BWC/AD HOC GROUP/51 (Part II), pages 17-19, paragraphs 15 and 16) (18 July 2000), pp.1-2.

48. For contrasting approaches to this declaration trigger see, BWC AHG, BWC/AD HOC GROUP/WP.313, 'Working paper submitted by China Proposed Text for Article III – Declarations' (23 September 1998) and BWC/AD HOC GROUP/WP.389, 'Working paper submitted by Finland on behalf of the European Union Submission of Declarations' (12 July 1999).

49. BWC AHG, BWC/AD HOC GROUP/WP.421 and BWC/AD HOC GROUP/51 (Part II), pp.17-19, paragraphs 15 and 16 (18 July 2000).

50. R J Jackson; Ramsay, A J; Christensen, C D; Beaton, S; Hall, D F; Ramshaw, I A., 'Expression of mouse interleukin-4 by a recombinant ectromelia virus suppresses cytolytic lymphocyte responses and overcomes genetic resistance to mousepox' *Journal Of Virology*, 75:3, February 2001, pp.1205-1210.

51. BWC AHG, BWC/AD HOC GROUP/WP.421.

52. Kelly, 'The Trilateral Agreement: lessons for biological weapons verification' p.95.

53. BWCAHG, BWC/AD HOC GROUP/51 (Part II), pp. 17-19 (18 July 2000).

54. Ibid.

55. BWC AHG, BWC/AD HOC GROUP/WP.130, 'The Declaration of Vaccine Production Facilities, Working paper by the United Kingdom of Great Britain and Northern Ireland' (6 March 1997) pp.1-2.

56. Ibid.

57. Ibid.

58. BWC AHG, BWC/AD HOC GROUP/31, 'Procedural Report of the Ad Hoc Group of the States parties to the Convention on the Prohibition of the Development, Production and Stockpiling of Bacteriological (Biological) and Toxin Weapons and on Their Destruction' (26 July 1996), p.13.

59. Wilson, 'Strengthening the BWC: Issues for the Ad Hoc Group' p.31.

60. Examples of the different approaches to this declaration trigger were provided by, BWC AHG, BWC/AD HOC GROUP/WP.313 'Working paper submitted by China, Proposed text for Article III – Declarations' (23 September 1998), BWC/AD HOC GROUP/WP.284 'Working paper submitted by the United Kingdom of Great Britain and Northern Ireland on behalf of the European Union, Declarations' (24 June 1998) and BWC/AD HOC GROUP/WP.393 'Working paper submitted by Finland on behalf of the European Union, Submission of Declarations' (16 July 1999).

61. BWC AHG, BWC/AD HOC GROUP/CRP.8 (Technically corrected version) (30 May 2001) Article 4, para. 13.

62. BWC AHG, BWC/AD HOC GROUP/WP.393 'Working paper submitted by Finland on behalf of the European Union, Submission of Declarations' (16 July 1999).

63. BWC AHG, BWC/AD HOC GROUP/CRP.8 (Technically corrected version) (30 May 2001) Article 4, para. 14.

64. Ibid., Article 4, para. 15.

65. Ibid., Article 6, section D, pp.36-47 and Article 8 pp.52-54.

66. Anonymous, 'Federation of American Scientists Working Group on BW Verification – Gradual Phase-in of Protocol Measures' (Draft, July 2000).

67. BWC AHG, BWC/AD HOC GROUP/WP.313.

Declarations

68. BWC AHG, BWC/AD HOC GROUP/WP.232, 'Working paper submitted by India, Indonesia and Mexico – Measures to strengthen the implementation of Article III of the Biological and Toxin Weapons Convention' (2 October 1997). See also BWC/AD HOC GROUP/25, 'Some Elements in a Verification Protocol, Working paper submitted by Sweden' (14 July 1995) p.2.

69. BWC AHG, BWC/AD HOC GROUP/WP.227 'Working paper submitted by Iran – Declaration on the implementation of Article X of the Convention' (1 October 1997)

70. VEREX, BWC/CONF.III/VEREX/9 p.12.

71. BWC 3RC, BWC/CONF.III/23 Part III, pp. 77-78 (UK proposal) and p.43 for the adopted CBM form.

72. Nicholas A. Sims, 'The Diplomacy of Biological Disarmament: Vicissitudes of a Treaty in Force, 1975-1985' (New York, St. Martin's Press, 1988) p.136.

73. Statement by the U.S. President's Senior Advisor for Arms Control, Non-Proliferation and Security Affairs, John D. Holum, Geneva 29 March 2000.

74. BWC AHG, BWC/AD HOC GROUP/WP.427 'Working paper submitted by South Africa – Proposed text for Article VIII' (2 August 2000).

75. BWC 3RC, BWC/CONF.III/23 Part III, p.80.

76. BWC AHG, BWC/AD HOC GROUP/WP.262, 'Working paper submitted by the Group of NAM and Other Countries – Investigations: Exclusion of all natural outbreaks of disease' (22 January 1998).

77. Anonymous, 'Federation of American Scientists Working Group on BW Verification – On the question of Outbreak Declarations under a Biological Weapons Convention Compliance Regime' (June 1999).

78. BWC AHG, BWC/AD HOC GROUP/WP.427 'Working paper submitted by South Africa – Proposed text for Article VIII' (2 August 2000).

79. BWC AHG, BWC/AD HOC GROUP/WP.409 'Working paper submitted by Ukraine – Article III, Section D, Subsection I' (6 December 1999).

80. VEREX, BWC/CONF.III/VEREX/WP.93 (4 December 1992) 'On Determining the Quantity of Microorganisms and Toxins Required for Protective Purpuses' [sic],Unofficial Translation, English only document.

81.. Gillian Woollett, Ph.D. Associate Vice President Pharmaceutical Research and Manufacturers of America before the Committee on Government Reform, Subcommittee on National Security, Veterans' Affairs and International Relations, U.S. House of Representatives, June 5, 2001.
http://www.house.gov/reform/ns/107th_testimony/gillian_woollett.htm

82. Barry Kellman, 'Bridling the International Trade of Catastrophic Weaponry' *The American Law Review* 43:3 (Spring 1994).

83. Of course, the initial lesson from the CWC in this regard was that such declarations identified discrepancies rather than assuaging concerns, and perhaps states parties were too quick to discount the utility of the measure on that basis.

Chapter 4

Visits and Clarification Procedures

Introduction

On-site measures in arms control agreements are intended to verify that states parties are adhering to their undertakings. Such measures are never the sole means by which states make assessments about compliance, because national technical means, intelligence, and other methods remain in use even though they may not be explicitly referred to in an agreement. Disquiet about the proliferation of biological weapons capabilities and the implications of the biotechnology revolution resulted in increasing doubts about the wisdom of an unverified BWC. The completion of the CWC also indicated that complex political and technical verification problems could be resolved given sufficient effort and will. Without oversimplifying the situation, many believed that if it could be done in the chemical weapons context, it could also be done in the BWC.

This was by no means a consensus view and the *minimalism-reform* divide remained significant. The modalities of on-site verification measures remained a source of much discussion, rancour and, ultimately, significant compromise by all states parties because it went to the heart of the debate. With the term 'verification' itself contentious the nomenclature of routine verification (inspections) was also problematic, hence the use of the term 'visits' emerged. More states parties were actively involved in the visits debate and had a real stake in the outcome than in any other area of the Protocol negotiations. It included, Australia, Brazil, Canada, China, France, Germany, India, Iran, Japan, the Netherlands, New Zealand, Norway, Pakistan, Republic of Korea, Russia, South Africa, Sweden, Switzerland, the UK, and the US, all of which had different views on the issue and all of which considered visits as critically important to shaping the Protocol to their national interests. The visits debate was an acid test of their diplomacy and its outcome the principal indication of *minimalist* or *reformist* ascendancy.

This chapter examines the evolution of a very complex debate on visits and clarification procedures. It does so by first examining why the very nomenclature of verification was contentious and what the envisaged purpose and function of on-site activities were, before outlining the generic evolution of the debate, and then examining the two principal types of on-site activity developed by the Ad Hoc Group; randomly-selected transparency visits and clarification visits. Under the former activity the chapter outlines how the concept was weakened from the inside out, that is to say the concept itself remained intact but the discrete variable aspects of visits, such as the period of notice before a visit, were weakened to the extent

90   *The Biological Weapons Convention*

that the final version of the provisions was far removed from the original procedures envisaged by key *reformists*. In the examination of the second type of on-site activity, clarification visits, the text outlines the metamorphosis of this measure from an alternative to randomly-selected transparency visits into a supplementary, but distinct, measure in itself. Overall, the on-site measures in the draft Protocol appear, at face value, to be weak, but as a package the measures offered significant potential to enhance transparency of a party's activities.

'Visits' not 'Inspections'

In the Ad Hoc Group the term 'verification' was not *verboten* but in the Western Group it did become a non-word because the US maintained its core position that the BWC was not verifiable. The US objective, as it stated at the Special Conference, was strengthening the Convention through, *inter alia*, benchmarks, clarification procedures, mechanisms to pursue specific concerns and engagement.[1] Within the Ad Hoc Group any reference to 'verification' usually drew a stock response from the US that in its view the BWC was not verifiable. In the end it became easier to stop using the term. Western states parties adopted terms such as 'compliance measures' and 'enhancing transparency' rather than 'verification' and thus the use of discourse associated with verification regimes such as the CWC or the IAEA – i.e. inspections – was eschewed in favour of more anodyne language, i.e. visits.[2] This was part of the attempt to distinguish between the effort at enhancing compliance and transparency in the BWC and verification under the CWC and the IAEA. As the UK noted:[3]

> It is ... not appropriate to think in terms of "routine inspections" as understood in the CWC, CFE and INF Treaties for example. A BW inspection or visit, in contrast, requires a more qualitative approach. In practice this means that inspectors have to make an evaluation of a broad range of interrelated factors such as the scale of specific facilities and the explanations provided for their use. A judgement needs to be formed on whether or not the facilities and activities are consistent with their stated purpose, with descriptions of the development of the site and with the BTWC itself.

While the nomenclature was important in the negotiations, the substantive issue was that visits involved routine on-site activity, which was distinct from investigations of use or alleged breaches of the Convention (by their nature extraordinary events) and constituted a separate element of the Protocol. Visits were concerned with routine monitoring of activities and facilities declared – or those that should have been declared – under the Protocol.

The purpose and function of on-site measures

The rationale for routine on-site activity was directly linked to the weaknesses of declarations if they stood alone as a compliance measure. VEREX identified the principal weakness of declarations as accuracy[4] because without the ability to check submitted declarations a state party could hide prohibited activities within a facility declared as undertaking legitimate activity free of any real concern of discovery. As one analyst noted, '[t]he accuracy of data provided by each party to an arms control agreement *must* be independently verified by the other party or parties.'[5] [my emphasis] Put simply, information submitted to the BWC states parties had to be checked, just as comparable information was checked by the OPCW and IAEA in the chemical and nuclear fields.

The potential, and practice, of using legitimate activities to cover prohibited activities had been exposed during the early 1990s in both the BWC and the NPT with the revelations of the Soviet Biopreparat biotechnology facilities, Iraqi production plants and nuclear facilities, and the North Korean nuclear facilities which masked offensive work in contravention of the BWC and the NPT respectively. These revelations had undermined confidence in arms control and the failure to resolve this problem in the BWC would not result in a significant increase in confidence about the veracity of the Convention. States parties were unlikely to sign up to a future agreement unless compliance measures could be used to assess the accuracy of claims of compliance. As a consequence the importance of ensuring declared activity was genuine, rather than acting as cover for prohibited activities, could not be underestimated.

Without routine on-site activity the Protocol would fall far short of contemporary standards of transparency under the CWC and the IAEA. However, simply because many of the countries involved in the Ad Hoc Group agreed to routine on-site activity in the CWC and the development of enhanced safeguards in the IAEA Additional Protocol, the inclusion of similar provisions – conceptually rather than technically – was not a foregone conclusion in the Protocol. To be specific, while the UK stated, '[i]t is highly unlikely that agreement could ever be secured for a protocol based exclusively on challenge inspections'[6] others noted correctly that 'the political climate had changed since the CWC negotiations were concluded, and States Parties seem to have become less willing to accept international on-site inspection and monitoring.'[7]

Reaching agreement on transparency and compliance mechanisms that could help differentiate between legitimate and prohibited activity to the satisfaction of states parties, while protecting national security and proprietary confidential information, was never going to be easy. It meant considering what was technically feasible *and* what was politically acceptable, but it took on additional significance because of the political importance inclusion or omission would send about the will of states parties to strengthen the BWC.

As the negotiations on the Protocol developed, three generic reasons could be identified as justifying the inclusion of visits as a compliance measure in the Protocol: deterrence, clarification, and co-operation.[8] The last function, co-operation, was a distinct issue within the BWC due to the obligations contained in Article X of the Convention. In the compliance architecture the co-operation aspect was largely irrelevant, but it served a useful purpose as an incentive to join the Protocol, as a means to sweeten visits for developing states parties, and as a specific obligation for co-operation in the biological sciences in line with Article X of the Convention.

92 *The Biological Weapons Convention*

During the negotiations visits developed another purpose as a method for resolving ambiguities in submitted declarations; the clarification role. In this clarification role a visit to a facility was the final mechanism for addressing ambiguities in declarations, including what had been declared and what had not been declared, after states parties had undertaken consultations with one another and/or the Organization. This role offered a mechanism between doing nothing and launching an investigation. Clarification visits were an alternative to some kind of random visit process in the initial development of the rolling text, but they developed into a distinct additional measure themselves.

In the deterrence role visits were intended to confirm the accuracy of declarations at visited facilities; encourage accuracy in all declarations; and, increase confidence and transparency into the BWC regime.[9] If visits were unable to fulfil their deterrence function and could not confirm the accuracy of declarations it follows that confidence in the declarations would be diminished, and from that the pressure on states parties to submit wholly accurate declarations was reduced. As one participant in the Ad Hoc Group commented, without visits to act as an incentive 'the good guys get lazy and the bad guys declare what they want.'[10] Those states parties that doubted the ability of visits to fulfil this deterrence-come-declaration-accuracy function argued that the burden imposed fell too heavily on compliant states. Within the Western Group that key point of contention was never resolved.[11] To be specific, the US argued that the deterrence function could not be fulfilled, and hence visits were a burden which served no useful purpose. Germany and Japan were sympathetic to this argument, but all others in the Western Group believed visits could fulfil a useful deterrence function.

The evolution of the visits debate

Although towards the end of the negotiations there were two types of visits, randomly-selected transparency visits and clarification visits, these ideas were distilled compromises of many other visions for routine on-site activity during the negotiations. At different stages the Ad Hoc Group had before it visits, inspections, information visits, confidence-building visits, familiarisation visits, short notice non-challenge visits, random non-challenge visits, ambiguity-related non-challenge visits, random visits, voluntary visits, clarification visits, consultation visits, randomly-selected visits, transparency visits, and finally randomly-selected transparency visits. In short, a complex and confusing set of overlapping concepts and terms to describe on-site measures. To understand the debate it is necessary to take a step back and examine the evolution of ideas and states parties' positions.

The debate moved through three stages. Between 1995 and the end of 1997 the proponents of what became randomly-selected transparency visits outlined the concept and developed text for insertion into the draft Protocol. In the period 1998-2000 supporters of the alternatives to these visits, clarification visits, developed their vision in greater detail. In addition, the alternative but less intrusive concept of 'transparency visits' was elaborated as a counter to randomly-selected visits (as they then existed). After 2000 the debates began to merge as the

Visits and Clarification Procedures

usefulness of some kind of on-site clarification visit was recognised, but proponents of randomly-selected transparency visits rejected them as an alternative and considered them a supplementary measure. Nevertheless, this was diplomacy and in order to press their case those opposed to only having clarification visits needed to convince those sceptical of randomly-selected visits that the latter visits had value. This is the period when the routine visits concept was diluted in order to gain greater support among sceptical states parties. Although the debates on the two types of visits – random and clarification – occurred in parallel for ease of explanation we will deal with each discretely.

Randomly-selected transparency visits

The UK was one of the leading proponents of some kind of routine on-site activity in the form of visits and held two important roles in the whole debate. First, the UK was in a large part the 'manager' of the concept as it developed between 1995-2000; it rarely worked alone, but it did tend to dominate discussions. Second, the UK held the Friend of the Chair position for compliance measures which meant its delegation was wearing two hats: its (*reformist*) national position and its attempts at seeking compromise on behalf of the Ad Hoc Group.

In one of its first submissions the UK argued that visits had five inter-related benefits: (1) validate declarations through on-site activities and encourage accuracy in declaration submissions; (2) facilitate transparency of national microbiological activities; (3) understand how national safety and rules and regulations operate and are implemented in practice; (4) facilitate the relationship between a state party and the Organization; and, (5) contribute to deterring potential proliferators.[12] This document also established the core UK theme vis-à-vis visits which it often repeated:[13]

> The key point is that visits are part of an integrated and balanced package of measures, each carefully crafted to complement the other constituent components of the protocol. These components would include: *declarations* covering military microbiology, BL4 containment laboratories, aerobiology, work with listed agents/toxins and production microbiology, and past activities; *challenge inspections* in response to specific compliance concerns; *investigations of alleged use*; and, in order to implement the regime effectively, *a professional inspectorate*. [Emphasis in original]

Central to understanding the UK view on this topic, and its approach in general, is the observation from VEREX that no *single* measure could offer complete confidence in ensuring compliance with the BWC, but a range of measures, working in combination with each other, did permit the BWC to be strengthened. Many others shared that view, but another proponent of visits, Sweden, initially took a different stance on their role and used a different nomenclature. Sweden argued that verifying the accuracy of declarations did require some kind of on-site inspection, but it should be limited to declared facilities and that the main function of inspections would be directed against undeclared facilities and facilities or activities of concern.[14] While the short-notice element of such visits was common to both approaches, and Sweden cited 24 hours as the period of notice, there was a distinction between the principal function of visits. At this juncture Sweden advocated a lower threshold for conducting clarification-come-challenge type inspections whereas the UK opted for greater reliance on routine visit activity and viewed challenge inspections as an exceptional tool.

The idea of both routine and challenge activity was common in other agreements and of itself not particularly controversial. Cuba, for example, supported routine and challenge activities from the very beginning.[15] It was the degree of intrusiveness being advocated for routine on-site activity that created the problems. Under the Protocol there would be no stockpiles of weapons to destroy and hence rigorous monitoring of the destruction process was not required. Second, there could be no equivalent of a schedule of chemicals which had no or few legitimate purposes. Quantitative limitations on possession of certain pathogens were meaningless in practical terms. Thus, as we have seen in the preceding chapter most of the required information about relevant activities involved the civil sector and all states parties were keen to have as low a burden as possible imposed on industry. South Africa advocated a system of voluntary confidence-building visits which would not involve inspectors, but experts nominated by states parties. The system, according to its sponsor, avoided unnecessary intrusiveness while permitting a state party to demonstrate its compliance with the BWC to the experts and keep open regular channels of communication between states parties and states parties and the Organization.[16]

What is interesting here is that three of the main proponents of a *reformist* BWC protocol – the UK, Sweden, and South Africa – all began with quite different ideas on the issue of visits. By the middle of 1996, however, *reformists* recognised they would have to present a common vision if they were to convince the *minimalists*. The paper of the EU was critical in this process because it forced the 15 EU states to agree upon a discussion paper which bore the hallmarks of a robust visits process. While it is significant that the EU discussion paper did not bind its members – only a formal Common Position did that – the EU claimed that so-called 'non-challenge visits' would provide additional mechanisms to deter non-compliance, provided they were short notice – deemed to be 'essential' and taken to mean 24 hours – and they could build transparency about activities by verifying declarations and resolving uncertainties.[17] Significantly, the EU stated that the likelihood of non-challenge visits 'uncovering concrete evidence of BW-related prohibited activities is low'[18] but the presence of expert personnel on-site meant that they might gather information which could arouse suspicion. The EU advocated visual inspection, interviewing, identification of key equipment, and auditing as basic measures to be employed on-site and favoured the possibility of using sampling and identification only if necessary to resolve any uncertainty. The lessons learned from both the Trilateral Process and UNSCOM are clearly in evidence here; not least in the importance placed on simply being able to get professional, high quality personnel on-site and have a look round a facility.

A second important element also appeared in the EU paper; the right of the Organization *to initiate* a visit where specific ambiguities or questions arose about a declaration or certain activities which could not be resolved by other means. The EU therefore brought different ideas together into two basic types of on-site activity: routine on-site activity related to the accuracy of declarations, and specific on-site activity related to discrete ambiguities or concerns. These became the foundations of what eventually emerged as 'Randomly-Selected Transparency Visits' and 'Clarification Visits'. The purpose of the former type of visit was well understood from other arms control agreements, but clarification visits were problematic – not least because of the power granted to the Organization to actually query a state party's declaration in detail – and the concept was further elaborated by Sweden and the Netherlands in late 1996 and the UK in early 1997.

By mid-1997 other Western states put their support behind the routine visit concept. Australia, Austria, Canada, the Netherlands, New Zealand, Sweden and Switzerland presented a paper on the general principles of such ideas[19] and Canada espoused the idea of visits as a means to instil additional confidence that the Protocol was being treated as a 'living document' rather than a 'paper' commitment, thus providing a means to demonstrate compliance to other states parties.[20] Demonstrating compliance is an important nuance in the debate. Visits were never intended by their proponents as a means to catch cheaters with the proverbial smoking gun: they were intended to check whether what was actually declared was consistent with what was actually happening at a facility.

Nevertheless, many others remained unconvinced. South Africa still favoured confidence-building visits and Brazil expanded ideas for visits of a more voluntary nature.[21] By 1998 the contest was not swinging in favour of the more intrusive vision. The *minimalists* were holding out and although they did not act as a concerted group the necessity of having to counter objections from states parties such as the US, India, Russia, China, Pakistan, South Africa, and Brazil led to stalemate in the text; it was neither moving forward nor reducing the number of options available in the rolling text itself.

It is from this point where we begin to see what Dando has correctly identified as 'erosion' coming into play[22], even though at the level of detail much was still to be worked out in relation to all types of visits. A part of this process can be seen as a result of the 29-state working paper under which the increasing frustration with the pace of the negotiations and the failure to make significant progress towards conclusion of the Protocol became clear. To facilitate greater progress these 29 states parties identified declarations, visits, investigations of non-compliance, and an organization as central elements of the legally-binding Protocol. However, while the text did not go into specifics on any of these items, the necessity for compromise on visits is obvious; the 29 could only agree that there would be '[p]rovision for visits to facilities in order to promote accurate and complete declarations and thus further enhance transparency and confidence.'[23] This was a move away from verifying the accuracy of declarations.

The UK paper of December 1998 is where dilution by *reformists* begins to become noticeable, because the UK proposed that the period of notice before a visit would now be five days – rather than 24 hours the EU paper had deemed 'essential' – and that the level of access to the facility and control over which activities could be conducted during the visit began to shift in favour of the visited

96 *The Biological Weapons Convention*

state party and the facility. For example, in the rolling text sampling would 'only be conducted if offered by *the facility*'[24], whereas in the new UK proposed text, sampling would 'only be conducted if offered by *the visited State party and visited facility personnel*'[25] [my emphasis] which provided an additional obstacle to the use of sampling as a technical measure. Granting power of refusal to both the facility and the state party – in effect a double veto – now became acceptable.

It was not all bad news for the *reformists*; one positive move was that South Africa shifted position and attempted to introduce some clarity into the debate through a package of different visits for different purposes.[26] Voluntary visits still existed, but random visits with the purpose of confirming that declarations were consistent with the obligations under the Protocol were also identified as a necessary measure. These would be non-confrontational and confidence-building in their nature, of two-day duration and with a five-day notice period, and while rigorous managed access provisions were identified as a right of the visited state party, interviewing, visual observation, identification of key equipment and auditing were all permitted, and sampling available if offered by the facility.

The package also included clarification visits to declared facilities and consultation visits to undeclared facilities, but despite some of the limitations in the South African proposal, the working paper highlighted important elements of common ground on which states parties could develop a compromise. In particular, as a South African proposal it permitted a number of other NAM states – essentially all but the hard-line non-aligned – to support random visits more attuned to their concerns. Some of the more detailed aspects were modified in a later paper[27] but a clear coherent alternative existed to the *reformist* model(s) on offer. The more positive role played by South Africa was critical to the process overall since as a moderate non-aligned state and as the Co-ordinator of the NAM, it wielded significant influence in the Ad Hoc Group. Unless South Africa could be persuaded that a concept was valid it was highly unlikely that more conservative states could be persuaded of its utility. In simple terms, the *reformists* needed South Africa on board if they were to succeed.

An additional factor to sweeten visits was the more detailed approach to their role in enhancing peaceful co-operation between states parties. While the possibility of using visits as a conduit for peaceful co-operation had been mooted, Brazil, Chile, New Zealand, and Norway expanded the concept to enable visits to have a recognised dual-purpose:[28]

> [i]n addition to strengthening the compliance regime, the improvement of States parties' capabilities through technical cooperation and assistance activities or programmes in the context of visits would be a cost-effective means for the Organization to simultaneously discharge some of its tasks under the various provisions of the Protocol.

In essence there was increasing support for some kind of random visit procedure among states parties including those outside the Western Group. There were disputes over their purpose, intrusiveness, and the power of the visiting team, as well as which specific measures could be employed on-site, but such visits had supporters. The trick was now to convince sceptics and opponents and in the

Visits and Clarification Procedures

1998-2000 period three states parties were crucial to the debate and its evolution: the US, Germany, and South Africa.

The US position

The US position is important because of its power in the negotiations, its dominant role in the Western Group, and the fact that its support or opposition to a concept could decide the concept's fate. However, the US position on visits evolved and was more complex than either consistent opposition or support for a particular measure. It was also difficult to work out exactly what the US wanted vis-à-vis visits because the position took so long to emerge and, when it did finally emerge, the Ad Hoc Group was literally three years ahead of the US in its thinking.

Chevrier has suggested that in the three-year period 1995 to 1998 'the United States took a back seat'[29] in the negotiations. To an extent this is a correct observation; certainly if the number of formal written proposals for the Protocol text – in the form of working papers – is taken as an indicator of a proactive approach then the US was less active than the UK, South Africa, Russia and many others. Quite correctly Chevrier also noted that the US was not the sole state party exhibiting an apparent lack of engagement; '[w]here is the substantive participation of China or Japan or India?'[30] However, these states parties and the US by no means sat back in the negotiations and allowed others to develop a Protocol which was unaffected by their concerns. The 'back seat' approach did not reflect a lack of interest by the US delegation in Geneva – which was not only the largest delegation but also one of the best informed and highly organized – but a lack of direction from Washington.[31] Up until 1998 the inability of the US to take a lead on certain issues was due to bureaucratic politics and deadlock over a negotiating position in Washington.[32] [33]

The change in the US position emerged in early 1998 when the three key agencies in the US – Defence, State, and Commerce – agreed on a compromise package of proposals released at the end of January 1998.[34] The US position on visits was outlined as being in favour of voluntary visits at the discretion of the facility concerned and with all decisions on the level access determined by the facility. The purpose of such visits was 'to address questions regarding the BWC or the protocol.'[35] In addition, the US stated it supported 'non-challenge clarifying visits' to clarify an ambiguity or anomaly or any uncertainty with annual declarations. Moreover, the US made clear it opposed routine or random visits.[36] Despite the fact that the US had a very different vision of the Protocol than many of its closest allies, this policy was entirely consistent with the US stated objectives for the Protocol: benchmarks, clarification procedures, and mechanisms to pursue specific concerns.

Levy opined that the January 1998 proposals on visits 'amounted to a middle ground between a new intrusive on-site monitoring regime and the status quo.'[37] That was a correct observation and it cannot be ignored that what the US proposed was a significant improvement on the available mechanisms in the Convention. The difficulty it presented to the *reformists*, however, was that the state party which had tipped the balance of power in their favour was opposed to one of the key *reformist* planks for the Protocol; a routine, random, intrusive on-site measure to check the accuracy of declarations. Compared to the ambition of other states parties, other arms control regimes, and what else was on offer in the Ad Hoc Group, the US proposal placed it back in the *minimalist* camp. The US position appeared to be unaffected by the debates of the last three years. In addition, 'for some in Washington, mostly in the Pentagon and the Department of Commerce, even the proposed provisions for clarification visits went much too far.'[38]

As a consequence the debate stalled in 1998. The *reformists* were not prepared to give up on routine visits simply because the US' initial position was against such a measure; they were going to attempt to change that position. In contrast the US was not going to be easily persuaded that it needed to change its position, especially after that position was a product of an inter-agency compromise. Compounding this, US opposition to routine visits sheltered other states parties whose positions were unknown in public but were thought to be against intrusive on-site measures; Russia, China, India, Pakistan, and Iran.

The debate only really began to move forward in 1999. The US position in the first half of 1999 remained opposed to random and routine visits and the emergence in public of a letter from the US Secretary of Commerce to the Secretary of State underlined that certain agencies did not support a 'negotiating strategy of attempting to mollify the most hard-line members of the Western Group.'[39] The attempt by the UK to develop a Western Group compromise on this issue led to a paper on transparency visits, but did not produce the necessary accommodation between the US and its Western Group allies, particularly those in the EU.[40] Wilson reported that there was a 'growing impatience with the United States' and that 'the US will not countenance any form of visits that are mandatory' and the 'position has been portrayed by US negotiators as immutable, having been fixed upon at cabinet level.'[41] In addition, a potentially destabilising issue was identified, whereby there was:[42]

> an increasing view among some delegations ... that they will have to choose between having a regime that accommodates the United States' reluctance for intrusive verification but that is weak, or proceeding with an effective mechanism in the knowledge that the United States may pull away and refuse to participate.

This may have been mooted, in part out of sheer frustration, but it was never a realistic option. However, by the end of October 1999 visits were causing significant political problems and the divisions were spilling over into the public domain. One report noted that, 'there are still differences within the Western Group on the necessary provisions for randomly-selected visits, and between the Western Group and the NAM on the necessary provisions for clarification visits.'[43] The UK compromise paper of the sixteenth session on 'transparency visits' was considered too weak by other members of the Western Group and too strong for the US, but although the US 'initially stated that it could not accept Britain's compromise paper, [it] then made it known that if everyone else in the Western Group accepted the paper it would too.'[44] Attempting to find a compromise was compounded by the NAM paper which in certain places was more intrusive than the UK, and later German, compromise proposals. A NAM paper on visits which advocated, at least in certain places, a more intrusive compliance regime than any corresponding 'Western Group' position was anathema to many of the *reformists* in the Western Group and only served to underline both the Western Group's weakness as an actor and the level of frustration many felt towards the US.

In effect the intra-Western Group frustration scuppered an opportunity to engage with the NAM and address those issues problematic to all Western Group members. States parties and observers alike now knew openly that there was a schism in the Western Group on visits which prevented real progress on the issue.[45] What weakened the Western Group strengthened the hard-line NAM and those within the NAM who were less enamoured with intrusive compliance measures knew they still had three cards to play in their favour: first, shelter behind the US position; second, play off the US and other Western Group members against each other; and third, simply wait and allow the negotiations to drag on interminably.

Interventions and efforts by South Africa and Germany effectively prevented the waiting strategy from coming into play, as it was during this period when 'transparency visits' emerged as a serious compromise option. The 'price' was the erosion of the vision of intrusive, routine visits.

Although publicly the US remained sceptical, in January 2000 details of an informal paper circulated by the US were published. It now appeared that the US did not reject the idea of transparency visits, but did oppose the concept of validating declarations, and questioned whether or not this activity could or should be done through visits.[46] US-sponsored visits would be an aid to transparency designed to maintain the expertise of the Technical Secretariat, but would not assess or validate the declarations of facilities. Such visits would therefore be co-operative in nature, although not necessarily voluntary, and designed to build confidence, although access would be at the discretion of the state party. One analysis of the US concept claimed it amounted to 'a guided tour of the facility.'[47] This negative assessment was supported by another analyst covering the negotiations in Geneva:[48]

> the US position is that transparency visits should not be considered as a way of ensuring declarations are accurate and complete, [and] should consist of only a tour of and a briefing at the facility and should take place at the discretion of the visited State Party. It resists any intrusive measures in this context.

This brought much needed clarity to the US position and was characterised as the US 'moving towards an acceptance of transparency visits', which offered hope for a coherent deal to emerge.[49]

However, the US was further isolated when Russia announced 'it could go along with the mandatory visits, but only to high containment BL-4 facilities.'[50] Russia had previously argued that neither random nor clarification visits were required; only voluntary visits were necessary to address anomalies in declarations.[51] The implication was that Russia would accept the other proposals contained in the NAM paper of 1999, but with limitations and concerns greater than those expressed by India. As an indication of the Russian position on visits, note that visits to biodefence facilities were deemed unacceptable; whatever was going on in the Biopreparat complex and the military biodefence facilities would remain unseen, subject to declarations (which could not be checked), clarification visits (which Russia sought to emasculate), and challenge inspections (which were unlikely). Russia was no supporter of meaningful transparency measures. With the official position of China known to favour visits only to 'high-risk' defence facilities, to be against clarification visits, and intent on avoiding visits becoming surrogate investigations[52] the US shielded Russia and China inadvertently. However, the Russian development left the US proposing the weakest 'set' of routine on-site measures related to declarations.[53] Testimony in September 2000 confirmed the limited vision of the US when the head of the Geneva delegation outlined transparency visits as having a notice period 'to allow thorough preparation of a facility in advance of a visit' and 'far less intrusive activities in any non-challenge visit' than comparable activity in the CWC.[54] Further corroboration of the US position noted that:[55]

> Compared to the CWC, the on-site activities that the United States is arguing for in a BWC Protocol would be less intrusive, far fewer in number, smaller in scale, shorter, and diffused among a dramatically larger universe of facilities. We are proposing visits to a limited number of BWC-relevant facilities to increase transparency, promote fulfilment of declaration obligations, and familiarize a BWC Technical Secretariat with a country's biotechnology and biodefense infrastructure.

In summary, the US position remained *minimalist* when compared to the positions of many of its closest allies and against the other alternatives available. Nevertheless, any assessment of the US position must recognise that its original objective was not to have routine on-site activity, no matter how weak, under the Protocol. Its position had been changed, but the cost of moving the US towards a compromise other states parties could agree to was high.

The German compromise

As a member of the EU Germany was bound by the Common Position of the 15 EU states which, *inter alia*, called for 'effective follow-up to ... declarations in the form of visits, on the basis of appropriate mechanisms of random selection, so as to enhance transparency of declared facilities and activities, promote accuracy of declarations, and ensure fulfilment of declaration obligations in order to ensure further compliance with the Protocol.'[56] The EU common position (actually supported by 28 European states) however, lacked specifics. Germany was acutely aware that both Russia and the US were not receptive to the idea of routine on-site measures, and neither was China nor the hard-line NAM. Furthermore, Germany's experience with the CWC during the first few years of implementation (1997-2000) influenced its position. The failure of the US to make its civil chemical industry declaration and submit its implementing legislation meant that the burden of OPCW inspections fell on other chemical industry producers, not least Germany.[57] Thus, it is fair to characterise the German position as being in favour of a robust BWC Protocol, but Germany opposed strong measures on paper which it did not believe others would actually be able to implement or measures others would step back from upon implementation. Germany worried about the gap between the visions of the UK, Sweden, and France and those of the US, Russia and China in terms of both the impact such a gap had on completing the Protocol negotiations and the possibility of non-implementation of such measures by certain states parties upon entry into force.

While the UK paper of June 1999 was an attempt at compromise it could not deliver consensus in the Western Group. Germany then took the initiative with a working paper which fleshed out the alternative vision of 'transparency visits' and proposed significant changes to the rolling text.[58] The UK compromise had itself been developed by the Friend of the Chair overseeing compliance measures (the UK Ambassador) and transparency visits were in fact the proposed compromise from the FOC.[59] Germany proposed to delete much of the contested language relating to the activities of the visiting team and replace it with more generic language that left the visited facility great scope to provide as much (or as little) transparency of its activities as it saw fit. Visits were solely about increasing transparency and would consist of a briefing, a tour of the facility and a question and answer session between the visited facility staff and the visiting team.

The significant changes to the concept of visits were in the detail related to the purpose of the visit, the level of access to the facility granted to the visiting team, the rights of the facility and the visited state party, and the on-site measures permitted to be undertaken by the visiting team. Confirming the accuracy of declarations was abandoned. In its place were two weaker aims: enhancing transparency of declared facilities and activities, and promoting accuracy in declarations. Interviewing of personnel and auditing of the facility's records were omitted. Any information provided to the visiting team and access to the facility was at the sole discretion of the facility, and, as such, there was no requirement for managed access provisions.

A member of the German delegation explained in a separate seminar that the rationale was, 'to overcome the problem of the different visit concepts by merging acceptable elements from the existing visit concepts to create a nonintrusive, transparency increasing approach based on a model for random selection of declared facilities to be visited.'[60] According to Beck such visits were designed to:[61]

leave the information provided by the visited facility to the discretion of the visited state party and the facility, which can show as much transparency as deemed necessary to convince the visiting team that the activities conducted at the facility are for legitimate purposes only. The concept includes no elements of intrusiveness like sampling, accounting, and so forth, which are inspection elements that a great number of non-aligned states parties and some major biotech industry states parties do not want for different reasons.

Three things are noteworthy: first, this was a German paper and not an EU paper suggesting the concept did not have broad support in the EU; second, that power

102   *The Biological Weapons Convention*

was shifting towards the facility and the visited state party as the actor that decided which activity could take place on-site, thus reducing the rights of the (future) Organization and, by extension, other states parties; and, third, the recognition of states parties opposed to intrusive visits implicitly uniting even though their opposition was for different reasons.

It was an attempt at compromise designed to bridge the gap between the *reformists* and the *minimalists*. It satisfied neither – no doubt as Germany expected – but its importance in establishing a new middle ground should not be underestimated.   Of itself, it provided no new, immediate, or dramatic breakthrough in the negotiations, but it did allow others who were in fact seeking compromise to pursue similar attempts to bring all states parties closer together.

South Africa

South Africa orchestrated and delivered one of the critical breakthroughs in the visits debate at the sixteenth session of the Ad Hoc Group in September 1999; a cohesive NAM vision for all visits.[62]   This narrowed the differences in opinion on visits. At the *reform* end of the spectrum, randomly-selected visits were accepted with a primary purpose to confirm that 'declarations are accurate and complete', but they would also enhance transparency and act as a conduit for technical assistance and co-operation programmes.   Visits could be extended beyond two days if necessary (and agreed by all concerned parties). The visit plan consisted of a briefing and the visit team would be permitted to review and discuss the facility's declaration, interview individuals if they so consented (and as long as such interviews were in the presence of representatives of the visited state party), review relevant documentation, and visually observe the appropriate parts of the facility. At the *minimal* end of the spectrum, differences still existed among the non-aligned about the types of facilities to which they would apply.   Furthermore, the notice period was proposed as seven days and access would be at the discretion of the state party, therefore limiting the utility of visits and making them dependent on the attitude of the individual state party.[63]

With respect to the specifics, China was understood to oppose elements of it[64] and the paper certainly contained provisions which were unacceptable to all the Western Group members.   The proposal that visits should apply only to biodefence and BL4 facilities (at the behest of India and supported by China), the fact that voluntary assistance visits to obtain technical assistance and voluntary clarification visits to address anomalies and ambiguities had priority, and therefore could reduce random visits to zero in a particular year, and the level of access to the facility determined by the visited state party (not the facility), were all problematic. Furthermore, the visited state party was granted wide ranging power over the content of the visit report because the visiting team was required to incorporate any comments from the state party and was under pressure to remove any information and data requested for deletion by the state party.

It was not a proposal that gained immediate support from other states parties, since it would severely limit the role of visits.   The possibility of confining randomly-selected visits to biodefence and maximum biological containment facilities meant that all other facilities would be subject only to declarations and investigations of non-compliance or, at best, voluntary clarification visits. Although some Western states reportedly welcomed the NAM paper as a way to take forward the debate, others used it to voice their unhappiness with the less rigorous proposals being mooted.

To be specific, rumours of a US proposal on transparency visits which had been circulated within the Western Group were rife in Geneva. The NAM paper was used as a conduit by other Western Group members to attack this US proposal and in doing so effectively confirmed in public that the Western Group was split. Wilson observed that 'the US is particularly keen to maintain an image of a united Western Group because it feels its own position may isolate it, revealing how close many of its actual positions are to those of China and India.'[65]

From this point onwards the *reformist* vision for visits was moribund; the US was known to oppose it and the NAM had its own carefully crafted compromise to protect and champion. Simply to retain visits the *reformists* had to compromise and bring on board the NAM states while diluting the more restrictive measures proposed, such as the limit on the types of facilities. The states parties were split five ways: the US vision, the hard-line NAM vision of restricted facilities and quotas, the moderate NAM vision, Western states such as Germany willing to compromise, and the *reformist* vision. At the time there was a feeling that the Western Group had not capitalised on the NAM proposal and failed to exploit the opportunity it presented to take the visits debate forward. The proposal was a carefully crafted compromise initiated by South Africa and it effectively created a critical mass of states parties in favour of routine on-site measures designed to promote the accuracy of declarations. Through that it placed states parties such as India, China, Russia and the US outside this cross-caucus grouping. The failure of the *reformists* to exploit this opportunity was remiss. In part, the more robust procedures had always been the European Union vision for the Protocol, and even that vision had been weakened by Germany.[66] With the South African proposal, the numbers began to move in favour of the *reformists*; the German compromise offered the middle ground; and the US position was not beyond further change. There was now considerable scope for developing a compromise across the Ad Hoc Group and as the Chairman of the negotiations noted, visits were becoming more coherent.[67]

The composite text

The actual strength of randomly-selected transparency visits depended on a number of variable factors, the inclusion or omission of which affected the ability of visits to fulfil their stated function. By early 2001 it was not a choice between two coherent visions; rather alternatives emerged through numerous compromises among states parties that crossed alliances and working groups.[68] This complicated the debate significantly. The key issues were as follows: what was the purpose of visits; were they mandatory or voluntary; how long was the notice period prior to a visit; what types of facilities could be visited; what was the selection criterion;

104 *The Biological Weapons Convention*

what level of access to the facility would be granted to the visiting team; and, which on-site activities were permitted. In the final analysis it is the outcome of the negotiations on these variable factors that provide the best indicator of how the *minimalist-reformist* contest was resolved.

The purpose of visits

In the early discussions on visits it was clear that a wide range of countries considered their purpose was to validate the information provided in declarations.[69] As the negotiations progressed this validation/verification requirement was rejected in favour of 'enhancing transparency' and 'promoting accuracy' of declarations.[70] Transparency visits were intended only to promote 'accurate fulfilment of the declaration obligations.'[71] A French expert remarked that the purpose of transparency visits was 'not verification of the declaration as such even if some elements of verification of the consistency of the declaration are there' and went on to imply that such a limited purpose was as weak as it could be, *if* a final compromise was to be agreed.[72] As Dando observed, 'we do not have a strong system ... to determine that the declaration is complete and accurate.'[73]

The change might be considered a nuance to accommodate different interpretations of what verification actually meant, but it actually goes much deeper than that. This can be illustrated by reference to the verification activities in the CWC with respect to *Other Chemical Production Facilities*, which offered the best (but still limited) comparison to the BWC problem. Inspection of OCPFs in the CWC were not tied to the scheduled chemicals or the destruction facilities, but those facilities in the civil industry sector that used chemicals of specific interest to the CWC's states parties. Thus, for OCPFs the *general aim* of inspections was 'to verify activities are consistent with the information to be provided in declarations' but the *particular aim* of the inspections 'shall be the verification of the absence of any Schedule 1 chemical.'[74] Had the Protocol adopted a similar strategy to the CWC randomly-selected transparency visits might have had the general aim of ensuring activities were consistent with the information provided in declarations, but a particular aim of verifying the absence of biological agents, toxins, materials and equipment in types and quantities that have no justification for prophylactic, protective or other peaceful purposes.

In the composite text, the purpose of randomly-selected transparency visits was to 'promote the overall objectives of the Protocol' via three identified means:[75]

> Increasing confidence in the consistency of declarations with the activities of the facility and encouraging submission of complete and consistent declarations; Enhancing transparency of facilities subject to [such visits]; Helping the Technical Secretariat ... to acquire and retain a comprehensive and up-to-date understanding of the facilities and activities declared globally.

If undertaken this would have been a significant improvement on the existing provisions of the BWC which offered no comparable mechanism. Such visits would, therefore, have strengthened the Convention. It was not verification of

Visits and Clarification Procedures 105

declarations as contained in the original vision(s) of *reformist* states. It was something less rigorous in accordance with the wishes of the *minimalists*.

Mandatory or voluntary visits

The second variable factor was whether or not visits were a mandatory measure or a voluntary undertaking. In basic terms, could a visit be refused? If the implementing organization requested a visit to a facility, but the facility had the right to refuse the request, any semblance of a deterrence factor was omitted entirely from the mechanism. Visits had to be mandatory if they were to have any role in denying 'a potential violator the means for concealing proscribed programmes under the cover of legitimate activities.'[76] In the composite text randomly-selected transparency visits were mandatory; an obvious, but important, victory for the *reformists*.

Short or long notice

The third variable factor was the notice period prior to a visit. As one analyst noted, '[i]f all non-challenge visits were to allow several weeks of advance notice, the compliance regime would forfeit the essential functions of deterrence at declared facilities and encouragement of (and confidence in) accurate declarations.'[77] The ability to clean up a laboratory in a short period of time was one of the principal reasons that visits had to be short-notice; however, industry specialists identified a total clean up of a facility as possible only in the rarest of circumstances. Evidence from the pharmaceutical companies and from inspections of other facilities in the USSR and Iraq did indicate that something usually escaped any attempt at clean-up. A professional, highly trained inspectorate would probably see a sufficient number of anomalies – even without sampling – to raise doubts. If, on the other hand, sampling was permitted, 'data can still be picked up after a room is decontaminated.'[78] In reality the short or long notice dispute was something of a proxy. Even with weeks of lead time beyond anything offered in the Protocol visits under the Trilateral process were able to reveal a sufficient number of anomalies between Soviet/Russian claims and what was actually occurring in facilities. Discrepancies were identified. In an ideal world the notice period would have been short, but the *reformists* could afford to give ground here. The options mooted in the negotiations ranged from 24 hours to twenty-one days. The 14 day notice period marked another victory for the *minimalists*.

Types of facilities

Within the architecture of the compliance regime there were two basic types of facilities: declared facilities and undeclared facilities. With respect to the latter, visits would have a role in assessing undeclared facilities, but that was a specific problem in the overall debate related to clarification procedures. It was uncertainty over which declared facilities visits applied to that became an important variable. Under the declarations envisaged in the composite text the *reformists* insisted visits

106   *The Biological Weapons Convention*

apply to all types of declared facilities, regardless of the activity that necessitated the declaration.

One alternative in the rolling text limited visits to those declared under the maximum biological containment trigger and/or those declared under the Biodefence trigger.[79] Thus, certain declared facilities would still offer scope for a violator to conceal a prohibited programme within an ostensibly legitimate declared facility. However, all members of the Western Group favoured visits to all declared facilities and this united position won out. In line with the preferences of the *reformists* randomly-selected transparency visits were to be made to all facilities.

Selection criteria

The fifth variable to consider was how facilities were selected for visits. The options were: in proportion to the declarations submitted by each state party; in proportion to the declarations submitted by each region; or, on some form of random basis. If visits were selected according to the proportion of declared facilities then those states with most facilities would receive the greatest number of visits. One possible way around this problem was the notion of a regional quota system for such visits[80] because under a system of proportionality the US and other Western states, particularly Japan and the European Union states, would receive most visits, whereas India and China, for example, would receive fewer visits. India supported selection based on proportionality.[81]

The alternative approach was random selection. Random selection would mean all declared facilities had an equal chance of being selected for a visit. A modification, weighted-random selection, gave certain facilities devised by agreed criteria a higher probability of selection. For example, if the weighting was placed on biodefence facilities, then biodefence facilities had a higher probability of being selected than other declared facilities. The key in this procedure was to weight selection without reducing the probability of visits to all countries and all types of facilities to zero, thereby significantly diminishing the utility of visits. Western states preferred visits to be 'distributed as widely and equitably as possible among those states submitting declarations.'[82]

Under those existing alternatives states with a large or a small number of facilities were protected from receiving a disproportionate number of visits, which became a cause for concern of states such as Australia, New Zealand, and South Africa. They did not fit neatly into either category and feared they would end up with a number of visits disproportionate to their relative size and number of declared facilities. South Africa and New Zealand proposed a cube-root system of allocating visits to achieve the objective of being fair to all states parties. This selection process would, according to their view, ensure a broad geographical spread of visits and a range of facilities visited in states parties with a large number of declared facilities.[83]

In a classic diplomatic compromise an amalgam of all variations found its way into the composite text. This meant that facilities subject to randomly-selected transparency visits were determined by a complex criteria based on a percentage of the annual maximum number of visits permitted under the Protocol in total, the maximum number of visits a facility could receive in any five year period, the maximum number of visits a state party could receive in any year, whether or not an individual facility had been visited in the last five years, that such visits must be spread across a representative range of facilities, and the proportion of the declared facilities in each state party.[84] Few people actually understood what this would translate into should the Protocol enter in force, but it was, at face value, sufficiently random, sufficiently proportional, and sufficiently fair to give the impression that it would work in practice. Of greater import, it represented no one's known public option.

Level of access and on-site activity

Another variable factor was the level of permitted access at facilities. The level of access could be judged against three options: access anywhere within the facility at the discretion of the visiting team; access at the discretion of the visited facility and/or visited state party; managed access devised by the visiting team and the visited facility and/or the visited state party. The first option was a non-starter and had no support among delegations. It was rejected because of the recognised need to protect confidential proprietary information (CPI) and national security information (NSI). Consideration of the impact on-site measures would have on CPI and NSI was an explicit requirement for the work of VEREX and subsequently formed one of the elements in the mandate of the Ad Hoc Group.

The second option was not conducive to an intrusive or robust compliance architecture because it permitted a facility to control the access of the visiting team and, in a worse case scenario, permitted a violator to control what could and could not be seen at the facility, thereby further reducing the chance of anomalies between that declared and that seen being uncovered. The final option, managed access, was based on concepts devised in the negotiations for the CWC and championed by the UK.[85] Under managed access the visited facility/state party could deny access to certain areas in order to protect CPI or NSI but was also under the obligation to provide alternative means of explanation if the visiting team required access to a laboratory or records to fulfil its mandate.

In the composite text access was to be at the discretion of the visited state party (not the facility), but was required to be sufficient to fulfil the visit mandate. This resolved the problem for both *minimalists* and *reformists* and put off the real decisions for another day, i.e. implementation.

The final variable factor was the types of activity permitted on-site. VEREX considered 21 activities as possible verification measures, including: visual inspection; interviewing; auditing; identification of key equipment; sampling and identification; and, medical examination. The Ad Hoc Group, of course, was no longer thinking in terms of 'verification', but certain measures were clearly far more intrusive than others; for example medical examination of staff in comparison to visual inspection. In that context medical examination was never an activity advocated under visits. All the other components might, however, have been necessary under a visit, but delegations had divergent opinions on permitted

108 *The Biological Weapons Convention*

activities. Sampling and analysis was a major source of contention and US industry representatives made known their objection to the use of sampling, as it considered the procedures represented a threat to CPI.[86]

Explicit references to the other types of activity under consideration were also left out of the composite text. The visit consisted of a briefing of up to three hours duration, a tour of the facility – not to exceed two hours – and a visit plan under which the visiting team could, with consent, undertake the following: discuss issues with facility personnel and/or representatives of the state party (providing *all* discussions were in the presence of a state party representative); review documentation at the facility; visit, and revisit, parts of the facility involved in the declared activities; and, other on-site activities granted by the visited state party.

At face value this appears weak, but while understanding that compromise was necessary to achieve consensus it is important to recognise that upon implementation precedent, development of latent possibilities, and interpretation of procedures through understandings usually served to strengthen an agreement's provisions. For example, how would a 'discussion' differ from an 'interview' or a 'review of documentation' be distinguished from an audit? While not suggesting the composite text was made up of semantic nuances, it is worth noting that latent possibilities existed within nearly all the identified measures. It is certainly possible to envisage that had the first few visits been to states parties such as the UK, Brazil, South Africa, Australia, Sweden, Italy, and Canada the 'standard' for co-operation, the level of access provided, and the measures permitted on-site would have been established as quite high. This would not have been the case if the first few visits were to states parties such as India, Russia, China, the US, and Pakistan.

In effect, the level of access and the permitted activities during a visit favoured the *minimalists*, but there was considerable strength in the text if interpreted correctly. Randomly-Selected Transparency Visits were stronger than many analysts have given them credit for.

Clarification visits

One of the lessons learned from implementation of other arms control agreements was that declarations were not a foolproof method of supplying information on activities and capabilities. While this could be exploited by the determined proliferator, it was also recognised that not all errors, omissions or mistakes were deliberate attempts to circumvent provisions of the treaty. Confusion, misunderstandings, and errors could occur and the utility of provisions for clarifying issues which arose following the submission of declarations were recognised by nearly all states parties. Divergence occurred, however, regarding procedures if a state party was unsatisfied with the outcome of the consultations and clarification procedures. This was particularly true of Western states parties who no doubt had the experience of the Sverdlovsk incident, the Trilateral Process and, even with all its rights, UNSCOM and the difficulties experienced by inspectors in Iraq. Hence, Western states parties wanted provisions inserted into the Protocol which permitted mandatory on-site activity *if* written consultations, exchanges of information, face-to-face meetings, or other means did not resolve a particular concern.

The rationale for clarification visits was outlined in early discussions, and at the fifth session of the Ad Hoc Group the Netherlands proposed a separate category of visits to address ambiguities.[87] [88] The concept was later elaborated by other states[89] and what emerged in the rolling text were two separate clarification procedures. Clarification visits were initially an alternative to randomly-selected transparency visits, but evolved into an important complementary measure to them, particularly in light of the weakness of the declaration-checking element of such visits. This added an additional point of dispute between Western and NAM states, because the NAM always opposed any mandatory element in clarification procedures, and especially mandatory clarification visits. In contrast, as the routine on-site activities became weaker, the ability to mandate and require a visit to resolve a clarification concern became ever more important to Western states parties, especially to the Europeans, Australia and New Zealand, all of whom thought they had compromised on routine activity to the maximum extent possible.

This resulted in a hardening of positions and two procedures emerged: one was related to declarations only and intended to clarify any anomaly or concern following the submission of declarations. The other was more generic and could be used to address any compliance issue under the Convention and the Protocol, including declarations. The two procedures existed side by side and attempts to rationalise the rolling text with one procedure always failed.

With respect to declaration clarification procedures, the US proposed that the purpose was to 'clarify an ambiguity, anomaly, omission or other issue related to a State Party's declaration' including consultations between the states parties with the possibility of a mandatory clarification visit. In the event of the clarification procedure being related to an undeclared facility a clarification visit could be initiated under a red-light procedure, i.e. the Executive Council of the Organization must vote to stop a clarification visit proceeding.[90] Similar concepts were supported by the UK and France[91] whereas South Africa, Iran, and China considered clarification visits would be wholly voluntary in nature.[92] Even in the NAM paper of 1999 on visits, a state party could volunteer a clarification visit, but there was no mandatory element to it.

The composite text had a difficult time reconciling divergent positions on this issue; acceptance of mandatory procedures would mark a defeat for the NAM and become a major point of contention in the endgame. Wholly voluntary procedures, however, would reduce the support for the Protocol from the Western Group, which was already becoming precarious. The Chairman and the drafting team therefore had a difficult task reconciling this issue, and understandably produced a compromise which attempted to be all things to all states parties.

Under the composite text any concern raised about a declaration or a facility could be dealt with using the declaration clarification procedures under Article 6, or the Consultation, Clarification and Co-operation (CCC) measures under Article 8, which applied to any area of the Protocol or the Convention.[93] Without over simplifying, Article 8 of the Protocol strengthened the provision of Article V of the

110 *The Biological Weapons Convention*

BWC, whereas Article 6 of the Protocol was concerned only with the declaration requirements and was, therefore, Protocol specific.

If the concern related to a facility which the state party seeking clarification believed should have been declared, but was not, the state party from which the clarification was requested had the right to choose which clarification procedure was followed; Article 6 or Article 8. This element of choice was referred to as *a fork in the road* and the compromise sought to allay concerns about having two types of clarification procedures in the text. Both procedures followed a similar pattern whereby information could be sought to clarify a concern or anomaly in the declaration(s). The controversy was what happened in the event that the concern or anomaly was not addressed to the satisfaction of the party which initiated the clarification process. Under Article 6 this point was reached when the state party seeking clarification believed that the consultative meeting had failed to provide such clarification and their concern was unresolved. In that event, the Director-General of the Organization could suggest the state party subject to a clarification request offer a voluntary clarification visit. If no such voluntary clarification visit was offered within 21 days, all the information was submitted to the Executive Council and considered at its next regular session. The Executive Council could then initiate a clarification visit by a green-light voting procedure of two-thirds majority of those present and voting.

It was the ability to initiate a clarification visit that was subject to continued debate within the Ad Hoc Group. The difference in views revolved around whether or not mandatory clarification visits were a specific and targeted way of resolving concerns and ambiguities about declarations or, alternatively, whether they implied an investigation by the back-door. Although the latter overstated the concern, because the provisions for clarification visits were the same whether voluntary or not and were significantly less intrusive than investigations, the concern remained. It would be a very weak investigation process given the lengthy time frame involved in the consultations, at least 60 days, but an element of challenge was implied by the notion of proving compliance/non-compliance vis-à-vis the declaration(s) requirements of the Protocol. The perspective of the NAM was reported as: [94]

> If states parties were concerned that a relevant facility was not included in a declaration, or a perceived problem was not resolved through consultation procedures, or there was a failure to volunteer to host a clarification visit, they could instigate an investigation against the facility.

Given the politically sensitive nature of challenge investigations such a procedure seemed highly unlikely to be used and thus it was something of a theoretical possibility rather than a realistic avenue for resolving problems. There was a widespread feeling among a majority of Western states that the clarification provisions of the composite text were not as extensive as they could be, particularly given the ability of the state party subject to clarification on undeclared facilities to choose the clarification procedure. Under Article 6 the procedures include 4 steps: submitting a request in writing to the Director-General; a response from the state party subject to a clarification within 30 days; a consultative meeting if the written response did not resolve the issue; and, forwarding the information, if no voluntary clarification visit was offered and the issue was still not resolved, to the Executive Council. That body, as noted earlier, could initiate a clarification visit.

Article 8 procedures, Consultation, Clarification and Co-operation, did not include explicit provisions for mandatory clarification visits, although a special session of the Executive Council could be requested by the party initiating the clarification request. That special session could recommend to the states parties involved any measures it deemed appropriate to resolve the issue. The concern of those in favour of stronger provisions was that Article 8 procedures would be chosen by states wishing to obstruct the consultation process and the *fork in the road* option therefore weakened the provisions.

Clarification procedures were considered as one of the principal methods of strengthening the Convention by some states; for example, the US was known to favour clarification procedures over other methods such as random visits to strengthen the Convention.[95] Such procedures could certainly be considered as one, if not the, method of strengthening Article V of the Convention. One of the reasons that other industrialised states felt quite strongly about the clarification process was the fact that, in their view, they had already compromised on the randomly-selected transparency visit provisions to accommodate the concerns of the NAM and the US. Therefore, in their view the clarification procedures should be stronger and carry a mandatory visit element because the kind of evidence required to launch an investigation was unlikely to be available for undeclared facilities and, more importantly, the clarification procedures could increase confidence about compliance at a low and non-accusatory level. As one non-governmental organization suggested, 'clarification visits must be mandatory in order to prevent suspicions arising and undermining the treaty ... [but] ... where the clarification visit is to be conducted at an undeclared site...some form of review is appropriate.'[96] This mirrored the proposals of the US and in the composite text it was such a formulation that survived, whereby clarification visits could be initiated after review by the Executive Council.

Even without automatic provision for a mandatory clarification visit the measures did strengthen Article V of the Convention and offered a useful complementary element to randomly-selected transparency visits. Furthermore, although quotas were envisaged on the number of clarification visits which could be conducted each year, the ability to use clarification procedures could be considered as a deterrent-type procedure. A clarification request on any facility would force the state party to recognise the concern and a mandatory clarification visit or an investigation could not be ruled out by that state party.

Minimalism or *Reform*

Writing in September 1998, when the Ad Hoc Group had begun the transition from adding elements to the rolling text of the Protocol to fine tuning those discrete elements into a coherent regime, some considered the challenge was to 'retain the original vision of an effective regime.'[97] As the authors remarked, 'visits are the crux of the matter.'[98] Others correctly identified that since the completion of the CWC, states parties seemed more reluctant to accept routine on-site activity. Throughout the life of the Ad Hoc Group, visits were not an assured inclusion.

As the Protocol developed two elements emerged. First, routine activity which at its core was concerned with the accuracy of declarations and second, some form of agreed clarification procedure, an objective congruent with strengthening Article V of the Convention. While these were discrete elements they were also complementary to each other in the overall compliance architecture.

Many of the states in the Western Group supported a strong visits regime, whereas others, including some in the Western Group, were more reticent or hostile to such intrusive activities. As a consequence, during the negotiations significant compromises were required to accommodate competing visions. As the negotiations progressed the extent of differences became more obvious and, as Wilson correctly observed, some of the European Union states, Australia, New Zealand, and Norway became frustrated with the dilution of visits to accommodate the positions of, among others, India, China, Pakistan, Iran, Russia and the US.[99]

Under randomly-selected transparency visits, two elements were drawn from the stated preferences of the *reformists*: the mandatory element and the application of such visits to all declared facilities. Three elements were drawn from the preferences of the *minimalists*: the purpose, to enhance transparency, the long-notice period prior to a visit, and the level of access, at the discretion of the state party. In terms of the permitted activity, the capabilities were drawn from the *reformist* model, but in all cases were weakened by the necessary consent of the state party before any activity could take place. There was latent potential in the provisions to visit and re-visit the parts of the facility however, and the option to request and conduct other on-site activities offered a certain amount of flexibility that was not immediately obvious, but might be turned to good effect by a skilled visiting team. On the weak side, such visits did not envisage determining that declarations were complete and accurate and the selection criteria implied more visits to the developed than to some of the developing states through the principle of proportionality.

While the provisions would strengthen the Convention the actual degree of strengthening was much less than the *reformists* advocated. The amount of compromise was a cause for concern; nevertheless, any doubts had to be tempered by the realisation that routine on-site activity was permitted and was mandatory for all declared facilities. These measures did, by their existence, strengthen the Convention. Moreover, the deficiencies in the provisions for randomly-selected transparency visits could have been compensated by stronger elements in the clarification visits. In the end, this was not the case, even though clarification procedures included provision for mandatory clarification visits which were more focussed. While it was still possible for the Executive Council to initiate a clarification visit under a green-light procedure, the initiation procedure suggested that there would be few mandated clarification visits, because the process could stall in the face of difficulties in acquiring the requisite number of votes in the

Visits and Clarification Procedures

Executive Council. Taking these deficiencies together the second pillar was weaker than the comparable function under the CWC and much weaker than the original vision proposed by *reformists*: the final draft of the Protocol favoured the preferences of the *minimalists*.

Notes

1. BWC Special Conference, BWC/SPCONF/1 p.89.
2. The use of 'visits' was not entirely new given the French proposal for 'reciprocal visits' to biodefence facilities in 1991 and the 'visits' conducted under the Trilateral Process involving the UK, US, and Russia.
3. BWC AHG, 'The Role and Objectives of Information visits' United Kingdom, BWC/AD HOC GROUP/21 (13 July 1995) p.2.
4. BWC VEREX, BWC/CONF.III/VEREX/9, pp.166-169.
5. George L. Rueckert, 'On-Site Inspection in Theory and Practice' (Westport, Praeger, 1998) p.80.
6. BWC AHG, BWC/AD HOC GROUP/21 p.1.
7. Tibor Tóth, Erhard Geissler and Thomas Stock, 'Verification of the BWC' Erhard Geissler and John P. Woodall (Editors) *Control of Dual-Threat Agents: The Vaccines for Peace Programme* SIPRI Chemical & Biological Warfare Studies No. 15 (Oxford, Oxford University Press, 1994), p.74.
8. An outline of the early thinking about visits was provided in, BWC AHG, BWC/AD HOC GROUP/31, 'Procedural Report of the Ad Hoc Group of States Parties to the Convention on the Prohibition of the Development, Production and Stockpiling of Bacteriological (Biological) and Toxin Weapons and on Their Destruction' (26 July 1996) pp.30-31.
9. Graham S. Pearson, 'The Necessity for Non-Challenge Visits' Bradford Briefing Paper Number 2 (Bradford, University of Bradford, 1997) p.25.
10. Based on private conversation at the twenty-third session of the Ad Hoc Group.
11. Within the Western Group this was a critical debate. It is covered in detail in: Malcolm R. Dando, 'Preventing Biological Warfare: The Failure of American Leadership' (Basingstoke, Palgrave, 2002) pp.113-131. The key issue was that the US did not believe that visits could in fact fulfil the task they were supposed to do. Reports on the trial and practice visits to which Dando refers were submitted to the AHG. The US also conducted two trial visits, but a report on those was never made available to the AHG as a whole. The status of those reports is unclear: see United States Department of Energy, 'DOE Exercise to Determine the Potential Impact of a Legally Binding BTWC Regime on DOE Sites' Pacific Northwest National Laboratory, prepared for the U.S. Department of Energy (June 1998) [available at: http://cbwtransparency.org/archive/doeexercise.pdf]. A good indication of the US debate is provided by Dr. Zelicoff at a Nonproliferation Policy Reform Task Force meeting on 'The Biological Weapons Protocol: How Practical, How Desirable?' available at http://www.npec-web.org/pages/projects.htm. In that report Dr Zelicoff indicates the US findings: 'What we found was that non-challenge visits do not achieve their goals, to put it another way, "confidence building" - doesn't, and "Transparency visits" - aren't. More questions were raised as result of confidence building visits and transparency visits than were answered. The visiting team and the visited team both came out with a sense that they had failed to accomplish their mission.'

12. BWC AHG, 'The Role and Objectives of Information Visits' Working Paper submitted by the United Kingdom BWC/AD HOC GROUP/21 (13 July 1995) p.3.
13. Ibid.
14. BWC AHG, 'Short Notice On-Site Information Visits and Inspections as parts of a Verification Regime for the BWC' Working Paper by Sweden BWC/AD HOC GROUP/WP.15 (29 November 1995).
15. BWC AHG, 'Elements for a Potential Verification Regime within the framework of the Convention on the Prohibition of the Development, Production and Stockpiling of Bacteriological (Biological) and Toxin Weapons and Their Destruction' Working Paper by Cuba, BWC/AD HOC GROUP/WP.22 (30 November 1995).
16. BWC AHG, 'A System of Confidence Building Visits' Working Paper by South Africa BWC/AD HOC GROUP/WP.64 (16 July 1996).
17. BWC AHG, 'European Union Discussion Paper regarding short notice non-challenge visits' Working paper submitted by Ireland on behalf of the European Union BWC/AD HOC GROUP/WP.67 (16 July 1996).
18. Ibid., p.2.
19. BWC AHG, 'Working paper submitted by Australia, Austria, Canada, Netherlands, New Zealand, Sweden and Switzerland' BWC/AD HOC GROUP/WP.178 (22 July 1997).
20. BWC AHG, 'Canadian views on Non-Challenge Visits' Working Paper submitted by Canada BWC/AD HOC GROUP/WP.193 (28 July 1997) p.3.
21. BWC AHG, 'Proposed new language for the sections on Request and Voluntary Visits' Working Paper submitted by Brazil, BWC/AD HOC/GROUP/WP.273 (March 1998).
22. Dando, 'Preventing Biological Warfare: The Failure of American Leadership' p.128.
23. BWC AHG, 'Working paper submitted by Argentina, Australia, Austria, Belgium, Bulgaria, Canada, Czech republic, Denmark, Finland, France, Germany, Greece, Ireland, Italy, Japan, Netherlands, New Zealand, Norway, Poland, Portugal, Republic of Korea, Romania, Slovakia, Spain, Sweden, Switzerland, Turkey, United Kingdom of Great Britain and Northern Ireland, and the United States of America' BWC.AD HOC GROUP/WP.296 (10 July 1998).
24. BWC AHG, BWC/AD HOC GROUP/43 (Part I) Annex I, p51 (paragraph 33).
25. BWC AHG, 'Random Visits – Proposed New Protocol Text' Working Paper submitted by the United Kingdom of Great Britain and Northern Ireland' BWC/AD HOC GROUP/WP.326 (2 December 1998) p.4.
26. BWC AHG, 'Visits' Working paper by South Africa, BWC/AD HOC GROUP/WP.336 (5 January 1999).
27. BWC AHG, 'Proposed Text for Annex B' Working paper by South Africa, BWC/AD HOC GROUP/WP.360 (26 March 1999).
28. BWC AHG, 'Proposed Language for the Section on Randomly-Selected Visits and Annex B' Working Paper submitted by Brazil, Chile, New Zealand and Norway BWC/AD HOC GROUP/WP.346 (19 January 1999).
29. Marie Isabelle Chevrier, 'Preventing Biological Proliferation: Strengthening the Biological Weapons Convention An American Perspective' Oliver Thränert (editor) *Preventing the Proliferation of Weapons of Mass Destruction: What Role for Arms Control? A German-American Dialogue* (Bonn, Froedrich-Ebert-Stiftung, 1999) p.90.
30. Marie Isabelle Chevrier, 'Progress and Peril in the Ad Hoc Group to Strengthen the BWC' *Disarmament Diplomacy* Issue Number 7 (July/August 1996) p.8.

31. The dynamics of the US delegation, its negotiation strategy, and its activities in Geneva is a subject in itself beyond the scope of this study. Whether or not an individual may agree with the position of the US, the team in Geneva went about its task and completed its job with some considerable skill if one assumes that without a meaningful and dynamic negotiating strategy the responsibility of the negotiators is to hold to the last high level agreed position on this issue.

32. Jonathan B. Tucker, 'Strengthening the BWC: Moving Toward a Compliance Protocol' *Arms Control Today* 28:1 (January/February 1998) p.22.

33. Leslie-Anne Levy, 'Clinton's record on Chemical and Biological arms control' *Disarmament Diplomacy* Issue Number 41 (November 1999) p.10.

34. See 'News Chronology' *The CBW Conventions Bulletin* Issue no. 39 (March 1998) 27 January, p.37.

35. USIS Washington File, 'Fact Sheet: The Biological Weapons Convention' 27 January 1998. http://www.fas.org/nuke/control/bwc/news/98022001_ppo.html.

36. Ibid.

37. Levy, 'Clinton's record on Chemical and Biological arms control' p.10.

38. Oliver Thränert. 'The Compliance Protocol and the Three Depositary Powers' Susan Wright (Editor) *Biological Warfare and Disarmament: new problems/new perspectives* (Oxford, Rowman & Littlefield Publishers, 2002) p.349.

39. Cited in, Dando, 'Preventing Biological Warfare' pp.136-137.

40. Henrietta Wilson, 'The BTWC Protocol: the debate about Visits' *Disarmament Diplomacy* Issue Number 40 (September/October 1999) p.23.

41. Ibid.

42. Ibid.

43. Henrietta Wilson, 'Strengthening the BWC: Issues for the Ad Hoc Group' *Disarmament Diplomacy* Issue number 42 (December 1999) p.33.

44 Ibid.

45. Ibid., p.34.

46. see 'News Chronology' in *The CBW Convention Bulletin* (Number 48) electronic version, p.1.

47. Oliver Meier, 'The US clarifies its position on 'visits'' *Trust and Verify* February 2000, issue number 89, p.2.

48. Jenni Rissanen, 'The BWC Protocol Negotiation 18th Session: Removing Brackets' *Disarmament Diplomacy* Issue Number 43 (January/February 2000) p.23.

49. Ibid.

50. Jenni Rissanen, 'Protocol Ad Hoc Group Enters Deeper into Consultations' *Disarmament Diplomacy* Issues Number 48 (July 2000) p.30.

51. Thränert. 'The Compliance Protocol and the Three Depositary Powers' p.356.

52. Zou Yunhua, 'China: Balancing Disarmament and Development' Susan Wright (Editor) *Biological Warfare and Disarmament: new problems/new perspectives* (Oxford, Rowman & Littlefield Publishers, 2002) p.228

53. There is a difficulty here when referring to a 'set' because of the importance of the different variables in the architecture (scope of facilities, notice period, on-site activity etc.); the US was not proposing to limit such visits to a particular type of facility, unlike Russia, China, and India, but the range of on-site measures which could be employed by the visiting team were extremely limited in the US proposal; considerably less intrusive than that advocated by NAM.

54. Testimony by Ambassador Donald Mahley, State Department Special Negotiator for Chemical and Biological Arms Control, to the House Committee on Government

116 *The Biological Weapons Convention*

Reform Subcommittee on National Security, Veterans' Affairs and International Relations, September 13, 2000, cited *Disarmament Diplomacy* September 2000, pp. 38-39.

55. Testimony by Susan Koch, Deputy Assistant Secretary for Threat Reduction Policy, to the House Committee on Government Reform, Subcommittee on National Security, Veterans' Affairs and International Relations, September 13, 2000 cited *Disarmament Diplomacy* September 2000, p.42.

56. Statement by State Secretary Wolfgang Ischinger, Federal Foreign Office Bonn, to the Ad Hoc Group of the States Parties to the Convention on the Prohibition of the Development, Production and Stockpiling of Bacteriological (Biological) and Toxin Weapons and on their Destruction, Geneva, 29 June 1999. The EU Common Position was agreed on 17 May 1999 and supported by 28 European states in total.

57. Alexander Kelle, 'Preventing Chemical Weapons Proliferation: Implementing the Chemical Weapons Convention A German Perspective' Oliver Thränert (editor) *Preventing the Proliferation of Weapons of Mass Destruction: What Role for Arms Control? A German-American Dialogue* (Bonn, Froedrich-Ebert-Stiftung, 1999) p.82. See also, Oliver Thränert. 'The Compliance Protocol and the Three Depositary Powers' p.359, footnote 43.

58. BWC AHG, 'Follow-up after submission of declarations' Working paper submitted by Germany BWC/AD HOC GROUP/WP.380 (29 June 1999).

59. The proposals to take the rolling text forward from the Friend of the Chair (FOC) were contained in the 'Part II' text of each report from the AHG. Thus, in this case BWC/AD HOC GROUP/45 (Part II) pp.41-50 related to visits.

60. Volker Beck, 'Preventing Biological Proliferation: Strengthening the Biological Weapons Convention A German Perspective' Oliver Thränert (editor) *Preventing the Proliferation of Weapons of Mass Destruction: What Role for Arms Control? A German-American Dialogue* (Bonn, Froedrich-Ebert-Stiftung, 1999) p.104.

61. Ibid.

62. BWC AHG, BWC/AD HOC GROUP/WP.402 'Working paper submitted by the NAM and other States – Proposed text for Visits' (22 September 1999).

63. Ibid.

64. Wilson, 'Strengthening the BWC: Issues for the Ad Hoc Group' p.33.

65. Ibid., p.34.

66. BWC AHG, BWC/AD HOC GROUP/WP.380 'Working paper submitted by Germany – Follow-up after submission of declarations' (29 June 1999). (The significant weakening Germany proposed was evident by the text which it proposed for deletion).

67. Ambassador Tibor Tóth, 'Time to Wrap Up' *The CBW Conventions Bulletin*, Issue No. 46 (December 1999) p.2.

68. Marie Chevrier, 'Strengthening the International Arms Control Regime' Raymond A. Zilinskas (Editor) *Biological Warfare: Modern Offense and Defense* (Boulder, Lynne Rienner 2000) p.160.

69. BWC AHG, BWC/AD HOC GROUP/8 'Working paper submitted by Cuba – Elements for a possible verification regime in the frameworks of the Convention on Biological Weapons' (9 July 199), BWC/AD HOC GROUP/21 'Working paper submitted by the United Kingdom – The Role and Objectives of Information Visits' (13 July 1995), BWC/AD HOC GROUP/25 'Working paper submitted by Sweden – Some possible elements in a verification Protocol' (14 July 1995), BWC/AD HOC GROUP/WP.67 'Working paper submitted by Ireland on behalf of the European

Union – European Union discussion paper regarding short-notice non-challenge visits' (16 July 1996).

70. BWC AHG, BWC/AD HOC GROUP/50 (Part I), Annex I, page 41, as an example.

71. BWC AHG, BWC/AD HOC GROUP/52 'Procedural Report of the Ad Hoc Group of the States Parties to the Convention on the Prohibition of the Development, Production and Stockpiling of Bacteriological (Biological) and Toxin Weapons and on Their Destruction' (16 August 2000) p.41.

72. Dando, 'Preventing Biological Warfare' p.110. Dando was citing Henri Garrigue's presentation to a NATO Advanced Research Workshop in Warsaw, November 2000 (see footnote 9).

73. Ibid.

74. Convention on the Prohibition of the Development, Production, Stockpiling and Use of Chemical Weapons and on Their Destruction, Verification Annex, Part IX, section B, paragraph 14.

75. BWC AHG, BWC/AD HCO GROUP/CRP.8 (Technically Corrected Version) 30 May 2001, Article 6, section B, paragraph 15, p.28.

76. Douglas J. MacEachin, 'Routine and Challenge: Two Pillars of Verification' *The CBW Conventions Bulletin* Issue number 39 (March 1998) p.1.

77. Anonymous, 'Federation of American Scientists Working Group on BW Verification – Visits are crucial' (September 1998) pp.1-2.

78. Stimson Center, 'House of Cards: The Pivotal Importance of a Technically Sound BWC Monitoring Protocol' A Joint Research Report of Academic and Institute, Pharmaceutical and Biotechnology Industry, Defense Contractor, and Inspection Veteran Brainstorming Groups, Report number 37 (May 2001) p.69 (see footnote 89).

79. BWC AHG, BWC/AD HOC GROUP/WP.402 'Working paper submitted by the NAM and other States – Proposed text for Visits.' 22 September 1999.

80. BWC AHG, BWC/AD HOC GROUP/WP.67 'Working paper submitted by Ireland on behalf of the European Union – European Union discussion paper regarding Short-Notice Non-Challenge Visits' (16 July 1996) p.3.

81. Jenni Rissanen, 'BWC Update' *Disarmament Diplomacy* (January/February 2000) p.23.

82. Ibid.

83. BWC AHG, BWC/AD HOC GROUP/WP.433 'Working paper submitted by New Zealand and South Africa – Selection Methodologies for Random Visits' (28 November 2000) p.1.

84. BWC AHG, BWC/AD HOC GROUP/CRP.8 (Technically Corrected Version) 30 May 2001, Article 6 pp.25-27.

85. BWC AHG, BWC/AD HOC GROUP/WP.247 'Working paper submitted by the United Kingdom of Great Britain and Northern Ireland – Investigations: Managed Access' (10 January 1998).

86. 'Summary of PhRMA's Position on a Compliance Protocol to the Biological Weapons Convention' (circulated 12th session of the Ad Hoc Group) p.3.

87. BWC AHG, 'Friend of the Chair on Compliance Measures' BWC/AD HOC GROUP/WP.37 (5 December 1995) p.3.

88. BWC AHG, BWC/AD HOC GROUP/WP.105 'Discussion paper by Sweden and the Netherlands – Further Elaboration of concepts of On-Site Visits (other than those to investigate a non-compliance concern)' (18 September 1996) pp.2-3.

118   *The Biological Weapons Convention*

89.   see for example, BWC AHG, BWC/AD HOC GROUP/WP.159/Rev.1 'Working paper submitted by the United Kingdom – Clarification and Consultation Procedures' (16 July 1997), BWC/AD HOC GROUP/WP.294 'Working paper submitted by the United States of America – Proposed Elements of Clarification Visits' (9 July 1998), BWC/AD HOC GROUP/WP.307 'Working paper submitted by Japan – Proposed Language: Article III – F. Visits and Investigation – I. Visits Clarification Visits' (17 September 1998), BWC/AD HOC GROUP/WP.336 'Working paper submitted by South Africa – Visits' (5 January 1999), BWC/AD HOC GROUP/WP.338 'Working paper submitted by China – Clarification Procedures and Voluntary Visit' (7 January 1999), BWC/AD HOC GROUP/WP.367 'Working paper submitted by the Islamic Republic of Iran – Voluntary Clarification Visits' (20 May 1999).

90.   BWC AHG, BWC/AD HOC GROUP/WP.294 'Working paper submitted by the United States of America – Proposed Elements of Clarification Visits' (9 July 1998) pp.1-3.

91.   BWC AHG, BWC/AD HOC GROUP/WP.311 'Working paper submitted by France and the United Kingdom of Great Britain and Northern Ireland – Clarification Visits: Initiation' (23 September 1998).

92.   BWC AHG, BWC/AD HOC GROUP/WP.336 'Working paper submitted by South Africa – Visits' (5 January 1999) p.15 and BWC/AD HOC GROUP/WP.338 'Working paper submitted by China – Clarification Procedures and Voluntary Visit' (7 January 1999).

93.   BWC AHG, BWC/AD HOC GROUP/CRP.8 (Technically Corrected Version) 30 May 2001. See Article 6 pp36-47 and Article 8 pp.52-54.

94.   Wilson, 'Strengthening the BWC: Issues for the Ad Hoc Group' p.33.

95.   BWC AHG, BWC/D HOC GROUP/WP.294, 'Working paper submitted by the United States of America Proposed Elements of Clarification Visits' (Geneva, 9 July 1998).

96.   Federation of American Scientists Working Group on BW Verification, 'Visits are crucial' (September 1998) p.3.

97.   Ibid., p.1.

98.   Ibid.

99.   Wilson, 'The BTWC Protocol: The Debate about Visits' p.23.

Chapter 5

Investigations

Introduction

Although the BWC contains provisions for the investigation of non-compliance, Article VI, the use of this mechanism remains at the mercy of the permanent five members of the United Nations Security Council because they can veto any investigation request submitted to the Security Council. This was the principal complaint many states parties had with the Convention because in their view the BWC lacked feasible provisions for an investigation of non-compliance. Indicative of the problems with these provisions was the fact that in seeking to strengthen the Convention up to 1991, states parties opted for clarification of the provisions of Article V of the BWC and did not attempt to address the inherent problems with Article VI. Those problems were, to an extent, less intractable following the UN resolutions that granted the Secretary-General the power to investigate use of chemical and biological weapons or suspected breaches of the Geneva Protocol from 1980 onwards.[1] Nevertheless, despite the fact that those procedures could circumvent the veto-related problems intrinsic to Article VI, any use of those procedures would underline further the weaknesses of the Convention: the provisions of the BWC would not be used to investigate or redress an alleged breach with its obligations.

These problems were well recognised by the states parties and during the Protocol negotiations detailed procedures for investigations were a guaranteed element of the future legally-binding instrument. In fact, developments in this area of the text were rapid; key aspects of the procedures were agreed quickly, and by the end of 1999 the remaining differences were largely endgame issues that would have to be resolved in a Chairman's text.[2] In the first section of this chapter the evolution of the Protocol related to investigations is explored before an examination of the main areas of contention, such as the size of the investigation area. As in other chapters, the final section places the composite text within the framework of *minimalism* and *reform* to determine which party gained the ascendancy in the area of investigations.

Broad agreement for investigations

Prior to the development of the rolling text of the Protocol many states parties had submitted working papers on the issue of investigations and, in general, there was broad agreement on the scope of investigations.[3] Australia, Canada, South Africa,

The Biological Weapons Convention

Sweden, Cuba, Ireland (on behalf of the 15 states of the European Union), the US, and Russia all issued working papers outlining key principles or specifics related to investigations. Many of these papers contained similar proposals and the same elements, albeit with different emphasis on certain issues. These elements included: the right to request an investigation to any facility anywhere whether declared or undeclared; a short notice period; investigations could only be requested by states parties; information and/or evidence was required to substantiate any compliance concern; an investigation had to be within the scope of the Convention; an investigated state party had the right to protect commercial proprietary and national security information; during an investigation managed access provisions would apply; the investigated state party had to make every reasonable effort to provide access to buildings or areas; an investigation had to be conducted in the least intrusive manner; a report on the investigation must contain only factual elements; and, a further (political) body would consider the investigation report and decide on further action, if necessary.

The similarity of these proposals does not mask that with the exception of Cuba and South Africa the proposals originated with Western states. However, all the indications were that a number of states parties favoured provisions similar to those agreed in the CWC. Absent from this list of formal papers and positions, as in nearly all others of the Protocol, was the view of states parties such as China, India, Iran, and Pakistan. Their commitment to intrusive compliance procedures and enhanced transparency could not be taken for granted. Indeed, neither could the commitment of the Russian Federation.

Russian thinking on the issue of investigations appeared to be in contrast to others. Russia's position was based on the assumption that, '[t]he Convention already provides for a mechanism for investigating alleged violations of its provisions. All that is needed is to spell out the details of the procedures involved.'[4] A true statement, but Russian thinking was based on maintaining investigations through the United Nations and it considered proposals for a new organization to conduct investigations as detrimental to its interests.[5]

Attempts to cast doubt on the acceptability of using the Security Council to investigate possible breaches of the Convention call in question the political effectiveness of the United Nations and of the Security Council as its principal organ, on the one hand, and, on the other, lay the ground for the review and amendment of the Convention with a view to the establishment of a new organization in place of the United Nations.

This was a *minimalist* view of the Protocol. Under the Russian vision there would not be a Technical Secretariat or professional inspectorate for the BWC or its Protocol; everything would 'be referred to a technical body, either an existing one, or one specially set up on the basis of an existing unit in the United Nations system.' The Russian position was not maintained, indeed it was unsustainable given the pressure from every Western state to establish some kind of professional BWC organization to implement the Protocol and the intense dislike – in practice and principle – of most states parties to the discrimination under the Security Council vis-à-vis its role in Article VI of the BWC.

Investigations 121

Following the introduction of the rolling text the inclusion of provisions for investigations *per se* was never a real issue in the negotiations. Rather the scope, modalities, and intrusiveness of the investigation process were the key points of contention. By the end of 1999 very few issues remained to be settled and nearly all of these were substantive endgame problems to be traded off in other areas of the text. The relative success of the negotiations on investigations cannot be easily explained but the fact that similar provisions had been negotiated in the Chemical Weapons Convention, and thus a basic blueprint existed to follow in terms of the scope of the provisions and a basic architecture, certainly assisted the Ad Hoc Group. A further factor was the leadership provided by South Africa, which held both the FOC position and acted as the brains behind much of the process. In addition, the cross-caucus like-minded party of *reformists* intent on developing a meaningful investigation process included the entire Western Group, much of the Eastern and Central European states, and a good proportion of the moderate NAM. Although the US created some specific problems, its attitude to investigations was not significantly different to that of its closest allies. The *minimalists* in this area were Russia, China, and the hard-line NAM.

The purpose of an investigation

An investigation had one specific purpose; 'determining the facts relating to a specific concern about possible non-compliance with the Convention by any other State Party.'[6] Hence, these provisions established the procedures and mechanisms to ascertain the facts (as far as was possible) about alleged treaty violations. Four types of investigations were envisaged in the rolling text: field investigations of alleged use of biological or toxin weapons; facility investigations of an alleged breach of the obligations in the Convention vis-à-vis development, production and stockpiling of biological or toxin weapons; investigations of unusual outbreaks of disease; and, investigations of alleged transfers in non-compliance with Article III of the BWC. Only two survived into the composite text. Field investigations:[7]

> conducted in geographic areas where the release of, or exposure of humans, animal or plants to, microbial or other biological agents and/or toxins has given rise to a concern about possible non-compliance under Article I of the Convention or use of bacteriological (biological) and/or toxin weapons.

And Facility investigations defined as:[8]

> Investigations of alleged breaches of obligations under Article I of the Convention, to be conducted inside the perimeter around a particular facility at which there is a substantive basis for a concern that it is involved in activities prohibited by Article I of the Convention.

Unlike the CWC, the BWC does not explicitly prohibit the use of biological or toxin weapons because during the original negotiations too many states believed an explicit prohibition on use in the BWC would undermine the 1925 Geneva Protocol and might, therefore, undermine the customary law against the use of chemical and biological weapons. However, thinking evolved in the 1980s and early 1990s and the CWC does explicitly prohibit the use of chemical weapons. Moreover, as Wheelis noted, 'although use is not specifically prohibited by the BWC, the preamble is very clear that preventing use is in fact the major goal of the convention ... [and] [a]llegations of use are in fact allegations of an egregious violation of the most fundamental purpose of the convention.'[9] Wheelis went on to note that 'any use whatsoever of biological or toxin agents as weapons is prima facie evidence, of the strongest kind, that a stock of agent was held in excess of that devoted to peaceful purposes, thereby proving antecedent violation of Article I of the convention.[10] This is precisely how the states parties viewed the matter and given that Iran had attempted to amend the BWC in 1996 with the addition of an explicit prohibition on use, and later sought to add such a prohibition to the general provisions of the Protocol, investigations of alleged use were in fact the easier of the investigations on which to reach agreement.

The two types of investigations were sub-divided when it came to the decision-making procedures of the Executive Council. As a result, the Protocol also contained provision for investigation of unusual outbreaks of disease under the broader rubric of a field investigation. Therefore, the only proposed investigation contained in the rolling text which did not make it into the Protocol was that related to a violation of Article III of the Convention. This was not a surprise since that investigation process existed in name only; no text was ever placed under the sub-titles relating to this type of investigation.

As the negotiations progressed it was clear that the provisions for investigations were modelled on similar provisions in the CWC, which Ruckert had referred to as 'the most intrusive provisions for on-site inspections of suspect facilities of any arms control agreement to date.'[11] In the last version of the rolling text the following represented the main outstanding issues which the composite text would have to resolve and the Chairman's task was in reconciling opposing positions on these key issues.

Outbreaks of disease as a basis for an investigation

An outbreak of disease was one of the signatures of the use of biological and toxin weapons and might also indicate the release of a pathogen from a facility acting in non-compliance with the provisions of the Convention. In Sverdlovsk the outbreak of anthrax was the key signature that something unusual had happened and which needed to be explained. The fact that this was never done to the satisfaction of those states parties which believed the Soviet Union to be developing biological weapons was one of the main reasons why concerns festered and undermined confidence in the Convention.

The CBMs agreed in 1986 required information on unusual outbreaks of disease and one of the proposed declarations for the Protocol related to disease reporting to the future Organization. South Africa attempted to explain some of the differences between an allegation of use of biological weapons and unusual outbreaks of disease in the early sessions of the Ad Hoc Group[12] but the NAM harboured suspicions about an outbreak of disease being used to initiate an investigation request. Since most outbreaks of disease occurred in the developing states it was possible to envisage an investigation request supported by developed states parties and opposed by developing states parties. A later working paper established in unambiguous language the concern of the non-aligned, 'that disease outbreaks due to natural causes may in future be the subject of frivolous requests for investigations ... and the future Protocol should prevent this as much as possible.'[13] The working paper went on to note that all disease outbreaks should be considered as natural and there was, therefore, no need for a state to prove that the outbreak was a natural event. Furthermore, if a state party believed that an outbreak of disease on *its* territory was not a natural outbreak, but due to non-compliance with the Convention, then it should have the right to request an investigation upon submission of evidence.[14] Implicit in this was the proposal that a state party should not have the right to request an investigation relating to an outbreak of disease on the territory of another state party.

In practice, this meant that the US would not have had the right to request an investigation into a Sverdlovsk-type outbreak but Russia would have had the right to request an investigation if it considered the outbreak to be due to non-compliance with the Convention. This was not a rationale or position supported by Western states parties, which expected to be able to request an investigation of a Sverdlovsk-type incident. The basic difference was one of principle. The Western Group did not anticipate requesting an investigation into every unusual disease outbreak, nor did they want to have to use the resources of the future Organization to investigate such outbreaks. They were unwilling, however, to foreclose the option because of the lesson from history. Russia and some of the NAM, however, were suspicious of investigation requests being used as a means to spy on them, not least because of the allegations about espionage activities under the rubric of UNSCOM.[15]

As a consequence, the latter group of states sought to put in place procedures whereby evidence required for such an investigation was high. To be specific, they inserted provisions which prevented anecdotal evidence being used to initiate an investigation: '[r]eports coming from the mass media cannot be considered as evidence. Information from private persons cannot be the sole evidence on the basis of which the request shall be made.'[16] Returning to the Soviet programme as an example, these restrictions would have ruled out an investigation based on the initial media reports in Germany about Sverdlovsk or the information provided by defectors such as Pasechnik at a later date.

Generic provisions were placed in the text of Article I of the rolling text on general provisions stating that, 'the Organization shall consider only such sources of information which are objective, unbiased, legal and do not violate the sovereignty of States Parties.'[17] Such language was so open to interpretation as to be meaningless, unless one wanted to actually prevent an investigation from taking place. Furthermore, the specific provisions to investigate an unusual outbreak of disease, as contained in Annex C, section V, stated that an 'outbreak of disease which appears to be unusual may be investigated *by the affected* State Party'[18] [my emphasis] thereby establishing a marker implying no other state party could request an investigation into the outbreak.

The Western Group was aware of, and sympathetic to, the concerns of certain other delegations and the composite text contained a number of safeguards on investigating unusual outbreaks of disease to assuage concerns. If there was a suspicion that an outbreak of disease was directly related to activities prohibited by the Convention then 'detailed evidence, and other information, and analysis substantiating why ... it considers the outbreak of disease not to be naturally occurring and directly related to activities prohibited by the Convention'[19] had to be provided by the state party requesting such an investigation. In accordance with the wishes of Russia and others the text stated that, '[r]eports coming exclusively from the mass media cannot be considered as evidence.'[20]

In addition, for any investigation request into an outbreak of disease the Executive Council had to determine that there was a basis for the concern[21] and information could be requested from the World Health Organization, the World Organization for Animal Health, and the Food and Agriculture Organization to assist this process (although how such information was to be provided to the Executive Council in the 24 hour period it had to consider the investigation request was not made clear in the text). In the event of a request being made for an investigation on the territory of another state party, that state party had the right to provide evidence and information indicating that the outbreak was in fact due to natural causes or unrelated to the prohibitions of the Convention.

The final safeguards were provided in the decision-making procedures for the initiation of an investigation. If the outbreak was on the territory of the state party requesting the investigation, the Executive Council must vote to stop the investigation proceeding by a two-thirds majority of those present and voting; thus a red-light procedure. If the outbreak was on the territory of another state party – not the state party requesting the investigation – the Executive Council must vote by a simple majority of those present and voting to permit the investigation to proceed; thus a green-light procedure.

Whether or not these safeguards would satisfy the concerns of those opposed to investigation of disease outbreaks remained to be seen. However, it was clear that for a number of states the ability to investigate a Sverdlovsk-type incident was of crucial importance. Had these provisions been omitted from the draft Protocol the scope of the investigation process would lean towards a *minimalist* vision and, more importantly, the Protocol would not have addressed one of the key lessons from the life of the Convention. The inclusion of these provisions indicated that the *reformists* were successful in developing robust procedures.

Consultation, Clarification and Co-operation (CCC)

One proposal in the final version of the rolling text would have undermined the investigation procedures had it been carried over to the draft Protocol. Throughout the negotiations on the rolling text certain delegations (Iran, Pakistan, China, and India) maintained support for the explicit principle that consultation and clarification procedures *must* be exhausted before an investigation could be initiated.[22] Under this provision, states parties were required to make full use of the consultation, clarification and co-operation (CCC) procedures under the Protocol prior to the submission of an investigation request. Such 'full use' would potentially require 90 days from notification of the concern by a state party to a decision by a Special Conference of the States Parties, in the event that the CCC procedures did not resolve the concern.

The origins of this debate could be traced to the fourth session of the Ad Hoc Group when it was noted that 'other measures especially consultation and clarification to address concerns could be explored in parallel to or prior to launching an investigation. Prior bilateral consultations could be important, with multilateral action a measure of last resort.'[23] While these measures would have provided a necessary bulwark against frivolous investigation requests, it indicated resistance to investigations through a specific procedure that would slow investigations down to the extent that evidence of non-compliance could be cleaned up or the incriminating activities halted, even though whether or not a total and successful clean up is actually possible is a moot point.

There was support for using the CCC procedures when possible but *reformist* states parties would not support provisions which required such consultations and slowed the investigation procedure down to an unacceptable extent. The agreement in the rolling text for the Director-General to propose to the requesting state party that it seek clarification from the state party to be investigated indicated the flexibility of some delegations but, in event of the requesting state party taking up that proposal, information was required within 24 hours.[24] This indicated two consultation procedures, one initiated by a state party, which could last up to 90 days, or one initiated following a proposal from the Director-General, potentially much shorter.

The composite text did not make the CCC procedures mandatory, but as in the CWC it did endorse their use noting that, 'States Parties should, whenever possible, first make every effort to clarify and resolve ... any matter which may cause doubt about compliance with the Convention'[25] in accordance with CCC procedures contained in Article 8 of the Protocol. This did remove what would have been a significant weakness in the provisions relating to investigations. Those states parties which had favoured mandatory CCC procedures in order to prevent frivolous investigations being carried out had to compromise in this area, but the 'should' in the language indicated that CCC ought to take place, but was not necessarily a mandatory requirement. The Chairman's text thus permitted supporters of both options to claim victory.

Information to be submitted for an investigation request

All delegations agreed with the principle that a state party would have to submit information to substantiate its request for an investigation. However, the experience of UNSCOM, and the use of intelligence-gathering beyond the remit of UNSCOM, made a number of states sceptical about how information was gathered. Certain provisions in the rolling text required a state party to 'provide relevant information about the source of such information in order to confirm that the

126 *The Biological Weapons Convention*

information is well-founded.'[26] Nonetheless, the proposal failed to include criteria on who would make any judgement on whether supporting information was, in fact, well-founded.

Requesting an investigation under the Protocol was tantamount to notifying the international community of alleged non-compliance. It went beyond a simple naming-names strategy because it signalled the intention of the requesting state party to challenge the assertion of compliance by another state party. As such, it therefore seemed highly unlikely that a party would request an investigation unless it was certain of non-compliance, had evidence to support its case, and was reasonably sure evidence of non-compliance would be uncovered. While requesting an investigation was different to indicating via other fora suspected non-compliance, for example declassified intelligence reports, evidence presented to the Executive Council in support of an investigation request had to be credible enough to prevent the investigation process from being stopped, under the red-light procedure, or permitted to proceed, under the green-light procedure. Only an inept state would bring information that was not well-founded to the Executive Council and the above proposal was, in certain ways, superfluous.

Quite a lot of information was required for the submission of an investigation request as detailed in Annex B of the Protocol. For a field investigation, information on eleven specific aspects were requirements in any request, and for a facility investigation seven specific aspects were identified. In addition, '[a]ll such evidence and other information shall be as precise as possible.'[27] Compared to the CWC the Protocol was more stringent, because under the former an investigation request into alleged use of chemical weapons *should* include information on nine specific issues, whereas under the BWC Protocol, the text was explicit in its requirement that the request *shall* include the eleven identified issues.[28] This indicated that, upon implementation, the investigation procedures would not be undermined by misuse. This was a further indication that the provisions for investigations would represent more than an evolution of the existing procedures and hence were *reformist* in scope.

Initiation of investigations

While only two basic types of investigations were provided for, Field and Facility investigations, there were different decision-making procedures for four scenarios relating to field investigations. Two have been referred to above; a field investigation of an outbreak of disease on the territory of the requesting state party and a field investigation of an outbreak of disease on the territory of another state party. In the case of a request for a field investigation relating to an allegation of use on the territory of the requesting state party, an investigation proceeded unless the Executive Council voted to stop the investigation by a three-quarter majority of its members present and voting; thus a red-light procedure. For an investigation request for a field investigation of alleged use on the territory of another state party, the investigation proceeded unless the Executive Council voted to stop the investigation by a simple majority of its members present and voting; thus a red-light procedure.[29]

Investigations 127

The decision-making procedures were a contentious issue. Those delegations in favour of rapid initiation of an investigation generally favoured a red-light procedure. Those in favour of slower procedures generally favoured a vote to permit an investigation to proceed; i.e. a green light procedure. Under the CWC a challenge inspection could be requested of any facility or any location on the territory of another state party. Such an inspection would proceed unless the Executive Council of the OPCW voted within 12 hours of receiving the request to stop it by a three-quarter majority of all its 41 members. As Kenyon noted:[30]

> This precise format was the result of long and difficult negotiation. In the end it was agreed that the assumption should be that a challenge inspection request would normally be implemented. In other words, no decision of the Executive Council should be necessary to allow the inspection to proceed. Only if there is a clear wish to prevent it is a decision required.

This requirement, according to Kenyon, was 'deliberately set high' because the *political* process 'of a body such as the Executive Council.'[31] Unlike the judicial processes of most states, whereby independent judges established whether or not there was a case to be answered relating to an allegation, the Executive Council of the CWC was made up of states parties and their representatives were under obligation to consider and take into account the interests of their government. Therefore, in the case of a challenge inspection request in the CWC the investigation decision-making process was reached on the understanding that:[32]

> Most Governments will have an interest in the proper operation of the Convention but they will also be obliged to consider their relations with both the challenging and the challenged States. Even if the evidence for concern about compliance with the Convention is strong it could be difficult for a Government to instruct its representatives to vote positively in favour of an investigation. An instruction to abstain to vote to stop an investigation would, however, be much easier to issue and would still have the effect of permitting the investigation to proceed.
> The level of three-quarters majority rather than simple majority was felt to be important because of the tendency in international bodies for States to vote in blocs. This construction meant that a group of States which commanded at least one quarter of the votes available could ensure that the inspection went ahead and no single group could prevent it without support from at least some members of other groups.

A red-light procedure in the BWC Protocol was not favoured by a number of states parties, least of all Russia which proposed a green-light procedure requiring a two-thirds majority of the full membership of the Executive Council for all investigations.[33] Unlike the CWC, the Protocol used different formulations for different types of investigation. In the case of a request for a facility investigation the procedure required a simple majority of the Executive Council members present and voting to vote to approve the investigation request. This green-light procedure was proposed by the US and supported by Russia, China, Iran, India, and Pakistan, among others.[34] This latter group had favoured a green-light procedure for facility investigations in order to prevent frivolous investigations being carried out. In contrast, and excluding the US, a majority of the Western states favoured a red-light procedure for all investigations.[35] It was highly unlikely that agreement could be reached on a simple all red-light or all green-light choice; not least because of US opposition to a red-light procedure for facility investigations.

The formulations in the composite text were a definite compromise designed to accommodate all delegations and balance out winners and losers in the red-light/green-light debate. Of greater import, however, was that the procedures established, *de facto*, a hierarchy of non-compliance concerns: use of biological weapons was considered a graver threat than the conduct of activities prohibited under Article I of the Convention in a facility. That may in fact have confirmed an implicit understanding among states parties, but while advocates of disarmament would be disappointed by the creation of an explicit hierarchy, it was difficult to argue that use of biological and/or toxin weapons was not more serious than other activities which were prohibited under the Convention. Once more the difference between the practice of getting agreement for a disarmament regime and the theory of devising an ideal model was thrown into focus.

The composite text therefore included both *reformist* and *minimalist* preferences; the inclusion of a red-light formulation for some investigations would be congruent with a robust Protocol. The green-light initiation for investigations of disease outbreaks on the territory of another state party was a necessary compromise to gain support for these provisions among other delegations. While that was understandable, the green-light procedure for initiating facility investigations indicated a weak Protocol. As Moodie commented:[36]

> a majority of Executive Council members must vote in favour of a request for an investigation of a suspect facility before such an investigation can proceed. This means that a simple majority – 26 votes in this case – could also block it. It should have been the other way round ... the investigation should proceed unless a significant vote – considerably more than a majority – is taken to block it.

The green-light initiation for Facility investigations was a major cause for concern among those who supported a Protocol modelled by the *reformists*.

The size of the investigation area

Another area of disagreement was the size of the investigation area for a field investigation. In the final version of the rolling text the size of the investigation area could, 'not exceed [300] [500] [1,500] square kilometres [in the case of human disease and 15,000 square kilometres in case of animal and plant disease in size.]'[37] Although evidence to support the large investigation area proposed and favoured by the European Union states was circulated during the formal negotiations,[38] Iran proposed an area of 10 square kilometres. The position of Iran was based on evidence it submitted in a working paper in which it was claimed that:[39]

Investigations 129

the ultimate travelling distance of bioaerosols could not be more than 10 km downwind from the source of release. This idea has been supported by many scientific literatures that propose 10 km limit for bioaerosol dispersion ... [and therefore] ... for a sound and effective field investigation, the perimeter dispersion for bioaerosols should not be more than 10 km.

Iran's claim was hotly contested in both the conference room and in the margins of the negotiations because scientific evidence did not support the claim of a 10km 'ultimate travelling distance.' For example, a 1961 study of an aerosol cloud of *Bacillus subtilis var. niger*, indicated that the 'cloud travelled at least 23 miles downwind (the most distance sampling station) and covered an area of approximately 100 square miles.'[40] The non-governmental investigation of the Sverdlovsk anthrax outbreak conducted in 1993 indicated a downwind hazard to animals 'out to a distance of 50km.'[41] Either the Iranian delegation was receiving poor scientific advice, or something else was at play in this proposal.

An additional problem was extending the area if the investigation team deemed it necessary to do so during the course of an investigation. If the investigated state party did not agree to an extension, those in favour of extending the investigation area proposed procedures whereby the investigation team would submit analysis and evidence to substantiate the request to the Director-General and the Executive Council. The Executive Council was then to decide on the extension by simple majority vote of those present and voting. These provisions were themselves a compromise formulation. The United States had initially proposed that that area could be extended by 50% by the Director-General of the Technical Secretariat.[42]

The composite text balanced these differences in a package deal. In terms of the investigation area, for human diseases it could not exceed 1000 km^2 and for diseases involving animals and plants it could not exceed 7,500 km^2. These areas were greater than those favoured by some NAM, however, there was no provision for the extension of the investigation area unless the receiving state party agreed to the request. In the event that such a request was not agreed to, the fact was simply noted in the final report of the investigation together with the explanations of the receiving state party. A (relatively) large investigation area was bought with the granting of veto power on any extension of that area.

A further key question was access to buildings during a field investigation; the transition from a field to a facility investigation. Certain historical lessons impinged here. Had an investigation of the Sverdlovsk outbreak occurred in 1979 the investigators in the field would have certainly recognised the need to examine the microbiological facility upwind of the outbreak. Wilson reported that, 'there is a nervousness about giving the investigation team too many powers to promote the transition ... in that field investigations might thus provide a quicker and easier access to sensitive facilities than a facility investigation. Several NAM countries – including India, Iran, Pakistan and China – are particularly anxious about this.'[43]

Under the Protocol, if the investigation team acquired information that indicated a facility engaged in prohibited activities on the territory of a state party – not necessarily the territory of the investigated state party – the information was passed to the receiving state party, together with information on how the indication was arrived at. The receiving state party had 24 hours to comment on the information. It was then passed to the Director-General and the Executive Council, which in turn submitted the information to the requesting and the receiving state party as well as the state party, if different, where the facility was located. Only these states parties, and states parties serving on the Executive Council, could then request a facility investigation. Thus, should a facility investigation proceed it was in fact a second investigation with its own mandate and investigation team. This was not too contentious because there was widespread recognition that a field investigation and a facility investigation required different personnel, but the timeline of at least 48 hours from request *in situ* to a decision by the Executive Council was not ideal. The inclusion of these additional safeguards or obstacles (depending on how you viewed it) indicated that delegations that preferred a balance of power erring towards the state party, rather than the investigation team, succeeded in this area of the text. The impact of these obstacles could only be gauged in the event of the situation arising, but their inclusion weakened the Protocol.

Access and specific measures

The final area of the rolling text where substantive differences still remained was the level of access permitted during an investigation and the balance of rights and obligations between the investigation team and the receiving state party. Differences of view related not only to the generic provisions but also the specific provisions for field and facility investigations.

The mandate of the Ad Hoc Group required the measures agreed to strengthen the Convention to be able to protect national security and confidential proprietary information. Furthermore, as could be been seen from the early working papers and discussions, there was broad agreement that any request for an investigation had to be within the scope of the Convention. As a result, general provisions such as 'access shall be for the sole purpose of establishing the facts relevant to the investigation mandate'[44] and the undertaking that the receiving state party, 'shall make every reasonable effort to demonstrate its compliance with the Convention ... to enable the investigation team to fulfil its mandate'[45] were agreed procedures.

Likewise, many of the managed access provisions used in the CWC were easily agreed upon. Areas where differences still existed related to the balance of the provisions between the investigation team and the state party, and the final say on access. One difference concerned the receiving state party's power to make the final decision on '[the nature and extent of such]' or '[regarding any]' access; a subtle but important difference, because the former implied some access had to be granted, whereas the latter implied the ability to deny access altogether.[46] The importance of this provision was illustrated through the existence of similar language, which granted to the receiving state party the right to make the final decision on the nature and extent of access, including the ability to deny access, to 'particularly sensitive places ... not related to the investigation mandate.'[47] A concern of the United States was the interaction between the rights enshrined in an international agreement and the rights of individuals and private companies under

Investigations

131

national law. As such, the US supported language which would require the receiving state party, 'to provide the greatest degree of access possible, taking into account any constitutional obligations it may have with regard to proprietary rights or searches and seizures.'[48]

In the composite text these provisions survived although repetitious obligations were edited out. Under the provisions the right of the receiving state party to 'make the final decision on the nature and extent of access' was included, but the state party was required to provide the greatest degree of access possible, taking into account constitutional obligations regarding searches and seizures.[49] Power of refusal was therefore granted to the state party, but it was not absolute, and this was not extraordinary in other agreements.

Field investigations

During a field investigation the following specific activities were proposed for the investigating team: interviewing eyewitnesses to the alleged activity; interviewing those exposed to biological and toxin weapons; interviewing other individuals; interviewing individuals not available in the investigation area; visual observation; sampling and identification; and, collection and examination of background information and data. All presented problems which had to be resolved in the composite text.

Interviewing A problem with all interviews was whether or not the interview took place in the presence of a representative of the receiving state party if the individual concerned indicated otherwise, i.e. if the individual to be interviewed requested representatives of the receiving state party not be present. All interviews required the explicit consent of the individual concerned, and in the composite text the individual could indicate that representatives of the receiving state party not be present.

The interviewing of individuals not available in the investigation area was contested and further limitations were proposed in the rolling text, including that such individuals would normally be resident in the investigation area and the consent of the receiving state party be obtained prior to such interviews. In the composite text these qualifiers were not included in the provisions, although the investigation team still had to provide 'etiological and/or epidemiological information indicating why such interviews are necessary to fulfil its mandate.'[50]

Visual observation Visual observation provided few difficulties, however in the provisions for disease/intoxination–related examination a similar problem to that referred to above, namely access to persons or animals not present in the investigation area, arose in the negotiations. Although the concept was contested, the composite text did include provisions for access to medical/veterinary examination and/or to body samples of affected persons or animals outside of the investigation area. This provision circumvented some of the limitations on investigations related to the inability to expand the investigation area unless the receiving state party consented. Of greater import was that it prevented a non-

132 *The Biological Weapons Convention*

compliant state party from gaining absolute assurance that the investigation could be thwarted by simply moving humans and/or animals outside the investigation area prior to arrival of the investigation team. With this provision, nothing was absolute. The point to stress with this issue is the interconnectedness of the provisions and the manner in which *reformists* and *minimalists* turned their attention to alternative and indirect means to achieve their objectives. In this case, guaranteeing access to persons or animals outside the investigation area became more important because of the limitations on the size of, and potential expansion of, the investigation area itself.

Sampling and analysis Two issues arose in the negotiations in relation to sampling and analysis: whether or not sampling and analysis could occur only with the consent of the receiving state party; and, were the samples to be analysed on the territory of the receiving state party or some other place? In the composite text, the consent of the receiving state party was not required; however, samples could only be taken when the investigation team deemed it appropriate and relevant to do so.

Balancing this *reformist* clause resulted in the requirement that analysis of the samples must be 'carried out on the territory of the receiving State Party and in the presence of the representatives of the investigation team and the receiving State Party.'[51] Specific provisions were made for the procedures to be followed in the event that analysis of samples could not be undertaken on the territory of the receiving state party. However, this principle represented acceptance and recognition of the US implementing legislation in relation to sampling and analysis in the CWC and the prevention of samples leaving the territory of the US. Other states have followed this US precedent and it was widely recognised that the US would institute similar measures for the Protocol, whether or not the Protocol contained such explicit provisions. VEREX identified how important sampling and analysis was, because it 'could provide key information to resolve certain ambiguities about compliance'[52] but of critical importance was the chain of custody for samples and the preservation of 'intellectual, individual and commercial proprietary rights in the case of legitimate activities',[53] if there was to be overall confidence in the investigations regime. These concerns meant that the provisions had to be balanced.

Collection of background information Similar questions arose in the context of access to, and the collection of, background information and data by the investigation team. Once again the investigation team did not require the explicit consent of the receiving state party, but any documents or data identified by the receiving state party as not relevant to the mandate of the investigation had to be returned to the state party, although such data was to be identified in the final report of the investigation team.

Facility investigations

In the event of a facility investigation the specific measures available to the investigation team were: interviewing; visual observation; identification and

Investigations 133

examination of key equipment; consideration of biological materials; examination of documents and records; examination of medical records; examination of clinical and pathological samples; and, sampling and identification. As in the case of field investigations, explicit consent was required for interviewing, although the presence of representatives of the receiving state party was mandatory and, in this case, the state party could object to questions posed to facility personnel and ultimately require answers not be provided to such questions. Visual observation was as for field investigations and the provision for the identification and examination of key equipment linked to the equipment declared by the facility and the list of equipment contained in Annex A of the Protocol. The measure related to the consideration of biological materials was linked to the concept of current and annual transparency thresholds, as provided for in Article 3, section C of the composite text.

The investigation team could only examine documentation and records available at the facility, which were relevant to its mandate, including information on the supply and consumption of media, the design and operation of equipment and the transfer of biological agents and toxins. The receiving state party could assist the investigation team in providing this information if it so desired, but was under no obligation to assist. Information on the types and quantities of the biological agents and toxins was not explicitly provided for, given that it was a contested proposal throughout the negotiations. However, that information might be interpreted as being provided for under the more generic information on the receipt and transfer of biological agents and toxins. Provision was also made in the composite text for access to records not held at the facility in question; again there was no obligation on the state party to provide such information to the investigation team. In the event information was provided, examination was subject to the provisions of managed access.

Medical records could only be examined by the investigation team at the discretion of the receiving state party, although the latter was required to 'endeavour to provide the greatest degree of access possible to such data.'[54] Examination of clinical and pathological samples previously taken by the facility required the permission of the receiving state party when a request was made by the investigation team.

Sampling and identification, as in field investigations, was provided for in the composite text. Greater control was, however, provided to the receiving state party because it could refuse a sample. In such an event the receiving state party was obligated to 'make every reasonable effort to demonstrate that the requested sample is unrelated to the non-compliance concern(s) contained in the investigation mandate.'[55] Samples would be taken by representatives of the receiving state party, rather than the investigation team, and analysis would take place on-site wherever possible, or if not possible, on the territory of the receiving state party. The text contained language that stated, '[i]f the removal of samples is agreed'[56] that implied removal of samples could be prevented, even though this was not an explicit provision in the text of the Protocol. All measures were tempered by the necessary general principle of managed access.

Minimalism or Reform

The relative strength or weakness of the Protocol depended, *inter alia*, on the overall balance of rights and obligations between the investigation team and the investigated state party. The overall scope of investigations built upon the obligation in Article VI of the Convention by permitting an investigation of any location or facility within a state party. A second element of central importance was the decision-making procedure to launch an investigation. The multi-tiered approach to the question of initiation, whereby investigations of alleged use and investigation of an outbreak of disease on the territory of the requesting state party were to be initiated by the red-light procedure, whereas an investigation of an outbreak of disease on the territory of another state party and a facility investigation required a green-light decision-making procedure, was not popular. The decision-making procedures were not ideal, but the crucial violation of the Convention, use of biological or toxin weapons, would require an investigation to be deliberately prevented from occurring. Although weaker than comparable challenge inspection provisions in the CWC, it was clear that in the Ad Hoc Group a compromise was necessary to resolve the red-light/green-light debate. In all cases the period of notice was short, rather than long, which further strengthened the provisions on investigations, even though the overall timelines for access to an area were a source of concern.

Access to the investigation area or facility was not limited to the decision of the investigated state party, which was obliged to provide access but also had the right to take measures it deemed necessary to protect CPI and NSI. Most of the on-site measures identified during VEREX were provided for, including: interviewing, visual observation, sampling and identification, collection of background material and documentation, examination of documents and records, examination of medical records, and examination of clinical and pathological samples. The balance of rights and obligations between the investigating team and the investigated state party shifted to the state party in certain areas, such as sampling and analysis, but no single measure undermined the ability of the investigation team to carry out its responsibilities. Furthermore, given the specificity of the provisions, the composite text might be considered as an improvement on similar provisions in the CWC, because there were fewer mechanisms to be decided upon following implementation.

Not to be ignored was the separation of powers: as the Netherlands remarked in the original negotiations in 1971, fact-finding should have been separated from judgement regarding non-compliance. Under the composite text the investigation team acted as the fact-finding element of the procedure and the Executive Council of the future organization would consider the report of the investigation team. However, the right of a state party to decide itself whether or not non-compliance had occurred was implicit in the provisions. Although it was expected that a separate body would undertake the judgement on non-compliance, the provision does strengthen the Convention. Taken together the Protocol's provisions on investigations were stronger rather than weaker and in the final analysis resembled the *reformist* vision.

Investigations 135

Notes

1. BWC AHG, 'Alleged Use Investigation – Authority to Trigger' Working Paper by Australia BWC/AD HOC GROUP/WP.13 (29 November 1995) contains a summary of the key UNGA resolutions from 1980 through to 1990 pp.4-5.

2. Henrietta Wilson, 'Strengthening the BWC: Issues for the Ad Hoc Group' *Disarmament Diplomacy* Issues Number 42 (December 1999) p.32.

3. See, for example, the following: 'Investigation of Alleged Use of Biological Weapons' Working Paper submitted by South Africa, BWC/AD HOC GROUP/11 (10 July 1995); 'The application of intrusive measures on-site inspections, auditing, sampling and identification in order to strengthen the BWC' Working paper submitted by South Africa, BWC/AD HOC GROUP/12 (10 July 1995); 'Alleged Use Investigation – Authority to Trigger' Working Paper by Australia BWC/AD HOC GROUP/WP.13 (29 November 1995); 'Use of investigative epidemiology as a tool in the investigation of unusual outbreak of disease and alleged use of biological weapons' working paper submitted by South Africa BWC/AD HOC GROUP/WP.11 (29 November 1995); 'The relationship between investigations of alleged use of BTW and unusual outbreaks of disease and challenge inspections' Working paper by South Africa BWC/AD HOC GROUP/WP.16 (29 November 1995); 'Investigation on the use or alleged use of biological or toxin weapons against a State Party to the Biological Weapons Convention' Working paper submitted by Cuba BWC/AD HOC GROUP/WP.21 (30 November 1995); 'Difference between investigation of alleged use of BTW and investigation of unusual outbreaks of disease' Working paper submitted by South Africa BWC/AD HOC GROUP/WP.54 (15 July 1996); 'Systems and tools for an investigation of alleged use of biological or toxin weapons' Working Paper submitted by South Africa BWC/AD HOC GROUP/WP.55 (15 July 1996); 'Concerns about abuse of challenge inspection' Working paper submitted by Canada BWC/AD HOC GROUP/WP.59 (15 July 1996); 'Unusual outbreaks of disease and their investigation' Working Paper submitted BY South Africa BWC/AD HOC GROUP/WP.62 (16 July 1996); 'European Union discussion paper on challenge inspections' working paper submitted by Ireland on behalf of the European union BWC/AD HOC GROUP/WP.66 (16 July 1996); 'Initiation of Challenge Inspections' Working Paper by Australia BWC/AD HOC GROUP/WP.68 (16 July 1996); 'Challenge Inspection: Key Principles' Working paper submitted by Canada BWC/AD HOC GROUP/WP.70 (17 July 1996); 'The role of epidemiology in unusual/suspicious outbreaks of disease' Working paper submitted by the United States of America BWC/AD HOC GROUP/WP.73 (17 July 1996); and, 'Investigations' Working paper submitted by the Russian Federation BWC/AD HOC GROUP/WP.125 (4 March 1997).

4. BWC AHG, 'Working paper submitted by the Russian Federation – Basic principles and procedures for consideration of requests relating to alleged violations of the Convention on the prohibition of Biological Weapons' BWC/AD HOC GROUP/WP.181 (22 July 1997).

5. Ibid.

6. BWC AHG, BWC/AD HOC GROUP/CRP.8 (Technically corrected Version) (30 May 2001) Article 8, p.55.

7. Ibid.

8. Ibid.

9. Mark L. Wheelis, 'Investigation of Suspicious Outbreaks of Disease' Raymond A. Zilinskas (editor) *Biological Warfare: Modern Offense and Defense* (Boulder, Lynne Rienner, 2000) p.115.
10. Ibid.
11. George L. Rueckert, 'On-Site Inspection in Theory and Practice' (Westport, Praeger, 1998) p.129.
12. BWC AHG, BWC/AD HOC GROUP/WP.54 'Working paper submitted by South Africa – Difference between investigation of alleged use of BTW and investigation of unusual outbreaks of disease' (15 July 1996).
13. BWC AHG, BWC/AD HOC GROUP/WP.369 'Working paper submitted by NAM and other States – Investigation of Disease Outbreaks' (29 June 1999).
14. Ibid.
15. Scott Ritter, 'Endgame' (New York, Simon and Schuster, 1999) pp.176-189.
16. BWC AHG, BWC/AD HOC GROUP/55-1 Annex I, p.80, paragraph 6.
17. Ibid, p.14, paragraph 6.
18. Ibid., p.253, paragraph 2.
19. BWC AHG, BWC/AD HOC GROUP/CRP.8, pp.55-56, paragraph 6.
20. Ibid., p.56, paragraph 6.
21. Ibid.
22. BWC AHG, BWC/AD HOC GROUP/55-1 Annex I Page 80, paragraph 10. Kenneth D. Ward, 'The BWC Protocol: a mandate for failure' *The Nonproliferation Review* 11:2 (Summer 2004) pp.196-197.
23. BWC AHG, BWC/AD HOC GROUP/31 'Procedural Report of the Ad Hoc Group of the States Parties to the Convention on the Prohibition of the Development, Production and Stockpiling of Bacteriological (Biological) and Toxin Weapons and on Their Destruction' (26 July 1996) p.25.
24. BWC AHG, BWC/AD HOC GROUP/55-1 Annex I p.83, paragraph 23.
25. BWC AHG, BWC/AD HOC GROUP/CRP.8 p.56, paragraph 10. The comparable formulation in the CWC is contained in Article IX (2).
26. BWC AHG, BWC/AD HOC GROUP/52 p.82.
27. BWC AHG, BWC/AD HOC GROUP/CRP.8 (technically Corrected Version) p.58, paragraph 18 and Annex B paragraphs 62 to 65 and 124 to 126.
28. CWC, Verification Annex, Part XI, section B, paragraph 3.
29. In addition to the red-light/green-light issue the actual number of Executive Council members required to block or permit an investigation was also important. See, for example: Lynn C. Klotz and Mark C Sims, 'The BWC: Challenge Investigation Voting Procedures' *The CBW Conventions Bulletin* Issue no. 41 (September 1998) pp.1-3.
30. Ian R. Kenyon, 'Non-Compliance Concern Investigations: Initiation Procedures' Briefing Paper Number 15 (University of Bradford, Bradford, 1998) p.7.
31. Ibid.
32. Ibid., p.8.
33. BWC AHG, BWC/AD HCO GROUP/WP.181 (22 July 1997) p.3
34. For the position of the US see, Michael Moodie, 'The BWC Protocol: A Critique' CBACI Special Report 1 (2001) footnote 14 and Leslie-Anne Levy, 'Clinton's Record on Chemical and Biological Arms Control' *Disarmament Diplomacy* (Issue Number 41) November 1999 p.10. For the position of most NAM delegations see Jenni Rissanen, 'Pressure Mounts at Protocol Negotiations' *Disarmament Diplomacy* Issue Number 54 (February 2001) p.35.

Investigations

35. Rissanen, 'Pressure Mounts at Protocol Negotiations' p.35.
36. Moodie, 'The BWC Protocol: A Critique' pp.19-20.
37. BWC AHG, BWC/AD HOC GROUP/55-1 Annex I p.224, paragraph 3 (c).
38. An in-room paper was circulated by the UK depicting the spread of anthrax on Gruinard Island following the BW testing conducted in the early 1940s. This paper, and distribution of anthrax indicated in the paper, supported the UK's, and other States Parties', proposals for a large investigation area.
39. BWC AHG, BWC/AD HOC GROUP/WP.434 'Working paper submitted by the Islamic Republic of Iran – Technical Justification for the limited size of the Area of Investigation' (28 November 2000) p.2.
40. LeRoy D. Fothergill, 'Biological agents in warfare and defence' *New Scientist* No. 263 30 November 1961, p.546.
41. Matthew Meselson, Jeanne Guillemin, Martin Hugh-Jones, Alexander Langmuir, Ilona Popova, Alexis Shelokov, Olga Yampolskaya, 'The Sverdlovsk Anthrax Outbreak of 1979' *Science* 266 (18 November 1994) p.1206.
42. BWC AHG, BWC/AD HOC GROUP/WP.348 'Working paper submitted by the United States of America – Determination of, and Modification to, Field Investigation Area(s)' (20 January 1999).
43. Henrietta Wilson, 'Strengthening the BWC: Issues for the Ad Hoc Group' *Disarmament Diplomacy* Issue Number 42 (December 1999) pp.32-33.
44. BWC AHG, BWC/AD HOC GROUP/55-1 p.84, paragraph 30 (a).
45. Ibid., p.85, paragraph 30 (g).
46. Ibid.,, p.85, paragraph 30 (e).
47. Ibid., p.85, paragraph 31 [(a)].
48. Ibid., p.85, paragraph 30 (f).
49. BWC AHG, BWC/AD HOC GROUP/CRP.8, Article 9, pp. 60-61, paragraphs 28 (c) and (e).
50. Ibid., p.137, paragraph 92.
51. Ibid., p.139, paragraph 104.
52. VEREX, BWC/CONF.III/VEREX/9 p.18.
53. Ibid.
54. BWC AHG, BWC/AD HOC GROUP/CRP.8 p.151, paragraph 168.
55. Ibid., p.152, paragraph 172.
56. BWC AHG, BWC/AD HOC GROUP/CRP.8 p.152, paragraph 174 and BWC/AD HOC GROUP/55-1 Annex I, p.247 paragraph 53.

Chapter 6

Export Controls

Introduction

After visits the other contentious area of the negotiations was the issue of non-proliferation and export controls. That this was going to present problems was not a surprise to any delegation. The issue of non-proliferation and the use of export controls had ossified to become a 'major stumbling block in several arms-control forums'[1] during the 1990s. This was a North-South issue that had potentially important implications for the future of all multilateral disarmament negotiations.

The issue was never about non-proliferation or export controls *per se*: all states parties maintained in public that proliferation of biological weapons was undesirable and contravened Article III of the BWC and export controls were one means to fulfil the non-proliferation obligation. Rather, it was about the non-proliferation policies of certain states parties and the manner in which they applied export controls to states parties and non-states parties. This was perceived to be discriminatory by those that bore the brunt of export controls: Iran, Cuba, Libya, China, India and Pakistan. As influential states in the NAM this sub-group of hard-liners were able to galvanise support among more moderate states such as Indonesia and Mexico for a policy that focussed on the elimination of the Australia Group. It is important to understand that the debate in the Ad Hoc Group was a proxy discussion about the existence of the Australia Group and the perception of broken promises from the final stages of the negotiations on the CWC and divisions about the application of export controls in the context of the NPT. Therefore, we must first examine the origins and evolution of non-proliferation and the development of export controls in the nuclear, biological and chemical weapons context. The chapter then moves on to explore the archaic and convoluted negotiations in the Ad Hoc Group through the identification of generic *reformist* and *minimalist* models for export controls. Finally we examine the composite text of the Protocol.

Non-proliferation and export controls

It is often forgotten that in the chemical and biological context attempts at non-proliferation can be traced back to the negotiations for the 1925 Geneva Protocol. In addition to the general prohibition of use in war, the US proposed 'to control the traffic in poisonous gases by prohibiting the exportation of all asphyxiating, toxic, or deleterious gases and all analogous liquids, materials and devices manufactured and intended for use in warfare.'[2] After further discussions the proposal was considered unworkable, not least because it 'would be very difficult to apply as it was practically impossible to discriminate between chemical products used for industrial, pharmaceutical or other purposes and those which might be used in chemical warfare.'[3] In other words, the dual-use problem; and so began a lengthy cycle of non-proliferation debates which evolved in their current format as a consequence of nuclear weapons and developed into a recognisable form following the completion of the NPT.

Nuclear export controls

Under NPT Article III:2, each party undertook not to transfer specific materials or equipment unless such materials were subject to the safeguards regime of the IAEA. That undertaking required some form of control on transfers, but the NPT did not define or identify the said materials or equipment. This 'uncertainty in what the relevant treaty language in this area meant, and therefore what items fell within its scope'[4] resulted in the Zangger Committee under which NPT states parties that were suppliers of nuclear materials met to decide and consider how to interpret the export control obligations. In particular, what did the obligation mean and what items fell under its remit? The Zangger Committee produced the so-called *Trigger List* containing items which when exported would trigger the necessity for safeguards. As Schmidt noted, the Zangger Committee did not determine the export control requirements of the NPT; rather, the Committee's members 'meet to negotiate what minimum requirements should be applied.'[5] Thus, the Zangger Committee had two main objectives: to reach common understanding of what the materials and equipment were, and to consider procedures for exporting such materials in order to fulfil the obligations of the NPT.[6] Under the NPT, or rather as a result of it, the development of an international nuclear trade policy guided by the NPT, the IAEA safeguards under INFCIRC/153, and the trigger list of the Zangger Committee, replaced that which had previously been primarily a national issue and, given the predominance of its industry, a US concern.[7]

The Zangger Committee was not an official or a subsidiary body of the NPT or the IAEA. It was a group of like-minded supplier countries party to the NPT. A second non-official body, the Nuclear Suppliers Group (NSG), formed after the nuclear explosion conducted by India in 1974 as an attempt to bring non-NPT parties such as France into the export control and nuclear trade policy regime. The NSG 'seeks to contribute to the non-proliferation of nuclear weapons through the implementation of two sets of guidelines for nuclear exports and nuclear-related exports' adopted by consensus and implemented through national export control systems.[8] As Walker noted:[9]

> However uncoordinated their actions, the 1970s therefore saw the assertion of authority over nuclear trade policy by the supplier countries, with only fleeting regard for the interests or feelings of importers. The universality approach to nuclear trade was effectively abandoned for the time being.

Furthermore:[10]

> The NPT rules had come to be regarded as insufficient, the guidelines appeared to contravene the spirit of cooperation in trade and development between suppliers and recipients and the leading suppliers could not agree among themselves on what constituted the proper conduct of trade.

The success of export controls in stemming proliferation was, and is, debated, but export controls were never intended as a means to guarantee non-proliferation. The nuclear programmes in South Africa, India, Pakistan, Israel, the DPRK, Libya, Iran, and Iraq illustrate that simple fact. They became, however, a central plank of Western non-proliferation policy over three decades and their application, and the dichotomy between nuclear controls and nuclear co-operation became contentious. At the 1995 NPT Review and Extension Conference Iran, Indonesia, Syria, Nigeria and Algeria, made clear their objections to the Zangger Committee and the NSG branding them 'as closed, secretive groupings inconsistent with Article IV and usurping the IAEA's role laid down in Article III [of the NPT].'[11] These states considered the application of export controls outside the IAEA/NPT as arbitrary and discriminatory. Iran and others sought to have the IAEA declared as the sole body responsible for verifying NPT compliance. The issue was revisited in 2000 at the Sixth Review Conference, as Johnson reported.[12]

> Much was made of the "inalienable right" to develop nuclear energy, and the [NAM Working] paper called for the removal of "unilaterally enforced restrictive measures" ... saying that no NPT party should be denied technology, equipment or assistance on the basis of "allegations of non-compliance not verified by the IAEA".

Other states wanted the Sixth Review Conference 'to recognise the role of the Zangger Committee and existing national export control mechanisms in the prevention of proliferation.'[13] The debate in the NPT context offered three lessons. First, the drafting of the NPT left the fulfilment of the non-proliferation objective to states parties, which a number interpreted as requiring export controls. Second, to improve the application of export controls based on national measures the controls were co-ordinated in different fora by the dominant supplier states. Third, discontent emerged about the application of such controls in developing states, such as Iran, because the interpretation of the proliferation threat rested with the supplier state not the official status of the recipient state according to the IAEA Board of Governors.

The perception that the application of regimes external to the formal treaty structures was discriminatory resulted in a demand to bring export control mechanisms inside the formal treaty systems and the dissolution of those mechanisms outside the treaty. In terms of the nuclear field that related to the Zangger Committee and the Nuclear Suppliers Group, while in the chemical and biological field, the focus was the Australia Group. Much of the debate in the Ad Hoc Group had its origins in the final stages of the negotiations for the CWC.

142   *The Biological Weapons Convention*

The CWC hangover

Without doubt the Ad Hoc Group's work was complicated by the perceived failure of the CWC-solution to the export control issue: namely the question of the Australia Group. Unlike the NPT and the BWC, the CWC did not contain explicit provisions linking disarmament and development, but it did contain clauses to avoid hampering economic development. The central issue was the fate of the Australia Group, an informal gathering of key suppliers of chemicals and related equipment which had sought to co-ordinate their controls of exports from 1985, as a result of the use of chemical weapons during the Iran-Iraq war.[14] The Australia Group soon found itself under the same scrutiny as the NSG and Zangger Committee. Argentina, then a member of the NAM, asserted in the final stages of the CWC negotiations that states which:[15]

> have given the international community satisfactory guarantees regarding their commitments with respect to the non-proliferation of weapons of mass destruction should not encounter limitations on their legitimate aspirations to develop and accede to dual-use technologies for the development and welfare of their peoples.

Such was the pressure on the Australia Group that in the final stages of the negotiations the then President of the Conference on Disarmament (Ambassador Paul O'Sullivan of Australia) was authorized to make a statement on the behalf of the Australia Group vis-à-vis its relationship to the CWC. In that statement he noted the aim of Article XI of the CWC, *inter alia*, to facilitate the fullest possible exchange in chemical activities, but noted also the:[16]

> use which can be made of certain chemical products and equipment for purposes prohibited under the convention should cause States which are future parties to the convention to exercise the greatest vigilance so that the desire to ensure the greatest chance of development to all does not as a consequence facilitate, for certain proliferators, prohibited activities which constitute a potential threat to global security.

Furthermore, the statement noted that the members of the Australia Group would:

> undertake to review, in the light of the implementation of the convention, the measures that they take to prevent the spread of chemical substances and equipment for purposes contrary to the objectives of the convention, with the aim of removing such measures for the benefit of States parties to the convention acting in full compliance with their obligations under the convention.
>
> They intend thus to contribute to an increase in commercial and technological exchanges between States and to the universal and full implementation of the convention on the prohibition of chemical weapons.

Australia Group members and states vociferously opposed to the existence of the Australia Group interpreted the meaning of this statement differently. Developing states interpreted the text as meaning that such a review would lead to the removal of export controls among states parties to the CWC; tantamount to the dissolution

Export Controls

143

of the Australia Group. Australia Group members interpreted the text as meaning that a review would take place and the objective would be to remove controls for those states parties to the CWC in full compliance with their obligations. No time frame was provided for the review intimated by O' Sullivan. In addition, whether or not a country was in 'full compliance' with the treaty was answered by each state party and not the OPCW.

Although the O'Sullivan statement eased the way to agreement on the CWC it left certain states, such as India, hopeful while others, such as Pakistan and Iran, unassuaged. Feakes noted that:[17]

India's permanent representative welcomed the Australia Group's commitment but added that it would have to be carried out "fully and promptly." He also expressed the opinion of many developing countries that "the Australia Group will have to dissolve itself in letter and spirit as far as trade in chemicals and related equipment is concerned in order to promote healthy universality and credibility for the Convention."

Others noted that 'no clear commitment has been incorporated to the effect that existing export controls on certain chemicals would be withdrawn once the verification provisions of the Convention come into effect.'[18] The CWC text was finalised following the O'Sullivan statement, but it was clear that a number of states were unhappy with the provisions relating to export controls. Pakistan expressed 'serious reservations on certain provisions'[19] including:[20]

[t]he language of Article XI does not address the essential concern of developing countries that existing discriminatory export control mechanisms, such as the 'Australia Group', should be dismantled once the Convention comes into force.

Egypt observed that the draft text was 'not fully satisfactory to us as long as it leaves room for the States Parties to absorb eventual damage to their economic and technological development as a result of the Convention.'[21] Iran noted that 'States Parties would have to rely on the faithful implementation of this Article by chemically developed countries and on their commitment to remove restrictions.'[22] China referred to the lack of balance in Article XI '[i]n spite of the persistent strong demand of the developing countries, this draft has not expressly provided for the removal of discriminatory restrictions on chemical trade and exchanges between States Parties.'[23] Upon implementation the Chinese perspective was later expanded:[24]

We do not deny the right of any country to stipulate stricter export controls than those required by the CWC and to establish small groups for that purpose. However, the existence of the Australia Group has resulted in discrepancies in the legal provisions of different countries, which has created a de facto split legal system within the CWC states parties. This inevitably causes confusion and affects the normal international trade of chemicals ... giving rise to international disputes.

Zukang envisaged two ways to resolve the difference in views; either dissolve the Australia Group or amend the CWC to bring it into line with the Australia Group,

144 *The Biological Weapons Convention*

because '[t]here must be a single standard rather than two.'[25] A very different perspective was taken by one analyst in 1994.[26]

> It must be made clear to opponents of continued controls, however, that the Australia Group will respond to potential proliferants' actual behaviour: parties in compliance will be rewarded with free trade; cheaters and non-signatories will be punished with continued controls. ... opponents of export controls should be reassured by the promise of that if they ratify and comply with the CWC, controls on dual-use chemicals will be removed.

Stern identified the key issue: the perception and understanding that export controls would be removed for those states that joined the CWC and complied with its provisions. Whether or not that actually happened was, and is, open to interpretation and those countries which perceived the Australia Group as still applying export controls when the OPCW had found (or reported) no evidence of non-compliance, such as Iran, hardened their position against mechanisms operating outside the formal structures of the Treaty. Moreover, within the OPCW the legitimacy of the Australia Group appeared to be slipping away, according to the First Director-General:[27]

> As more States join the CWC, and as their chemical producers support it, the arguments originally advanced for the continuing maintenance of restrictions on chemicals outside a credible, reliable international legal framework become increasingly redundant. Given this fact, the continuing existence of export controls by some states parties against others is hard to understand, and very difficult to justify.

It remained clear that the Australia Group would not disband itself until there was greater confidence in the CWC regime as a whole and confidence in the export control system within the CWC was low. Although, 'the CWC has the potential to develop a strong and nearly universal regime for the regulation of toxic chemicals that could eventually eliminate the need for the Australia Group'[28] confidence was not at a level where the Australia Group would allow its chemical controls to wither away for CWC states parties. This was illustrated (and justified) by the figures for import-export data, which according to the OPCW did not correspond in 70-80% of cases.[29] Until the import and export data supplied to the OPCW corresponded to a much greater degree the Australia Group was unlikely to be convinced that an effective export control regime for chemical weapons-related materials and equipment was in place. These different perceptions demonstrated two streams of thinking. The first was a philosophy long held by Western states, that the existence of a control mechanism was not the same as effective implementation: as illustrated by the Argentinean statement, the other philosophy was that signing up to an international agreement was sufficient by itself.

Non-proliferation and export controls in the BWC

Different opinions about export controls began to be aired in 1986, but it was in 1991 that the issue began to emerge as a stumbling bloc in the BWC. The spectre of biological warfare during the Gulf War had alerted Western states to their contribution to biological weapons proliferation in Iraq and, as with chemicals in 1985, they began to act in a co-ordinated fashion under the aegis of the Australia Group. Fearing an expansion of the Australia Group's reach those demanding unimpeded access to technology attempted to reign in export controls.[30] The anodyne language of the Final Declaration, whereby implementation of the article 'should continue to be the subject of multilateral consideration'[31] masked the divisions among states parties.

Export controls were, however, beginning to be re-evaluated, particularly the application of controls and the responsibilities of exporting states. In the early part of the VEREX negotiations Australia proposed that following the elaboration of Article I of the BWC to include a list of agents and toxins of concern, Article III of the Convention would need to be strengthened 'to include export controls on these agents' because it would then be possible 'to track transfers and to verify their legitimacy.'[32] In the academic and policymaking community a re-evaluation of how to apply export controls and achieve non-proliferation was under way.[33] Moodie called for a change of emphasis whereby:[34]

> [t]he focus of restraint efforts ... must shift away from attempts to deny technology itself to increasing the certainty about the uses to which that technology is put ... away from prohibiting technology exports to more emphasis on knowing what happens to them ... a multilateral strategy of technology management.

The 'technology management' strategy was in line with the proposal put forward by Australia during VEREX, but rhetoric over and dispute about export controls in the CWC meant that by the time VEREX came to report Australia's proposal had been abandoned by the Western states and its implications – true multilateral export controls – hidden away. In the final report of VEREX, information on transfers was viewed as background material, which might be effective if combined with other measures. Such information was likely to be supplied in the form of a declaration on imports and exports of materials and equipment deemed relevant to the BWC.[35] The key aspect of the emerging debate was that the more radical thinking was tantamount to a multilateral strategy for technology management, akin to Kellman's 'traceable paper trail from the exporter to the final destination'[36] to enhance confidence in what was really happening with critical technologies. The problem with that approach was that it would require action on a multilateral basis, which would undermine the legitimacy of the Australia Group as it existed and would risk a lowest common denominator approach in terms of what was controlled and how effective such controls were in reality. By 1994, with the CWC negotiations completed, the Australia Group had become a key point of contention in the BWC.

The Special Conference

During the first three meetings of the Special Conference competing visions of the potential mandate were aired. Germany, and those that followed, Finland, US,

146   *The Biological Weapons Convention*

Sweden, and Australia, did not mention provisions relating to export controls. It fell to Brazil to raise the issue.[37]

> It was neither possible nor desirable to stop the spread of technology, for that might jeopardize the industrialization of the countries of the South and destroy the basis of that cooperative international framework that was required for the achievement of disarmament and non-proliferation objectives.

Furthermore, as the delegation went on to note, 'the purpose of export controls must be straightforward: to prevent the proliferation of weapons of mass destruction, and not obscure trade for peaceful purposes.'[38] While Brazil did not rule out export controls, Romania very much counted them in, noting that an effective BWC verification regime, 'would rely on a number of interwoven measures such as data exchanges, *export controls*, analysis of data to determine consistency, national technical means and routine as well as challenge inspections.'[39] [My emphasis] South Africa stated it 'was compelled to control the technology, equipment and material that could be used in the production of [weapons of mass destruction]'[40] but, export controls should be used to prevent proliferation, not to prevent development. South Africa 'would work to ensure that such controls did not prevent developing countries from obtaining access to the advanced technologies needed for their development.'[41]

Similar sentiments were expressed by Indonesia.[42] In what was to become a familiar approach Iran adopted a confrontational strategy to what it perceived as the real problem.[43]

> The expansion of the "Australia Group" list and the inclusion of 65 biological substances and related equipment in only two to three years, constituted an indication of what lay ahead. The list was in contravention of the text of the Convention, and the restrictions must be lifted. If members were expected to accede to the demands of verification, existing arbitrary export control regimes must be removed.

The Nigerian delegate, however, noted the key point and opened up a possible route to compromise.[44]

> Broad political support for a strengthened treaty would depend <u>inter alia</u>, on the transparency of the export-control policies of exporting States, which would ensure that their implementation of the treaty did not hamper the economic and technological development of the parties, but rather promoted international cooperation in all fields of peaceful biological activities. [Emphasis in original]

The identification of *transparency* in export control policies was a nuance in the debate and whether or not it was deliberate that concept later proved to be of critical importance. China required 'the removal of any restrictions, including those in any international agreements, incompatible with the obligations undertaken under the Convention, Article 10 [sic] in particular.'[45] This objective was stated with greater force in the trilateral working paper of Iran, India and China, in which it was stated that 'there shall be no restrictions for the States

Parties in this regard. All existing restrictions against States Parties must be removed.'[46] Hence, as the Ad Hoc Group embarked upon its work baseline positions were well known; action was required on the issue of export controls if the Protocol was to be agreed.

The Protocol negotiations

During the negotiations themselves very little time was devoted to strengthening Article III of the Convention because of the difficult political issues it addressed. To be specific, negotiation on this issue was avoided because every debate on it soured the relationship between delegations on all other subjects. After any open discussion on Article III co-operation between states parties went out of the window. This, obviously, damaged the prospects for progress in other areas of the text and negotiations were held only when they could no longer be avoided. Iran, Pakistan, Cuba, India, Libya, and China, maintained that the Australia Group must be disbanded and export controls should not be applied to states parties. Australia Group members maintained that the co-ordination of export controls was necessary to fulfil the non-proliferation objectives contained in Article III of the BWC and that it was a national responsibility which could not be dictated by international regulations.[47]

Different strategies were adopted to promote these competing objectives in the Protocol. For those opposed to the Australia Group the strategy was based on the acceptance of export controls within the formal treaty framework contingent on the Protocol containing a universal standard applicable to all parties. Export controls applied by certain states parties but not by others were deemed ineffective in achieving their objectives and thus not required. This could be broadly interpreted as bringing into existence a universal Australia Group-type list of controlled items agreed by all states parties, i.e. what Australia had mooted during the early stages of VEREX. It was an approach most often articulated in formal statements which called for universal, non-discriminatory export controls.[48] In addition, recognising there would be a transitional period between the implementation of new standards the review procedure for existing export control arrangements, adopted in the CWC, was to be carried over to the Protocol and bolstered by the inclusion of a specific timeframe for such reviews. These states proposed also some kind of complaints procedure for dealing with any denial of a transfer request, i.e. denial of an export licence.

Australia Group members based their strategy on a rigid interpretation of the existing obligation in Article III of the Convention: that the non-proliferation objective was to be implemented at the national level and was therefore a national responsibility. Moreover, decisions about compliance with the BWC and its future Protocol were national decisions: the future organization would not, in their view, define and decide which states parties were in compliance and which states parties were in non-compliance with the BWC. Certain members of the Australia Group adopted a more transparent approach to the application of export controls and undertook outreach activities to explain the working and decision-making

148 *The Biological Weapons Convention*

procedures for national export licensing and export controls. In a repackaging of export controls the measures taken were not defined as a blanket ban on certain items, but rather as licensing procedures for items deemed sensitive for proliferation purposes. The UK also challenged Iran and other NAM delegations to present evidence of their claims that biological weapons-related export controls were hampering their peaceful economic development: no such evidence was presented in public.

The veracity of claims that export controls hampered economic development was also being tested. Roberts conducted a review of US chemical and biological restrictions and concluded that:[49]

> the conventional wisdom about export controls on items and materials sensitive from the point of view of biological weapons have it wrong. They are not trade restrictions but trade enablers. The trade that results is not controlled in a traditional sense, but licensed. The export control system is most accurately described as a system that licenses, channels, and renders transparent trade in dual-use materials.

The UK later reported to the Ad Hoc Group that only two export licences were denied in 1999/2000.[50] Finally, Western states began to accept that there was a role for a consultation procedure in the event of a denial of an export to another state party to the Protocol.

Competing models in the rolling text

The two identified strategies were not developed under a strict bloc-orientated approach. Iran and China still maintained a public position that called for the abolition of the Australia Group. Conversely, the UK still maintained a public position which rejected any encroachment on its national prerogative to determine export controls, as did the US and Germany. As the negotiations progressed the debate was marked by increasing divisions rather than a narrowing of differences. Indeed, formal meetings were rarely rational and even mentioning the Australia Group by name in the formal negotiations led to something akin to apoplectic responses from certain delegations. In any debate one thing could always be counted upon: those with hard-line views never failed to reiterate their baseline positions in public.

Due to this the provisions and proposals to strengthen Article III of the Convention were never fully developed. As a consequence the rolling text itself was poorly drafted. Two competing visions on how to strengthen Article III of the Convention however can be identified; one was a *reformist* vision for an integrated regime of export controls, while the other was a *minimalist* proposal that amounted to little more than a reaffirmation of the existing obligations and national-led implementation. In contrast to other areas of the Protocol, where the Western Group usually supported the adoption of stringent provisions that left little room for interpretation at the national level and NAM states preferred to draft general principles which left significant room for interpretation upon actual implementation, the positions were reversed. The NAM proposed and supported

Export Controls 149

the *reformist* integrated model, whereas the Western states supported *minimalist* proposals opting to stay as close to the status quo as possible.

It is important to note that these competing visions were never fully developed and it was not at all clear that all Western states supported one vision and all NAM supported the other.[51] In addition, the two competing models were not immediately obvious in the language of the rolling text; indeed neither model was proposed as a coherent or integrated regime for export controls before the shift to the composite text.[52] However, it was clear from different areas of the rolling text that the proposals put forward would, if joined up, provide for the kind of multilaterally negotiated export control system many delegations had repeatedly called for. It was also clear that one had greater depth than the other, as illustrated in Table 6.1.

The NAM favoured a system which involved, *inter alia,* declarations, transfer guidelines, reporting of transfers of specified equipment and materials, consultation and dispute settlement procedures, prohibitions of transfers to non-states parties and states that developed biological or toxin weapons, and the possibility of clarification and investigation procedures. In contrast, the model favoured by the Western states was based on national measures and additional transparency through reporting and consultations. The failure by any delegation to present a coherent joined-up vision is not easy to understand. Perhaps they believed they had in fact presented coherent models; or they did not believe such models were workable or feasible; or the proposals were part of the negotiating process that was stymied by the confrontational atmosphere in this area of the text; or states parties were well aware that this was an endgame issue that simply required them to go through the motions of being seen to be doing something. Either way, the rolling text remained in stark contrast to other areas of the Protocol and the proposals themselves were inferior in terms of how they were introduced, presented, explained, revised, and discussed by all states parties.

At the sixteenth session the NAM stated that there was a 'need for effective national export control mechanisms in accordance with obligations of Article III of the Convention.'[53] Specific measures were proposed for consideration, including guidelines on transfers for states parties and non-states parties, declarations on denial of transfers, guidelines to promote harmonization of national, regional and other regulatory mechanisms with those included in the Protocol, transparency and confidence-building measures, and provisions for review mechanisms.[54]

While this statement made no specific textual proposals it introduced two important nuances into the debate. First, the explicit recognition of 'the need for effective national export control mechanisms', and second, the reference to 'concerns arising from any undue restrictions on exports to States Parties to the Convention.' The former nuance indicated NAM acceptance of export controls in the Protocol. The latter – 'undue restrictions' – implied recognition that certain restrictions on exports were in fact 'due'. This statement offered an opportunity to move the debate forward, as the NAM paper on visits had done in the same session of the Ad Hoc Group. However, just as the Western states botched their response to the NAM proposals on visits, the significance of the statement on export controls was undermined by the accompanying statements of certain delegations.

The Biological Weapons Convention

Table 6.1. Export control models

	Reformist model	*Minimalist* model
General obligations	(1) Reaffirmation of Article III	(1) Reaffirmation of Article III
Prohibitions	(2) Prohibited to non-states parties (3) Prohibited to states found to have developed BW	(2) Prohibitions on transfers unless for prophylactic, protective or other peaceful purposes
Review	(4) Review of existing national measures	(3) Review of existing national measures
Declarations	(5) Mandatory declarations on transfers & toxins listed in Annex A (I) and equipment in Annex A (II) by supplier and recipient	
Guidelines	(6) Reporting of transfers to BL4 laboratories (7) Reporting of transfers related to delivery systems (8) Reporting of transfers related to aerosolization equipment (9) Reporting of transfers related to stabilization of agents & toxins to environmental stress	(4) Reporting of transfers of fermenters over 100 litres, Aerosol chambers, Aerobiology equipment, & Aerosol analytical equipment
Transparency	(10) End-use certificates indicating final destination	(5) Mandatory reporting of national measures taken to implement Article III (BWC) (6) Annual reporting of aggregated transfers
Consultations	(11) Consultation & clarification via Article V (BWC) (12) Settlement of disputes procedure	(7) Bilateral consultations for genuine problems
Other measures	(13) Declaration subject to visits and investigations (14) Investigation of transfers in violation of Article III (BWC)	(8) Encouragement to go beyond specific controls in the Protocol

As Wilson reported all knew that it was a moderate expression by the NAM that did not reflect the national positions of all states.[55] The statement by South Africa was made in plenary session and in a public forum hard-liners never missed an opportunity to express their national position. This is exactly what happened, and the NAM position was undermined by follow-up statements from India, Iran, Cuba, and later China, that supported the statement from South Africa, but stressed that this was as close to a maximum compromise as they were willing to accept. Furthermore, reciprocal gestures from the Western Group were expected sooner, rather than later. Rather than bolstering the moderate position, the follow-up statements focussed attention on the obvious divisions between hard-line and more

Export Controls 151

moderate NAM states. By stating that the NAM position was a significant compromise and that at least some states parties still expected the Australia Group to disband, these statements illustrated to the Western Group that the NAM could be split on this issue. It was now clear that a majority of the NAM were prepared to work on the issue, whereas a vocal minority remained hard-line in their approach. Instead of placing the onus on the Western Group to make a response, the attempt only served to indicate that the Western Group simply had to bide its time and wait for the NAM to split so they could be played off against one another.

From mid 1999 much of the negotiation on export controls was done in private early morning meetings and while some progress was made the fragile nature of tentative agreements meant they were not included or reflected in the rolling text. An exchange of working papers outlining national positions in late 2000 and early 2001 marked the point where real negotiations began. The use of working papers for this debate underlined the paucity of real progress, because in no other area of the rolling text did an exchange of national positions occur in this way towards the end of the negotiations. The UK both chaired the sessions on this topic and issued its own working paper on export controls noting that:[56]

> some States appear to believe that implementation of the Protocol will mean that national controls on exports between states parties to the Protocol should be immediately and automatically relaxed, or even eliminated, in order to promote technology exchange and co-operation. This argument seems to be based on the assumption that the Protocol will provide a regime of declarations and on-site measures which will instantly, unambiguously and universally confirm compliance with the BTWC, and that all states parties will always act in good faith. Accordingly, it is argued that, in the case of transfers of materials or equipment between states parties to the Protocol, national export controls are unnecessary, hamper economic development and should either be relaxed or removed. The United Kingdom believes that these arguments are flawed and that a blanket relaxation of national export monitoring and control arrangements would undermine the fundamental objectives of the Convention. It is not a case of *either* the Protocol *or* export controls: the two are mutually complementary means which contribute to the same end – the strengthening of the Convention.

With reference to the case of Iraq and the UNSCOM investigations the UK noted that verification and national export controls were necessary factors and that states parties could not be expected to abandon export controls on transfers to other states parties on the basis that they had signed the Protocol.

Iran still maintained that the Australia Group had to disband, but recognizing that this was unlikely proposed a procedure for the settlement of disputes arising from denial of transfers.[57] The proposal was resubmitted to the Ad Hoc Group sponsored by Iran, China, Cuba, India, Indonesia, Mexico, Pakistan, Libya and Sri Lanka.[58] The procedures outlined a series of measures a state party denied an export could take to address its concerns. These procedures were in fact similar to those used in the envisaged CCC mechanism for declarations. Compared to other measures in the draft Protocol much of it was uncontroversial. The new element was recourse to a panel for dispute settlement, under which the panel was required to make a ruling or recommendation within six months. This juridical element was

152 *The Biological Weapons Convention*

innovative but wholly out of line with any other measures in the Protocol. There was, for example, no comparable proposal from any *reformist* related to verification or compliance. As Rissanen noted, '[t]he proposition is widely considered unrealistic, and is not likely to gain support of countries in the Australia Group.'[59] In fact, the insertion of a dispute settlement procedure into the rolling text resulted in a response from nine Western states (Australia, Austria, Belgium, Canada, Germany, Italy, Republic of Korea, Sweden, and the UK)[60] which underlined that the procedure had no chance of being accepted in the Protocol. These states parties made three points: first, no provisions on the denial of transfers, or on any consultations or review were needed in the Protocol; second, they would not countenance provisions which obliged states parties to transfer items if they were not completely satisfied they were consistent with the non-proliferation objectives of the Convention; third, in their view:[61]

> no multilateral organization can ever address, consider, decide upon, review, or overturn any decision taken by a State Party that a potential transfer is inconsistent with the non-proliferation obligations undertaken by that State Party as its national responsibility under the Convention.

By the end of 2000, the level of debate - or rather the lack of debate - meant that the rolling text was still heavily bracketed. The actual proposals in the text were first or second drafts that lacked the nuances and implicit understandings evident in others areas of the Protocol. Nevertheless, the rolling text contained five concepts around which a final article might be constructed: general obligations, transfer guidelines, transparency measures, prohibitions, and review.

The composite text

The early morning meetings had developed some ideas and provided the Chairman with some room for manoeuvre, but drafting the provisions was not an easy task, as the Chairman reported to the Ad Hoc Group.[62]

Implementing legislation

The provisions first sought to strengthen Article III of the Convention by requiring each state party to 'review and, if necessary, amend or establish any legislation, regulatory or administrative provisions to regulate the transfer of agents, toxins, equipment and technologies'[63] considered relevant to the obligations in the Convention. This reaffirmation of the basic obligation contained one additional requirement, whereby each state party would report to the Technical Secretariat of the Organization the measures it had adopted, as well as whenever amendments where made to such measures. The timeframe was 180 days and in essence this was a mandatory initial declaration by another name. To assist in the fulfilment of implementing such measures any state party could request assistance from the Technical Secretariat or any state party on meeting its obligations under the article.

Transfer guidelines

Reminiscent of other arms control treaties the transfer guidelines established under the Protocol were broad in principle but narrow in terms of specifics. The principal obligation contained in the first sentence required each state party to 'undertake all measures they deem necessary to ensure that obligations under Article III of the Convention are implemented fully and effectively.'[64] This reinforced the notion that each state party was responsible for the implementation of Article III of BWC and was the favoured position of the Australia Group.

The broad scope of the measures was underlined by the inclusion of *they deem necessary*, language which ruled nothing out and provided legal cover under the Protocol for any measure taken to ensure non-proliferation. It was balanced by the second sentence which established that 'such measures shall be implemented in a manner designed to avoid hampering the economic and technological development of States Parties or international co-operation.'[65] Although standard language the use of *in a manner designed to avoid* rather than *in a manner that shall avoid* provided an obvious defence for any state party to claim that the measures were in fact designed to avoid such hampering, but might have failed to do so upon implementation. This was nuanced, and rather clever, drafting.

The guidelines included four measures which *may* be taken; thus, the guidelines were not mandatory. Such measures included information on end-use, an end-use certificate and a written undertaking that the requested item would not be re-transferred outside the jurisdiction or control of the receiving state party without permission of the supplier or the supplying state. Information could also be requested from the recipient state on its national measures to prevent transfer of items in contravention of the Convention. The exporting state party could also take into account 'the nature and implementation in the requesting State Party or State of measures ... to comply with the purpose of the Convention, and the extent to which these measures are effective in fulfilling the purpose of the Convention.'[66] This meant that the requesting state had to supply information and the supplying state was free to interpret the stringency of the provisions. The guidelines then identified four specific dual-use items linked to aerosol-related work.

In the final paragraph the guidelines stated that all states parties 'shall consider the status of implementation of the Convention and this Protocol in a potential recipient when considering a request for a transfer.'[67] This text was supposedly designed to encourage ratification of the Protocol and the Convention, but it reiterated one of the above voluntary measures, and appeared to make it mandatory. If this was the case that was a factor which may have led to some confusion upon implementation.[68]

Notifications

One of the long-standing objectives of the developing states, some form of notification, was also included in the article. The scope of notifications, however, fell short of the original proposals from, among others, India, and included only specialised aerosol-related equipment. Exports of the specified equipment were to

154 *The Biological Weapons Convention*

be notified to the Director-General of the Organization in annual aggregated retrospective format, using the reporting form contained in Appendix I of the Protocol. Such reports were intended to 'promote transparency and to enhance confidence-building'[69] among states parties. To further this aim, annual reports on exports were available to other states parties on request and states parties could consult and exchange additional information among themselves to avoid discrepancies in the data and information reported.[70] The critical element here was that the provisions strengthened Article III of the Convention and provided the information-sharing practice of the Australia Group with legitimacy.

Consultations

The penultimate section of the article related to consultations. These were wholly voluntary and relied on both or all states parties involved in the consultations to agree to them. Furthermore, the language was drafted in a manner that effectively legitimised the Australia Group's states' practice of consulting with each other on requests related to materials and equipment of a sensitive nature. This was an improvement on the provisions of the Convention, but the notion that all states parties could partake in such consultations was diminished by the inclusion of 'if it deems it appropriate' which permitted any state party to rebuff a consultation request. The scope, tenor and voluntary nature of the consultations were established in the opening paragraph of the section:[71]

> States Parties may consult among themselves on the implementation of the provisions of this Article. States Parties may, as they deem it appropriate, inform other States Parties of the outcome of their national authorising procedures and any background relating to the approval of a requested transfer.

It is also worth nothing that one Western diplomat characterised the provisions for consultations as the maximum achievable.[72]

Review

The First Conference of States Parties after the First Review Conference of the Protocol (6 years after entry into force) was mandated to consider restrictions and prohibitions on transfers to non-states parties to the Convention and the Protocol. This was in line with the NAM view of a prohibition on transfers to non-states parties, but against the wishes of states who considered such a change an amendment to the Convention's 'any recipient whatsoever' formulation.[73] It therefore balanced the competing objectives by pleasing no state party.

Responses to the composite text

At the beginning of the twenty-third session a coalition of nine states parties reiterated their position that states parties which fulfilled their responsibilities should not be 'subjected to measures which in effect constitute a denial of their rights under the relevant Articles of the Convention.' They considered 'a fair transparent and multilateral export regulation mechanism within the future Organization for the implementation of the Protocol'[74] essential. As per practice, their uncompromising position vis-à-vis the Australia Group was reiterated in the final paragraph.[75]

The key issue for these states was that they were not opposed to export controls *per se* but the continuation of the status quo vis-à-vis the application of export controls outside the formal regime was unacceptable to them. China then went one step further in a separate working paper and called for a system based on the incorporation of the Australia Group control lists in the Protocol, declarations of transfers of listed items, end use certificates, a prohibition on transfers to non-states parties, declarations on denial of transfers and the establishment of mechanisms to settle dispute arising from such denials.[76] Apart from the composite text, this working paper was the first, and only, proposal to put together the separate elements in an integrated package. China delivered the text on 8 May 2001, thirty-five days after the Chairman had delivered the composite text to all delegations and seven years after the negotiations had begun.

The initial response to the composite text was negative. China, Iran, Pakistan, Cuba, and Libya all expressed concerns about the balance of the text in Article 7 in statements eerily reminiscent of the debate on Article XI (economic and technological development) of the CWC in 1992.[77] Mexico also reiterated the request for a multilaterally negotiated framework that would be both legally-binding and the sole basis for regulating trade in this area. Furthermore, Mexico expressed the view that the concerns of states who had proposed a separate dispute settlement mechanism were ignored; a view Libya echoed.[78]

Sweden made a brief statement on behalf of the European Union which noted the position of the Western Group: '[t]he strengthening of Article III can in no case mean weakening or the replacement of national controls or of the consultation mechanisms that exist between certain countries.'[79] According to the EU, the provisions of the text went further than similar mechanisms in other agreements, particularly in the institutionalisation of consultations, and as such, the EU was 'hesitant about the provisions [on consultations]'[80] because such institutionalisation had always been opposed.

Germany objected to the possibility of prohibitions on trade with non-states parties. While accepting the legitimacy of similar provisions in the CWC and the principle that countries that joined the Protocol should be treated differently from those that did not, Germany upheld the common Western Group view that the provisions of Article III of the Convention applied to any recipient, and the Protocol could not amend the Convention by introducing general trade restrictions on non-states parties, or mandate its parties to consider such restrictions in the future. Furthermore, a separate review mechanism was not a necessary additional procedure above the standard review conferences and Germany's preference was the deletion of the entire section on review. Canada and Australia aligned themselves with the European Union and the position of Germany on the provisions for review, as did South Korea and New Zealand.[81] Italy considered the

156 *The Biological Weapons Convention*

concerns of some developing countries about the misuse of export controls to deny economic development to be overstated, whereas France made a formal statement noting that the provisions 'go well beyond what is contained in the international legal instruments which exist and are comparable to our future Protocol. We are still very reluctant about these proposals.'[82]

Of those with a moderate approach, Chile repeated its opposition to any proposal which provided a jurisdictional role for the Organization in the area of transfer disputes, but supported the Brazilian approach of including some kind of policy or political response mechanism to the problems under Article 14 (peaceful co-operation) of the Protocol. In that respect, Chile stated that it could live with the composite text. The UK followed the French statement and reiterated its support for the European Union position, but noting that it was prepared to achieve an acceptable conclusion on the text but only if others were also prepared to set aside national positions. In effect, these responses identified four groups: a majority of the Western states indicated their interest and support for the composite text subject to certain concerns (which were widely interpreted as negotiation points for the endgame); the NAM had focussed on the absence of dispute settlement provisions, thus suggesting acceptance of the text subject to one additional element being added; others, such as Chile, indicated they supported the composite text as it stood; finally, the group of states such as the US, which had not made their position clear in public. Therefore, hard-liners in both the Western Group and the NAM were marginalized by the indications that an agreement on the composite text on non-proliferation and export controls was possible for the vast majority, despite the rhetoric still being put forward at this late stage.

Minimalism or *Reform*

The export control debate in the Ad Hoc Group was marked by competing political objectives which sought to either abolish the Australia Group or retain the Australia Group at any cost. The pursuit of these objectives prevented rational debate and promising proposals were never fully developed. This was in stark contrast to the debates in other areas of the text, such as visits. Although the Ad Hoc Group did strengthen Article III of the Convention it failed to internationalize the controls and, ultimately, failed to strengthen non-proliferation objectives in any significant way. Overall, the composite text reaffirmed the basic non-proliferation obligation and maintained the national implementation emphasis of that obligation. In the provisions greater transparency was provided by the *de facto* declaration requirement to report on national legislation, and the consultation procedures. However, the voluntary nature of many of these provisions weakened them and the lack of mandatory declaration requirements for import and export of agents and toxins identified in Annex A was a significant omission.

In providing guidelines on the implementation of such measures it rectified one of the key deficiencies of the BWC. Furthermore, in providing for consultations the provisions sought to address one of the key political problems in this area; the lack of transparency. Nevertheless, the degree of strengthening was minimal. The

Export Controls 157

clarification aspect of the provisions and the voluntary nature of many of its measures indicated that the text followed the course of action adopted at preceding review conferences by clarifying understandings and indicating what states parties might do to implement their obligations. An additional factor which could not be ignored was that the provisions in Article 7 legitimised the activities of the Australia Group states vis-à-vis the consultation procedures and the co-ordination of controls if certain states parties deemed it appropriate to do so.

Any assessment of the negotiations must also draw attention to a number of errors in the negotiation strategies of states parties. These errors cut across the Protocol as a whole and indicate the interconnectedness of the separate elements. The objection to a formal declaration on the national measures taken to implement the Protocol could be considered short-sighted. In opposing the declaration on national measures greater transparency of the provisions to implement Article III of the Convention was lost. Of greater import, Western states were less likely to be convinced that the developing states had the necessary measures in place to fulfil their non-proliferation objectives and safeguard the most critical materials and equipment. The unavailability of that information was unlikely to engender immediate confidence in the regime vis-à-vis export controls and failure to require a declaration was a lose-lose solution to the immediate problems of the NAM. The failure of the Ad Hoc Group to develop proposals for declaration or reporting requirements of transfers for certain agents, toxins and equipment was also an error. As such the Ad Hoc Group delivered a solution based on the only area where states parties could reach agreement: reaffirmation of existing objectives and language which was known to contain ambiguities that could be interpreted differently by delegations.

Given the protracted difficulties in this area of the negotiations the response to the Chairman's proposals was quite muted. No delegation rejected the text outright, although most had indicated further changes were necessary. The text was a compromise which did not reflect the publicly-stated preferred option of any delegation. The provisions went further than the Western states would have liked, but not as far as many of the NAM had wanted: at least based on their respective public claims. One must exercise caution here, however, because in this area of the negotiations the debates in the public arena are of limited use to our understanding. Virtually every significant aspect of the 'negotiations' on this article were conducted in private, often by the states parties themselves. While it was, and is, possible to see the potential of the measures contained in Article 7 of the Protocol, past practice and political realities vis-à-vis export controls did not encourage much hope that the mechanisms would fulfil their potential. In the area of export controls, there was a victory for the *minimalists*, which in this case, were to be found in a united Western Group.

Notes

1. Michael Moodie, 'Beyond Proliferation: The Challenge of Technology Diffusion' *The Washington Quarterly* 18:2 (Spring 1995) p.183.

2. Jozef Goldblat, 'The problem of Chemical and Biological Warfare' Volume IV *CB Disarmament Negotiations 1920-1970* (Stockholm, Almqvist & Wiksell, 1971) p.60.
3. Ibid., p.64.
4. Fritz Schmidt, 'NPT Export Controls and the Zangger Committee' *The Nonproliferation Review* 7:3 (Fall-Winter 2000) p.137.
5. Ibid.
6. Ian Anthony and Jean Pascal Zanders, 'Multilateral security-related export controls' *SIPRI Yearbook 1998 Armaments, Disarmament and International Security* (Oxford, OUP, 1998) p.380.
7. William Walker, 'Nuclear trade relations in the decade to 1995' John Simpson (Editor) *Nuclear non-proliferation: an agenda for the 1990s* (Cambridge, Cambridge University Press, 1987) p.70.
8. Anthony and Zanders, 'Multilateral security-related export controls' pp.384-385.
9. Walker, 'Nuclear trade relations in the decade to 1995' p.72.
10. Ibid.
11. Rebecca Johnson, 'Non-Proliferation Treaty: Challenging Times' Acronym 13 (February 2000) p.14.
12. Rebecca Johnson, 'The 2000 NPT Review Conference: A Delicate, Hard-Won Compromise' *Disarmament Diplomacy* Number 46 (May 2000) p.11.
13. Ibid.
14. Information on the Australia Group including its origins, can be found on the website of the Group: http://www.australiagroup.net/index.html
15. United Nations, Conference on Disarmament, CD/PV.613 (20 February 1992) cited Amy Smithson, 'Separating Fact from Fiction: The Australia Group and the Chemical Weapons Convention' The Henry L. Stimson Center Occasional Paper No. 34 (March 1997) p.19.
16. United Nations, 'Final Record of the Six Hundred and Twenty-Ninth Plenary Meeting' 6 August 1992, CD/PV.629 p.7.
17. Daniel Feakes, 'Export Controls, Chemical Trade and the CWC' Jonathan B. Tucker (Editor) *The Chemical Weapons Convention: Implementation Challenges and Solutions* Monterey Institute of International Studies, April 2001 p.47.
18. Counsellor Shahbaz, 'A Perspective on the OPCW Preparatory Commission' *Chemical Weapons Convention Bulletin* Number 19 (March 1993) p.6.
19. United Nations, 'Report of the Ad Hoc Committee on Chemical Weapons to the Conference on Disarmament' CD/1170 (26 August 1992) p.19.
20. Ibid.
21. Ibid., p.22.
22. Ibid., p.28.
23. Ibid., p.25.
24. Sha Zukang, 'China's Perspective on Non-Proliferation' Joseph Cirincione (Editor) *Repairing the Regime* (New York, Routledge, 2000) p.129.
25. Ibid.
26. Jessica Eve Stern, 'Co-operative Security and the CWC: A comparison of the Chemical and Nuclear Weapons Non-proliferation regimes' *Contemporary Security Policy* 15:3 (December 1994) p.43.
27. José M. Bustani, 'Opening Statement by the Director-General to the Conference of the States Parties at its Fifth Session' OPCW CSP document C-V/DG.11 15 May 2000.
28. Feakes, 'Export Controls, Chemical Trade and the CWC' p.50.

Export Controls   159

29. News Chronology *The CBW Conventions Bulletin* Issue No. 51 (March 2001) pp. 43-44.
30. BWC 3RC, BWC/CONF.II/23 pp.66-70.
31. Ibid., p.12.
32. VEREX, BWC/CONF.III/VEREX/WP.10 'Working paper submitted by Australia - The BTWC: A possible verification regime' (1 April 1992) p.2.
33. Henry Sokolski, 'Best of Intentions: America's campaign against strategic weapons proliferation' (Westport, Praeger Publishers, 2001) pp.63-86.
34. Moodie, 'Beyond Proliferation' p.198.
35. VEREX, BWC/CONF.III/VEREX/9, p.11.
36. Barry Kellman, 'Bridling the international trade of catastrophic weaponry' *The American University Law Review* 43:3 (Spring 1994) p.834.
37. BWC Special Conference, BWC/SPCONF/1 p.92.
38. Ibid.
39. Ibid., p.95.
40. Ibid., p.102.
41. Ibid.
42. Ibid., pp.109-110.
43. Ibid., p.111.
44. Ibid., p.106.
45. Ibid., 'China's view on Follow-Up Mechanism for Strengthening the BWC (Working Paper 13) p.42.
46. Ibid., 'China, India, Iran (Islamic Republic of)' Working Paper 15 pp.44-45.
47. For a summary of an early general debate on export control issues see: BWC AHG, BWC/AD HOC GROUP/32 'Procedural Report of the Ad Hoc Group of the States Parties to the Convention on the Prohibition of the Development, Production and Stockpiling of Bacteriological (Biological) and Toxin Weapons and on Their Destruction' (27 September 1996) pp.69-77.
48. See for example, 'Statement by Ambassador Carmen Moreno, Under-Secretary of Foreign Affairs of Mexico to the Ad Hoc Group of the States Parties to the Convention on the Prohibition of the Development, Production and Stockpiling of Bacteriological (Biological) and Toxin Weapons and on Their Destruction' Geneva, 21 March 2000.
49. Brad Roberts, 'Export Controls and Biological Weapons: New Roles, New Challenges' *Critical Reviews in Microbiology* 24:3 1998 p.241.
50. BWC AHG, BWC/AD HOC GROUP/WP.424 'Working paper submitted by the United Kingdom of Great Britain and Northern Ireland – Fulfilling the Objectives of the Biological and Toxin Weapons Convention: Resolving the issue of Trade and Exchange of Technology' (20 July 2000) p.3.
51. The proposals put before the Ad Hoc Group in working papers included the following: BWC AHG, BWC/AD HOC GROUP/WP.126 'Working paper submitted by India – Guidelines to ensure compliance with the Obligations under Article III of the Convention on the Prohibition of the Development, Production and Stockpiling of Bacteriological (Biological) and Toxin Weapons and on Their Destruction' (5 March 1997); BWC/AD HOC GROUP/WP.142 'Working paper submitted by Austria and New Zealand – Implementation of Article III of the Convention on the Prohibition of the Development, Production and Stockpiling of Bacteriological (Biological) and Toxin Weapons and on Their Destruction (BWC)' (14 March 1997); BWC/AD HOC GROUP/WP.147 'Working paper submitted by the Friend of

the Chair on Compliance Measures – IV Measures to Strengthen the Implementation of Article III' (19 March 1997); BWC/AD HOC GROUP/WP.148 'Working paper submitted by the Islamic Republic of Iran – Transfer Guidelines' (19 March 1997); BWC/AD HOC GROUP/WP.184 'Working paper submitted by Austria – (H) Measures to Strengthen the Implementation of Article III of the BWC' (23 July 1997); BWC/AD HOC GROUP/WP.407 'Working paper submitted by the NAM and Other States – Statement on behalf of the Group of Non-Aligned Movement and Other States: Measures to Strengthen the implementation of Article III of the Convention' (8 October 1999); BWC/AD HOC GROUP/WP.424 'Working paper submitted by the United Kingdom of Great Britain and Northern Ireland – Fulfilling the Objectives of the Biological and Toxin Weapons Convention: Resolving the issue of Trade and Exchange of Technology' (20 July 2000); BWC/AD HOC GROUP/WP.426 'Working paper submitted by the Islamic Republic of Iran – Settlement of Disputes on Transfer Denial' (2 August 2000); BWC/AD HOC GROUP/WP.432 'Working paper submitted by China, Cuba, India, Indonesia, the Islamic Republic of Iran, Mexico and Pakistan – Settlement of disputes arising as a result of denial of transfers' (23 November 2000); BWC/AD HOC GROUP/WP.443 'Working paper submitted by Australia, Austria, Belgium, Canada, the Federal Republic of Germany, Italy, Republic of Korea, Sweden, and the United Kingdom of Great Britain and Northern Ireland – Article III, section F' (26 February 2001); BWC/AD HOC GROUP/WP.444 'Working paper submitted by the United Kingdom of Great Britain and Northern Ireland – Suggested amendments to Article III, section F, paragraph 2' (23 February 2001); BWC/AD HOC GROUP/WP.452 'Working paper submitted by China, Cuba, India, Indonesia, Iran (Islamic Republic of) Libyan Arab Jamahiriya, Mexico, Pakistan and Sri Lanka' (7 May 2001); BWC/AD HOC GROUP/WP.453 'Working paper submitted by China – The Issue of Export Control' (8 May 2001).

52. Prior to the working paper by China, BWC/AD HOC GROUP/WP.453, India's vision of an export control regime contained in BWC/AD HOC GROUP/WP.126 was the only coherent proposal which covered most aspects of the export control issue.

53. BWC AHG, BWC/AD HOC GROUP/WP.407 pp.1-2.

54. Ibid., p.2.

55. Henrietta Wilson, 'Strengthening the BWC: Issues for the Ad Hoc Group' *Disarmament Diplomacy* Issue number 42 (December 1999) p.30.

56. BWC AHG, BWC/AD HOC GROUP/WP.424, pp.1-2.

57. BWC AHG, BWC/AD HOC GROUP/WP.426.

58. BWC AHG, BWC/AD HOC GROUP/WP.432 and BWC/AD HOC GROUP/WP.432/Rev.1.

59. Jenni Rissanen, 'Protocol Ad Hoc Group enters deeper into consultations' *Disarmament Diplomacy* Issue number 48 (July 2000) p.30.

60. BWC AHG, BWC.AD HOC GROUP/WP.443 'Working paper submitted by the Australia, Austria, Belgium, Canada, the Federal Republic of Germany, Italy, Republic of Korea, Sweden, and the United Kingdom of Great Britain and Northern Ireland' (26 February 2001).

61. Ibid., p.2.

62. Jenni Rissanen, 'Hurdles Cleared, Obstacles Remaining: The Ad Hoc Group Prepares for the Final Challenge' *Disarmament Diplomacy* (April 2001) p.22.

Export Controls   161

63. BWC AHG, BWC/AD HOC GROUP/CRP.8 (Technically Corrected Version) 30 May 2001 Geneva, p.48.
64. Ibid.
65. Ibid.
66. Ibid.
67. Ibid., paragraph 6.
68. Onno Kervers, 'Strengthening Compliance with the Biological weapons Convention: the draft Protocol' *Journal of Conflict and Security Law* 8:1 2003 p.186.
69. BWC AHG, BWC/AD HOC GROUP/CRP.8 p. 48, paragraph 7.
70. Ibid., page 50, paragraph 9.
71. Ibid., paragraph 10.
72. Kervers, 'Strengthening Compliance with the Biological weapons Convention: the draft Protocol' p.187
73. Rissanen, 'Hurdles Cleared, Obstacles Remaining: The Ad Hoc Group Prepares for the Final Challenge' pp.23-24.
74. BWC AHG, BWC/AD HOC GROUP/WP.452.
75. Ibid., p.2.
76. BWC AHG, BWC/AD HOC GROUP/WP.453.
77. Rissanen, 'Hurdles Cleared, Obstacles Remaining: The Ad Hoc Group Prepares for the Final Challenge' pp.16-27.
78. Ibid.
79. Katarina Rangitt, Oral statement in Plenary session by Sweden on behalf of the European Union, 3 May 2001.
80. Ibid.
81. Rissanen, 'Hurdles Cleared, Obstacles Remaining: The Ad Hoc Group Prepares for the Final Challenge' pp.23-24.
82. Statement by Ambassador Hubert de la Fortelle on behalf of France, 10 May 2001.

Chapter 7

Peaceful Co-operation

Introduction

Peaceful co-operation in the biological sciences was, and is, seen as a key component of the BWC by a significant number of its states parties. As we have seen in chapter two, these parties succeeded in ensuring the mandate of the Ad Hoc Group reflected both their concerns and their objectives during the Protocol negotiations. Developing states had long argued that in order to promote universality of the BWC it was essential to give effect to the co-operative aspects of the Convention, namely Article X.[1] In this chapter we examine how that debate evolved in the Protocol negotiations and the measures agreed by the Ad Hoc Group to strengthen Article X of the Convention.

Article X had two elements, one promotional and one regulatory:[2]

(1) The States parties to this Convention undertake to facilitate, and have the right to participate in, the fullest possible exchange of equipment, materials and scientific and technological information for the use of bacteriological (biological) agents and toxins for peaceful purposes. Parties to the Convention in a position to do so shall also cooperate in contributing individually or together with other States or international organizations to the further development and application of scientific discoveries in the field of bacteriology (biology) for the prevention of disease, or for other peaceful purposes.

(2) This Convention shall be implemented in a manner designed to avoid hampering the economic or technological development of States parties to the Convention or international cooperation in the field of peaceful bacteriological (biological) activities, including the international exchange of bacteriological (biological) agents and toxins and equipment for the processing, use or production of bacteriological (biological) agents and toxins for peaceful purposes in accordance with the provisions of the Convention.

The article encapsulated the other side of the dual-use problem; namely how do national and international agreements prohibiting the use of certain technologies for specified purposes ensure that the control mechanisms do not hinder or prevent the use of the same technology for legitimate purposes? In short, peaceful co-operation, and Article X in particular, cannot be separated from the BWC. Any assessment must also take into account the non-proliferation obligation under the Convention's Article III. The relationship between the two articles has evolved into an uneasy balance and one analyst went so far as to claim that there was 'an obvious contradiction between Articles III and X.'[3]

The chapter begins with a brief historical analysis of the origins of the article and is followed by a summary examination of the divisive nature of the debate at

164 *The Biological Weapons Convention*

successive review conferences of the Convention. In doing so the purpose is to underline that the contest between *minimalists* and *reformists* in this area of the BWC shifted the Western Group into the *minimalist* camp and the NAM into the *reformist* camp. By the early 1990s for the developing states parties the issue of co-operation had to be given equal status in any negotiations to strengthen the Convention. The chapter then examines how the measures contained in the composite text were developed during the negotiations, and concludes that the Ad Hoc Group developed explicit co-operation measures which went beyond any other agreement to date.

History of Article X of the Convention

A reading of the United Nations document provided to the First Review Conference in 1980 suggests that peaceful co-operation was 'one of the central issues in the negotiations.'[4] This is not a conclusion one would automatically draw from the documentation of the ENDC and CCD during the 1968-1971 period. Few calls for co-operative activities were made by the non-aligned according to the official documentation. While Sweden did recognise that trade in dual-use goods and materials was pertinent to the BWC, it was in the context of verification through a prohibition on transfers of agents which might be used as a means of warfare. However, the Swedish proposal did note that such controls 'would be implemented in a manner which would avoid hampering the scientific, technical or economic development of the parties, or international co-operation in peaceful activities.'[5] As the Swedish representative correctly noted, 'that idea is taken from the Non-Proliferation Treaty, which has a similar clause in its Article III.'[6]

The origins of the modern disarmament-development relationship can be traced back to Eisenhower's *Atoms for Peace* programme in the 1950s. *Atoms for Peace* was founded on a basic nuclear bargain between the US and any recipient of US atomic knowledge. Nuclear technology and information would be transferred from the US to the recipient state providing that state committed itself to use the technology for peaceful purposes.[7] The policy was rather simplistic and both the US and the USSR contributed to proliferation of nuclear technology:[8]

> One of the most striking parallels between the U.S. and Soviet nonproliferation policy is that both countries, for extended periods of time, nurtured the misleading idea that there exist clearly good "atoms for peace" and bad "atoms for war." This perspective was most pronounced during the Atoms for Peace period, when the U.S. and the Soviet nuclear policies promoted the development of civilian – and presumably safe – nuclear activities abroad with little regard for their military or dangerous implications. One of the ironies of this period was the development of a U.S.-Soviet peaceful nuclear energy and prestige race in tandem with the superpower arms race.

The notion of whether or not an atom was 'good' or 'bad' rested on the intention of the party that possessed it, which in essence encapsulated the dual-use problem. This disarmament-development link was enshrined in NPT Articles III and IV and one analyst viewed this bargain as 'legitimising a link between peace and economic development.'[9]

Although the initial UK working paper presented to the ENDC contained no provision for peaceful co-operation in biological sciences it did note, 'that most of the microbiological agents that could be used in hostilities are also needed for peaceful purposes.'[10] The dual-use nature of the problem was, therefore, known, but a subsequent UK draft Convention of 1969 also contained no provisions recognisable as Article X language. The first indication of the need for such provisions came from Sweden in 1970 during the debates on verification issues.[11] A co-operation clause was, however, in line with the views of Joshua Lederberg, one of the leading US non-governmental proponents for biological weapons control. Lederberg argued in an informal meeting on 5 August 1970 that:[12]

> The promulgation of an international agreement to control biological warfare in a negative sense should, therefore, be accompanied by steps urgently needed to build positive efforts at international co-operation, a kind of defensive biological research against natural enemies of the human species.

According to this view there should be a balance between controls on the deliberate use of disease as a weapon and the response of the world community to address the problem(s) posed by disease as a natural occurrence; a commitment to wage war on disease and not war with disease in Sims' parlance.[13]

In the October 1970 draft of the Convention Article VIII was clearly recognisable as what today we know as Article X.[14] Once introduced the article remained essentially unaltered, suggesting its obligations were uncontentious. The similarities in the language of Articles III and IV of the NPT and Article X of the BWC are obvious, but if there were few calls for enhanced peaceful co-operation in the negotiations themselves why, and how, did it become such an important issue post-negotiation?

The shift in priorities of the NAM from disarmament to development played an important role, because disarmament became a means to achieve development objectives and conferences dealing with disarmament became 'a bargaining chip in the larger context of North-South dialogue.'[15] This factor was multiplied in the BWC with the promise of the biotechnology revolution. In addition, after 1986 the demands of the developing states for access to dual-use biological-related materials increased at a time when the developed states became more reluctant to export biological weapons-related dual-use technology for fear of proliferation. In basic terms competing interests over different obligations in the Convention clashed.

It is this clash which is the most contentious aspect of the Article X debate in the contemporary period, but this itself is a later development. From 1980 onwards, as Sims noted in his study of the First Review Conference, development became more important to the NAM.[16] This resulted in the two separate obligations in Article X being 'conflated into a single unwarranted obligation to promote development.'[17] This is the crux of the matter because in successive final declarations of their review conferences states parties, collectively, reinterpreted Article X of the BWC. This reinterpretation means Article X is a key part of the

166 *The Biological Weapons Convention*

biological disarmament regime balanced on two pillars: disarmament and development. Whether or not all states parties subscribe to this view in the contemporary period is open to question. In fact, the whole notion of a 'bargain' between security and development is being challenged in the BWC and in the NPT. However, the significance of the bargain was illustrated by the statement of Morocco's King Hassan II to the UN Security Council in 1992:[18]

> We believe that disarmament will have no true significance unless it engenders in the countries of the North the dynamics of cooperation with the countries of the South to help the latter to free themselves from underdevelopment.

In other words, the security benefits derived from the BWC have little meaning to states such as Morocco unless development is given equal prominence. Conversely, states parties from the industrialised world view the BWC and disarmament treaties as security agreements and the co-operation aspects as ancillary or subordinate to the core obligations.[19]

VEREX paid scant attention to peaceful co-operation because the process was clearly driven by the notion of verification, but two working papers by Iran pointed to problems vis-à-vis co-operation under the BWC.[20][21] The former drew attention to the increasing reluctance of developed states to trade technology 'under the pretext that they might be used for [biological weapons] production.'[22] The latter detailed the impact of infectious disease in developing states and concluded that assistance to combat such diseases was imperative.[23]

One of the four specific areas identified in the mandate of the Ad Hoc Group was directly related to Article X of the Convention, but the inclusion of this was itself a compromise deal. Even in 1994 very different ideas existed about the meaning of co-operation under Article X of the Convention. Brazil's view was that low participation in existing CBMs was an indicator of the difficulties developing states had in keeping track of their industry.[24] Any future BWC organization, according to Brazil, would have to assist national authorities in preparing their declarations and training personnel to fulfil the obligations of the future compliance regime. Such activities, 'inevitably ... lead to the provision of technical assistance'[25] which Brazil proposed.[26]

> A framework for donor countries who might be interested in providing additional assistance for the improvement of biosafety practices in other countries ... [and] provide a strong incentive for many countries to sustain active participation in the implementation of the Convention.

Other states went further than Brazil; South Africa stated that it believed 'an integral objective of the proposed protocol should be the facilitation of international co-operation and technical assistance.'[27] The draft mandate included provision for 'the formulation of specific measures to promote international cooperation and to provide technical assistance which will enhance effective participation in verification and improve national bio-safety standards and practices.'[28] In essence, the Brazilian proposal. A number of delegations did not consider the Brazilian approach as going far enough and China, India and Iran had a key role in re-drafting the mandate of the Ad Hoc Group to reflect their concerns, and under the final version the Ad Hoc Group had to consider:[29]

> Specific measures designed to ensure effective and full implementation of Article X, which also avoid any restrictions incompatible with the obligations undertaken under the Convention, noting that the provisions of the Convention should not be used to impose restrictions and/or limitations on the transfer for purposes consistent with the objectives and the provisions of the Convention of scientific knowledge, technology, equipment and materials.

Disputes over the mandate were therefore a continuation of previous *minimalist-reformist* contests and, in particular, the 1991 disagreements about taking the BWC to the next phase of its development. In summary, to gain agreement to *negotiate* a Protocol the mandate would have to include a requirement to strengthen international co-operation and address the regulatory aspects of Article X of the Convention. It is important here to note the change in the debate as the mandate reveals where the real dispute actually was, because the majority of this element of the mandate addressed the regulatory paragraph of Article X and not the promotional aspect of the Article. This pitted the moderate NAM and its supporters, such as Brazil, against the real priorities of the hard-line NAM in the negotiations.

As a consequence, by the time the Ad Hoc Group began its work, the peaceful co-operation dispute was itself a proxy for the more important contest related to the issue of export controls for states parties such as India, Iran and China, but the peaceful co-operation aspect remained important because, as Sims outlined; 'the obligation "to avoid hampering" development had been converted into the idea that the implementation of Article X should positively promote it.'[30] Prior to the Fourth Review Conference in 1996 a member of the Chilean government noted that: [31]

> What developing countries require is a substantial exchange of equipment, material and information; increased technical assistance between States; and adequate institutional means in the framework of the United Nations or other existing international organizations.

The language in the 1996 final declaration of the Fourth Review Conference is more strident than in preceding review conferences, with an opening sentence that 'once more emphasizes the increasing importance of Article X,'[32] providing adequate demonstration of the concerns of the developing states. Many of the proposals re-iterated that called for in the final declarations of previous review conferences and a summary of the statements and proposals contained in Table 7.1 and Table 7.2 illustrate that the issues were not new.

As the head of the Iranian delegation at the Special Conference stated, peaceful co-operation 'as prescribed in article X of the Convention, had proved to be a mirage.'[33] The debate has not been a static one and the link to export controls and the perceived and claimed impact of such controls on development became the real

Table 7.1 Statements related to Article X in Final Declarations 1980-1996

Statement	1RC	2RC	3RC	4RC
1. Disarmament should promote economic development	•	•	•	•
2. Implementation has not hampered economic development	•			
3. Increasing importance of Article X			•	•
4. Science has increased potential for co-operation		•	•	•
5. Recognise measures already taken		•	•	•
6. Specialized agencies (WHO) should improve co-operation		•	•	•
7. States urged to promote co-operation		•	•	•
8. States urged to undertake specific measures		•	•	•
9. States should use UN system for co-operation			•	•
10. Establish programme of vaccine development			•	•
11. Implementation must be consistent with BWC obligation				•
12. Article X is a legal obligation				•
13. Provisions should not be used to impose restrictions				•
14. Note mandate of AHG				•
15. Notes 1992 Rio Conference, Agenda 21, & CBD				•
16. Concern over emerging / re-emerging diseases				•
17. Organizations/Institutions to support vaccine production				•

Table 7.2 Specific measures for Article X in Final Declarations 1980-1996

Measure	1RC	2RC	3RC	4RC
1. Increase scientific and technical co-operation	•	•	•	•
2. Transfer / Exchange of information	•	•	•	•
3. Training of personnel	•	•	•	•
4. Transfer of equipment / materials	•	•	•	•
5. Information on implementation	•	•	•	•
6. Transfer / exchange information on research programmes		•	•	•
7. Promotion of contacts between scientists		•	•	•
8. Technical training programmes		•	•	•
9. Conclude bilateral, regional, & multilateral agreements		•	•	•
10. Co-ordinate national and regional programmes		•	•	•
11. International public health & disease control		•	•	•
12. Use UN system		•	•	•
13. UN body to assess means to improve co-operation	•	•	•	
14. Epidemiological & data reporting systems for disease			•	•
15. Establish world data bank			•	•
16. Develop institutional mechanisms			•	•
17. Study enhanced radioactivity on micro-organisms			•	
18. System for global monitoring of disease				•
19. Exchange and training programmes for scientists				•
20. Vaccine production projects in developing states				•

Peaceful Co-operation 169

point of dispute from the early 1990s, as it had done in the NPT and in the final stages of the CWC negotiations. Nevertheless, just as Iran was able to speak openly of the 'mirage' of peaceful co-operation, the Western Group was under no illusion about the level of expectations in this area: 'as one insider put it ... "the road to a Protocol goes through Article X."'[34]

The Ad Hoc Group

In one of the first working papers submitted to the Ad Hoc Group Brazil reiterated its view from the Special Conference that compliance measures and measures related to Article X 'should be mutually reinforcing and ... form a coherent regime.'[35] Brazil proposed that co-operative measures might be implemented in conjunction with compliance measures, such as visits, and envisaged a series of regional or national seminars to precede such visits.[36] While Brazil took a holistic view of the issues facing the Ad Hoc Group in this area the US adopted a more sceptical approach. The first US working paper on this topic made its position clear:[37]

> Agreeing to consider specific measures designed to ensure effective and full implementation of Article X does not infer that Parties to the BWC conclude Article X is presently not fully implemented. It means there is agreement to explore potential additional proposals for mutual benefit of all States parties.

No state, least of all the US, suggested that agreeing to consider compliance measures implied the Convention was not fully implemented; it was precisely because of non-compliance that the Protocol was being negotiated. The US went on to note that states parties would have to consider the issues involved very clearly and that 'identification of needs may be required before programs can be developed.'[38] Thus, just as the Ad Hoc Group had to consider what was required to strengthen compliance with the Convention – its needs – it should consider which aspects of Article X had to be strengthened. The UK took a similar position in the third session:[39]

> discussions on Article X could encompass a very wide range of diverse issues. Although given the terms of Article X, this may be to some extent inevitable, it might be useful for the AHG to focus its attention on a more specific range of activity.

The UK's view was that the Ad Hoc Group had to recognise that 'much of the work in these fields was the preserve of commercial companies. States parties could not replicate activities of the private sector, nor dictate to biotechnology companies what information they should release.'[40] This latter statement was a hostage to fortune because the compliance measures envisaged under the Protocol dictated to biotechnology companies precise information they had to release about their activities in declarations. While the context was different, the principle was the same and it gave succour to the hard-line NAM throughout negotiations.

170 *The Biological Weapons Convention*

The strategy proposed by the UK was for the Ad Hoc Group to begin its work by defining activities directly relevant to the Convention and to consider the extent of such activities undertaken by existing organizations and programmes. According to the UK's view the Ad Hoc Group would then be able to determine whether or not a new role for Article X actually existed. Pre-empting this strategy, the UK paper went on to note that:[41]

> the most appropriate and efficient role may be as a collector and disseminator of information about these activities, as relevant, and as a possible coordinator of advice and assistance on subjects related to implementation of the Convention and the Protocol.

In effect, the creation of an information clearing house, similar to that envisaged under the Convention on Biodiversity.

Given the context of the debate and the number of specific measures identified in the review conferences the early sessions of the Ad Hoc Group were surprisingly marked by a dearth of actual proposals. This was a source of frustration to certain delegations. The NAM had consistently proposed measures in successive review conferences, yet not one of the measures proposed in that forum had been amended or tabled as a formal proposal to the Ad Hoc Group. This might be considered part of a wider negotiating strategy which allowed the developing states to see how much the developed states were willing to offer in this area of the negotiations. It might also be considered as confirmation that the real issue in this debate was not about co-operation at all, but about export controls. The paucity of concrete proposals permitted other delegations to propose that co-operation based on implementation assistance, rather than development represented the way forward. Inactivity by the NAM allowed others to determine the direction of the debate.

The US had explicitly noted that although the NAM had called for specific proposals, they had contributed none to the discussion[42] and US analysis concluded that the measures adopted by the Ad Hoc Group to strengthen Article X must meet three criteria: be reasonably inexpensive, easy to implement, and not require commercial entities to publicly disclose proprietary information. Based on these criteria the US recommended that states parties establish access to the internet 'in countries, or regions of countries, currently underserved, or minimally served by reliable communications.'[43] It is illustrative of the static thinking among most delegations that the significance of this proposal – and the prospects of what it offered – was ignored in favour of more traditional approaches that favoured open-ended commitments to outcomes such as vaccine production facilities.

Brazil and the UK collaborated on the holistic approach to co-operation and submitted a joint paper on a practice non-challenge visit which had, *inter alia*, explored opportunities to address Article X cooperation.[44] The Brazilian approach of mutually reinforcing objectives was deemed a success because the report demonstrated that a visiting team could carry out both compliance and co-operation activities. It noted that:[45]

Peaceful Co-operation 171

this exercise showed that clarification by site personnel, with a view to demonstrating compliance, can be complemented by technical advice from the IT [Investigation Team] to help identify possible improvements to site activities.

Furthermore, there was no conflict between compliance and co-operation; indeed the report claimed that, '[a]s it transpired the two were complementary.'[46] The conclusion presented an endorsement of the Brazilian approach to the problem. A further Brazilian paper at the fifth session posed similar questions to those taken up by the US and the UK on the envisaged scope of any specific measures adopted by the Ad Hoc Group. In particular, how could any future Organization best integrate its activities with existing activities of other organizations and second, what activities should become the sole responsibility of the future OPBW to fulfil the mandate and strengthen the compliance regime?[47] Accepting that there were no easy answers to these questions Brazil proposed five specific measures for further consideration: assistance with declarations; assistance with national legislation; co-operative elements in visits; national and regional seminars; and, promotion of institutional and technical co-operation among institutions involved in the compliance mechanisms.[48]

This practical approach was taken up by the Friend of the Chair in a separate paper that noted, '[t]he need to focus on a more specific range of activities and on "areas directly relevant to the Convention."' [49] In that paper five areas of activity were identified: transfer and exchange of information concerning research in biosciences; active promotion of professional contacts between scientists and technical personnel; encouragement of publication of results of biological research directly related to the Convention in scientific journals generally available to states parties; increased level of technical cooperation and assistance; and, greater co-operation in international public health and disease control.[50]

Those advocating a practical approach were able to demonstrate both their support for Article X and their willingness to mine existing politically-binding agreements – the review conference final declarations – in pursuit of specific measures which could garner widespread support in the Protocol. The need for a practical approach to the issue was underlined further by the final comment in the FOC's paper, in that it introduced 'a note of caution and a dose of realism with regard to the possibilities ... for discussion; and provides some criteria for the establishment of priorities, the concentration on "core areas" relevant to the BWC.'[51]

By the end of the sixth session the elements discussed were structured into a draft article.[52] Although the Ad Hoc Group made its transition to a rolling text, progress on the Article X was initially very slow. The NAM attempted to regain the initiative by inserting new commitments in Article VII (which dealt with co-operation issues). Real divisions emerged at the tenth session in March 1998 with an attempt to narrow the scope of the co-operation aspect by limiting the specific measures required by the mandate. The title of Article VII, *Scientific and Technological Exchange for Peaceful Purposes and Technical Cooperation*, was amended by the Western Group to read, 'Implementation Assistance and Technical Cooperation.'[53] Western states also introduced alternative language to limit the

172 *The Biological Weapons Convention*

future BWC Organization to providing only two types of co-operative support: first, to 'provide a forum for consultation and cooperation in matters to promote implementation assistance and technical cooperation for peaceful purposes.'[54] And second, the Organization would 'assist States parties, upon request, in obtaining implementation assistance.'[55] Although additional elements were inserted into a third sub-paragraph, references to enhancing co-operation and avoiding hampering economic development were omitted.

The proposed amendments were resisted fiercely and were (correctly) interpreted as activity which 'cast doubt on the willingness of the Ad Hoc Group to address measures to implement Article X of the Convention.'[56] This was an interpretation shared by the NAM, which issued a statement to the Ad Hoc Group on the final afternoon of the tenth session in which states parties expressed 'their concerns at attempts to reduce the scope and importance of issues related to Article X of the Convention.'[57] Such concerns were also reiterated at the fourteenth NAM Summit in South Africa, where the final document established a clear position vis-à-vis the negotiation of the Protocol.[58]

> Substantive progress in strengthening the application and full operationalisation of Article X is thus crucial for the conclusion of a *universally acceptable* and legally binding instrument to strengthen the Convention. [Emphasis added]

Stripping away the diplomatic language the message to the Western Group was unequivocal; if there was to be no strengthening of Article X of the Convention there was to be no Protocol. Dismay at these developments was also echoed by non-governmental observers who criticised this retrograde step.[59] The differences about the very purpose of the article continued throughout 1998, but a compromise at the first session of 1999 led to the title of the article reverting back to its original formulation. This resulted in a clear step forward for both the article in question and the approach taken by all parties towards the question of peaceful co-operation. In fact, it marked the beginning of a period where the text of the article was streamlined and the commitments within it developed into a much more coherent whole. By mid-1999 the scope of the article included international co-operation, promotion of trade, and measures to avoid hampering economic development. By the end of 1999 the sole dispute related to the regulatory aspects and the question of export controls.

Development of the rolling text: the promotional aspects

While the rolling text of Article VII did develop into a more coherent whole during the 1999-2000 period it remained a mish-mash of repetitions with similar obligations spread across its discrete sections. The specific co-operation (promotion) measures can be best identified and understood in eight categories. First, the publication, exchange and dissemination of information, which included workshops, training programmes and conferences as modalities for information exchanges, as well as publications, access to publications and a database of useful sources. Second, measures related to combating disease, which was no surprise given that Article X called for states to co-operate in the development and application of science for the prevention of disease. Third, proposals related to improving and developing research capabilities. Fourth, the issue of vaccines, which proved to be a source of division among the states parties, and divergence over the responsibility of the future Organization to develop and finance vaccine production facilities, a proposal which the developed states considered beyond the remit of the future Organization. A fifth cluster included obligations related to technology transfer, while a sixth focussed on co-operation in biodefence. As with vaccine development and production, biodefence split the Ad Hoc Group along North-South lines, with the developed states extremely reluctant to incorporate biodefence into the article, not least because in their view Article 13 on *Assistance and Protection Against Bacteriological (Biological) and Toxin Weapons* incorporated aspects of co-operation. A seventh cluster addressed communication and contacts between states parties and the future Organization, while the eighth focussed on specific training programmes. Practically all of the specific measures contained in the above obligations could be traced back to proposals made at the review conferences.

States parties, however, developed a further category of measures which were Protocol-specific. These measures included capacity building, such as providing support to upgrade laboratories which could then fulfil the criteria for designation and certification by the Organization. Others were more generic, such as biosafety practices and regulations, Good Laboratory Practice, Good Manufacturing Practice, occupational health and safety practices, environmental protection, and biological containment. Many of the developed states actively supported the adoption of these types of measures among states parties and lobbied for the Organization's Technical Secretariat to take a lead role in promoting such activities. Support for such measures by Western states was in part due to the specific and tangible nature of these provisions when compared to the open-ended commitments contained in other areas of the text. For example, the commitment to promote and support the 'monitoring, diagnosis, detection, prevention and control of outbreaks of diseases, and international co-operation on the research, development and production of vaccines'[60] was so open-ended and unquantifiable it was practically meaningless in terms of specific actions individual states parties could implement. How would a state party, or the states parties, ever assess the implementation of such a measure and whether or not the obligation was being fulfilled? The triumph of rhetoric and vacuity over substance in certain measures was all too obvious.

Another area of the text that the developed states strongly supported was the provisions for Protocol implementation assistance. In this area any state party could receive assistance related to the establishment and functioning of the required National Authority, the preparation of declarations, the necessary internal legislation, and training for national authority personnel.

States parties were also innovative in the creation of mechanisms to facilitate co-operation upon implementation. Provisions existed in the text of the article for agreements and arrangements to be reached with the FAO, the International Centre

174 *The Biological Weapons Convention*

for Genetic Engineering and Biotechnology, the International Vaccine Institute, the OIE, the OPCW, the United Nations Environment Programme, the United Nations Industrial Development Organization, the WHO, and the Secretariat of the Convention on Biological Diversity. However, it was the mechanisms within the Protocol that were truly innovative, such as the Co-operation Committee and the decision to use visits as a conduit for technical co-operation, as well as the requirement for annual declarations on the measures taken to implement co-operation aspects of the Convention and the Protocol. These would have gone a long way to fulfilling the politically-binding commitments from 1980 onwards.

The Co-operation Committee

It had been a long-standing objective of the NAM to develop specific institutional frameworks to facilitate the implementation of Article X of the BWC, but it was not until 1999 that a framework of institutional mechanisms began to emerge: in particular, the proposal for a Co-operation Committee.[61] Like Article X itself, the genesis of this committee can be found in the NPT particularly Article V of the NPT and its 'appropriate international body' intended to promote and ensure the benefits of peaceful nuclear explosions were made available to the non-nuclear weapons states. While the IAEA and the UN General Assembly agreed that the IAEA was in fact the 'appropriate body' referred to in Article V of the NPT, during the actual NPT negotiations the developing states had wanted to leave the door open for a new international body responsive to their needs, rather than those of the nuclear weapons states.[62] The Co-operation Committee would also have represented the fulfilment of developing states' objectives for the BWC, first expressed in 1980, for co-operation on an institutionalised basis. These states parties were also taking on board developments in the CWC, in ensuring that co-operation would not be sidelined or subordinated in the new Organization, which many feared was happening in the OPCW.

During 1999 different visions of the Co-operation Committee emerged within the Ad Hoc Group. The original NAM vision ascribed to the Committee a dominant role in the future Organization for the promotion and co-ordination co-operation under the Protocol. It granted to the Committee five functions and powers, the fifth of which permitted the Co-operation Committee to adopt 'specific measures to promote international exchange in the field of biotechnology for peaceful purposes.'[63] Thus, under these powers the Co-operation Committee would be able to commit the OPBW and the states parties to new and additional measures for co-operation upon entry into force of the Protocol. This was too open-ended for the Western states parties, but the main difference between the developed and the developing states was whether or not the Committee dealt only with the co-operative aspects of the Article or addressed the co-operative and regulatory aspects of the Article, given its envisaged function in the receipt and assessment of the annual declaration on peaceful co-operation. The Netherlands, New Zealand, Australia, France, Germany, Sweden, Switzerland, and the UK all supported the Co-operation Committee, but the implicit function of the Committee to 'judge' the level of compliance with the peaceful co-operation obligation

Peaceful Co-operation 175

inherent to the NAM proposal and its ability to adopt and commit states parties to new measures was rejected.[64] These states parties were willing to accept a Committee which made recommendations to the Conference of States Parties, but they were unwilling to permit the establishment of a Committee which might develop new commitments unchecked by all states parties. Hence, by the end of 1999 the key sticking point was the structure and role of the Committee and the power of the Committee within the Organization.[65]

Although differences did exist relating to its exact powers and functions, the Co-operation Committee was always envisaged as a subsidiary organ of the Organization which, as its name suggested, would serve as a forum for consultation to promote the implementation of Article X of the BWC and co-operative and assistance provisions in the Protocol. Potential sticking points in the make up and function of the Committee, in particular whether its membership was open to all states parties or it was an Executive Council-type body with elected members taking decisions for all were resolved in the composite text. (It ended up with 57 elected members, but any state party could attend and had access to the deliberations of the Committee.) Other areas of contention were hived off to separate sections of the article or, in one case (export controls) a different article of the Protocol. Thus, the judicial nature of the Committee implied by its hard-line NAM proponents throughout 1999 and 2000 was headed off by the separate section which established mechanisms to review and consider any concerns about the implementation of Article X that ostensibly dealt with the regulatory aspects and export control issues, and the requirement for annual declarations under section G of the Article (see below). Separating these elements from the original vision allowed all states parties to accept and support the idea of an appropriate institutional body to focus on co-operation in the BWC, thus realising a long standing objective of the developing states.

Visits

Although many of the ideas put forward during the early debates on the provisions of this article were subsequently revised and changed beyond recognition, Brazil and a number of other pragmatic states never gave up on achieving a holistic approach to co-operation and compliance. Once the states parties had agreed in principle to establish a new organisation for the BWC, the Technical Secretariat was allocated a clear role in co-operation activities through the provisions for *Co-operation and assistance in the context of visits*.[66] This built upon the proposals mooted by Brazil at the Special Conference and in the early sessions of the Ad Hoc Group and envisaged measures aimed to capitalise on the non-challenge nature of the visits. The idea was to provide practical advice and assistance to facilities in a number of areas, such as biosafety, diagnostic techniques, national and international regulatory mechanisms, marketing and sale of products, training requirements, access to information and publications, and more specialised assistance. This achievement in early 2000 indicated that the Ad Hoc Group was able to devise and agree on practical structures for the delivery of scientific and technical co-operation. As such, it gave many delegations a sense of hope during a

176 *The Biological Weapons Convention*

period when the negotiations appeared to be stalling and, in a separate context, sweetened routine on-site activities and raised the bar further for those developing states looking to weaken – or in some cases omit – routine on-site activities.

Annual declarations

As one commentator noted in 1980, 'those countries which had hopes of benefiting from the "peaceful co-operation" clauses of the Convention ... will want to know what agreements have been made which might come under this rubric.'[67] This did indeed prove to be the case and in 1980 Brazil and Argentina proposed that 'the next Review Conference should receive information collated by the Secretariat on the implementation of Article Ten.'[68] Such a request was repeated at each successive review conference. The proposal subsequently found its way into the rolling text[69] and was later developed by Iran[70] and, later still, an actual format for the declaration requirement was submitted.[71] It was accepted by a majority of states parties and by the end of the eighteenth session the Ad Hoc Group had agreed on the principle of annual declaration on the implementation of Article X of the Convention and Article 14 of the Protocol (as it became), as well as on the mechanism for consideration of the annual reports by both the Director-General and the Co-operation Committee. The problem was the duplication of such activities maintained by the contested similar declaration under Article III of the rolling text on declarations. The key difference being that declarations under Article III were subject to on-site activities and specific clarification procedures; declarations under other articles were not subject to such explicit procedures. Even though Iran, among a few others, attempted to maintain Article X declarations under both articles, the inclusion of such declarations in the composite text under Article 14 only was no great surprise. Nevertheless, the anodyne language was very carefully constructed.

Although the actual text did not say as much, the implication of a declaration was that the future Organization, or its subsidiary organs, would have to make some kind of judgement on the activities of states parties concerning their implementation of these Articles. This was implicit in the Director-General's role of 'suggesting specific practical steps' for the enhanced implementation of peaceful co-operation; clearly, if both the Director-General and the Co-operation Committee were to make recommendations on how to strengthen the implementation of Article X of the Convention and Article 14 of the Protocol, a judgement about the level of compliance based on the submitted declaration(s) had to be made. This was a factor everyone understood, but was never brought out in the negotiations themselves.

Development of the rolling text: regulatory aspects

Three areas in Article 14 of the Protocol related to the regulatory aspects of provisions of the BWC's Article X. In the general provisions section the text reiterated the obligation contained in Article X:2. This commitment was itself

Peaceful Co-operation 177

expanded in a separate section on *Measures to avoid hampering the economic and technological development of States parties.* The language in this section of the Article drew from similar provisions in Article XI of the CWC, but was itself supplemented by a third section outlining the procedures to review and consider any concerns related to actual implementation. This was basically short-hand for considering export control issues, and the context of the debate must be understood by the linkage of the export control issue in the NPT, the CWC and the BWC, as discussed in the preceding chapter.

The contentious element was whether or not the language sought to abolish the Australia Group – or other similar export control mechanisms – or recognised the existing obligations under Article III of the Convention: in particular, the non-proliferation commitment to 'any recipient whatsoever' regardless of whether or not the recipient was a state party. As early as 1997 the Chairman of the Ad Hoc Group had noted that:[72]

> The solution which was agreed in respect of the CWC was an undertaking to revisit the need for export control regimes in a couple of years time. A similar solution seems unlikely to be acceptable to the developing countries in respect of the BWC. These countries consider that the undertakings under the CWC are too weak and that these undertakings are not being met, and consequently the developing countries are keen to see a true elimination of export control regimes in the verification protocol. However, several industrialised countries regard export control regimes both now and in the future as being a necessary element to meet their obligations under Article III of the BWC as an important ingredient of an integrated non-proliferation regime.

In completing the CWC negotiations the O'Sullivan statement might have been an acceptable constructive ambiguity for the CWC. In the Ad Hoc Group it haunted and soured the negotiations in Geneva. A number of states parties required what could be considered as a *CWC-plus* solution to the problem. This would entail an obligation to review national measures to prevent proliferation within a specified timeframe. The other contentious issue was to what extent, if any, the Executive Council or the Conference of States Parties could make recommendations to states parties to bring their national regulations into line with the obligations of the Convention and the Protocol. As in other areas of the text, there was a dichotomy and contradiction in the approach of states parties.

In this particular case, the NAM preferred the Executive Council to pass judgement on whether or not a state party had complied with reviewing its export control legislation with an emphasis on not hampering peaceful development. These states parties also proposed the Executive Council have the power to require a state party to change its legislation. As might be expected, the Western Group opposed this. However, in the area of national implementation legislation the preference of the Western Group supported an explicit requirement for such legislation and an implicit assessment of it through the submission of information on the legislation, regulations, and other measures in the proposed annual declaration in another article of the Protocol. As we have seen in chapter three, the NAM opposed this. In different areas of the Protocol different states parties were

178 *The Biological Weapons Convention*

not willing to accept that the Organization could pass judgement on their national regulations and, potentially, find such procedures or practices were out of line with the requirements of the BWC and its Protocol.

Delegations attempted to circumvent this problem by incorporating specific procedures to review and consider any complaints related to the implementation of the Convention and the Protocol. While all delegations agreed that a review mechanism was a worthwhile procedure, opinion diverged on the powers and functions of the Executive Council and, ultimately, the Conference of States Parties. At the end of 1999 the existing proposals were revamped in a separate *Implementation Follow-Up* section.[73] This built upon the earlier proposals and affirmed the right of any state party to raise a concern about the implementation of Article X of the Convention, and the attendant article in the Protocol, and bring it to the attention of the Executive Council.

The basis of the review procedure had been agreed by early 2000 and the one remaining difficulty related to the powers of the Executive Council and its ability to recommend a solution(s) to states parties to resolve any dispute. Given that under Article IX of the rolling text (on the Organization) the Executive Council could 'request a State Party to take measures to redress the situation within a specified timeframe'[74] objections to a similar procedure related to peaceful co-operation and the regulations linked to non-proliferation commitments indicated a lack of consistency in the Ad Hoc Group. It was clear that the provisions of Article IX applied to *all* areas of the Protocol and no state party could reasonably claim that the provisions did not apply to the question of export controls. In that respect, this additional section was superfluous; but the NAM insisted on attempting to spell out a judicial process to review the implementation of export licensing regulations. It is significant that no comparable process existed in any area related to compliance issues. The resolution to the problem was found through a finesse of language. Explicit reference to the power(s) of the Conference of States Parties was omitted and so future difficulties would have become a question of who could control the Executive Council and the decisions of the Conference of States Parties. In short, who could muster sufficient support to block criticisms of their implementation of the Protocol and the BWC.

The composite text

Despite the early difficulties by the middle of 1999 all delegations appeared to have accepted the general scope of the Article and a framework of specific measures had been developed in the rolling text. As the negotiations continued the differences among delegations were narrowed and by the end of 2000 very few issues required attention. Many of these related to very specific measures, such as the inclusion of co-operation on biodefence matters, the powers and functions of the Co-operation Committee and the provisions related to the regulatory aspects of the article. In drafting the composite text the Chairman was able to draw from a series of informal consultations and the main area of concern was the actual scope of the regulatory measures within the article related to Article III of BWC.

Peaceful Co-operation 179

Table 7.3 Co-operation principles in the composite text

Statement	Article 14	Comment
(1) Disarmament should promote development		Implicit in Article
(2) Implementation has not hampered development		
(3) Increasing importance of peaceful co-operation		Preamble #14
(4) Scientific developments have increased potential for co-operation		Preamble #14
(5) Recognition of measures already undertaken	#4	
(6) UN agencies should have a role in co-operation	Section (F)	
(7) States parties urged to promote co-operation	Section (A)	
(8) States parties urged to undertake specific measures		Explicit throughout Article XIV
(9) States parties should use existing institutional mechanisms of UN	#4 and Section (F)	
(10) Efforts to establish international programme of vaccine development		Implicit in #4, #21(a) and #25
(11) Implementation to be consistent with obligations under the BWC	#2, #3, and Section (C)	Plus review & compliant procedures under Section (E)
(12) Legal obligations under Article X	#1(c) and Section (C)	Plus review & complaint procedures under Section (E)
(13) Provisions should not be used to impose restrictions	#1(c) and Section (C)	Plus review & complaint procedures under Section (E)
(14) Note mandate of AHG		Not applicable
(15) Link to 1992 Rio Conference, Agenda 21, and CBD		Implicit in Section (F)
(16) Concern over emerging/re-emerging diseases		Implicit throughout Article XIV
(17) Support vaccine production projects		Implicit in obligations, & #21(a)

The extent of strengthening achieved by the Ad Hoc Group in its drafting of the Protocol is illustrated by Tables 7.3 and 7.4. Of the seventeen identified principles and general statements made at the review conferences, eight were not explicit in Article 14 of the composite text. Of those eight, four were implicit within the article: disarmament should promote economic and technological development; United Nations specialised agencies should participate in discussions to improve institutional co-operation; efforts to establish a programme of vaccine

180   *The Biological Weapons Convention*

development; and, multilateral organisations should support vaccine production projects.

Table 7.4   Co-operation measures in the composite text

Measure	Article 14	Comment
1. Scientific & technical co-operation	#1(a); 3; 4; 29(c)	
2. Transfer & exchange of information	#1(a); 4(a); 21(h); 23(g)-(j); 29(a)(i); 29(a)(v); 29(d)	
3. Training of personnel	#4(i); 21(e); 23(e)	
4. Transfer of equipment & materials	#1(a)-(b); 4(g)	
5. Information on implementation	Section (E), (G), #33	
6. Transfer & exchange information on research programmes	#4(a); 4(d); 21(g)	
7. Promote contacts between scientists	#29(c)	
8. Technical training programmes	#21(e); 23(e)	
9. Conclude bilateral, regional, & multilateral agreements	Section (F)	
10. Co-ordinate national & regional programmes		Co-operation Committee and Section (F)
11. International public health & disease control	#4(b)-(d); 4(h); 21(d); 29(b)	
12. Use UN system	Section (F)	
13. UN body to assess means to improve co-operation		Implicit (and superseded) by future OPBW and Co-operation Committee
14. Epidemiological & data reporting systems for disease	#29(b)	
15. Establish world data bank	#4(e); 29(a)(iv)	
16. Develop institutional mechanisms	Section (D)	Co-operation Committee, Visits, & implementation assistance
17. Study enhanced radioactivity on micro-organisms		Not mentioned
18. Global monitoring of disease	#4(c), (f), (g)	
19.Exchange & training programmes	#4(i)	
20. Vaccine production projects	#21(a)	

A further two issues were addressed by the Preamble of the Protocol, the increasing importance of the Article X and the increased potential for co-operation.[75] Of the remaining issues, one would no longer be valid – the mandate of the Ad Hoc Group – if the Ad Hoc Group completed its work by the 2001 deadline. Therefore, only one statement had neither an explicit nor implicit

Peaceful Co-operation 181

reference in the composite text; that implementation of the BWC had not hampered economic and technological development. That statement was made only at the First Review Conference in 1980 and not repeated at subsequent review conferences.

Of the twenty proposals for specific measures made at previous review conferences, only one had not been transformed into a specific obligation within the Protocol, or was implicit in the obligations undertaken; namely a study of the effect of enhanced radioactivity on micro-organisms. A further ten areas of co-operation were developed and adopted by the Ad Hoc Group during the negotiations: Designation of laboratories; Biosafety; Environmental protection; Occupational health; Good Laboratory Practice/Good Manufacturing Practice; Diagnostics; International Regulations; Protocol implementation assistance; Information sharing on genetically-modified organisms; and, Regulations governing handling and transportation, use and release of agents.

Taking all this together the Ad Hoc Group had translated general statements and principles into specific legally binding obligations for co-operation under the future Protocol. Although the promotional aspects of the Article could not be viewed in isolation from its regulatory aspects, much greater progress had been made on strengthening co-operation and assistance provisions. However, in the regulatory aspect the composite text went further than the CWC with its adoption of a specific timeframe for the first review of national measures taken to implement non-proliferation obligations. Moreover, in providing a specific review mechanism for any state party to bring its concerns about the implementation of the provisions of Article X of the Convention and Article 14 of the Protocol, the composite text had addressed the principal objective of states in the NAM.

Western states were reluctant to accept a separate review mechanism, but any compliance issue brought to the attention of the future Organization related to co-operation would have to demonstrate that the application of provisions of the Convention and/or the Protocol had hampered the economic and technological development of a state party. Statements would not be enough: evidence would be required. Thus, this actually acted as a safeguard because the review mechanism of this article could be used to the advantage of the Western Group upon implementation to rebut any future claims about their activities hampering the development of other states parties.

Minimalism or *Reform*

The Ad Hoc Group established a new benchmark for the co-operative elements of multilateral disarmament treaties. It also established new mechanisms and institutions to facilitate such activities, such as the Co-operation Committee and the requirement for annual declarations, and it developed the use of a compliance measure, visits, as a conduit for co-operation. Any assessment of the degree of strengthening of Article X of the Convention must take into account that all but one of the specific measures identified at the review conferences had found their way into the text of the Protocol. On that evidence alone the co-operation aspect of

182　　　*The Biological Weapons Convention*

the article was strengthened to a significant degree in line with the objectives of *reformists*.

Less clear in the final stages of the negotiations, before they collapsed, was the extent to which the Ad Hoc Group had strengthened the regulatory aspects of the article. Although it appeared that most delegations accepted the provisions of Article 14 of the composite text, the sections related to the regulatory aspect contained language drawn from, and included in, the CWC. It is too early to draw definitive conclusions about the CWC, but the implementation, and interpretation, of the obligations within Article XI of the CWC suggested that the same language or obligations within the Protocol might encounter problems. However, Article 14 had gone further than the CWC in some respects, particularly its separate review mechanisms, and when the regulatory aspects of the article were considered in conjunction with the measures and obligations contained in Article 7 (non-proliferation) the Convention had, quite clearly, been strengthened. The final draft was a victory for the *reformists* which in this area were the NAM states.

Notes

1.　See for example statements made at the Fourth Review Conference: 'Statement by Ambassador Munir Akram at the Fourth Review Conference of the Parties to the Convention on the Prohibition of the Development, Production and Stockpiling of Bacteriological (Biological) and Toxin Weapons and on their Destruction' Tuesday, 26 November 1996; 'Statement by H. E. Mr. Sirous Nasseri Ambassador and Permanent Representative of the Islamic Republic of Iran to the United Nations Office in Geneva to the Fourth Review Conference of the States parties to the Biological and Toxin Weapons Convention' Geneva 26 November 1996 (pp. 5-6); 'Statement by H.E. Ambassador Ejoh Abuah, Permanent Representative of Nigeria to the United Nations in Geneva to the Fourth Review Conference of the Biological Weapons Convention' 25 November 1996; and 'Statement by H.E. Ms. Arundhati Ghose, Ambassador, Permanent Representative of India to the Fourth Review Conference of the Parties to the Convention on the Prohibition of the Development, Production and Stockpiling of Bacteriological (Biological) and Toxin Weapons and on their Destruction' Geneva, 26 November 1996.
2.　Convention on the Prohibition of the Development, Production and Stockpiling of Bacteriological (Biological) and Toxin Weapons and on Their Destruction.
3.　Erhard Geissler, 'Arms control, health care and technology transfer under the Vaccines for Peace programme' Erhard Geissler and John P. Woodall (Editors) *Control of Dual-Threat Agents: The Vaccines for Peace Programme SIPRI Chemical & Biological warfare Studies No. 15* (Oxford University Press, Oxford, 1994) p.27.
4.　BWC 1RC, BWC/CONF.I/4 (20 February 1980) p.1.
5.　ACDA, 'Statement by the Swedish Representative (Myrdal) to the Conference of the Committee on Disarmament: Chemical and Biological Weapons, April 9, 1970' *Documents on Disarmament 1970* (Washington, U.S. Government Printing Office, 1971) p.138.
6.　ACDA, 'Statement by the Swedish Representative (Myrdal) to the Conference of the Committee on Disarmament: Chemical and Biological Weapons, July 21, 1970'

Peaceful Co-operation 183

(CCD/PV.480 pp 5-10) *Documents on Disarmament 1970* (Washington, U.S. Government Printing Office, 1971) p.336.

7. William C Potter, 'Managing Proliferation: problems and prospects for US-Soviet Cooperation' Dagobert L Brito, Michael D Intriligator, Adele E Wick (Editors) *Strategies for Managing Nuclear Proliferation: Economic and Political issues* (Lexington, Massachusetts, Lexington Books, 1983), pp.245-246.

8. Ibid., see note 62, p.247.

9. Amy E Smithson, 'Separating Fact from Fiction: The Australia Group and the Chemical Weapons Convention' Occasional Paper Number 34, March, The Henry L Stimson Center (Washington, 1997) p.17.

10. Jozef Goldblat, 'The Problem of Chemical and Biological warfare: A study of the historical, technical, military, legal and political aspects of CBW, and possible disarmament measures' *Volume IV CB Disarmament Negotiations, 1920-1970* (Stockholm Almqvist & Wiksell, 1971) p.256.

11. 'Statement by the Swedish Representative (Myrdal) to the Conference of the Committee on Disarmament: Chemical and Biological Weapons, July 21, 1970' (CCD/PV.480 pp. 5-10) p.336.

12. ACDA, 'Remarks on Biological Warfare by Dr. Joshua Lederberg to the Conference of the Committee on Disarmament" August 5, 1970 (CCD/312, August 27, 1970) *Documents on Disarmament 1970* (Washington, U.S. Government Printing Office, 1971) p.361.

13. Nicholas A. Sims, 'The Evolution of Biological Disarmament' (Oxford, OUP, 2001) p.146.

14. ACDA, 'Revised Communist Draft Convention Submitted to the General Assembly: Prohibition of the Development, Production and Stockpiling of Chemical and Bacteriological (Biological) Weapons and on the Destruction of Such Weapons' October 23, 1970 *Documents on Disarmament 1970* (Washington, U.S. Government Printing Office, 1971) p.535.

15. Avi Beker, 'Disarmament Without Order: The Politics of Disarmament at the United Nations' (London, Greenwood Press, 1985) p.77.

16. Nicholas A Sims, 'The Diplomacy of Biological Disarmament: Vicissitudes of a Treaty in Force, 1975–1985' (New York, St. Martin's Press, 1988) p.145.

17. Sims, 'The Evolution of Biological Disarmament' p.120. See Sims' chapter on 'The Regime of Development' pp.119-150 for a full discussion of the changing context of Article X of the BWC.

18. Smithson, 'Separating Fact from Fiction' p.20.

19. See for example 'Statement by Ambassador Donald A. Mahley United States Special Negotiator for Chemical and Biological Arms Control Issues' to the Ad Hoc Group on 25 July 2001, in which it was stated that the concept of technological development was a subordinate element to compliance enhancement under the Protocol.

20. VEREX, BWC/CONF.III/VEREX.WP.27 'Concerns and views of a vaccine producer of the developing countries' Working paper by the Islamic Republic of Iran, 7 April 1992.

21. VEREX, BWC/CONF.III/VEREX.WP.26 'Natural Biological Bomb: a need for biotechnology in Developing countries' Working paper by the Islamic Republic of Iran, 7 April 1992.

22. Ibid., p.5.

23. VEREX, BWC/CONF.III/VEREX.WP.27 p.3.

24. BWC SPCONF, BWC/SPCONF (19-30 September), Part III, p.22.
25. Ibid., pp.22-23.
26. Ibid., p.23.
27. Ibid., p.39.
28. Ibid., p.66.
29. Ibid., p.10
30. Sims, 'The Evolution of Biological Disarmament' p.130.
31. Camilo Sanhueza, 'The Obligation to Cooperate in Technology Transfer: Article X of the BTWC' *UNIDIR Newsletter*, Number 33/96 p.80.
32. United Nations, 'Fourth Review Conference of the States parties to the Convention on the Prohibition of the Development, Production and Stockpiling of Bacteriological (Biological) and Toxin Weapons and on Their Destruction, BWC/CONF.IV/9 (December 1996) p.23.
33. BWC SPCONF, BWC/SPCONF/1 p.111.
34. Amy E Smithson, 'Tall Order: Crafting a Meaningful Verification Protocol for the Biological Weapons Convention' *Politics and the Life Sciences* (March, 1999) p.82.
35. BWC AHG, BWC/AD HOC GROUP/22 'Working paper submitted by Brazil – Specific Measures for Implementation of Article X in the Context of a Compliance Regime for the BWC' (13 July 1995) p.1.
36. Ibid., p.2.
37. BWCAHG, BWC/AD HOC GROUP/23 'Working paper submitted by the United States of America – Discussion of Potential Article X Issues' (12 July 1995) p.1.
38. Ibid., p.2.
39. BWC AHG, BWC/AD HOC GROUP/WP.7 'FOC Article X: Areas of Biological Activity of Direct Relevance to the Convention' (Working paper submitted by the United Kingdom) (28 November 1995) p.1.
40. Ibid., p.2.
41. Ibid., p.3.
42. BWC AHG, BWC/AD HOC GROUP/WP.25, 'Paper submitted by the United States of America – Computer Networking as a means of Strengthening the BWC' (1 December 1995) p.1.
43. Ibid.
44. BWC AHG, BWC/AD HOC GROUP/WP.76 'Working paper submitted by Brazil and the United Kingdom of Great Britain and Northern Ireland – Report of a Joint UK/Brazil Practice Non-Challenge Visit' (18 July 1996) p.1.
45. Ibid., p.7.
46. Ibid., p.8.
47. BWC AHG, BWC/AD HOC GROUP/WP.104 'Working paper submitted by Brazil – Article X Implementation in a BWC Compliance Regime: Aspects of Cooperative Approach' (17 September 1996) p.4.
48. Ibid., p.5.
49. BWC AHG, BWC/AD HOC GROUP/31 'Procedural Report of the Ad Hoc Group of the States Parties to the Convention on the Prohibition of the Development, Production and Stockpiling of Bacteriological (Biological) and Toxin Weapons and on Their Destruction' (26 July 1996) p.73.
50. Ibid., pp.64-66.
51. Ibid., p.77.
52. BWC AHG, BWC/AD HOC GROUP/WP.150 'Working paper submitted by the Friend of the Chair on Article X' (21 March 1997).

53. Graham S. Pearson, 'Progress at the Ad Hoc Group in Geneva' Quarterly Review Number 3, *The CBW Conventions Bulletin* Issue No. 40 (June 1998) p.2.
54. BWC AHG, BWC/AD HOC GROUP/40 'Procedural Report of the Ad Hoc Group of the States Parties to the Convention on the Prohibition of the Development, Production and Stockpiling of Bacteriological (Biological) and Toxin Weapons and on Their Destruction' (17 March 1998) Annex I, p.17.
55 Ibid.
56. Pearson, 'Progress at the Ad Hoc Group in Geneva' Quarterly Review Number 3, p.2.
57. BWC AHG, BWC/AD HOC GROUP/40
58. Non-Aligned Movement 'Final Document XII NAM Summit' Durban, 29 August – 3 September 1998 p.30.
59. Pearson, 'Progress at the Ad Hoc Group in Geneva' Quarterly Review Number 3, p.3.
60. BWC AHG, BWC/AD HOC GROUP/CRP.8 (Technically Corrected Version) 30 May 2001, p.75.
61. BWC AHG, BWC/AD HOC GROUP/WP.349 'Working paper submitted by the Group of NAM and Other Countries – Establishment of a Cooperation Committee' (January 1999).
62. David Fischer, 'History of the International Atomic Energy Agency' (Austria, IAEA, 1997) p.151.
63. BWC AHG, BWC/AD HOC GROUP/WP.349 (21 January 1999).
64. Jean Pascal Zanders and Maria Wahlberg, 'Chemical and biological weapon developments and arms control' *SIPRI Yearbook 2000* (Oxford, Oxford University Press, 2000) pp.525-526. See particularly the reference to the Australia, France, Germany, Sweden, Switzerland, UK non-paper on the Committee.
65. Henrietta Wilson, 'Strengthening the BWC: Issues for the Ad Hoc Group' *Disarmament Diplomacy* Issue number 42 (December 1999) p.30.
66. BWC AHG, BWC/AD HOC GROUP/CRP.8 (Technically Corrected Version) 30 May 2001 pp.80-81.
67. Nicholas A. Sims 'Prospects for the Biological Weapons Convention Review Conference' (January 1980), *ADIU Report* II.1 (March 1980) pp.6-7 by the University of Sussex Armament and Disarmament Information Unit, cited in Sims, 'The Diplomacy of Biological Disarmament' p.145. See footnote 42.
68. Sims, 'The Diplomacy of Biological Disarmament' p.147.
69. BWC AHG BWC/AD HOC GROUP/36 p.54, paragraph 5.
70. BWC AHG BWC/AD HOC GROUP/WP.227 'Working paper submitted by the Islamic Republic of Iran – Declaration on the implementation of Article X of the Convention' (1 October 1997).
71. BWC AHG, BWC/AD HOC GROUP/WP.350 'Working paper submitted by the Group of NAM and Other Countries – Information to be Provided in the Declaration of Implementation of Article X of the Convention' (21 January 1999).
72. Tibor Tóth, 'A window of opportunity for the BWC Ad Hoc Group' *The CBW Convention Bulletin* Issue Number 37 (September 1998) p.2.
73. BWC AHG, BWC/AD HOC GROUP/49/Add.3, p.78.
74. BWC AHG, BWC/AD HOC GROUP/51 (Part I) p.118 (see paragraph 34).
75. BWC AHG, BWC/AD HOC GROUP/CRP.8 see Preamble, 13th and 14th paragraphs.

Chapter 8

The Organization

Introduction

Although the focus of concern among most states parties has always been the lack of effective compliance mechanisms, institutional and organizational issues related to the BWC have been an issue of interest for many of the external observers of the Convention. Indeed as one of the principal proponents of creating institutional mechanisms for the BWC has correctly remarked, even before the negotiations were completed in 1971 it was noted that the BWC would require 'continuous definition and a serious administration'[1] to be effective.

In this final chapter on the negotiation of the Protocol our attention is focussed on the issue of a BWC implementing organization. As we have seen in the opening chapters, by the early 1990s states parties were themselves making proposals at the review conferences for some kind of standing administrative unit to oversee implementation of the Convention and, more specifically, the new additional (politically-binding) commitments such as the CBMs. By the time the Ad Hoc Group began its negotiations the IAEA had revamped and improved the institutional mechanisms to assist its implementation of the Safeguards agreements intrinsic to the NPT, the OPCW had been created and a provisional secretariat was in place to assist entry into force of the CWC, and the negotiations on the Comprehensive Test Ban Treaty were on course to produce a new organization to oversee implementation of that Treaty. As in all others areas, the BWC looked increasingly out of step with other comparable disarmament and non-proliferation agreements. While not an issue to grab the headlines the lack of supporting institutional mechanisms was widely considered a major flaw in the BWC. As a consequence, the Protocol negotiations were expected to produce a new international organization to implement the Protocol *and* the Convention, even though they were separate legal agreements.

The need for an institution

Writing after the demise of the Protocol Nicholas Sims asked; '[w]hy is there no Organization for the Prohibition of Biological Weapons (OPBW)? The world has had its OPCW for 5 years. No one would want to suggest that biological weapons constitute a lesser threat than chemical weapons, or that biological disarmament is less in need of strengthening than chemical.'[2] The fact that it was a UK academic asking such questions accurately reflected a central issue in the debate about a

188 *The Biological Weapons Convention*

BWC organization. Rather than the states parties, it was 'Friends of the Convention' such as Sims who initially highlighted the need for institutions to support the BWC and later, the creation of a fully fledged international organization. Only at the Third Review Conference in 1991 did the states parties themselves push for the creation of a small, two-person secretariat, to assist in collating, distributing, and analyzing the CBMs. However, with the failure of even that proposal, the *reformists* increased their demands during the VEREX process, via the Special Conference, and eventually in the Ad Hoc Group.

The importance of an OPBW – or something akin to it – in the contemporary period has in fact been underlined by the failure of the negotiations, but many of the arguments put forward to support the creation of such an institution were first articulated in the early to mid 1980s by non-state actors.

After outlining the vicissitudes of the first ten years of the BWC in *The Diplomacy of Biological Disarmament* Sims developed a twelve point 'Agenda for Recovery', the eighth of which read.[3]

> Installation of a limited set of permanent institutions ... sufficient to ensure 'continuous definition and a serious administration' of the treaty régime and to encourage the maximisation of its benefits to all.

This vision was outlined in a subsequent chapter and central to the call for arresting the decline of the BWC was 'management of the treaty régime' and a commitment from the states parties to 'devote far greater resources' to the BWC. Sims, himself, was taking up the theme developed by Leonard Beaton and the latter's observation and analysis on the possibility of a BWC in the early 1970s. Beaton stated that:[4]

> it is clear a general Convention must be backed up by continuous definition and a serious administration. Otherwise, it could become a screen behind which one or more powers came to mobilize the full military potential of modern medical advances while more amiable peoples deceived themselves that they were safe.

Until 1991 the failure of the BWC to ensure complete biological disarmament and the failure of the states parties to both admit this (and to challenge forcefully non-compliance) did in fact result in a situation where more amiable peoples deceived themselves they were safe. It permitted states parties such as the USSR to deceive others. International treaties are living documents; international law, like any other law, requires enforcement if the obligations are to be met and the desired outcome (in this case disarmament) realised. However, the situation in the BWC was aptly described by the UK Minister present at the Fourth Review Conference in 1996.[5]

> A general perception held that the biological weapons problem was solved; that it did not present a real risk or threat; and that it did not merit a place on serious arms control agendas .... But over the last decade, we have seen these comfortable assumptions overturned.

As he later went on to note, 'a simple, international ban on biological weapons alone is not enough.'[6] Not everyone was as indifferent to the shortcomings of the

The Organization

BWC as the states parties. In particular the notion of the BWC being in force meaning that the Convention required no on-going attention was coming under attack even in the mid 1980s, as Sims noted:[7]

> It is precisely that 'serious administration' which is lacking. Those who took the British initiative of 1968 and watered it down into the Convention of 1972 gave the world biological disarmament on the cheap: a disarmament régime of minimal machinery which would cost next to nothing to sustain. It is now painfully evident that these short-term savings have been outweighed by the long-term costs of a régime lacking the means to sustain its credibility in the face of suspicious events which cannot be resolved one way or the other.

In other words, states parties were remiss in their attention to actually ensuring implementation of the BWC. This was not a BWC-specific phenomenon; rather it was a problem across nearly all disarmament and arms control agreements and there was a growing realisation as the Cold War came to an end that agreements needed to be 'tended':[8]

> The means by which these agreements survive and adapt to changing conditions after they enter into force deserve as much attention as the negotiations that produced them in the first place. They cannot be left simply to fend for themselves.

According to Flowerree, successful implementation required 'effective treaty implementation mechanisms' able to cope with issues related to compliance, changing conditions, the necessity of interpreting treaty language when ambiguities arise (as they inevitably do), dealing with new technological developments, and developing implementing procedures.[9]

The incremental development of the Consultative Committee under the Convention's Article V was an important step for the BWC, but even with a procedure agreed under which a state party could bring a complaint or a concern about compliance to the attention of other states parties *and* act on this under the Treaty, a variant of the question Kissinger asked about European security remained: who do you call for the BWC? Even if a call was placed to one of the depositaries there was no agreed forum to address the issue because the BWC had no equivalent of the IAEA Board of Governors, no Agency for the Prohibition of Nuclear Weapons in Latin America and the Caribbean under the 1968 Treaty of Tlateloco, no Standing Consultative Commission as under the ABM Treaty, no Special Verification Commission as under the INF, no Joint Compliance and Inspection Commission as under the START I Treaty, nor even an alternative as envisaged under the INF which permitted the use of other institutional mechanisms – the Nuclear Risk Reduction centres – and certainly not an equivalent to the OPCW. The BWC had the depositaries and the United Nations Security Council and if the depositaries were willing to act, by the mid 1980s one of the depositaries was widely suspected (and now known) to be in non-compliance (USSR), the Administration of another depositary was reported to consider the BWC 'irrelevant' (US), and the UK could act only as guardian or 'honest broker' in certain circumstances, but was not going to push against the wishes of its closest ally. For the UK the BWC was a poor second to the importance of the 'Special Relationship'. Notwithstanding the incremental improvements made to Article V of the BWC, the Convention lacked precisely what Beaton, Flowerree, and Sims identified: a body to manage and oversee the Convention. Paradoxically, even before certain states parties began to realise that institutions were required for the BWC to bolster its principal security function, the paucity of institutional mechanisms was actually being flagged as an issue of concern in the co-operation element of the Convention via the calls for 'institutional mechanisms' to enhance peaceful co-operation. States parties were able to recognise that enhancing peaceful co-operation required institutional mechanisms as 'early' as 1986, but ignored the same problems in the security dimension until 1991. The consequences of this failure to manage the Convention had a detrimental effect on it:[10]

> From ... the after-life of the BWC it is apparent that a treaty considered of secondary importance when it was negotiated became the source of considerable bilateral and international friction, in part through its failure to provide a permanent body to facilitate consultations on compliance questions. In the matter of the Sverdlovsk incident, U.S. suspicions could have been raised in a less confrontational manner had such a body been in existence.

The references to institutions to enhance co-operation in the BWC were made in the context of the UN system, and the Secretary-General of the UN was expected to allocate resources to the functioning of the Convention at its five-yearly review conferences and, after 1986, absorb the costs imposed by receiving, collating, and distributing the CBMs to the states parties. The view was that the BWC entailed few additional commitments for the UN and its depositaries were happy to pass additional commitments they were ostensibly supposed to fulfil onto the UN whenever possible. That process failed and was known to be failing by the mid 1980s. Hence, the first call for institutional support sought to make use of existing mechanisms through the creation of a Standing or Treaty Consultative Committee (later referred to as the Committee of Oversight), served by a small, permanent secretariat, and any sub-groups of experts the Committee of Oversight might establish as either standing advisory bodies or as ad hoc requirements, such as a Legal Advisory group and/or a Scientific Advisory group.[11]

By 1991 Sims had elaborated further on the issue of supporting mechanisms for the BWC and drew attention to the importance of the review conferences themselves to the Convention as the only existing means to manage the Treaty. The 'thoroughly inadequate'[12] arrangement of minimal activity undertaken by the Depositaries and the UN (together and separately) underscored the importance of particular states parties such as Sweden and other committed *reformists* who not only acted as the conscience of the Convention but also provided the impetus for further development. The 'modicum of institutions' now proposed by Sims were deemed necessary to ensure that the BWC could better withstand 'the vagaries of international reputation and to the impact of more substantial changes in its diplomatic, scientific and military environments.'[13] A Committee of Oversight,

Scientific Advisory Panel, Legal Advisory Panel, and a BWC-specific secretariat were called for by Sims and others.[14] At this juncture certain states parties were also picking up these ideas, notably the UK, and during the Third Review Conference a significant number of states parties did in fact commit themselves to the idea of supporting institutions. As Sims later recounted:[15]

> The most clear-cut failure of this [Third] Review Conference was the blocking, on spurious grounds of cost and more understandable disagreements over composition, of all proposals for supportive institutions to underpin the treaty regime. Proposals for a standing or interim committee to facilitate the operation of the Convention, particularly its CBMs, received much support from governments and NGOs alike; but in the end there was insuperable Third World opposition to the concept under any of its suggested titles ... and likewise to proposals for a small CBM-processing unit within the UN Secretariat with staff specially funded by the parties to the Convention.

Whether or not it actually was only developing states which blocked the creation of such basic institutional support is unclear: others have hinted at an 'unholy alliance' between Cuba and the US being the principal obstacle to the creation of the CBM unit in 1991.[16]

Whatever the real reason for the failure, by 1991 the *reformists* had embraced the ideas promulgated by Sims and others and began to support creation of some kind of Organization; namely a future OPBW. This support emerged in part because of the frustration generated by the Third Review Conference, in part because organizational aspects and institutional support for treaties became more the norm rather than the exception, and in part because vision of the *reformists*. Returning to Flowerree, *reform-minded* governments began to realise that the benefits they sought in agreements required some officials to live with the Convention and its obligations fulltime, all of the time.[17]

The shift in states parties' attitudes was evident in VEREX[18] but became explicit at the Special Conference, the Fourth Review Conference in 1996, and following the introduction of the rolling text of the Protocol in July 1997. As in all other areas of the text, however, states parties were far from consensus agreement. Brazil, for example, recognised the need for a BWC organization but sought to exploit as many economies of scale and synergies with existing international and intergovernmental organizations as possible, notably the WHO.[19] Japan was also seeking to reduce costs to a minimum[20] and China, India and Iran stated that any future implementation arrangements 'should try to make better use of existing facilities in order to prevent the creation of a large bureaucracy.'[21] By 1996, at the Fourth Review Conference other states parties were explicitly supporting the creation of a new organization, including South Africa, and all the European Union states.[22] Sweden, as usual, had begun thinking about such issues earlier and had noted at the second session of the Ad Hoc Group that a 'Committee of States Parties ... and a Secretariat will be required'[23] to implement the new legally binding agreement. By 1998 the EU was formally committed to 'a cost-effective and independent organization, including a small permanent staff, capable of implementing the Protocol effectively.'[24] Similarly, the US was in favour of 'a

192 *The Biological Weapons Convention*

professional organization to implement the Protocol ... talented, small, and cost-effective.'[25] Work by non-governmental organizations appeared to support the creation of a 'lean and mean' OPBW and few, if any, believed that an organization of the scale of the OPCW was required.[26] As Pearson noted:[27]

> there will need to be an organization to implement the legally binding instrument. The organization will need to liaise with the National Authorities of the States Parties to collect, analyse and evaluate the mandatory declarations, carry out the non-challenge visits ... and conduct investigations of non-compliance concerns and of alleged use of biological and toxin weapons. There is broad agreement that such an organization should be "lean and mean" – and that it should concentrate on those activities that it **has** to do to strengthen the BTWC. [Emphasis in original]

The vision of the *reformists* required an OPBW. A strengthened BWC which required mandatory declarations, liaison with national authorities in each state party, some form of on-site activity to assess the accuracy of declarations, investigation procedures, enhanced peaceful co-operation, as well as rapid assistance and protection in the event of the use of biological or toxin weapons could not be achieved without a professional organizational hub. The alternatives to a new organization (whether large or small) were the depositaries or the UN, both of which had failed to fulfil their existing commitments to the required standard. The states parties had no other feasible choice before them except the creation of an OPBW if the Protocol was going to be agreed and enter into force.

The rolling text

It was only with the introduction of the rolling text that the language for the development of a new international organization to implement the Protocol, and at least implicitly the BWC itself, emerged. Many of the proposals either drew directly from those made at the review conferences of the BWC or from other international organizations, the OPCW in particular. In addition, the negotiations for the CTBT also required the creation of a verification organization – the Comprehensive Test Ban Treaty Organization (CTBTO) – and the tide appeared to be flowing in the direction of a new institution.

Thus, the idea promulgated by France in 1991 for increased disease surveillance was resubmitted and France proposed an international epidemiological monitoring network and electronic reporting modality be created as an 'integral part of the' organization.[28] South Africa proposed that the future organization include a 'Scientific Support Centre' which could provide advice to the states parties and the organization itself, undertake technical monitoring and information gathering, and provide the core of staff for non-challenge visits, among other duties.[29] In fact, the first version of the rolling text demonstrates that thinking on the organization was quite well established even though there was a contest of ideas between those who supported the creation of a new organization, *reformists*, and those who favoured using existing mechanisms, *minimalists*. Hence from a *reformist* perspective the outline of the organization was already well established in other arms control treaties and agreements. The (final) name of the new organization was lifted from the CWC – the Organisation for the Prohibition of Bacteriological (Biological) and Toxin Weapons – and it was charged with strengthening the BWC and implementing the Protocol. A three tier structure within the organization of a Conference of States Parties, an Executive Council, and a Technical Secretariat was envisaged, with a Director-General at the head of the permanent secretariat that would include the epidemiological network. In addition, the granting of privileges and immunities to the Organization was established (in principle) upon completion of the first version of the rolling text.

Others were less convinced and proposed that existing organizations and mechanisms be used. For example, during VEREX Iran suggested that the 'WHO may carry out annual routine monitoring on all declared biological facilities'[30] and at the Special Conference stated that a new organization for the BWC was 'ambitious and unnecessary', again proposing the WHO 'be entrusted with the verification responsibilities determined by this Protocol and with rendering of conference, logistic and infrastructural support required by the Organization.[sic]'[31] This linkage to the WHO was only deleted at the twelfth session in 1998.[32] Iran's position was widely viewed as 'unrealistic' both within the Ad Hoc Group and outside it.[33]

Russia also did not support the creation of a new organization. As with investigations of non-compliance, Russia saw no need for the creation of an organization that would alter, amend, or dismiss the role of the UN Security Council; hence the alternative one and half page option in the rolling text for implementation of the Protocol.[34] Russia did accept the existence of a BWC Organization at the thirteenth session of the Ad Hoc Group in January 1999, ostensibly removing the final obstacle to the creation of an OPBW, but its *minimalist* vision was evident in its position.[35] For example, Russia stated that the absence of declarations of BW stockpiles and destruction of BW production facilities (because theoretically no state party had any) had to be considered, that clarifying declarations could be achieved by voluntary visits and bilateral agreements between states parties, and that investigations of outbreaks of disease did not fall under the BWC (because they were a natural phenomenon). This meant that states parties could 'avoid mechanically replicating existing organizations set up under other international disarmament treaties (primarily OPCW).' Thus, for Russia, 'there is no obvious room for the more costly part of the work of a standing body – the organization and implementation of mandatory non-challenge visits.'[36]

As expected the text on the organization developed in line with the substance of the compliance architecture contained in other articles, as had happened in other regimes.[37] In the initial versions of the rolling text the Technical Secretariat would have conducted non-challenge visits but not have conducted investigations related to non-compliance. Furthermore, as other areas of the Protocol developed, language was removed from the article on the Organization (e.g. that on investigations and initiation of investigations) or added to it (e.g. the Co-operation Committee).

194 *The Biological Weapons Convention*

Although progress was dictated by developments in other areas of the text, the *reformists* were in the majority throughout the negotiations. In fact, although the whole article of the rolling text remained in square brackets and was, therefore, contested, the development of the provisions was rapid. The working paper submitted by the Chairman of the negotiations (who chaired the discussions on the organization) at the Eleventh session in mid 1998 provided adequate demonstration of the progress. With the acceptance by Russia of an organization in January 1999 the main obstacles to progress centred on developments in the rolling text (visits, investigations, confidentiality provisions, and the legal architecture particularly) and settlement of two divisive questions: the Executive Council and the question of liabilities. For the Executive Council it was the question of its composition[38] and under the issue of liabilities the liability of the Organization in the event of a breach of confidentiality and the loss of proprietary commercial information pitted a few states parties against the majority. Indeed, leaving aside the decision on where the new organization would be located (Geneva or The Hague) these were the only two substantive issues left by the end of 1999. They remained unresolved until the composite text emerged.[39]

The Executive Council

As in more recent negotiations on the OPCW and the CTBTO the real questions here related to how representative would the executive organ of the Convention and the Protocol actually be? Those states parties with a major stake in the operation of the OPBW and the implementation of the Protocol sought to ensure their own permanent or semi-permanent status in the Executive Council. Those with global and regional ambitions for status and power sought the same, but also became embroiled in a contest with each other over status.

This was particularly acute in the Asia question where meeting the ambitions of all states parties within Asia was practically impossible if Asia was to be one regional bloc stretching from Beirut to Beijing and Damascus to Dunedin. In the former camp we can assume that the P-5 (China, France, Russia, UK, and the US) placed themselves as being major players even though arguably only the US, Russia and China should be included and the US was itself *primus inter pares*. The second tier contest was more nuanced. Within North America, what role for Canada arose; in Europe the obvious question of Germany had to be addressed, and within Europe the role of states such as Italy, Spain, and Sweden, among others, who were loath to be pushed aside. This was all further complicated by the Western Group politics and how Japan, Australia, Argentina, New Zealand, Republic of Korea, and Israel (if admitted) fitted into the equation *if* the Protocol allocated seats on the Executive Council according to the Cold War triumvirate of Western Group, Eastern Group, and NAM and other states. (Israel remains outside any of these groups although it would join the Western Group if permitted.) In Asia, however defined, the jostling for position among the Middle Eastern states, linked in with Iran, Pakistan, India, which itself impacted on China, Japan, Republic of Korea, Indonesia, and Malaysia; and assuming a pure geographic basis what happened to Australia and New Zealand. Latin America and, if included the

The Organization 195

Caribbean, posed it own problems with Brazil, Argentina, Cuba, Mexico, and Chile jostling for status. Africa was simpler with South Africa and Nigeria being obvious candidates for semi-permanent status, but Eastern Europe was open to question given that much of the Former Soviet Union could be construed as being in Asia, and much of the former Cold War Eastern Bloc (i.e. Warsaw Pact states) were, or were soon to be, members of the European Union and/or NATO. Thus, at least a portion of them (unless reassigned to the Western European and other States) would share similar objectives and preferences to the Western states.

Given that none of the other appropriate organizations allocated representatives to their executive bodies on the Cold War caucus groups, a geographic basis of some kind was inevitable. In the Statute of IAEA the Board of Governors was designated according to technological capabilities and geographic representation. The 35 members of the Board are now designated and elected by the General Conference of the IAEA, derived from the most advanced states in terms of technology for atomic energy, while ensuring an adequate geographical distribution drawn from Latin America (5), Western Europe (4), Eastern Europe (3), Africa (4), Middle East and South Asia (2), South East Asia and the Pacific (1), and the Far East (1), plus one further member from either the Middle East and South Asia, South East Asia and Pacific, and the Far East, and one further member from either Africa, the Middle East and South Asia, and South East Asia and the Pacific. (This formula is itself subject to amendment pending acceptance of the October 1999 Resolution of the IAEA.)

Under the CWC, the Executive Council consisted of 41 states parties from five geographic regions: Africa (9); Asia (9); Eastern Europe (5); Latin America and the Caribbean (7); Western European and other states (10); and, the other single available seat rotated consecutively between Asia, and Latin America and the Caribbean. Within the regional groups there was a separate quota of allocations related to 'the most significant national chemical industry in the region as determined by internationally reported and published data', which in Africa accounted for three of the nine members, whereas in Eastern Europe it accounted for only one of the five members, and, in addition, the regional group could take into account other specific regional factors. In the CTBTO the Executive Council consisted of 51 states parties from six geographic regions: Africa (10); Eastern Europe (7); Latin America (9); the Middle East and South Asia (7); North America and Western Europe (10); and, South East Asia, the Pacific and the Far East (8). One third of these seats were to be filled based on particular criteria which included political and security interests, location of the International Monitoring System (IMS) facilities, nuclear capabilities relevant to the treaty determined by international data, and budgetary contributions to the CTBTO. The remaining two-thirds of the seats were to be nominated by the states parties in each region by rotation or election. As Johnson reported:[40]

This formula was designed to provide equitable regional participation, ensure no State is permanently excluded, and give States which regard themselves as major players the assurance of continuous seats on the Council, while avoiding the political overtones of providing 'permanent' seats to the nuclear-weapon States or others.

The CTBTO remained purely geographic, with Israel in the Middle East and South Asia bloc and Australia and Japan in the Pacific grouping, whereas the CWC used a mix of geography, politics and existing practice mixing purely regional geographic groups (Latin America and the Caribbean) with geo-political groups (Western European and other States).

The composite text merged aspects of all these. During the negotiations most states parties favoured the creation of six regional-political groupings, although at least one state party must have held out for five towards the end of the negotiations. In terms of actual size the options ranged from 35 to 51 states parties and a balance between the efficiency of a smaller executive organ and a more representative body was at the crux of the debate. The other issue was how to allocate the seats within the regional groups. The Chairman opted for 51 members in the Executive Council drawn from six geographical-political regions: Africa (11); East Asia and the Pacific (7); Eastern Europe (7); Latin America and the Caribbean (9); Western European and other States (12); and, West and South Asia (5). In that respect both the CTBTO and the OPBW illustrate that they are products of the post-Cold War world being more representative in multilateral terms and reflecting a broader geographic base. Even this, however, was a compromise and subject to the vagaries of change. As only one example, the rationale for an Eastern European bloc is open to serious question. Within these geographic regions seats on the Executive Council were not allocated solely by rote or election.

As the composite text outlined under each regional group it was understood (but not actually required) that the political and security interests of the region and/or its states parties and the states parties with the most significant national biotechnological industry and relevant pharmaceutical industry sectors across the region (according to reported and published data), and the number of declared facilities, would be taken into account. As with the CTBTO, certain states parties would therefore have *de facto* permanent seats on the OPBW Executive Council. The basis for the text was the cross-group working paper of Italy, Pakistan, and Poland which offered a compromise for two areas of contention: first via the inclusion of an explicit reference to the number of declared facilities and second, in the identification of those states parties with the most significant biotechnology related pharmaceutical industry *determined* by internationally reported and published data through the deletion of 'determined' and its replacement with 'indicated'; a more flexible approach. In addition, the paper expanded the 'other regional factors' within this to explicitly reference political and security interests. While the composite text itself reflected a few minor changes to this, the substance remained the same and, in effect, the Chairman moved the debate out of the Ad Hoc Group and into the realm of the future regional groups.

Immunity

Commercial proprietary information and the protection of intellectual and other property was one of the significant 'side' issues throughout the negotiations. It cut

The key question was what happened in the event of confidentiality being breached and legal redress for loss of earnings and/or legal redress for abuse of privileges were pursued by a state party. Those exercised by this issue correctly pointed out that theoretically the possible damages of the loss of confidential information was extremely high (in financial terms) and, thus, explicit and special protection was required against the leaking of confidential information and to protect industry from abuse of privileges and immunities granted to OPBW staff. This, it was argued, would provide industry with greater confidence in the Protocol. Japan was particularly attentive about this issue.[42] Waiving the immunity of individual staff members of the OPBW in the event of breaches of confidentiality was one thing most states parties could agree on and it was principle and practice in other organizations. However, waiving the immunity of the Director-General of the Organization and the immunity of the Organization and making them both responsible for, and punishable in the event of, a breach of the regulations by an individual member of staff was quite another. Leaving aside the question of whether or not an Organization likely to be starved of funding would ever be able to carry such a financial liability (and it would be its states parties that paid such a liability anyhow in reality) the bigger question revolved around the signal the inclusion of such a measure sent to the states parties. As Pearson noted, 'providing for the waiver of immunity for the Organization or the Director-General is tantamount to a prior expression of no confidence in either ... [and] this provision should be deleted from the draft Protocol.'[43] Such provisions did not make it into the composite text because they never gained widespread support among delegations.

Minimalism or *Reform*

By the time the rolling text of the Protocol appeared in July 1997 almost every state party active in the negotiations accepted the notion that some kind of institutional support would be required to make the actual Protocol work. Understandably given the recent creation of the OPCW and the CTBTO states parties were keen to exploit as many economies of scale and synergies as possible. In addition, the dual-use nature of the biological weapons problem, as well as the overlap on the issue of toxins between the BWC and the CWC, meant that any future OPBW would have to establish some kind of relationship with other international organizations. The Iranian proposal to sub-contract the implementation of the Protocol to the WHO was unrealistic and the Russian Federation emerged as the main opponent of the creation of a new international organization. However, with the acceptance of the requirement for an organization in January 1999 delegations were able to make rapid progress. Put simply, the Protocol required an OPBW and in this particular case there is no doubt that the

198 *The Biological Weapons Convention*

creation of an OPBW represented a *reformist* vision in terms of its scope, size, and powers and functions.

Notes

1. Leonard Beaton, 'The Reform of Power: A Proposal for an International Security System' (London, Chatto & Windus, 1972) p.197. (Readers should note that it was Sims' own work that both identified Beaton to me and drove me back to assess the original source.)
2. Nicholas A. Sims, 'Route-Maps to OPBW: Using the Resumed BWC Fifth Review Conference' *The CBW Conventions Bulletin* Issue No. 56 (June 2002) p.2.
3. Nicholas A Sims, 'The Diplomacy of Biological Disarmament: Vicissitudes of a Treaty in Force, 1975–1985' (New York, St. Martin's Press, 1988) p.269.
4. Beaton, 'The Reform of Power: A Proposal for an International Security System' p.197.
5. Statement by Mr David Davis, MP Minister of State for Foreign & commonwealth Affairs, Foreign & Commonwealth Office, United Kingdom of Great Britain and Northern Ireland to the Fourth Review Conference of the States Parties to the Biological and Toxin Weapons Convention, Geneva, Tuesday 26 November 1996, p.4.
6. Ibid., p.6.
7. Sims, 'The Diplomacy of Biological Disarmament' p.290.
8. Charles C. Flowerree, 'On Tending Arms Control Agreements' *The Washington Quarterly* (Winter 1990) p.199.
9. Ibid., pp.202-203.
10. Ibid., p.207.
11. Sims, 'The Diplomacy of Biological Disarmament' pp.298-306.
12. Nicholas A Sims,' Reinforcing Biological Disarmament: Issues in the 1991 Review' *Faraday Discussion paper No 16* The Council for Arms Control (January 1991) p.6.
13. Ibid., p.20.
14. Ibid., pp.20-24; see also Federation of American Scientists, 'Proposals for the Third Review Conference of the Biological Weapons Convention' *Contemporary Security Policy* 12:2 (September 1991), pp.240 and 250.
15. Nicholas A. Sims, 'Biological and Toxin Weapons Convention' *CDS Bulletin of Arms Control* Number 4 (November 1991) University of London, p.9.
16. News Chronology, *Chemical Weapons Convention Bulletin* Issue No. 14 (December 1991) 27 September 1991, p.13. During 1998-2003 I heard former members of the UN staff, former diplomats and other serving diplomats, as well as members of the NGO community, apportion blame for the failure of the CBM unit in 1991 on the US, Cuba, Mexico, and hard-line NAM states (i.e. Pakistan, Iran, et al). The Cuba-US 'alliance' is the most oft-cited reason, but it is not possible to determine whether this is an entirely accurate or a complete picture. My best guess on this would be that certain states parties objected to this proposal but were able to 'hide' behind states such as the US and thus avoided being 'blamed' for the failure.
17. Flowerree, 'On Tending Arms Control Agreements' p.213.
18. See for example, VEREX, 'The Biological Weapons Convention: A possible verification regime' Australia, BWC/CONF.III/VEREX/WP.10 (1 April 1992) p.2.
19. BWC SPCONF, 'Working paper by Brazil: Strengthening the BWC: Elements for a possible verification system' BWC/SPCONF/WP.4 (21 September 1994) p.5.

20.	BWC SPCONF, 'Illustrative guidelines for considering a mandate of an Ad-Hoc Working Group on measures to strengthen the BWC' Proposal of the Government of Japan, BWC/SPCONF.WP.9 (22 September 1994) pp.2-3.
21.	BWCSPCONF, 'Working paper by china, India, Iran (Islamic Republic of)' BWC/SPCONF/WP.15 (23 September 1994) p.2.
22.	Statement by H.E. Mr J. S. Selebi Permanent Representative of the Republic of South Africa at the Fourth Review Conference of the States Parties to the Convention on the Prohibition of the Development, Production and Stockpiling of Bacteriological (Biological) and Toxin Weapons and on Their Destruction, Geneva 26 November 1996; Statement by Mr Mervyn Taylor Minister for equality and Law Reform of Ireland on behalf of the European Union, Geneva, 25 November 1996.
23.	BWC AHG, 'Some possible elements in a verification protocol' Working Paper submitted by Sweden BWC/AD HOC GROUP/25 (14 July 1995) p.5.
24.	BWC AHG, 'Working paper submitted by the United Kingdom of Great Britain and Northern Ireland on behalf of the European Union' BWC/AD HOC GROUP/WP.272 (9 March 1998) p.4.
25.	BWC AHG, Statement by John D. Holum Acting Under Secretary of State for Arms Control and International Security Affairs and Director, U.S. Arms Control and Disarmament Agency to the Biological Weapons Convention Ad Hoc Group session XII' 6 October 1998.
26.	Federation of American Scientists Working Group on the Biological Weapons Convention, 'Preliminary Paper: The Cost and Structure of a BWC Organization' June 1998.
27.	Graham S. Pearson, 'An Optimum Organization' Strengthening the Biological Weapons Convention Briefing Paper No 5 (Bradford, University of Bradford, 1998) p.18.
28.	BWC AHG, Working paper submitted by France, 'Proposal concerning the establishment of an international epidemiological monitoring network' BWC/AD HOC GROUP/WP.134 (10 March 1997).
29.	BWC AHG, 'Scientific Support to a future organization' Working paper by South Africa BWC/AD HOC GROUP/WP.152 (11 July 1997).
30.	VEREX, 'Islamic Republic of Iran, Elements of Biological Weapons Monitoring Systems' BWC/CONF.III/VEREX/WP.25 (7 April 1992) p.5.
31.	BWC AHG, BWC/AD HOC GROUP/36 Annex I (4 August 1997), p.63.
32.	Graham S. Pearson, 'Progress in Geneva: Quarterly Review no 5' *The CBW Conventions Bulletin* Issue No 42 (December 1998) p.20.
33.	See for example the footnote attached to the relevant paragraph of the rolling text, and opinion offered by Pearson: Graham, S. Pearson, 'An Optimum Organization' Strengthening the Biological Weapons Convention Briefing Paper No 5 (Bradford, University of Bradford, 1998) p.19.
34.	BWC AHG, BWC/AD HOC GROUP/36 Annex I (4 August 1997), pp.79-80.
35.	Graham S. Pearson, 'Progress in Geneva: Quarterly Review no 6 *The CBW Conventions Bulletin* Issue No 43 (March 1999) p.14.
36.	BWC AHG, 'Working paper submitted by the Russian Federation: Some aspects of the establishment of the organization for the implementation of the Protocol' BWC/AD HOC GROUP/WP.341 (12 January 1999) pp.2-3.
37.	Thomas Bernauer, 'The Chemistry of Regime Formation' (Aldershot, Dartmouth Publishing Company Limited, 1993) p.34.

200   *The Biological Weapons Convention*

38. BWC AHG, 'Working paper submitted by the Chairman' BWC/AD HOC GROUP/WP.281 (29 June 1998).

39. It is understood that had the Protocol been accepted the seat of the Organization would have been in Den Haag, with the OPCW. Kervers informs us that a straw poll undertaken in May 2001 showed a clear preference for The Hague. This is also my personal understanding of the outcome of the question related to the Seat of the future OPBW. 'Onno Kervers, 'Strengthening Compliance with the Biological Weapons Convention: The draft Protocol; *Journal of Conflict and Security Law* 8:1 2003, p.189, see footnote 49.

40. Rebecca Johnson, 'CTB Negotiations – Geneva Update No. 30' *Disarmament Diplomacy* Issue Number 7 (July/August 1996) p.21.

41. BWC AHG, BWC/AD HOC GROUP/CRP.8 (Technically corrected version) 30 May 2001 pp.68-69 and 156-162.

42. See for example, BWC AHG, 'Working Paper submitted by Japan Proposed Language on Privileges and Immunities' BWC/AD HOC GROUP/WP.195 (28 July 1997) and 'Working paper submitted by Japan Proposed changes of text' BWC/AD HOC GROUP/WP.354 (23 March 1999).

43. Graham S. Pearson, 'Progress in Geneva: Quarterly Review no 12' *The CBW Conventions Bulletin* Issue No 49 (September 2000) p.23.

PART III
FAILURE AND ITS IMPLICATIONS

Chapter 9

The Protocol: Useful or Useless?

Introduction

Whether or not the composite text of the BWC Protocol was a useful or a useless additional tool in the efforts to manage the biological weapons problem is a moot point. The Protocol was not agreed, the negotiations failed and the Protocol (as it stands) is dead. Indeed, the conceptual approach of a single treaty silver-bullet 'solution' to the biological weapons problem is moribund for the foreseeable future, if not permanently: and, such a solution never existed in reality given the existing tripartite approach based on the Geneva Protocol, BWC, and Australia Group. Making an assessment of the Protocol is therefore something of a hollow exercise and may serve only to underline the scale of what was 'lost' during the 1991-2001 period – if one is a proponent of the Protocol – or what was 'lost' from an opportunity cost perspective in terms of wasted effort during the negotiations – if one believes the negotiations were an exercise in futility. An assessment, however, must be made; not least because the rush to judgement in 2001 about the utility of the Protocol was far from objective or measured. Rhetoric, politics, myth, and reality, were all thrown into the mix in July-August 2001 and what was actually happening in Geneva came second to the pursuit of political objectives. In this chapter a more measured view of the Protocol is undertaken with reference to the expressed views of both states parties and analysts.

The context

After years of negotiations and over twenty years of effort to strengthen the BWC referring to the context in which the Protocol should have been judged may appear unnecessary. However, after such intense involvement in the minutiae of the negotiations delegations, states parties, and other interested parties tended to ignore the real context of the Protocol and what it was supposed to actually do. During the negotiations many compromises had been made by all states parties on different issues. The nuances in the mandate had been forgotten and the negotiations had reached an all or nothing stage once the Chairman had delivered the composite text. Although constant reference was made to the BWC, the focus of most states parties was on the Protocol itself, not the fact that the Protocol was supposed to strengthen the Convention. The Protocol, it should not be forgotten, was an additional legally-binding agreement intended to supplement the Convention; to rectify some – not all – of the weaknesses in it which had been

204 *The Biological Weapons Convention*

identified over the last twenty years. In that respect Sims' observation from the mid-1980s that states parties must live and work with what they created was pertinent: '[w]e do not have *tabula rasa*, which would allow us to start drafting a satisfactory treaty from scratch.'[1] Likewise, the Ad Hoc Group did not have a *clean slate* to redraft the BWC: rather it was a necessity to build on and improve what actually existed. Any flaws or weaknesses in the BWC had to be addressed without changing (amending) the formal Treaty itself. This presented certain dangers as Ipsen observed: '[e]very attempt to improve ... [a treaty] may, therefore, lead to the exact opposite, to the total or partial destruction of the compromises which had been achieved by the terms of the ... treaty.'[2] Opponents of the Protocol might justifiably claim that if the foundations of an agreement are weak then any additional structure will be built on this weak foundation(s) and itself be not particularly robust. Of course, if the foundations of the agreement are strong, such as the general-purpose criterion, then additional structures can further enhance the BWC. A second important contextual issue was the nature of diplomacy itself, or rather the nature of diplomacy in arms control agreements. As remarked in the opening chapter, by the time an agreement reaches its final form few states parties can say it represents their preferred objectives or means to resolve a certain problem; the question is, is the agreement still in the national interest of the state party and are its provisions acceptable to the state party? The outcome may not necessarily be the lowest common denominator, but it certainly will be based on compromises.[3]

> Once concluded, an arms control agreement very often reflects a fragile construction of compromises – of a minimum consensus that has been reached with regard to highly controversial issues.

This was certainly applicable to the Protocol, even though states parties appeared to be moving towards consensus agreement that the composite text would be the basis of the last phase of their negotiations in August 2001.

A third contextual factor to bear in mind when assessing the BWC Protocol is the changed international environment, which is explored fully in the next chapter. However, recall that the BWC was a superpower deal, presented in 1971 as a *fait accompli* to the CCD in Geneva as a take it or leave it treaty. Other states parties took it, but many were unsatisfied from the start and sought upon implementation in 1975 to begin rectifying what they perceived as flaws and weaknesses. There can be little doubt that even if the Protocol had been agreed the *reformist-minimalist* contest would have continued, not least in the areas related to certain production facilities due to be listed but not declared, trade with non-states parties, and the operation and functioning of the OPBW. In 2001, neither the US nor Russia was in a position to present the other states parties with a similar two-state *fait accompli*, not least because of their different approaches. Any state could block consensus and prevent an agreement, but no state was in a position to present a take it or leave it deal to all states parties. The US probably could have presented such a deal to the Western Group and, if they took it, a united Western Group would quite likely have been able to build a significant majority in favour of that deal, but this could not be assured because of the number of players in the process. The demise of the Cold War superpower hierarchy meant that throughout the 1990s other states parties – and particularly those with visions of being global or regional powers – had asserted their authority and wielded their power of veto on the Protocol (which all had under the consensus rule) as a means to achieve their objectives. Put simply, the number of states parties with real influence had increased between 1971 and 2001. The Protocol, as it existed, reflected that reality: it was not a treaty with the fingerprints of the US and Russia all over it, but a treaty that reflected a balance of the concerns and objectives of the US, Russia, Canada, France, the UK, Germany, Sweden, South Africa, Australia, New Zealand, Japan, China, Iran, India, Pakistan, Cuba, Brazil, and other NAM states, as well as other Western Group and Eastern Group states parties.

The text reflected 'decades of thinking on biological weapons' verification, years of preparation and thousands and thousands of hours of consultation and negotiation in the period between 1995 and 2001.'[4] Taking up Westing's theme, the Protocol of July 2001 reflected exactly how far the states parties were (probably) prepared to go as a collective body responsible for the BWC. Its strengths were not there through luck; its weaknesses not due to ineptness of the drafters. The Protocol reflected what was thought to be possible: not the strongest possible deal; not the weakest possible deal; not what was necessarily required in every area of concern; and, certainly not what was ideal. Among the states parties was a delicate balance of power and the Protocol of 2001 reflected the politically and technically demanding task of attempting to keep all states parties on board.

Strengthening the Convention

The states parties were mandated to draft proposals to strengthen the Convention. It is worth recalling what the principal weaknesses of the BWC were based on lessons learned up to 2001, through the decisions of the review conferences and events in related areas. The principal deficiency with the BWC was that states parties had to trust one another to implement the Convention. It lacked a detailed and agreed architecture for demonstrating compliance, ensuring compliance and, if necessary, enforcing compliance. The ability to investigate non-compliance was dependent on UN Security Council agreement; the consultation procedures were not sufficiently detailed in the Convention; scientific and technological developments were reviewed only once every five years; there was no requirement to report the fulfilment of any destruction of biological or toxin weapons under Article II; the relationship between non-proliferation and peaceful co-operation was ill-defined and unclear; there was no reporting requirement for national implementation measures; specific measures for assistance and protection in the event of an attack were not established; the relationship to the Geneva Protocol and the impact of the BWC upon any reservations under the Geneva Protocol was not adequately considered; peaceful co-operation was high on intent but low on specifics; there was provision for only one review conference under Article XII;

206   *The Biological Weapons Convention*

and, the Convention lacked effective implementation mechanisms and supporting institutions.

It was possible to clarify, elaborate, or resolve some of these problems at the review conferences (as past practice demonstrated), but the power of states parties within the review conference mechanism was limited even when innovative solutions like the CBMs were created. Coupled with the broader development of known non-compliance (USSR), actual proliferation (Iraq), scientific and technical developments in biotechnology, and the lessons of other security agreements, as well as the development of new treaties such as the INF, CFE and eventually the CWC, by the completion of VEREX in 1993 all states parties had a good idea of where the practical and political problems with the BWC existed. The mandate of the Ad Hoc Group – a hard won compromise in itself – reflected those issues which states parties were willing to address. The Protocol of 2001 reflected the outcome of the consideration of appropriate measures over seven years and the drafting of proposals in a legally binding instrument. Despite the fact that such things only had to be considered, the Protocol included definitions of terms and objective criteria, some confidence building measures, a system of declarations, on-site activities and provision for investigations to promote compliance with the BWC, and measures designed to implement Article X of the Convention. In addition it created a new legal architecture to implement the Protocol and the BWC, an international organization, provisions to protect CPI and NSI, and additional assistance and protection undertakings. In short, it brought the BWC up to date, making it comparable in both form and available procedures with other treaties. That said, recent achievements in the NPT, the IAEA, the CWC, or the CTBT were irrelevant: the sole basis for assessing the utility of the Protocol was the BWC and the extent to which it fulfilled the mandate of *strengthening the Convention.*

Observers' reactions to the composite text

As Chevrier noted, 'everyone, whether they are with national delegations, international organizations, private companies, or nongovernmental organizations, has his own pet peeve regarding the protocol.'[5] Most observers focussed on the weaknesses, and in particular picked up the biodefence declaration:[6]

> A state could therefore keep much of its biodefense operations legally exempt from routine international scrutiny, subject only to the unusual process of facility investigation that will be difficult to initiate. ... it does not provide for comprehensive transparency of biodefense programs. Exempted facilities will be a natural source of suspicion, potentially capable of negating whatever reassurance the mandatory declarations convey.

The biodefence declaration was, however, a necessary compromise: it was simply not feasible to seek agreement on a declaration that required all biodefence facilities to be declared. The US would not countenance such a requirement and Russia (albeit not publicly) preferred a limited biodefence declaration but took a different approach to its specific concerns through the definitions of terms and the issue of threshold quantities, its approach to the actual declaration formats, and its objections to on-site activity. As Ward observed, 'Russia's efforts to reinterpret the convention and prevent international scrutiny were so obvious that it was not difficult to infer a direct link between its negotiating position and its suspected offensive BW activities.'[7] At the crucial level the question became a simple one: was the weak biodefence declaration in the Protocol better and more useful in assessing a state party's compliance with its undertakings than the existing available information under the CBM? Even with all its weaknesses the answer to that question had to be 'yes'. Whether or not a weak biodefence declaration was a price worth paying overall was a different question.

In the area of visits views diverged considerably. Pearson referred to them as a 'remarkably effective way of enhancing transparency and generating confidence in the consistency of declarations' and was careful to underline that the 'purpose is to demonstrate compliance and to deter would-be violators rather than find cheaters or catch out States Parties.'[8] Others considered the utility of visits highly questionable[9] or the whole conceptual basis for them flawed.[10]

> The draft protocol specifies so few total visits annually and such a limited number of visits for any one country or facility that it may, in fact, be difficult to develop the "mosaic" that serves as the baseline from which unusual behaviour can be distinguished.

There were also concerns about the dilution of the powers granted to the visiting team:[11]

> if the protections against unreasonable intrusiveness during on-site measures are assertively applied, as they undoubtedly would be in many instances, they could readily compromise the overall degree of transparency actually achieved and would certainly diminish the impression of transparency even among cooperative parties.

These were very real and legitimate concerns – as opposed to the asinine 'industrial spies, posing as arms control inspectors'[12] – but, again, the fact remained that simply to get close to a possible agreement, the *reformist* vision had to be diluted. Moreover, a closer examination of the provisions implied greater flexibility than many assumed and the lessons from the Trilateral Process suggested that claims of compliance could be assessed by visits as long as the visiting team was able to have a look round a facility. The provisions on visits and clarification were far from ideal, but they did offer routine on-site activity which was not available under the Convention. In contrast the provisions for investigations were generally welcomed and viewed as going 'a long way toward redressing the current limitations of the BWC ... [and a] substantial step forward.'[13] Another observer characterised investigations as 'probably the most valuable element of the draft protocol.'[14]

As could be expected, most observers formed opinions based on the overall balance of the package of compromises inherent to the Protocol. There was outright opposition to the text – with references to it being a 'malignant, fraudulent

208 *The Biological Weapons Convention*

draft' of a treaty'[15] – as well as scepticism that the Protocol offered any real benefits.[16] Some felt let down by the 'verification lite' approach of the composite text, and argued that 'negotiators should agree the strongest protocol possible and let the US come on board when it is ready.'[17] US analysts supportive of the Protocol argued that US demands in the text left no real scope to deal with the opposition of other states to more effective measures. As such, '[m]any US allies consider the Chairman's text to be the best that can now be achieved ... [but] consider it the bottom line and want no further compromises.'[18] In contrast those more sceptical of the Protocol approach to strengthening the BWC stated that, '[i]t is difficult to avoid the conclusion that, as a total package, the chairman's draft protocol falls far short of even the limited objective of bolstering confidence in compliance with the BWC.'[19] Moreover, even among supporters of disarmament efforts the conclusion was that 'it is admittedly an uncomfortably close question whether implementation of the chairman's text would do more good than harm.'[20] The former US Ambassador James Leonard, who oversaw the original BWC negotiations in Geneva, suggested that '[m]uch more than intergovernmental agreements and treaties will eventually be needed if disasters are to be avoided – domestic legislation must be developed and the scientific community must elaborate its own rules and procedures – but the protocol is an essential first step.'[21] In the UK community there was more support for the Protocol, even with its known weaknesses, and a strong line of argument was pushed that the provisions in the Protocol had to be considered against the provisions in the BWC – not the CWC, NPT, IAEA Additional Protocol, or CTBT – and the benefits it offered over the existing mechanisms. As such, 'the Protocol regime brings significant and worthwhile benefits' to states parties, improving 'health, safety, security and prosperity.'[22]

Industry representatives were not convinced. It was not the case that industry's views were ignored. Many states parties undertook detailed consultations with their own industry representatives and sought to protect CPI. However, unlike during the CWC negotiations industry played no useful role in the BWC Protocol. Its professional organizations distributed their 'industry positions' in Geneva but undertook little outreach to the states parties in Geneva itself. Western industry organisations such as PhRMA claimed that 'our input to date has fallen on deaf ears'[23] but that belied the role such organizations had adopted. Indicative of the professional organizations' approach was the redistribution of a 1998 European, Japanese, and PhRMA position paper in late 2000 which failed to reflect any of the developments in the text of the Protocol from 1998. The view from Geneva was that these bodies had not even attempted to keep themselves up to date with developments and as a consequence, if industry was not going to take the Protocol seriously many delegations were not going to take 'industry position papers' seriously.[24] The professional organizations were considered obstructive having offered a position which identified their concerns, but making no move after that to offer solutions. The industry, or more particularly PhRMA, debate was also viewed as an internal US contest played out on the international stage.[25] As a consequence, despite the fact that industry was a very important constituent of the BWC Protocol and it could have undertaken substantial efforts to improve the text,

The failure of industry to engage with the Geneva process meant its position was aligned to that of China, Russia, Pakistan, Iran, and India. Nevertheless, the views of observers, analysts, industry, and NGOs counted for little: what mattered were the positions adopted by states parties.

States parties' reactions to the composite text

At the twentieth session (10 July-4 August 2000) the Chairman and the Friends of the Chair divided the remaining areas of disagreement into issues relatively easy to resolve, those where there was a medium level of agreement, and issues where strong conceptual differences still existed. These included definitions of terms and thresholds, declarations, visits, investigations, non-proliferation and export controls, peaceful co-operation, legal issues, and the Organization. In certain cases the 41 problems identified in the latter category (Table 9.1) included more than one issue or part of the text.[26]

In effect, these were the issues that the Chairman had to deal with in the composite text, a good number of which have been explored in the preceding chapters. Rather than issue compromise ideas in one document states parties were drip fed a series of papers at the end of 2000 and the beginning of 2001, which ostensibly explored possible solutions to the remaining problems. In actual fact, many of these ideas were compromises developed in the drafting of the composite text. The Chairman presented the composite text to states parties on 30 March 2001. He proceeded to explain its provisions – and the compromises within it – to delegations at the twenty-third session of the Ad Hoc Group. Each state party was requested to submit, in writing, any changes it would like to see. By the opening of the twenty-fourth session the composite text contained three types of problems: typographical errors, technical inconsistencies, and omissions or changes requested by delegations which were of a technical nature; specific requests for changes to the text which were not controversial and, probably, could be accommodated; and, the outstanding issues of a substantive nature. While it is understandable that the rejection of the composite text by the US has skewed interpretations of events at the twenty-fourth session, prior to the US speech on 25 July completion of the Protocol was still far from an assumption. Much has been made of 'some 50 of the approximately 55 participating states – including all the major players save for the United States – making plenary statements supporting the Chairman's text as the basis for the necessary political decisions to adopt the Protocol.'[27] But, as we have seen, pledging support is one thing; delivering compromise is quite another issue altogether.

Iran, for example, implied it would block consensus agreement if its concerns about the entry into force criteria were not addressed. Iran had proposed that a provision similar to that in the CTBT whereby named states would have to ratify the Protocol before it could enter into force. Given that the Iranian list included states which were not even a party to the BWC (e.g. Israel) and was devised on criteria few considered objective, the proposal was viewed as an attempt to prevent the Protocol entering into force in the near future.

210 *The Biological Weapons Convention*

Table 9.1   Areas of strong differences in views

Generic Area	Problem
General Provisions	Prohibition on 'use' in the Protocol
	The explicit inclusion of 'pests and vectors' in the prohibition under the BWC
Definitions	Basic definitions on: biological and toxin weapon; biological agents; toxin
	Threshold quantities
Declarations	Date of initial declarations (1925/1946/1975)
	Current biodefence declaration
	High biological containment (BL3)
	Work with listed agents
	Other production facilities
	Other facilities
	Outbreaks of disease
	Notification on threshold quantities
Visits	Scope – all declared facilities or sub-set of them
	Selection of facilities: random/proportional
	Right of visiting team to ask and pursue questions/answers
	Level of access during a visit
	Access to documentation
	Sampling and analysis
	Drafting of the visit report
	Clarification procedures for undeclared facilities
	Ability to mandate a clarification visit
Export controls	Application on certain materials, equipment & technology
	Controls outside the Protocol, i.e. Australia Group
Investigations	Investigating outbreaks of disease
	Initiation process (red light/green light)
	Mandatory consultation process prior to an investigation
	Final decision on access to investigated area/facility
	Access to documentation
	Sampling and analysis
	Drafting and distribution of the investigation report
Assistance & protection	Whether or not a request for assistance should be conditional on a request for an investigation
Peaceful cooperation	Membership of the Co-operation Committee
	Peaceful co-operation in biodefence
	Relationship to Article III (export controls)
Legal issues	Measures to redress a situation & ensure compliance – report to UN Security Council or UN General Assembly
	Entry into force criteria
	Reservations on the Protocol
Organization	Seat of the Organization (The Hague or Geneva)
	Composition of the Executive Council
	Waiver of immunity for the Director-General & Organization

The Protocol: Useful or Useless? 211

Furthermore, Iran made a sudden call for the deletion of all reference to CPI from the Protocol, despite the fact that the Ad Hoc Group explicitly required that CPI be given consideration. In addition Iran demanded '[a]ny parallel export control regimes have to be dissolved after the Protocol enters into force.'[28] All this may have been bluster and brinkmanship by Iran, but it identified serious obstacles to progress. Likewise, India identified that the declarations related to biodefence, high biological containment, and production facilities 'need to be rectified.'[29] The deputy of the US delegation has recently claimed that Russia 'was deeply dissatisfied' with the composite text, and that China, Iran, Cuba, India, Indonesia, Pakistan, Libya, Mexico and Sri Lanka still demanded changes to the non-proliferation and export control provisions. Furthermore:[30]

> Russia demanded that the mechanism for investigating suspicious outbreaks of disease be eliminated ... leaving only investigations of alleged use. ... China joined Russia in insisting that it be stricken from the text. Iran, Pakistan, China, and India strongly emphasized the failure of the Chairman's Text to provide for mandatory consultations before a request for a challenge investigation could be acted upon. And finally, Pakistan stated that its support for the protocol was dependent on the incorporation of its proposal allowing a state to refuse a challenge investigation on "national security" grounds.

These are only some of the remaining objections that can be derived from the public domain. The US was rumoured to have 38 substantive problems with the text, which, if correct was the longest list but not by a long way.[31] The EU, or its constituent states, never submitted requests in writing, but many of their problem areas were well known. The EU *demarche* of 5 June 2001 to the US identified the biodefence declaration, the declaration on production facilities, and on-site activities as being major compromises to the US with which they were less than happy. Furthermore, according to the EU the weaknesses in the Protocol included clarification visits to undeclared facilities and the initiation of investigation procedures.

At the end of 24 July nearly 300 comments, views, and requests for changes on individual paragraphs and provisions had been recorded. In total 28 states parties explicitly requested changes to the composite text: Australia, Austria, Brazil, Canada, Chile, China, Cuba, France, Germany, Guatemala, India, Ireland, Iran, Italy, Japan, Libya, Mexico, Netherlands, New Zealand, Norway, Pakistan, Peru, Republic of Korea, Russia, South Africa, Spain, UK, and the US. The total number of required changes was 87. Most of these were in the well-known areas: general provisions (Article 1); definitions of terms (Article 2); lists and criteria (Article 3); declarations (Article 4); visits (Article 6); non-proliferation (Article 7); consultations (Article 8); investigations (Article 9); the Organization (Article 16); the entry into force criteria (Article 27); and, reservations to the Protocol (Article 28). The list, however, was expected to increase, not diminish in the near-term.

A lot was still to be decided and few realise that 28 states parties made known very specific requirements for certain changes, most of which were diametrically opposed to each other. For example, the argument over the declaration of all biodefence facilities or just a sub-set of them still raged; and even if that had been

212 *The Biological Weapons Convention*

resolved, one state party claimed that information required in the appendices related to biodefence was far too detailed and required the deletion of appendices B, C, and D (which would have left virtually nothing to declare). The declaration on high biological containment was still unresolved, and if two states parties had their way, there would have been no declarations on production facilities except for production using high biological containment. None of the above examples involved directly requests from the US (although the US had strong views on the outcome of those debates).

Substantive disputes in the rolling text were still live, still unresolved, and still subject to divergent opinions. These were not insurmountable problems, but given that China, Cuba, Iran, Indonesia, Libya, Pakistan, and Sri Lanka called for a return to negotiations based on the rolling text in May 2001 (effectively attempting to reject the composite text) the political will of all except the US to complete the Protocol in August 2001 could not, and cannot, be taken for granted.[32] In fact, in addition to the US, the political will of the above states parties was under very serious question. Of course, there was grandstanding, playing to the public gallery, endgame politics, and brinkmanship, but the fact remained that every substantive difficulty in the rolling text phase of the negotiations was still a point of contention in the composite text and the US was not the only problem.[33]

China had not yet accepted the text as a basis for further negotiations. Pakistan was not too positive and Iran not satisfied with the provisions on international co-operation and entry into force. The Russian Federation admitted that the text contained some reasonable compromises, but also retained some elements unacceptable to it.

With the exception of the Western Group (minus the US), the Eastern Group states in NATO and soon to be members of the EU, and the likes of South Africa, Chile, and Brazil, most active states parties were seeking further concessions and a weaker set of provisions than those in the composite text. Achieving anything stronger than the composite text as it stood was not possible. The process was now about holding onto existing strengths, as later testimony in the UK made clear.[34]

We would have liked to see something which was more robust ... [but][t]hat was not something which was going to happen. ... the balance of benefits versus the burden was in favour of the Protocol, but that is not to pretend we thought this was going to be the answer to all our problems.

The US rejection

So much has been written about the rejection of the Protocol by the US that there is no need to (re)cover much of that ground.[35] The points to understand about the US rejection of the Protocol are that it was comprehensive and final, leaving little room for manoeuvre for the US and other states parties; it was based on judging the Protocol against an objective the Protocol was never intended to fulfil; and, the identified problems of on-site activity, CPI, constitutional and ratification issues, and, particularly, export controls, were red herrings. The real question came down to biodefence, but even this was misleading, because at its heart the rejection of the Protocol represented a different approach to the whole issue of disarmament, arms control, and non-proliferation under which not all states parties were equal. In particular, it is instructive to note that the crucial issue was the question of the burden of verification and whether or not it hampered more the verifier or the violator.[36] A return to the argument of the early 1990s.

The debate over export controls is an interesting one because no where in his speech of 25 July 2001 did Ambassador Mahley claim or infer that the Protocol undermined US export controls or threatened the existence or activities of the Australia Group. As he noted, the preferred positions of certain states parties did imply such a threat, but such provisions were not included in the composite text. The text of the Protocol did not undermine export controls; it provided them (and the information-sharing and consultations under the Australia Group) with legitimacy. The US and its Western Group allies were all robust in their defence of export controls. They would have comprehensively rejected any Protocol that undermined existing export controls and did resist at all costs such efforts. Rather than undermine export controls the Protocol legitimised them. This is clear from an examination of the text of the Protocol, the interpretation of some non-governmental observers[37] and supported by the official UK view.[38]

> On the question of the Australia Group ... our conclusion was that the protocol helped to strengthen the concept of export controls and the need for multilateral export controls in this area. The Protocol as it was drafted in August did not seem to us to undermine the export controls of the Australia Group. We felt it legitimised them in a way in that these multilateral export control regimes are often criticised by countries that believe they are discriminatory, that feel themselves on the receiving end of the export controls. We felt that the Protocol as drafted in fact helped to strengthen the case for export controls, so that I think is a point where our interpretation did differ from that of the Americans.

The constitutional and ratification issues the US identified were not specific, but throughout the negotiations all were aware that ratifying an international agreement was an additional problem for the US. Nevertheless, this was a particular US problem they had faced before and one they would face again in the future. Each state party could assist the US as far as possible in ameliorating any problems, but no state party was going to draft a treaty on the political whims of the US Senate and shenanigans of individual senators. It was the task of the US team to protect their constitutional interests. Admission of constitutional difficulties with the Protocol reflected not the failure of the Protocol but the failure of the negotiating strategy of the US.

US objections to on-site activities were well known and on 25 July they related to the actual purpose and function of the devised activities in the Protocol, and the threat posed to CPI and NSI. According to the US position one of the principal objections was that 'safeguards are insufficient to eliminate unacceptable risks to proprietary or national security information.'[39] Others disagreed, but even so this was not an issue for which there was no solution. The US pharmaceutical and biotechnology industry is subjected to a plethora of regulations and a variety of on-

214   *The Biological Weapons Convention*

site activities, inspections and assessments and the 'threat' posed by a maximum of seven visits each year to the US, when access was subject to the approval of the state party and managed access provisions were in place, was dubious at best.

None of the above issues were unsolvable; certainly they would have created new problems and prolonged the negotiations, but had the US turned to its allies in early July 2001 and stated that these issues required further consideration if the US was to accept the text, then the Western Group would have almost certainly capitulated to the US demands. At this stage of the negotiations the US was in a position to present a *fait accompli* to its allies if it chose to go down that route. It did not do so, and the rejection of the composite text resulted in so much ire because of the lack of any effort whatsoever to address problems which could have been resolved. Again, it was not the text of the Protocol that was the problem *per se*; it was the politics in Washington and the change in political criteria under which the draft Protocol was judged that was used to reject the composite text. The sudden reappearance of 'verification' as a means to assess the utility of the Protocol and the claim that '[o]ne central objective of a Protocol is to uncover illicit activity'[40] were particularly galling and factually incorrect. The very term 'verification' had been eliminated from the Protocol because of US sensitivity to it. Furthermore, because verification was not the objective or purpose of the Protocol, the composite text (and the rolling text before that) developed the means the US had stated it sought when it joined the *reformist* camp in 1994: benchmarks for identifying discrepancies or ambiguities pertaining to facilities or activities; means to seek clarification of such ambiguities; a mechanism for pursuing specific activities of concern; and, agreed measures for direct diplomatic engagement to resolve compliance concerns. The only area of the Protocol explicitly intended to uncover alleged illicit activity was investigations of non-compliance, and even here the weaknesses of facility investigations, especially their initiation, was due to US demands. The US shifted the political goalposts and rejected the text without any serious or sustained effort to find solutions to their (stated) concerns. As Rosenberg noted:[41]

> The text is generous to the United States on every count that Washington has considered critical, ... U.S. allies, having already made many concessions to Washington's demands see no point in continuing to spar unproductively with the United States. If consensus cannot be reached through minor adjustment of the Chairman's text during this summer's negotiating session, most countries will conclude that the political will to strengthen the BWC does not exist.

The lack of political will was the key point. For those with a historical understanding of the BWC and its development there was an unnerving symmetry to the rejection. The position of the early 1990s had returned – bad verification was worse than none – and the suppleness of the US position of 1994 overturned. To paraphrase Robinson *et al* the US decided it would feel more confident in a world of the status quo rather than that regulated by an enhanced biological weapons disarmament package in the Protocol. As in August 1971, when the original superpower *fait accompli* of the BWC was presented to other states, the

US found itself in July 2001 with even its closest allies unable to support its position. Compounding this was a sense of déjà vu that the US had picked up the mantle of the USSR and was now preventing the adoption of specific measures which would strengthen the BWC and replacing them with a hollow promise of unspecific improvements at some later date. The rejection of the very approach to a Protocol destroyed the Chairman's composite text, prevented any return to the rolling text, and effectively signalled the end of the Ad Hoc Group. After tipping the balance of power in favour of the *reformists* in 1994, the US killed off a twenty-year *reformist* effort on 25 July 2001. And, just to underline the scale of the failure of the Ad Hoc Group, at precisely the point when the *reformists* needed to rise to the occasion and form a cross-caucus mass of states parties determined to support the Protocol, they withdrew into regional group positions and committed the single greatest error of the twenty-fourth session of the Ad Hoc Group.

Compounding failure

The rejection of the composite text was a shock to the states parties – though not entirely out of the blue – but the rejection of the whole process of the negotiations and the effective veto on any attempt to 'fix' the Protocol was a different matter. Understandably the states parties turned their attention to procedural issues as a means to buy time to think through the rejection and prepare for the Fifth Review Conference in November of 2001. Although the discussions on the drafting of the procedural report of the Ad Hoc Group were tortuous, by the final week the outlines of an agreed deal were taking shape. A report to the Fifth Review Conference would recall the mandate of the Ad Hoc Group in full, outline the work undertaken since 1996, and provide an unambiguous statement that the Ad Hoc Group had not been able to fulfil its mandate:[42]

> it was not able to complete its work and submit its report, to be adopted by consensus, including a draft of a legally-binding instrument to the States Parties to the Convention. This mandate, as agreed by the Special Conference in 1994 ... remains in force and determines the future work of the Ad Hoc Group.

The mandate remained valid and was to be fulfilled. It is important to understand here the nuances in the mandate of 1994 and the flexibility provided by 'determines the future work of the Ad Hoc Group' in the draft report of 2001. The common interpretation of the mandate was that the Ad Hoc Group would draft a Protocol and that such a Protocol would contain measures related to those identified in its sub-paragraphs: namely definitions, lists, CBMs, measures to promote compliance, and peaceful co-operation, while protecting CPI and NSI, and avoiding harming scientific research, co-operation, and development. The mandate was much more nuanced than that collective interpretation because there was no actual requirement for all these kinds of measures, no actual requirement for a single legally-binding instrument, and no actual requirement for all the measures proposed for strengthening the BWC to be included in the Protocol. The Ad Hoc

216 *The Biological Weapons Convention*

Group could equally have come up with a legally-binding agreement and a range of politically-binding or other measures if it so desired. This vagueness in the mandate was seen as a weakness, but in August 2001 (and beyond) the nuances and possibilities in it offered a way out of the impasse. All the states parties had to do was buy some time to think through the possibilities open to them and protect the mandate of the Ad Hoc Group. It is here where the states parties failed.

The principal difficulty was divergence on whether or not simply to report the failure of the Ad Hoc Group to achieve its mandate to the Review Conference, or to offer, in addition, an explanation for that failure. The vast majority of states parties favoured the former: two pursued the latter. As a consequence, hard-line positions were allowed to emasculate the Western Group and hijack the NAM, and all other states parties were complicit in permitting that to happen. Iran and Cuba bear the brunt of the blame for the failure of the Ad Hoc Group to report to the Review Conference. These two states parties sought short term political capital at the expense of the interests of the Ad Hoc Group by attempting to single out and name the US as the sole cause of the failure of the negotiations. For Cuba, it was purely political and the continuation of the propaganda war waged between it and the US. For Iran, it was much more disingenuous. The state party that less than two days before the US rejected the composite text had stated that it required significant changes to the text and implied it would block consensus on the Protocol if its demands were not met now claimed that had the US accepted the composite text the Ad Hoc Group would be signing off an agreed Protocol at the end of the twenty-fourth session. Somewhere between 23 July and 26 July, Iran had become a *reformist*.

Political theatre was to be expected and nearly all states parties apportioned blame to the US, but all understood the key rule of consensus: nothing was agreed until everything was agreed. Furthermore, none of these states parties would have agreed to the establishment of the Ad Hoc Group if the mandate had stated that only a majority had to agree to the text. They all required the consensus rule and they all understood that the Ad Hoc Group succeeded or failed as the Ad Hoc Group. Iran and Cuba, so protective of the consensus rule up until 25 July and so eager to retain the rolling text and put aside the composite text in May 2001, attempted to single out the US for political capital at the expense of everything else. Neither of these states parties would ever have agreed to themselves being named and identified as a problem state party in any report and the hypocrisy was there for all to see. The Western Group, even divided as it was, was not going to accept the breach of such a principle and swung behind the US stating that under no circumstances would it accept a report that named and identified the US as the sole reason for the failure of the negotiations. It was not only a partial truth; it set a precedent which might in the future be turned against other states parties. When the US made it clear that it would not accept any report that singled it out for blame, Iran immediately countered claiming that the factual report of the Ad Hoc Group should include the details of what happened, which country caused the difficulty (erroneously claiming there was only one), and why the negotiations had ended. This now became a competition between the US, Iran and Cuba. In supporting the US unreservedly the Western Group made no real effort at compromise and as the final days of the twenty-fourth session drew to an end, the stakes of this debate simply became higher and higher. The NAM allowed Iran and Cuba to dictate a position. Unlike in 1994, when the *reformists* in the NAM had exposed Iran, India and China and forced a compromise agreement, the NAM remained wedded to caucus solidarity. In the end the intransigence of Iran and Cuba, the failure of the NAM to face down their unreasonable demands, the failure of the Western Group to seek a solution, and the failure of the US to permit the obvious solution of simply annexing all the official statements to the procedural report, meant that the Ad Hoc Group did not issue a report to the states parties.

The scale of the error was only revealed in December when the US proposed to terminate the mandate of the Ad Hoc Group as the price for agreement to a new set of annual meetings between 2002 and 2006.[43] That demand was too great for any state party and caused the suspension of the Fifth Review Conference, the loss of the final declaration, perpetuation of bad feelings, and the minimal agreement of 2002.[44] While agreement on a procedural report of the Ad Hoc Group may not have prevented such an outcome it would have done two things: first, made the political cost of the US proposal to terminate the mandate of the Ad Hoc Group much higher; and, second, provided the states parties with substantial room for manoeuvre at the Fifth Review Conference. The opportunity, like so many others, was lost and the attempt to revolutionize the BWC and its implementation mechanisms had failed.

Conclusion

The BWC Protocol was not embraced by any state party or anyone in industry, the NGO or the academic community, with great enthusiasm. It was well known that many states parties had their own demands for changes to the text. This was not a done deal waiting for US approval and the Protocol was not less robust than many desired solely because of US positions. To suggest otherwise is to misunderstand the negotiations and to ignore the reluctance of more than one state party to see even a limited Protocol enter into force. In the end, we will never know how many of the 87 changes requested would be required and how those requests diametrically opposed to each other would be resolved. With all these known weaknesses, requested changes, and the distinct lack of enthusiasm for the Protocol text, did it have any value? Was it a useful or useless part of the effort to manage the biological weapons problem?

Kadlec observed that, '[t]he approach often quoted in medicine, *primum non nocere* or "first, do no harm", may be appropriate in considering the chairman's text.'[45] This was correct, but many observers appeared to ignore the corollary to the maxim: do no harm to what? The BWC was not in a better position than it had been in 1991 when the decision to pursue a real effort at strengthening the Convention was taken. No measure in the Protocol undermined or harmed the BWC: all supplemented it. Quantitative approaches to compliance had been rejected, definitions of terms underpinned the general-purpose criterion rather than weakened it, and all the prohibitions remained valid and in place. The declarations

218   *The Biological Weapons Convention*

were a substantial improvement on the CBMs; on-site activity and clarification procedures were spelled out; investigations of alleged non-compliance were freed from the veto of the United Nations Security Council; non-proliferation obligations and export licensing requirements for certain equipment were effectively legitimized; specific co-operation provisions were provided for; assistance and protection mechanisms were enhanced; a new legal architecture for implementing the Protocol, and *de facto* the Convention, was established; and, not least, institutional mechanisms to support the BWC were developed. The Protocol did no harm to the BWC: it potentially could have done great harm to those reluctant to enhance transparency. Kervers made two observations.[46]

> The negotiators never expected the Protocol to provide complete deterrence against violation of the BWC, and certainly not on day one of its existence. It was expected to provide a quite reasonable deterrent against violation of the BWC and to build a transparency regime, which over time would have further allowed for increasing confidence in compliance with it. ... By strengthening confidence in compliance with the norm, the Protocol could also have contributed to solidifying that norm. This in turn would have given the international community even more legitimacy to act against BW-proliferation.

And:[47]

> Under the Protocol, it would eventually not have been an attractive option to start developing a BW-programme for the large majority of states parties. This does not mean that the Protocol would prevent a state that wished to acquire biological weapons at all costs from doing so, even if such a state would be a party to it. But the Protocol would not have created a false sense of security if the very large majority of its states parties would continuously have been aware of that risk, and if their multilateral, regional and national actions would be aimed at preventing such a situation or restoring it.

The Protocol was a means to an end – enforcing biological disarmament – not an end in itself. Had the Protocol been adopted and entered into force, the Convention would have been tended by a dedicated group of professionals all of the time; would require its states parties to pay constant attention to it; and, would, as a consequence, remove the vagaries of quinquennial lip-service to biological disarmament that went hand in hand with the existing set up. The Protocol established, unambiguously, the procedural and legal framework for states parties to demonstrate their compliance and, if necessary, for the international community to pursue, pressure, and enforce compliance. The Convention as it stood offered no comparable mechanisms to give real effect to its obligations. Hence, the most important fact to understand about the Protocol was that it required every state party to demonstrate compliance with its obligation for biological disarmament.

Between 1991 and 2001 the international political climate had not developed into a new world order of peace and prosperity (and it was about to become increasingly dangerous); intelligence estimates hinted state, as well as non-state, interest in biological weapons becoming an increasing concern; scientific and technical developments coupled with globalization enhanced the difficulties of the

The Protocol: Useful or Useless? 219

dual-use problem; the international community had failed to uphold its own law vis-à-vis Iraq, and, the Trilateral process had been sacrificed on the altar of broader political objectives. The BWC Protocol could not prevent such events by providing an unequivocal guarantee, but it did permit those who wished to act against the use and proliferation of weapons considered repugnant to humankind to do so. Whether or not collectively the states parties or the international community was up to the task of enforcing its own law was (and still is) an entirely different question, but to uphold an agreement with multilateral legitimacy requires a legal text as a precondition.[48] That is what the BWC Protocol provided. And that is what made it a useful addition to the tools available to manage the biological weapons problem.

Few observers gave serious thought at this stage to what the alternative to the Protocol actually was. Of those that did, an unpromising future was described:[49]

> Those who actively oppose the composite text, in contrast to the many who express regret that it is not all that it could or should be, should ask where we will be in 10 years without a protocol. The advances in biotechnology and genomics are likely to magnify the already horrifying aspects of the BW threat. Some states out of fear, miscalculation, or malevolence may decide to establish offensive programs. Without a protocol, it is hard to imagine reaching agreement on an effective, multifaceted international system including export controls, robust defenses, and responses to violations to suppress proliferation.

The BWC Protocol was not about removing forever the threat of biological weapons: it was concerned with reducing the weaknesses in the existing law that prohibited their use, development, production, stockpiling, and acquisition. It was far from perfect, but no state party, international organization, industry, or NGO devised a feasible alternative approach for addressing the whole range of weaknesses with the BWC that had any chance of being accepted. For all the weaknesses in the Protocol, and there were many, the BWC still needs to be strengthened and as Steinbrunner *et al* observed: 'one cannot endorse the draft protocol with supreme and immediate confidence, but one can hold firm to the conviction that in the end its suggested provisions – and far more extensive ones – will have to be enacted.'[50]

Notes

1. Nicholas A. Sims, 'The Diplomacy of Biological Disarmament: Vicissitudes of a Treaty in Force, 1975-1985' (New York, St. Martin's Press, 1988) p.255.
2. Ibid.
3. Knut Ipsen, 'Explicit methods of arms control Treaty evolution' Julie Dahlitz and Detlev Dicke (Editors) *The International Law of Arms Control and Disarmament* Proceedings of the Symposium, Geneva 28 February-2 March 1991 (New York, United Nations, 1991) p.77.

4. Onno Kervers, 'Strengthening Compliance with the Biological Weapons Convention: the draft Protocol' *Journal of Conflict and Security Law* 8:1 2003, p.197.
5. Marie Isabelle Chevrier, 'A Necessary Compromise' *Arms Control Today* 31:4 (May 2001) p.15.
6. John Steinbruner, Nancy Gallagher, and Stacy Gunther, 'A Tough Call' *Arms Control Today* 31:4 (May 2001) p.23.
7. Kenneth D. Ward, 'The BWC Protocol: Mandate for Failure' *The Nonproliferation Review* 11:2 (Summer 2004) p.188
8. Graham S. Pearson, 'The Composite Protocol Text: An Evaluation of the Costs and Benefits to States Parties' The BTWC Protocol Evaluation Paper No 21, (Bradford, University of Bradford, 2001) p.15.
9. Robert P. Kadlec, 'First, Do No Harm' *Arms Control Today* 31:4 (May 2001) p.17.
10. Michael Moodie, 'Building on Faulty Assumptions' *Arms Control Today* 31:4 (May 2001) p.20.
11. Steinbruner *et al*, 'A Tough Call' p.24.
12. Kathleen C. Bailey, 'Why the United States Rejected the Protocol to the Biological and Toxin Weapons Convention' National Institute for Public Policy, October 2002, p.14 http://www.nipp.org/publications.php.
13. Kadlec, 'First, Do No Harm' p.16.
14. Moodie, 'Building on Faulty Assumptions' p.21.
15. Fred C. Ikle, 'The New Germ Warfare Treaty is a Fraud' *Wall Street Journal* July 27, 2001.
16. Moodie, 'Building on Faulty Assumptions' p.21.
17. Oliver Meier, 'A biological weapons protocol: verification lite?' *Trust and Verify* Issue Number 97 (May-June 2001) p.2.
18. Barbara Rosenberg, 'US Policy and the BWC Protocol' *The CBW Conventions Bulletin* Issue No 52 (June 2001) p.1.
19. Moodie, 'Building on Faulty Assumptions' p.22.
20. Steinbruner *et al*, 'A Tough Call' p.23.
21. James F. Leonard, 'An Essential First Step' *Arms Control Today* 31:4 (May 2001) p.18.
22. Pearson, 'The Composite Protocol Text: An Evaluation of the Costs and Benefits to States Parties' p.6.
23. Gillian Woollet, 'Associate Vice-President Pharmaceutical Research and Manufacturers of America before the Committee on Government Reform, Subcommittee on National Security, Veterans' Affairs and International Relations' U.S. House of Representatives, June 5, 2001.
24. This reality is perhaps best reflected by a private comment from a senior member of a delegation that not only favoured the BWC Protocol but also had a substantial biotechnology industry to protect. Upon re-release of the 1998 paper, the view was expressed that 'if that's the best they can do, they don't deserve to be taken seriously.'
25. Oliver Thränert, 'The Compliance Protocol and the Three Depositary Powers' Susan Wright (Editor) *Biological Warfare and Disarmament New Problems/New Perspectives* (Lanham, Rowman & Littlefield, 2002) pp.351-352.
26. For a comprehensive overview of these issues see: Graham S. Pearson, 'Strengthening the Biological and Toxin Weapons Convention' Progress in Geneva,

The Protocol: Useful or Useless? 221

Quarterly report no 12 *The CBW Conventions Bulletin* Issue no 49 (September 2000) pp.15-23.

27. Malcolm R. Dando, 'Preventing Biological Warfare: The Failure of American Leadership' (Basingstoke, Palgrave, 2002) p.174.

28. Statement at the 24th session of the Ad Hoc Group of States parties to the Biological Weapons Convention by Ambassador Al Ashgar Soltanieh, Geneva 23 July 2001.

29. Statement by Ambassador Rakesh Sood at the 24th session of the Ad Hoc Group of the States Parties to the Biological Weapons Convention, 25th July 2001.

30. Ward, 'The BWC Protocol: Mandate for Failure' pp.196-197.

31. Barbara Hatch Rosenberg, 'Allergic reaction: Washington's Response to the BWC Protocol' *Arms Control Today* 31:6 (July/August 2001) p.6.

32. BWC AHG, BWC/AD HOC GROUP/WP.451 Working Paper submitted by China, Cuba, Islamic Republic of Iran, Indonesia, Libyan Arab Jamahiriya, Pakistan and Sri Lanka 'Joint Statement on the Process of the BTWC Ad Hoc Group Negotiations (4 May 2001).

33. Onno Kervers, 'Strengthening Compliance with the Biological Weapons Convention: the Protocol Negotiations' *Journal of Conflict and Security Law* 7:2 2002, p.290.

34. Tim Dowse, 'The Biological Weapons Papers: Uncorrected evidence presented by Mr Tim Dowse and Mr Patrick Lamb on 22 October 2002' HC1248, 25 October 2002, p.29.

35. Dando, 'Preventing Biological Warfare'.

36. Guy B. Roberts, 'Arms Control without Arms control: The failure of the Biological Weapons Convention Protocol and a new paradigm for fighting the threat of biological weapons' The United States Air Force Institute for National Security Studies, Occasional Paper number 49, (March 2003) p.34 http://www.usafa.af.mil/inss/OCP/OCP49.pdf.

37. Chevrier, 'A Necessary Compromise' p.14.

38. Dowse, 'The Biological Weapons Papers' p.21.

39. Statement by Ambassador Donald A. Mahley United States Special Negotiator for Chemical and Biological Arms Control Issues, Geneva, July 25, 2001.

40. Ibid.

41. Rosenberg, 'Allergic reaction: Washington's Response to the BWC Protocol' p.3.

42. Draft procedural report of the 24th session of the Ad Hoc Group. From the author's personal files.

43. Daniel Feakes and Jez Littlewood, 'Hope and Ambition turn to Dismay and Neglect: the Biological and Toxin Weapons Convention in 2001' *Medicine, Conflict and Survival* 18:2, 2002, pp.161-174.

44. Jez Littlewood, 'Back to basics: verification and the Biological Weapons Convention' Trevor Findlay (editor) *Verification Yearbook 2003* (Nottingham, Russell Press Ltd, 2003) pp.85-102.

45. Kadlec, 'First, Do No Harm' p.17.

46. Kervers, 'Strengthening Compliance with the Biological Weapons Convention: the Protocol Negotiations' p.292.

47. Kervers, 'Strengthening Compliance with the Biological Weapons Convention: the draft Protocol' p.199.

48. Kervers, 'Strengthening Compliance with the Biological Weapons Convention: the Protocol Negotiations' p.292.

49. Chevrier, 'A Necessary Compromise' p.33.
50. Steinbruner *et al*, 'A Tough Call' p.24.

Chapter 10

The Implications of Failure

Introduction

As Stuart Croft noted, 'the form of arms control practised is always a product of the international political culture and context of its time.'[1] The BWC illustrates this in its actual obligations and how they are drafted, its mechanisms and procedures for implementation, and what is absent from a contemporary perspective. The CWC represents another international political culture and context. The failure of the BWC Protocol indicates a new culture and context; but what is that culture and context? And what can we learn from the failure of the revolution and the lost decade of 1991-2001?

Events cannot be disentangled from the broader trends in international security and arms control, even though the negotiations were discrete and occasionally appeared to occur in a vacuum. Underlying trends did have an impact on the negotiations themselves and, more particularly, the attitude of states parties to the strengthening process. Three years on from the collapse of the Protocol negotiations and the mandate of the Ad Hoc Group being put into abeyance it is necessary to ask some difficult questions. This is because the post-Protocol strategy to strengthen the BWC – the one that required 'out of the box' thinking – was supposed to be based on 'effective innovative measures.'[2] What emerged in November 2001 was a significant disappointment.[3] The origins for every measure proposed by the US could already be found in the final declarations of the review conferences. This does not negate the importance or the utility of calling for the enactment of national legislation, for example, but it begged the question of why a strategy based on politically-binding agreements among states parties which had not worked in 1980, 1986, 1991, or 1996, would now work? It would not, and virtually every state party and informed commentator held that view.[4] Attempts to claim that these proposals constituted effective or innovative measures was fallacious. Even this back to the future strategy failed at the Fifth Review Conference, because the new meetings required to elaborate on the ideas the state parties developed in November-December 2001 were contingent on the demand from the US that the mandate of the Ad Hoc Group be terminated. This was too high a price to pay. With the suspension of the Review Conference for one year, the eventual solution established in 2002 was a series of three expert and annual meetings to be held in 2003, 2004 and 2005. At the sixth Review Conference of the BWC (2006) any recommendations from these meetings will be considered and, if the states parties decide, further action mandated.

224   *The Biological Weapons Convention*

The 2002 outcome was not unlike the compromise of the Third Review Conference. In 1991 the VEREX agreement granted states parties no power to negotiate, no power to agree binding decisions, and ensured further progress was contingent on additional consensus agreement. It was, however, at least holistic in its examination of the verification issue. Moreover, VEREX was not the only outcome of 1991: states parties had delivered a useful Final Declaration in 1991. In 2002 states parties were even more parsimonious than they had been in 1991 failing to agree a Final Declaration and delivering what can only be described as a VEREX-minus solution. There was, once more, no power of negotiation, no ability to make binding decisions, and further progress was contingent on a new consensus decision in 2006. The focus on discrete aspects of the BWC – with each year's activity independent and unconnected from the other – underlined the extent of what had been lost: a strategy.

Following the death of the *reformist* project no alternative coherent strategy has been devised by, or made available to, the states parties. The ideas from the US are unimaginative; the response from other states parties to US proposals, embittered; and, the commitment of state parties to the new process of 2003-2005 questionable. The *minimalists* have been uncovered for what they always were: reactionaries against something they did not support rather than states parties with any alternative strategy. In contrast, the *reformists* have yet to re-emerge from their capitulation in July-August 2001. In the BWC there is a pervasive lack of ambition at precisely the period when the threat of biological weapons development, and possibly use, is increasing. Historically the states parties have returned themselves to a position similar to that between 1981 and 1986. The BWC has been pushed to the periphery, considered unimportant, and become a forum where political concerns take precedence over actual implementation.

Why have states parties proved themselves so unequal to the task? The purpose of this final chapter is to assess the implications of the failed revolution and to put those implications into a broader perspective. I contend that the *reformist* project of an all-embracing single legally-binding additional agreement to the BWC is dead. Of equal importance politically-binding measures will not strengthen the Convention to the required degree. What is required is a new strategy. A focus on the biological weapons problem itself rather than the Biological Weapons Convention, and recognition that managing the biological weapons problem is a strategy that encompasses all the risks from the individual to the international. The BWC is a part of that strategy – indeed an important part – but the states parties must recognise that it only one part of a much broader effort.

The death of the *reformist* vision

In the *minimalist-reformist* context it is quite clear that the origins of the Protocol can be traced back further than 1991; indeed to the First Review Conference in 1980. Each meeting of the states parties moved a little closer to the decision to negotiate an additional legally-binding instrument to the BWC. It began with enhanced consultation procedures, developed to include requests for information to

The Implications of Failure

enhance transparency, and finally encompassed all the key areas of the BWC, including non-proliferation and peaceful co-operation. In the end the *reformist* project failed and much of the blame has been placed at the door of the US, and more particularly the Administration of President George W. Bush.

The US certainly has to be recognised as the principal cause of the failure of the negotiations in July 2001, but it is not the sole reason for that failure. Throughout the 1990s other developments, not immediately obvious in their impact on the negotiations, influenced the positions of states parties and what they attempted to secure in the Protocol. Two trends are of particular note here: the rise of true multilateralism in international negotiations and the problem of compliance. Other trends and developments also influenced the outcome of the negotiations, such as the on-going biotechnology revolution, globalization, weak state structures, the overall international security environment, and the shift away from multilateral approaches to problem-solving. These latter trends have a more direct impact on how managing the biological weapons problem will develop in the next decade. For the Protocol, true multilateralism and the problem of compliance undermined the negotiations to the extent that when it was necessary to take a hard look at the final outcome (the composite text as it stood in May 2001) practically all found it wanting in certain areas and the US was unable to accept the deal(s) inherent within it, given its international outlook.

True multilateralism

The BWC Protocol was possibly the last of the WMD treaties. The CWC was a product of the Cold War and at its heart still represented a superpower deal which in its final form had to be accepted as a *fait accompli* once the limits of US and Soviet/Russian concessions had been made. A CWC was a long-standing objective of the international community and its breadth and depth are a testament to the continued efforts to achieve that objective and of the importance of political will and leadership – not least by the US – in fulfilling that goal. States such as China, India, Iran and Egypt may have complained about the final form of the CWC, but they could not afford to scuttle it at the crucial moment.[5] They could, of course, decide not to sign or ratify the CWC. Similarly, the CTBT was a long-standing objective of the international community finally realized during the mid-1990s after intense negotiations. The path to completion of the CTBT, however, represented something new. In the final year of the negotiations India adopted a 'blatantly obstructive role'[6] which meant the Treaty could not be signed off by the CD in Geneva. That body had to be circumvented by Australia, which took the final form of the CTBT out of the CD and submitted it to the UN on behalf of others. Much was made of the fact that this circumvention did not set a precedent for other treaties, but in reality it did set a precedent. In addition, it said something about the nature of negotiating in the post-Cold War environment. India had to publicly show its hand to force that situation, but it is instructive to note that in the UN General Assembly, Libya and Bhutan joined India in voting against the CTBT and Cuba, Lebanon, Mauritius, Syria, and Tanzania abstained.[7] As Arnett noted, several members of the CD did not vote for the CTBT 'suggesting that they were simply allowing India to take the heat.'[8] This was nothing new in itself. However, the decision by Australia and others to bypass Indian objections did illustrate the operation of the consensus rule in treaty-making and the willingness of states to publicly and substantively challenge the 'global' view was changing. India challenged the global view on the CTBT and Australia and others in essence said, 'fine, but we want this Treaty and we'll go ahead without you.' In the previous era the negotiations would have stalled or collapsed. Here they did not, even though the actual prospect of entry into force of the CTBT remains distant. A CTBT-type solution to the BWC Protocol problem was mooted by a number of NGOs, but in July 2001 and after not a single state party spoke in favour of such an option. This may indicate that the CTBT was politically important and the BWC was not.

In the NPT other forms of power have been asserted over the last decade. Indefinite extension of the NPT in 1995 was not taken by consensus, or a majority vote in favour, but as a result of the minority recognising their 'inability to prevail.'[9] The corollary of this is the recognition by the majority of their ability to prevail, call the bluff of the minority, and extend the NPT. In effect, binding all whether or not they wanted or supported such an outcome. Here consensus did not rule; it was put aside. There was, however, a price to such a decision. If not quite legally, then at least in spirit, the indefinite extension of the NPT was linked to amendments to the review process, the identification of specific 'yardsticks' for evaluation of implementation, and – at least by certain Arab states – the resolution on the Middle East for the creation of a WMD free zone in that region. Indefinite extension was a package deal in the eyes of many states parties. This reformed process of the NPT was itself expanded in 2000 at the NPT Sixth Review Conference with the identification of 'practical steps' to implement nuclear disarmament under Article VI of the NPT. Implementation of the '13 steps' and the new review process has itself run into trouble and is widely perceived as either not delivering the envisaged transparency, accountability, and disarmament, or failing to meet the new challenges in the nuclear non-proliferation area.[10]

The BWC Protocol was a post-Cold War negotiation. There was no superpower *fait accompli* or deal to be struck; the driving forces behind the Protocol were not the superpowers and there was no overt distinction between the different classes of states parties within the Convention. The *reformists* gained the ascendancy over time, but were able to pursue their aim of a strengthened BWC only when the more propitious climate emerged. The Cold War was not however completely shaken off. In the negotiations the states parties interacted in numerous ways and the balance between the caucus groups, the developed and the developing states, East-West, North-South, and the *reformists* and the *minimalists* all came into play.

During the 1990s states that had traditionally adopted the rhetoric of disarmament and verification now had to deliver; but in reality many of them had no intention of being subjected to intrusive verification when it became feasible to negotiate a BWC Protocol. Principal among these are Russia, China, India, Pakistan, and Iran. The US represents a special case because of its singular obsession with 'effective' verification and the abandonment of that in 1994. In the BWC all these states systematically frustrated the development of a robust

The Implications of Failure 227

compliance architecture. All put their own interests before the broader interest of ensuring biological disarmament. This is nothing new; indeed it is acceptable, legitimate, and the nature of diplomacy. Crucially, however, Russia, China, India, Pakistan, and Iran all offered statements throughout the negotiations which implied acceptance of multilaterally negotiated verifiable disarmament. They retained the rhetoric of multilateralism, yet each used every available opportunity to slow progress, create problems, weaken the provisions, and sideline important issues. The US, also, followed a similar approach, but there was no talk of a multilateral 'verification' regime, except at the point of rejection in 2001.

Translating these positions into something familiar we can see that the Cold War verification arguments between the superpowers have not come to an end: they simply involve more players. Russia is no more in favour of intrusive verification, transparency, or openness in the biological weapons area than its Soviet predecessor. The US has shifted back to its position that the BWC is unverifiable and is wholly unwilling to even discuss the prospect of negotiations on strengthening the Convention. China, India, Pakistan, and Iran have opted for the Soviet/Russian approach to disarmament: high on rhetoric and low on substance; to invoke special interests, ever ready to offer obstacles, slow down negotiations with calls for greater consideration by 'experts', and seek lowest common denominator solutions crafted by caucus groups. Under such strategies they can hide their own reluctance to actually deliver on verifiable disarmament. These states favour general principles of intent; language in agreements that leaves (too) much open to interpretation upon implementation. Sovereignty is paramount and they adopt an approach under which their declarations of compliance are sufficient in themselves. For these states their word is good enough and demonstrating compliance, accepting intrusive verification of compliance, and actually enforcing compliance with agreements is to be avoided. The lesson from history is somewhat different: the word of no state is good enough, whether it is the US or the UK, Russia or China, South Africa or Brazil.

Without doubt every state party active or present at the negotiations presented problems at some point in time. The issue here is the overall pattern of activity: who provided solutions to problems; was willing to seek compromise; was proactive rather than reactive; considered issues in depth and offered innovative and feasible solutions to the Ad Hoc Group and the problems of biological disarmament? And who reacted to issues; waited for solutions to emerge; lacked urgency or political will, offered unrealistic solutions, and opposed compromise? The latter group predominantly consists of the US, Russia, China, India, Iran, and Pakistan: the former group predominantly the European Union, South Africa, Canada, Switzerland, Australia, New Zealand, Chile, Brazil, and Norway to a greater or lesser extent. The degree to which these *reformists* could carry other states parties with them was crucial, but also significant was the ability of the US, China, Russia, India, Pakistan, and Iran to seek support in caucus groupings to mask and protect their position.

It is instructive that the breakthrough at the 1994 Special Conference occurred when the Western Group was united and the NAM as a caucus group was sidelined by non-aligned states acting in their own interests. Conversely, caucus solidarity in

August 2001 destroyed the Ad Hoc Group. The failure to issue a report which reaffirmed the mandate of the Ad Hoc Group left it defenceless. Opponents of it seized that chance. The August 2001 failure opened the door to the US attempt to terminate the mandate in December 2001 and as a consequence of the fallout from that, the current mess.

In the new multilateralism, real, powerful proponents of arms control and disarmament are actually few in number. Most of Latin America and the Caribbean with the exception of Brazil and Cuba, support efforts but do not forge the agenda: Africa remains poorly represented in the negotiations and is essentially led by South Africa, the former WMD poacher turned disarmament game-keeper. In North Africa and the Middle East, key states are not represented at the BWC negotiating table simply because they refuse to be bound by the Convention and are unwilling to undertake a legal undertaking to forego biological weapons: Egypt, Israel, Syria, to name only three who refuse to accept and bind themselves to a treaty outlawing weapons considered repugnant to humankind. Within Europe, the EU of 25 and states which usually associate themselves with the policies and positions of the EU constitute a bloc of approximately 30 states in favour of multilateral disarmament. Shifting East, with the exception of Russia and the Ukraine, most of the Former Soviet Union (minus the three Baltic Republics now in the EU) is not active in disarmament negotiations and it is assumed that these states would accept the will of the majority if any new agreement was to emerge in the future. Asia represents a conundrum: bound in group solidarity in most cases by the NAM these states parties remain reactive to events with the key NAM states of South Africa, Iran, India, Pakistan, and Brazil and China as the 'other' in many cases, battling for supremacy and leadership. In essence, because South Africa stands apart from the remainder of this group – and Brazil is certainly not as obstructive as the others – NAM positions are lowest common denominator and offer little in the way of substance. This is balanced in the BWC by the non-existence of the Eastern Group as an actor and the failure of the Western Group to act.

The new multilateral environment contains numerous positions which are increasingly difficult to narrow down into caucus groups or two party blocs such as developed versus developing, or East versus West, or, indeed North versus South. Of itself, this may not be an adverse development because the utility of many of these Cold War orientated groupings has to be seriously questioned. It is not their effectiveness that keeps them alive; it is conservatism and apathy, the lack of alternatives, geopolitical considerations, and an unwillingness to break them down and replace them with something more useful and truly representative. To borrow Alva Myrdal's phrase, the game of disarmament is now even more complicated with a greater number of states adopting the roles and positions formerly taken by the US and the USSR. Reality means it will become even more difficult to achieve agreement on arms control and disarmament treaties in any globally representative forum. Indeed, it may be impossible to secure any further disarmament or arms control agreements multilaterally unless there is a significant shift in the political will of states such as the US, China, Russia, Iran, and India. Likewise, unless states in Latin America, the EU, Africa, and the likes of Canada, Japan, Australia,

The Implications of Failure   229

and New Zealand are willing to break out of the caucus groups and form an alliance or coalition of the willing determined to pursue solutions to the problems of disarmament and apply real pressure to these states, there is little chance of further development in the multilateral arena. (Re)Solving the current crisis in disarmament and multilateralism will not stem from policies put forward by the likes of the US, China, Russia, and India. Only if the more *reform-minded* states decide to act will any solutions emerge. The emergence of real multilateralism had a significant impact on the dynamics of the negotiations. It was, itself, however, compounded by consistent failure to answer the most important question in arms control and disarmament: after detection, what?[11]

Compliance and enforcement

Why did so many states parties believe a Protocol was required to strengthen the BWC? It was certainly not out of a desire to push forward the development of international law *per se* or to create some kind of existential regime; it was because there were serious concerns about the level of compliance with the Convention and the ability of states parties to resolve compliance problems. Such concerns still exist and the problem has not gone away. By late 2001 the US had returned to a BWC policy not dissimilar to that of 1991. There could be no strengthening of the BWC without the issue of compliance being addressed. To some extent the renewed focus on compliance may have been a smokescreen in the BWC, masking the lack of detailed policy proposals put forward by the US and because its naming-names strategy at the first round of the Fifth Review Conference in relation to Iraq, the DPRK, Iran, and Libya (as well as Syria and Sudan), was announced with great fanfare but offered no substance in late 2001. However, the problem of compliance went much deeper than that: in particular the unwillingness and seeming inability of the international community to enforce its own agreements over time. In 1991 the attempts under the Trilateral Process to assess the scale of Soviet non-compliance with the BWC and the decision to forcibly disarm Iraq offered the prospect of enforcement of compliance. Iraq was the test case which the international community failed. Even now few seem to be embarrassed that it took the threat of war to even get the international community – in the form of the UN Security Council – to put pressure on Iraq to comply with its obligations of the previous decade and UN Security Council Resolution of 2002.

The US and the UK, however, are not paragons of virtuous compliance, giving up the Trilateral Process in the face of Russian obfuscation vis-à-vis its biological weapons infrastructure. Other developments paint a similar picture: the reaction to the Indian and Pakistani nuclear tests; the ability of the DPRK to frustrate the IAEA; and the willingness to permit Iran to offer less than full co-operation or honesty on its nuclear activities. The international community has adopted a soft stance on compliance; it wants the treaties, conventions, protocols, and law for its multilateral order but not the hard politics of enforcing such agreements. Far too many states consider upsetting the 'order' of the treaties and regimes by challenging suspected non-compliance as more unacceptable than actual non-compliance itself. Breaching norms, agreements and international arms control law has become overtly acceptable. This has permitted those opposed to multilateral solutions to claim multilateralism is synonymous with soft security and the avoidance of invidious issues. Proponents of multilateralism have yet to counter this in an effective manner.

Enforcing treaties and challenging non-compliance is not easy; indeed, it is easier to ignore non-compliance until it is too late. Challenging non-compliance requires difficult political decisions, a willingness to upset the consensus, and sustained and determined action by the state or states seeking to uncover or challenge suspect activity. Without glossing over the problems challenging non-compliance may in fact bring with it, a decision to act against alleged non-compliance and make states account for – or prove – their compliance requires concerted action. Those wishing to frustrate the process have time, geopolitical considerations, apathy, and the dynamic nature of international politics as their allies. And, as numerous cases have demonstrated, providing a 'smoking gun' to convince other states is not at all easy.

There are many lessons still to be drawn from this – as well as its partial reversal in 2002-2003 in relation to Iraq and Iran – but fundamental among them is a lesson that it is either overlooked or considered undiplomatic to draw attention to it. It is, however, a fact that cannot be ignored if a new disarmament agenda is to be developed. Most states are in compliance with their undertakings. Of the 152 states parties in the BWC the vast majority are not suspected of any non-compliant activity. Suspected non-compliance cannot, however, be ignored, and the majority must bear the burdens imposed by a small number of hard cases. In the BWC the hard cases included Iraq (until recently), the DPRK, and Russia. For both Iraq and Russia, the compliance issue was taken outside the BWC. The Russian case is still outstanding. The DPRK has never been addressed in public, even though its nuclear activities are being addressed under the Six-Party talks. States have a tendency to deny categorically biological weapons programmes. For example, Ambassador Summerhayes of the UK stated in 1980 that the UK had 'never possessed any of the agents proscribed by the Convention in quantities other than those explicitly permitted.'[12] The USSR repeatedly claimed concerns about its compliance with the BWC were unfounded and propagandistic, while Iraq claimed initially not to have had an offensive biological weapons programme to UNSCOM.

The lesson is simple: states lie. This is not to say that all states lie all of the time. Neither is it to say that some states lie all the time and others are unfailingly honest; nor that some states lie some of the time and are honest in most, or some, cases. The issue here is not that only certain states deserve special attention. Some do, but the lesson is much broader: claims by a state can neither be trusted nor treated with authority unless evidence is presented to back up that claim. One should not assume that every state is in non-compliance, but if historical anomalies or concerns exist, or if what is said differs from what is done, or a state has, or had, a nuclear, biological, or chemical weapons programme (past or present) much greater transparency and openness must be provided to demonstrate compliance and assuage concerns. In the BWC this must include at least those states with past offensive programmes of different types, nuclear weapon states, those with declared chemical weapons programmes, and those subject to on-going compliance concerns with the NPT, BWC, or CWC. In short, at least the following: Albania, Brazil, Canada, China, DPRK, France, Germany, India, Iran, Iraq, Japan, Libya, Pakistan, Poland, Republic of Korea, Russia, South Africa, UK, and the US. This is before the issue of Signatories to the BWC are taken into account – such as Egypt, Myanmar, and Syria – or non-states parties such as Israel and Sudan.

The word of a state – any state – is no longer satisfactory and proponents of disarmament must grasp this reality for a number of reasons. First, citizens and nationals cannot trust their own state's claims about compliance with an agreement unless evidence is available to substantiate it; verification of compliance begins at home. Second, it is no longer sufficient to pursue agreement on a treaty and hope that compliance with that agreement will take care of itself; there must be a willingness to devise mechanisms in an agreement which permit the enforcement of compliance on a graduated scale, but include provisions for worse-case scenarios. Third, there must be a willingness to uphold agreements and an acceptance that if the many will not fulfil their responsibility to ensure compliance, the few may have to take matters into their own hands. Fourth, penalties for breaching the agreement must be severe, and enforceable.

The few hard cases may make for bad law and these developments inevitably raise difficult questions about power, trust, accountability, equality, and sovereignty. The hard cases cannot, however, be ignored: either the international community drafts and accepts lowest common denominator 'law' designed for the majority (compliant) and as a corollary accepts that hard cases will have to be addressed outside such structures, or the international community gets serious about nuclear, chemical, and biological weapons in the hands of any state or any actor. The international community, and in this case the states parties to the BWC, must accept that disarmament of any kind is not achieved overnight and as a process it never ends: like domestic law disarmament needs constant attention and enforcement if it is to have any meaning.

The series of setbacks in recent years should not blind proponents of disarmament to possibilities, but neither should expectations of the past and past agreements become sacrosanct models. New ways of managing problems must be embraced. A multilaterally negotiated verifiable biological disarmament agreement is not on the agenda and from the evidence of the last decade opponents of that 'solution' are much greater in number than a single state. One of the principal misperceptions in the international community is that the current problems in 'multilateralism' rest with the US Administration of President Bush. Too many believe that 'if only Mr Bush would go away, the world would revert to the status quo ante, a mythical world of brotherly love and UN-mandated multilateralism.'[13] There is a significant element of truth in this observation and in the BWC it has manifested itself in two ways. Most states parties have adopted a 'battening down' approach whereby they are content to wait until the US Administration changes (now in 2008) with the belief that such a change will lead them back to the holistic, protocol-type approach to the BWC. Others have adopted an obstructive approach to US-led or US-supported proposals, driven by politics and an inability (or unwillingness) to recognise what else has been happening over the last decade. Reality must invoke a willingness to think about

232 *The Biological Weapons Convention*

arms control and disarmament differently. To do what the US correctly indicated was necessary; to think outside the box, even if its policy proposals for the BWC have been among the most unimaginative. *Minimalism* has not only been ascendant in the BWC since 2001, it has been unchallenged. With the demise of the Protocol came the death of the *reformist* project and its loss left the *reformists* bereft of ideas. New Zealand, Canada, Australia, South Africa, and the states of the European Union have so far failed to rise to the challenge at critical moments and this has allowed the US to ignore the concerns of its allies. Of greater import it permitted other *minimalists* (China, Russia, Iran, Cuba, Pakistan, and India) to mask their true positions and continue their reactive approach.

The mindset in the BWC created by the impasse in the negotiations is one where everyone else is content to simply wait until the US returns to the negotiating table and falls into line with the 'majority' world opinion that the BWC Protocol was, and is, the 'solution' to the biological weapons problem. It will be a long wait for anyone expecting that to happen; and in the meantime the biological weapons problem is only going to increase. In the new environment upholding the norm against biological weapons and providing the states parties to the BWC with the means to strengthen the Convention requires a new strategy. When one considers the negotiations on the BWC Protocol together with developments in international politics from 1991 through to the present day the fundamental lesson for the Convention is a simple one: there will be no BWC Protocol. It has too many enemies and there is no political will to pursue that solution. In light of that, what, if anything, can be done to manage the threat posed by biological weapons?

The individual to the international

The biological weapons problem is the issue not the BWC, or biological disarmament, or bioterrorism, or biocrimes involving assassination or deliberate contamination or harm using a pathogen. There is no single solution to the biological weapons problem. Whether or not a pathogen is used deliberately by an individual, a group to achieve political objectives by terror and violence, or by a state; whether or not the use of the pathogen is against humans, animals, or plants; and whether or not the pathogen is lethal or incapacitating, the problem is still one that involves the deliberate use of a biological agent. The biological weapons problem represents a spectrum, and just as action at the national level cannot resolve or manage all the security problems within this spectrum, neither can action only at the international level resolve nor manage this problem. A balance needs to be struck between national and international. Under the Protocol insufficient attention was paid to demonstrating implementation of the necessary national measures – viz. the willingness to delete a declaration on national implementation – whereas under the US alternatives the focus is orientated too much to national and like-minded measures, with a deliberate avoidance of international means to tackle the problem. The balance between national and international responsibilities that underpins the success of the CWC was not replicated in the Protocol.

The Implications of Failure   233

Since then the US has deliberately employed a policy of sidelining the BWC. Its preference in 2002 was for no further action except to agree to meet in 2006 at the Sixth Review Conference. It only supported and accepted the 'new process' under duress, after intense pressure from the UK and other allies, as an effort to build a coalition of support to act against Iraq, and on the condition that the proposal was a take it or leave it deal with a work programme that 'contained no flexibility ... which would potentially resurrect the "verification" protocol.'[14] US paranoia about the return of the Protocol or the creation of a Protocol by stealth means that is has ignored and undermined the linkages which exist between its preferred policy options – national implementation, export controls, biosecurity, penal legislation, an investigation process, biodefence, national and international public health responses to outbreaks of disease – and the BWC. Much of what the US desires could be achieved via the BWC *if* the US was to demonstrate serious leadership in the Convention. The BWC is certainly not the only answer to the biological weapons problem; but the biological weapons problem cannot be seriously addressed without a meaningful and effective BWC.

Therein lies the real political problem at this juncture. The US will not return to the negotiating table for fear of a Protocol-type approach and others will not take seriously the kind of measures which would have been required to bolster the BWC even with a Protocol. The states parties have backed themselves into a 'catch 22' situation where they cannot go back to the Protocol but anything other than the Protocol is not taken seriously. Someone has to break the impasse because as Smithson observed:[15]

> it should be considered foolhardy to neglect of any viable mechanism that can reduce the threat of weapons of mass destruction. Given America's singular status in the international community, custodianship of the ... BWC begins here, in Washington, DC.

The failure of American leadership, to use Dando's observation, also harms the US and its interests. As a result, what is happening in the BWC is a process not dissimilar to what Slaughter argued was happening with the state: disaggregation.[16]

The 2003-2006 work programme of the BWC is the manifestation of disaggregation within the BWC, but the process itself has been going on for a while outside the Convention. The 'broadening and deepening'[17] of arms control in the last three decades was accompanied by the multilateral tendency to centralisation: bringing together the constituent elements of arms control under one organization or institution as the central component of the regime such as the IAEA, the OPCW, and the CTBTO. This focus on the central component has ignored the other elements which have long provided support and supplemented the NPT, BWC and the CWC. In the nuclear area the discrete elements include the NPT, CTBT (and its predecessor), the IAEA, nuclear weapon free zones, export controls, and other national security and safety measures. In essence, a multiplicity of arrangements to manage the nuclear weapons problem.[18] In the biological weapons context two treaties compose the international legal architecture underpinning the norm against biological weapons. These two international agreements should have been bolstered and supplemented by separate national laws and regulations outlawing biological weapons at the national level. Additional components also developed from the need to co-ordinate export control policies while ensuring such co-ordination would not be the lowest common denominator solution: the Australia Group and the Wassenaar agreement. The BWC itself developed additional means such as the CBMs. None of these measures developed out of a desire by any state party to create a regime *per se.* These mechanisms developed because the BWC was not implemented effectively.

The objective of the Protocol was to bring as many of these arrangements under a single organization as possible: aggregation. In contrast, the future will consist of disaggregated arrangements devised by like-minded groups of states. The key to exploiting this development is not to dismiss disaggregation or the adoption of new policies by like-minded groups – no matter how large or small – as the abandonment of multilateral disarmament, but as a means to ensure that the norm against biological weapons is strengthened. The 1925 Geneva Protocol and the 1972 Biological Weapons Convention provide the legal authority from which countering the use, development, production, stockpiling, transfer and acquisition of biological weapons can base its legitimacy. The legal underpinning itself reinforces the normative aversion to such weapons and the moral authority to act against any preparations to use such weapons.

Much is already happening; indeed quite a bit of it was already in existence under the notion of a 'web of deterrence' involving arms control and disarmament agreements, export controls, protective measures (biodefence/public health), and penalties for the use of such weapons.[19] The various developments to counter the 'new' threat posed by biological weapons – most of it emerging as a result of both the failure of the Protocol and fear about terrorism since 11 September 2001 – still fit under the 'web of deterrence', or, as the International Committee of the Red Cross has termed its framework, a 'web of prevention' under its *Biotechnology, Weapons and Humanity* project.[20] This is clearly a broader framework than traditional arms control or disarmament, or the 'web of deterrence', but as the ICRC noted:[21]

> The responsibility to prevent hostile uses of biotechnology lies with each State. But it extends beyond governments to all persons, especially to military, scientific and medical professionals and those in the biotechnology and pharmaceutical industries.

The new reality is quite simple. Action is required at all levels; individual, sub-national, national, regional, like-minded, and international, public, private, government, and intergovernmental levels. Managing the biological weapons problems requires a rubric of measures from the individual to the international. There is no shortage of ideas or proposals in existence, as Table 10.1 illustrates. It is not that the means to give effect to biological disarmament and prevent either states, non-state actors or individuals from developing or using biological weapons are limited in number, or are too difficult to develop, or too existential. The means and methods do exist. Rather political will, and at this juncture, imagination, vision, ambition, and a strategy are lacking.

The Implications of Failure 235

Individual and national measures

Individual undertakings may be pledges by scientists not to be involved in offensive biological weapons programmes, similar to those proposed by Pugwash or other bodies.[22]

Table 10.1: From the individual to the international

Level	Measure	BWC link
Individual	Scientific pledges	Article IV
	Codes of Conduct	Article IV
Sub-National	Professional Body guidelines	Articles I, III, IV
	Research oversight	Articles I, III, IV
	Research publication guidelines	Articles I, III, IV
National	Health and Safety	Article IV
	Environmental regulations	Article IV
	Good Laboratory Practice	Articles IV, X
	Good Manufacturing Practice	Articles IV, X
	Product licensing standards	Articles IV, X
	Biosafety	Article IV
	Biosurety	Articles I, III, IV
	Biosecurity	Articles I, III, IV
	Public health	Article VII
	Biodefence	Articles I, III, IV, VII
	Export licensing	Articles I, III, IV
	National defence	Articles I, IV, VII
	BWC National Authority	Article IV
Regional	Mendoza agreement	Article IV
	European Security Strategy	Articles I, III, IV, V, VI, VII
Like-Minded	NATO	
	Australia Group	Articles III, IV
	Cooperative threat reduction	Articles I, II, III, IV, V, X
	G8	Articles I, II, III, IV, V, X
	Proliferation Security Initiative	Articles I, III, IV
International	Geneva Protocol	
	BWC	
	CWC	
	ENMOD	
	ICRC	
	International disease surveillance	Article X
	UN Resolutions	Articles I, III, IV
	UN CTC	Articles I, III
	Task Force Scorpio	Article VII
	WHO emergency response	Articles VII, X
	UN Secretary-General Investigations	Article VI
	No first use agreements	Articles I, VIII
	Criminalization	Articles I, III, IV, VIII

236   *The Biological Weapons Convention*

This approach may be expanded in various codes of conduct as the states parties to the BWC will discuss in 2005. Central to efforts overall will be the attitude of the scientific, biotechnology and pharmaceutical community; previously the community has been remiss in its overall engagement with the biological weapons problem. It was less than supportive of the efforts at the international level to strengthen the BWC. The community as a whole needs to recognise its responsibilities.[23] At the institutional level individual companies or professional associations such as PhRMA may develop their own codes of conduct or best practice guides relating to the biological weapons problem. These in turn may be bolstered and supported by the academic and scientific communities in various ways. One method explored recently was the research guidelines for publication of potentially dangerous information. Another would be through the development of ethics or professional committees to provide oversight about the conduct of certain scientific programmes to oversee what Kwik *et al* have termed the 'Persephone effect.'[24]

Such actions are supported by existing national and international efforts, best practice, regulations, and guidelines related to health and safety legislation, environmental legislation, biosafety and other mechanisms.[25] These represent in one very specific way the implementation of Article IV of the BWC, but the development of penal legislation and implementing legislation is another expected method of countering the threat posed by biological weapons at whatever level it occurs. Prosecution and proof of action and enforcement of such laws will generate further confidence in the discrete elements of the system.

Another new national measure can be seen in the development of laboratory security now under the rubric of 'biosurety' and 'biosecurity'.[26] This brings with it its own set of problems particularly when it occurs under an expanded biodefence programme resulting in a greater number of individuals having access to select agents. At the national level the US Government is very pro-biosecurity.[27] This makes a lot of sense, however, as other states parties and experts pointed out, in a country such as South Africa the utility of spending $1 million on biosecurity still fails to prevent an individual going into Kruger National Park and digging up anthrax spores. This is not to excuse inaction or assert biosecurity has no role to play, but biosecurity is neither a panacea nor an immediate global solution. It may make sense in the UK, other Western states and the US, but it misses other problems in other states; not least inadequate biosafety procedures in some states. Furthermore, as a recent US Inspector General report noted, enhanced security and safety for dangerous pathogens has not yet been translated into real security at the level of laboratories. Of the 11 University laboratories inspected all 11 failed basic tests of security and oversight of dangerous pathogens.[28] Biosecurity sounds good on paper, but there is much to work out conceptually at the global level and much to do practically at the level of facilities before it becomes a safeguard in which any trust can be placed. We must also recognise that different pathogen security measures may be appropriate.[29]

The next level of the new approach is one rooted in public health and biodefence. Again, recent events have thrown this neglected aspect into focus, but just as prior to 1995 few thought about the biological weapons problem in public

The Implications of Failure 237

health terms, the danger here is that the new focus on biodefence and public health preparedness is failing to think about biological weapons in an international context. Thus, while there is recognition that public health 'is just one layer in a comprehensive biological defence'[30] its link to a broader international effort has been lost. National measures such as Project Bioshield have some value (and present some new dangers), but in practical terms strengthening international health preparedness is equally important As Chyba noted, 'effective biological security demands that the United States act to improve global disease surveillance and response capacity – an element of "defense" that has no good nuclear or chemical analogue.'[31] The US – and other states – may not be as secure as they think unless response plans include an international component. Hence, even the most critical observers of an approach such as the BWC Protocol have suggested that an international disease surveillance mechanism would bring with it benefits linked to security in addition to the partial fulfilment of the Article X of the BWC.[32] The WHO or non-governmental groups such as ProMed have the expertise and experience to take the lead in this area. The next level would be emergency response and assistance, as required by Article VII of the BWC. In an ideal world the WHO would be best placed to take on this task, but the use of biological weapons may mean other mechanisms have to be put in place. Prior to the First Gulf War (1991) Swiss Disaster Relief in collaboration with the WHO established 'Task Force Scorpio' as a team of specialists to assess the degree of contamination from any use of weapons of mass destruction and how such use affected the civilian population. The UN Secretary-General had the authority to dispatch Scorpio and in the future such a group could be reconstituted as a first line of emergency assistance.

Regional, like-minded, and international measures

All these elements require some kind of co-ordination at different levels, but in addition what may be most important within the individual to the international context is a recognised national authority in each state. Traditionally, arms control and disarmament agreements have focused on national compliance through inspections or visits to military or civil facilities which meet the relevant criteria. With a complex dual-use problem such as biological weapons – particularly when the debate is politically fractious – the facility approach may not be the best means to move forward. The state party is responsible for the enforcement and application of its international undertakings at the national level. Ensuring biological disarmament in the UK is the responsibility of the UK Government; not the responsibility of, for example, PowderJect (or Chiron). It may be necessary to abandon the focus on actual facilities. Rather, states parties should focus on the implementation of the obligation(s) by the state party. A declaration by the state party on how it implements its obligations and a visit to the national authority to discuss and assess the extent to which such methods of implementation work may be the best starting point for demonstrating and assessing compliance. If there are concerns about the extent to which a state party carries out and enforces its obligations then the international community is faced with potential non-

238 *The Biological Weapons Convention*

compliance; moreover, in such a situation other states can have no confidence in implementation. This may require immediate remedial measures to be employed, such as the prevention of trade in certain materials, suspension of peaceful co-operation, and deliberate scrutiny of items and personnel originating or transiting that state. If there is no confidence in the ability of the state to enforce its obligations, what goes on in each facility is an additional concern – not the principal concern itself.

Bilateral agreements and regional agreements form the next level of activity. These can take on various forms such as licensing agreements for the production of certain goods to a particular standard (in this case bringing in standards of biosafety etc.) to Prior Informed Consent and biocontrol agreements, import and export of goods, disease surveillance at the regional level, export controls such as Wassenaar, through to a strategy for dealing with proliferation, such as the European Security Strategy (ESS). It could also take more declaratory forms, such as the Mendoza agreement in Latin America, or develop into a whole new concept of Biological Weapons Free Zones (BWFZs). Nuclear Weapon Free Zones have long standing acceptance, but in the absence of an international agreement to strengthen the BWC there is nothing which precludes regional groups of states parties developing an enhanced BWC structure at the regional level. Returning to the Mendoza agreement, these states parties could in principle take elements of the Protocol, amend it by agreement among themselves, and adopt it. Setting regional standards for access to pathogens, what is and is not permitted in terms of release of pathogens, or genetically-modified organisms, and other measures is acceptable.

Outside the regional context like-minded groups form the next level. In the area of export controls there is long standing precedent with the Nuclear Suppliers Group and the Australia Group. More recently, the development of the Proliferation Security Initiative and the activities of the G8 form the less-than-multilateral approach which has been so heavily criticised in some quarters.[33] It could, however, be developed by other like-minded groups of states beyond the EU, NATO, G8, Western Group and taken up by the likes of Association of South-East Asian Nations, the African Union, or the Organization of American States. Furthermore, the activities may not necessarily only be in the area of putative action and enforcement (although these are necessary), but could include regional disease surveillance, agreements on assistance and protection in the event of the use or threat of use of biological weapons, or indeed co-operation agreements related to the transfer of certain materials.

At the international level the traditional focus on the Geneva Protocol, the BWC and the CWC (because of the toxins overlap) should not be lost. Even internationally, however, the treaties are not the sole means of action. The role of UN Security Council under Article VI of the BWC for investigations remains important. More recently, UNSC Resolution 1540 of 2004 extended the issue of weapons of mass destruction beyond states to non-state and other actors. The next step for the UN is to permit both the Security Council and the Counter-Terrorism Committee to develop mechanisms to give effect to these sentiments. Another area where the UNSC may act is to co-ordinate with relevant bodies and outline a plan of action in the event of the use of biological weapons. This will serve both to

The Implications of Failure   239

reassure states parties that such commitments are being taken seriously and act as a deterrent in putting on notice any state or non-state actor that any use of biological weapons will result in an effective response at the humanitarian, political, and security level.

One dimension that is missing is the legal authority and determination to pursue and punish under the law those who use such weapons and assisted such use: the criminalization of the use of biological weapons.[34] Flowing from that is a requirement to be able to investigate use, or alleged use, of biological weapons. In considering how to do that in practice, lessons from the Trilateral Process, UNSCOM, UNMOVIC, the investigations conducted under the authority of the UN Secretary-General, the experience of the CWC and the IAEA, and the Protocol negotiations all come into play.

Many of the above measures can be tied into and linked to the articles of the BWC and the spirit and letter of the Geneva Protocol. The restrictive element has been either an assumption that giving effect to these agreements must happen by consensus agreement among all the states parties via the BWC or that because the BWC is 'ineffective' is has no useful role to play. This is not the case. All states parties should have a right to know what other states parties have undertaken to give effect to their obligations. Furthermore, all have a right to pass comment and discuss the measures taken by another state or group of states. The BWC does not, however, preclude a state party from adopting measures to prevent and ensure biological disarmament; indeed it requires them. Few realise what is actually happening at the different levels and how these discrete and disaggregated approaches contribute to the overall objective: preventing the use of biological weapons.

Conclusion

The history of the BWC indicates that it always required other measures to support it. The attempt to pursue and achieve 'disarmament on the cheap' did allow more amiable people to deceive themselves that they were safe from disease as a weapon. The world is not safe. Much has been achieved by the BWC but from the very beginning it was clear that certain states parties were not willing to accept disarmament that depended on the good will of others or take a willingness to trust other states as an adequate means to imbue confidence in the Convention. These concerns led to attempts to improve the BWC incrementally. The failure of the states parties to implement effectively the BWC gave rise to the evolution of the Convention at the review conferences, to the development of the export control arrangements, and the granting of authority to the UN Secretary-General to investigate alleged use of chemical and biological weapons. Between 1975 and 1991 what was technically and politically feasible gave rise to a series of evolutionary changes to the BWC and the way in which it was implemented. Some of these measures were innovative, such as the CBMs, but ultimately they failed to defeat the challenges posed by the biotechnology revolution, globalization, non-compliance by states parties, proliferation, and the rise of new threats. When the evolutionary approach failed the states parties agreed to attempt legally-binding improvements. The ideas and mechanisms within the BWC Protocol were not revolutionary *per se* but the attempt to bolster an existing disarmament agreement through the adoption of a Protocol which addressed nearly all the known weaknesses in the Convention was. It had not been tried before and it was the attempt itself that was revolutionary.

That revolution failed and the *reformist* effort foundered in the face of intransigence, prevarication, and sophistry by a powerful group of *minimalists* determined to prevent the BWC's states parties being collectively empowered with the mechanisms and legitimacy to require all to demonstrate their compliance with the obligation for biological disarmament. The contest of ideas between the *minimalists* and the *reformists* had been going on for so long that when the outcome was decided in July-August 2001 the *reformists* were not only defeated, but their vision destroyed. In its wake the triumph of the *minimalists* revealed there were no feasible ideas on how to strengthen the BWC. Incremental, evolutionary, and politically-binding measures had been tried before and failed. The legally-binding route to strengthening the Convention was no longer open. The failure of the BWC Protocol negotiations represents the end of approaches designed during the period of the Cold War. However, no one has any good ideas on how to overcome that failure and address the problems that still exist in the BWC. A strategy is missing. That is the most important implication of the failure of the BWC Protocol.

At a time when governments warn of the threat of biological weapons and when the print and academic media is awash with articles and warnings of a seemingly inevitable and impending doom perpetrated using biological weapons, solutions to the problem and threat remain partial, inconsistent, and non-binding. The states parties to the BWC have so far proven themselves unequal to the task. If any action is taken to reduce the scale and scope of the biological weapons problem in the twenty-first century it will be require a range of policies. At this period of time, these are most likely to be a series of *ad hoc*, casual and unco-ordinated strategies to combat the proliferation and potential use of such weapons. It is insufficient. Because the BWC Protocol negotiations failed and because the strategies put forward to replace the Protocol have been so unimaginative and hampered by the politics of the Convention, the BWC has been pushed to the periphery as a means to counter the biological weapons problem. The failure of the states parties has itself reinforced the disaggregation process. Those in favour of traditional multilateral undertakings have yet to articulate a new vision. The way back to multilateralism will have to include an acceptance of robust implementation and compliance mechanisms. States lie, cheat, and fail to live up to their obligations and until the most important question – after detection, what? – is grappled with multilateralism in the BWC will not be taken seriously again.

Until that time, the emergence of a biological disarmament governance structure implemented by a few like-minded states parties in one or two regions of the world will continue. Expanding this nascent structure to cover the whole of the biological weapons problem, co-ordinating it, and being aware of the breadth and depth of activities in this area actually requires an effective BWC. Indeed, the

The Implications of Failure

BWC is the lynchpin of the system if such a structure is to have an impact on the biological weapons problem as a whole. Ensuring disarmament requires, as Kervers noted, a legal underpinning and legitimacy. The BWC provides that, but the measures developed to give effect to the obligations in the BWC *must* be linked to it even if they are not developed under it in the traditional manner.

A framework exists for doing so, but it is not one with which many states parties will be familiar. The greatest problem in implementing effective biological disarmament remains getting states to act. The effort required is, however, worth it. The biological weapons problem cannot be 'solved' and biological disarmament is never 'achieved' because the dual-use nature of the knowledge, materials, and equipment needed to develop, produce, stockpile, and use biological weapons requires constant oversight, management, and enforcement. Doing that effectively requires action by all states parties to the BWC, the international community, regional, national, and sub-national bodies. A single treaty is never enough. As Moon noted: '[t]he more baffles that can be put in place while peace prevails, the greater the chance an international community has to prevent the use of a weapon it considers abhorrent'[35] The BWC is one such baffle, but it is not the only one. It is, however, at the centre of the legal, normative, and moral authority under which action is taken to counter biological weapons.

Notes

1.   Stuart Croft, 'Strategies of Arms Control: a History and Typology' (Manchester, Manchester University Press, 1996) p.31.
2.   Statement by Ambassador Donald A. Mahley, United States Special Negotiator for Chemical and Biological Arms Control Issues' Geneva, 25 July, 2001.
3.   U.S. Department of State, Washington File, 'Text: Bush Proposes to Strengthen the Biological Weapons Pact' 1 November 2001. See also, U.S. Department of State, 'Biological Weapons Convention (BWC): Summary of Proposals Within the U.S. Alternatives Package' Fact Sheet, Bureau of Arms Control, Washington, DC, October 19, 2001 http://www.state.gov/t/ac/bw/fs/2001/7912.htm.
4.   Jonathan B. Tucker and Raymond A. Zilinskas, 'Assessing U.S. Proposals to Strengthen the Biological Weapons Convention.' *Arms Control Today* 32:2 (April 2002) pp.10-14.
5.   United Nations, 'Report of the Ad Hoc Committee on Chemical Weapons to the Conference on Disarmament' CD/1170 (26 August 1992).
6.   Eric Arnett, 'The Comprehensive Nuclear Test-Ban Treaty' *SIPRI Yearbook 1997: Armaments, Disarmament and International Security* (Oxford, OUP, 1997) pp.403-407.
7.   Rebecca Johnson, 'CTBT Special Report' *Disarmament Diplomacy* Issue Number 8 (September 1996) p.22.
8.   Arnett, 'The Comprehensive Nuclear Test-Ban Treaty' p.407 (see footnote 14).
9.   John Simpson, 'The nuclear non-proliferation regime after the NPT Review and Extension Conference' *SIPRI Yearbook 1996 Armaments, Disarmament and International Security* (Oxford, OUP, 1996) p.563.
10. John Simpson, 'The nuclear non-proliferation regime: back to the future?' *Disarmament* 1:2004, pp.5-16.

11. Fred Ikle, 'After Detection – What?' *Foreign Affairs* January 1961. See also Brad Roberts, 'Revisiting Fred Ikle's 1961 Question, "After Detection – What?"' *The Nonproliferation Review* 8:1 (Spring 2001) pp.10-24.

12. BWC 1RC, BWC/CONF.I/4 p.27 and BWC/CONF.I/SR.3 p.9. Some caution is warranted here because the summary record is not a verbatim transcript and the exact words used by the UK Ambassador may have included an important proviso. However, the implicit claim of this statement is that the UK has never had an offensive biological weapons programme and that is untrue.

13. Gerard Baker, 'Bush should not be demonised' *Financial Times* 2 October 2003, p.21.

14. Guy Roberts, 'Arms Control without Arms Control: The failure of the Biological Weapons Convention Protocol and a new paradigm for fighting the threat of biological weapons' The United States Air Force Institute for National Security Studies, Occasional Paper number 49, March 2003 p.104 (see footnote 136) http://www.usafa.af.mil/inss/OCP/OCP49.pdf.

15. Amy E. Smithson, 'Prepared Statement Before the Senate Committee on Government Affairs Subcommittee on International Security, Proliferation, and Federal Services, 12 February 2002.

16. Anne-Marie Slaughter, 'The Real New World Order' *Foreign Affairs* 76:5 (September/October 1997) p.184.

17. Croft, 'Strategies of arms control: A history and typology' pp.58-60.

18. Jez Littlewood, Nuclear Weapons Proliferation: From arms control Regimes to Governance?' CEEISA/ISA International Convention, Budapest 26-28 June 2003. Simpson, 'The nuclear non-proliferation regime: back to the future?' pp.5-16

19. Graham S. Pearson, 'Prospects for Chemical and Biological Arms Control: The Web of Deterrence' Brad Roberts (Editor) *Weapons Proliferation in the 1990s* London, The MIT Press, 1995) pp.287-304.

20. ICRC, 'Biotechnology, Weapons and Humanity' See the website at http://www.icrc.org/Web/Eng/siteeng0.nsf/htmlall/bwh?OpenDocument

21. ICRC, 'Biotechnology, Weapons and Humanity' Summary report of an informal meeting of government and independent experts, Montreux, Switzerland, 23-24 September 2002, p.3.

22. Jacqueline Simon and Melissa Hersh, 'An Educational Imperative: the role of ethical codes and normative prohibitions in CBW-applicable research.' *Minerva* 40:1 2002 pp.37-55.

23. Claire M. Fraser & Malcolm R. Dando, 'Genomics and future biological weapons: the need for preventive action by the biomedical community' *Nature Genetics* online 22 October 2001.

24. Gigi Kwik, Joe Fitzgerald, Thomas V. Inglesby, and Tara O'Toole, 'Biosecurity: Responsible Stewardship of Bioscience in an Age of Catastrophic Terrorism' *Biosecurity and Bioterrorism* 1:1 (2003) pp.27-35.

25. Graham S. Pearson, 'The Complementary Role of Environmental and Security Biological Control Regimes in the 21st Century' *JAMA* 278:5 (August 6, 1997) pp. 369-372.

26. Michael Barletta, Amy Sands & Jonathan B. Tucker, 'Keeping track of anthrax: The case for a biosecurity convention' *Bulletin of the Atomic Scientists* May/June 2002 pp.57-62. Kathleen Carr, Erik A. Henchal, Catherine Wilhelmsen, and Bridget Carr, 'Implementation of Biosurety Systems in a Department of Defense Medical Laboratory' *Biosecurity and Bioterrorism* 2:1 (2004) pp.7-16.

The Implications of Failure

243

27. U.S. Department of State, Washington File, 'Interview with Assistant Secretary of State for Arms Control Stephen Rademaker' March 2003.

28. Department of Health and Human Services Office of Inspector General, 'Summary Report on Select Agent Security at Universities', March 2004, A-04-04-02000. Available at http://oig.hhs.gov/oas/reports/region4/40402000.htm.

29. John D. Steinbruner and Elisa D. Harris, 'Controlling dangerous Pathogens' *Issues in Science and technology online* 19:3 (Spring 2003) http://www.issues.org/19.3/steinbruner.htm.

30. Rebecca Katz, 'Public Health Preparedness: The Best Defense against Biological Weapons' *The Washington Quarterly* 25:3 (Summer 2002), p.70.

31. Christopher F. Chyba, 'Toward Biological Security' *Foreign Affairs* 81:3 (May/June 2002).

32. Alan P. Zelicoff, 'An Impractical Protocol' *Arms Control Today* 31:4 (May 2001) p.27.

33. Charles L. Thornton, 'The G8 Global Partnership and the Spread of Weapons and Materials of Mass Destruction' *The Nonproliferation Review* 9:3 (Fall/Winter 2002) pp.135-152.

34. 'A Draft Convention to Prohibit Biological and Chemical Weapons Under International Criminal Law' *The CBW Conventions Bulletin* Issue No. 42 (December 1998) pp. 1-5. 'International Criminal Law and Sanctions to Reinforce the BWC' *The CBW Conventions Bulletin* Issue No. 54 (December 2001) pp.1-2.

35. John Ellis van Courtland Moon, 'Biological and Toxin Warfare: Lessons from History' *The ASA Newsletter* Issue 77, 2000.

Index

Ad Hoc Group (of the BWC)
  Mandate, 215, 216
  Procedural reports, 215, 216, 217
aerobiology/aerosol dissemination, 76, 152
anthrax, 3, 13, 19, 76-77
Anti-Ballistic Missile Treaty, 189
Argentina, 17, 142, 176
Association of Southeast Asian Nations (ASEAN), 238
Atoms for Peace, 140, 164,
Australia, 17, 20, 29, 49, 52-53, 225,
  and export controls, 146, 152, 155
  and investigations, 119
  and peaceful co-operation, 174
  and special conference, 55
  and visits, 95, 106, 109, 112
Australia Group, 139, 141, 142, 143, 147, 151, 203, 234, 238,
Austria, 20, 28, 95, 152

Bacillus anthracis (see anthrax)
Bacillus subtilis var. niger, 129,
biodefence, 173
biological agents
  dual-use nature, 13, 75, 77, 232, 233
  production facilities, 77-79
Biological Weapons Convention (BWC)
  article
    I, 12, 13, 32
    III, 14, 24, 32, 139, 145, 157, 163
    IV, 157
    V, 18, 22, 24, 119
    VI, 18, 22, 119, 134, 189
    VII, 173, 237
    X, 24, 163, 237
    XII, 10, 16
  meeting of experts (1987), 23
  new process (2002-2005), 223-224
  original negotiations, 15-17, 24, 164-165, 204,
  review conference(s)

Fifth (2001-02), 6, 10, 12, 217, 223, 229
First (1980), 4, 10, 12, 16-19, 165
Fourth (1996), 10, 59, 188, 191
Second, (1986), 4, 10, 19-23, 145, 190
Sixth (2006), 223
Third (1991), 4, 10, 12, 23, 25-35, 57, 187, 224
special Conference (1994), 145, 166,
VEREX, 4, 5, 33, 35, 37, 47-54, 93, 132, 145, 166, 224
Biopreparat, 91
biosecurity, 236
biosurety, 236
biotechnology, 225
Botulinal toxin, 13
Brazil, 17, 53, 95, 96, 146, 156, 166, 169, 170, 171, 175, 176, 191
BWC Protocol
  article
    1 (general provisions), 123
    4 (declarations), 65-82
    6 (visits), 89-113
    7 (export controls), 139-157
    8 (CCC), 78, 110-112
    9 (investigations), 119-134
    14 (co-operation), 163-182
    16 (organization), 187-198
  clarification procedures, 5, 18, 108, 109, 110, 111, 124, 125, 211
  compliance, 9, 226, 230, 231, 232
  confidence-building measures (CBMs), 80, 122, 190
  co-operation committee, 174, 175, 181, 193
  declarations, 65-82
    accuracy, 91
    and China, 69, 70, 73, 74, 75, 78
    and European Union, 71, 75, 76, 77, 78
    and France, 69

BWC Protocol cont.

and Germany, 69, 71
and Japan, 69
and NAM, 70, 79, 80
and Netherlands, 73
and Russia, 69, 71, 72, 80, 81, 82
and South Africa, 69, 71, 73, 74, 80
and Sweden, 69, 71
and UK, 69, 73, 74, 77, 80
and Ukraine, 81
and US, 69, 70, 71, 72, 76, 77, 80, 82
annual, 70-79
  biodefence, 70-72, 206, 211, 212
  high biological containment (BL3), 72-74
  maximum biological containment (BL4), 72
  other facilities, 79
  plant pathogen containment, 74
  production facilities, 77-79
  other facilities, 77-79
  vaccine facilities, 77
  thresholds, 81
  transfers, 79,
  work with listed agents/toxins, 75-77
composite text, 67-68
initial, 68-69
  offensive programme, 68-69
  defensive programme, 69
notifications, 79-80
purpose, 66-67
VEREX, 67
declaration trigger, 67
definitions and terms, 12
Director-General, 197
disease outbreaks/reporting, 31, 122, 123
Executive Council, 109-111, 194-196
export controls, 5, 139-157
and Argentina, 142
and Australia, 146, 152, 155
and Austria, 152
and Belgium, 152
and Brazil, 146, 156
and Canada, 152, 155

BWC Protocol cont.

and Chile, 156
and China, 139, 143, 146, 147, 148, 150, 151, 155, 211
and Cuba, 139, 147, 150, 151, 155, 211
and European union, 155
and Finland, 145
and France, 140,
and Germany, 145, 148, 152, 155
and India, 139, 140, 143, 146, 147, 150, 151, 153, 155
and Indonesia, 139, 146, 151, 211
and Iran, 139, 142, 143, 146, 147, 148, 150, 151, 211
and Iraq, 142, 145
and Italy, 152, 155
and Libya, 139, 147, 151, 155, 211
and Nigeria, 146
and Mexico, 139, 151, 155, 211
and NAM, 139, 142, 148, 149, 150, 156, 157
and New Zealand, 155
and Pakistan, 139, 143, 147, 151, 155, 211
and Republic of Korea, 152, 155
and Romania, 146
and South Africa, 146, 150
and Sri Lanka, 151, 211
and Sweden, 146, 152
and UK, 148, 151, 152, 156
and US, 145, 148, 213
Australia Group, 139, 141, 142, 143, 147, 151
consultations, 154
guidelines, 153
in BWC, 144-147
in composite text, 150, 152-156
in CWC, 139, 142-144
in NPT, 139, 140, 141
legislation, 152
notifications, 153
Nuclear Suppliers Group (NSG), 140, 141
reviews, 154
Zangger Committee, 140, 141
investigations, 5, 119-134, 207
access, 130-133
alleged use, 121, 128

Index

247

BWC Protocol cont.
  and Australia, 119
  and Canada, 119
  and China, 120, 121, 124, 127, 129
  and Cuba, 120
  and European Union, 120, 128
  and India, 120, 124, 127, 129
  and Iran, 120, 122, 124, 127, 128, 129
  and Ireland, 120
  and NAM, 121, 123, 129
  and Netherlands, 134
  and Pakistan, 120, 124, 127, 129
  and Russia, 120-124, 127
  and South Africa, 119, 122
  and Sweden, 120
  and US, 120-123, 127, 129-130, 132, 214
  area, 128-130
  background information, 132
  CCC, 124-125
  equipment, 132
  facility, 121, 128, 132-133
  field, 121, 131-132
  initiation, 124-128, 134
  interviewing, 131, 132
  outbreak of disease, 122-124
  purpose, 121-122
  request for, 125-126
  right of refusal, 131
  sampling and analysis, 132, 133
  transfer, 122
  visual observation, 131, 132
 national authority, 238
 national legislation, 237
 non-compliance, 9, 188
 organization (OPBW), 171-172, 176-178, 187-198, 204
  and Brazil, 191
  and China, 191
  and European Union, 191
  and India, 191
  and Iran, 191, 193, 197
  and Japan, 191, 197
  and Pakistan, 196
  and Poland, 196
  and Russia, 120, 193
  and South Africa, 191, 192
  and US, 191
  Conference of States Parties, 193

BWC Protocol cont.
  co-operation committee, 193
  Executive Council, 193, 194-196
  liability, 196-197
  seat, 194
  Technical Secretariat, 193
  visits, 193
  waiver of immunity, 196-197
 peaceful co-operation, 163-182
  and Argentina, 176
  and Australia, 174
  and Brazil, 166, 169, 170, 171, 175, 176
  and China, 167
  and Chile, 167
  and France, 174
  and Germany, 174
  and India, 167
  and Iran, 166, 167, 169, 176
  and NAM, 165, 167, 169, 170, 171, 172, 174, 175, 177, 178
  and Netherlands, 174
  and New Zealand, 174
  and South Africa, 166, 172
  and Sweden, 164, 174
  and Switzerland, 174
  and UK, 165, 169, 170, 171, 174
  and US, 169, 170, 171
  article X (BWC), 163, 168
  co-operation committee, 174-175, 181
  declaration, 176
  disease surveillance, 173
  promotion, 172-176
  regulation, 176-178
  visits, 175-176
 review conferences, 4
 verification, 47, 213, 214
 visits, 5, 89-113, 207
  and Australia, 95, 106, 109, 112
  and Austria, 95
  and Brazil, 95, 96
  and Canada, 95
  and Chile, 96
  and China, 95, 97, 98, 100, 101, 102, 103, 106, 109, 112
  and Cuba, 94
  and European Union, 94, 95, 100, 103, 106, 112
  and France, 101, 104, 109
  and Germany, 99, 100-102

248   *The Biological Weapons Convention*

BWC Protocol cont.
  and India, 95, 97, 98, 99, 103, 106, 112
  and Iran, 98
  and Japan, 97, 106
  and NAM, 96, 98, 99, 100, 102-103, 109, 110, 111
  and Netherlands, 95, 109
  and New Zealand, 95, 96, 106, 109, 112
  and Norway, 96, 112
  and Pakistan, 95, 98, 112
  and Russia, 95, 97, 98, 99, 100, 101, 103
  and South Africa, 94, 95, 97, 99, 102-103, 106, 109
  and Sweden, 94, 95, 101
  and UK, 90, 91, 93, 94, 98, 101, 109, 112,
  and US, 90, 95, 97-100, 101, 103, 106, 108, 109, 111, 112
  clarification visits, 96, 108-111
  co-operation visits, 96, 174-175
  notice period, 105
  purpose of, 90-92, 104-105
  random visits, 93-108
  scope, 105-106
  selection criteria, 106-107
  transparency visits, 98, 99, 101
  voluntary, 105

Canada, 17, 53, 95, 119, 152, 155
CFE (Conventional Forces in Europe Treaty), 25
Chemical Weapons Convention (CWC), 21, 25, 33, 35, 57, 66, 90, 107, 177, 214, 225, 233, 238, 239
  challenge inspections, 120, 122, 126, 130, 132, 134
  declarations, 100, 104
  OPCW, 187, 189, 192, 195
China,
  and BWC review conferences, 20, 31, 32, 35, 36, 37
  and declarations, 69, 70, 73, 74, 75, 78
  and export controls, 139, 143, 146, 147, 148, 150, 151, 155, 211
  and investigations, 120, 121, 124, 127, 129
  and OPBW, 191

and peaceful co-operation, 167
and special conference, 54, 56-57
and VEREX, 53
and visits, 95, 97, 98, 100, 101, 102, 103, 106, 109, 112
codes of conduct, 236
Committee of Oversight, 190
compliance, 225, 229-232
Comprehensive Test-Ban Treaty (CTBT), 50, 59, 187, 233
Comprehensive Test ban Treaty Organization, (CTBTO) 187, 192, 195, 225, 233
Conference of the Committee on Disarmament (CCD), 164
Conference on Disarmament (CD), 15
confidence-building measures (CBMs), 22, 28, 31, 65, 67, 70, 77, 80, 122, 190, 191
Confidential Proprietary information (CPI), 107, 134, 208-209, 211, 213
consultative committee, 18, 22, 23, 31, 189
Convention on Biodiversity, 170, 174
co-operation committee, 174
Criminalization, 239
Cuba, 216
Cyprus, 17

disaggregation, 233,
disease Surveillance, 192, 237
DPRK, 91

ENDC, 15, 164,
entry into force, 209
European Security Strategy, 238
export controls, 5, 24, 139-157

Finland, 20, 54, 145
Food and Agriculture Organization, 173
France, 16, 29, 35, 48, 53, 69, 101, 104, 109, 140, 174, 192

general-purpose criterion, 12, 13, 204
genetic modification, 75-76
Geneva Protocol, 122, 139, 203, 238
Germany, 14
  and declarations, 69, 71
  and export controls, 145, 148, 152, 155
  and peaceful co-operation, 174

Index

and special conference, 54
and VEREX, 48, 53
and visits, 99, 100-102
Ghana, 17
Group of 8 (G8), 238
Gulf War

Hungary, 24

India, 37, 49, 51, 53-54, 56-57, 167, 191, 211, 225
  and export controls, 139, 140, 143, 146, 147, 150, 151, 153, 155
  and investigations, 120, 124, 127, 129
  and visits, 95, 97, 98, 99, 103, 106, 112
Indonesia, 56, 139, 146, 151, 211
industry, 208-209, 236
Intermediate Nuclear Forces Treaty (INF), 25, 189
International Atomic Energy Agency (IAEA), 65, 66, 90, 91, 140, 174, 187, 189, 195, 233, 239
International Centre for Genetic Engineering and Biotechnology (ICGEB), 174
International Vaccine Institute (IVI), 174
Iran, 14, 37, 49, 53, 54, 56-57, 98, 211, 216
  and export controls, 139, 142, 143, 146, 147, 148, 150, 151, 211
  and investigations, 120, 122, 124, 127, 128, 129
  and OPBW, 191, 193, 197
  and peaceful co-operation, 166, 167, 169, 176
Iraq, 25, 30, 49, 108
Italy, 196, 152, 155

Japan, 97, 196

Kuwait, 25

Legal Advisory Panel, 190, 191

managed access, 107
Meeting of experts (1987), 23
Mendoza agreement, 25, 238
Mexico, 20
Morocco, 166

mousepox, 76
multilateralism, 225-229

National Authority, 173, 237
national security information (NSI), 107, 134, 213
Netherlands, the, 18, 21, 48, 50, 53, 55, 73, 95, 109, 134, 174
Nigeria, 17, 20, 146
Non-Aligned Movement (NAM), 14, 54, 55, 57, 70, 79-80, 96, 98-100, 102-103, 109-111, 121, 123, 129, 139, 142, 148-150, 156, 157, 165, 167, 169, 170-174, 175, 177, 178
non-compliance, 206, 229-232
non-governmental organizations (NGOs), 26-27, 81
Non-Proliferation Treaty, 33, 50, 59, 65, 91, 164, 177, 187, 226, 233
Norway, 20, 96, 112
Nuclear Suppliers Group (NSG), 140-141, 238
nuclear weapon free zones, 238

Organisation for the Prohibition of Chemical Weapons (OPCW), 65, 187, 189, 192, 195
Organization for the Prohibition of Biological Weapons (OPBW), 4, 171-172, 176-178, 187-198, 204
Organization of American States (OAS), 238

Pakistan, 37, 95, 98, 112, 120, 124, 127, 129, 139, 143, 147, 151, 155, 196, 211
peaceful co-operation, 5, 24, 33, 163-182
Pharmaceutical Research and Manufacturers of America (PhRMA), 208-209
Poland, 196
project bioshield, 237,
proliferation Security Initiative, 238
Pugwash movement, 235

ricin, 3
Russian Federation, 53, 204, 205, 206,
  and declarations, 69, 71, 72, 80, 81, 82
  and investigations, 120-124, 127
  and OPBW, 120, 193
  and visits, 95, 97-99, 100-101, 103

Scientific Advisory Panel, 190, 191
South Africa, 205, 228
   and declarations, 69, 71, 73, 74, 80
   and export controls, 146, 150
   and investigations, 119, 122
   and OPBW, 191, 192
   and peaceful co-operation, 166, 172
   and visits, 94, 95, 97, 99, 102-103,
   106, 109
Soviet Union (USSR), 122, 188, 189
   and BWC review conferences, 15,
   19, 21, 28, 37
   and non-compliance with BWC, 36,
   206
special conference (1994), 47, 54-59
Stockholm International Peace Research
Institute (SIPRI), 35
Sverdlovsk, 19, 27, 108, 122, 123, 124,
129, 190
Sweden, 13, 16, 17, 21, 30, 55
   and declarations, 69, 71
   and export controls, 146, 152
   and investigations, 120
   and OPBW, 190, 191
   and peaceful co-operation, 164, 174
   and visits, 94, 95, 101
Switzerland, 17, 20, 30, 55, 174
START, 25, 189

Task Force Scorpio, 237
Treaty of Tlateloco, 189,
Trilateral Process, 48, 71, 76, 94, 108,
207, 219, 229, 239

United Kingdom (UK), 15, 21, 27, 29,
50, 53, 189
   and declarations, 69, 73-74, 77, 80
   and export controls, 148, 151-152,
   156
   and peaceful co-operation, 165, 169,
   170, 171, 174
   and visits, 90-91, 93-94, 98, 101,
   109, 112
United Nations (UN), 174, 190

Security Council, 119, 229, 238
UNMOVIC, 239
UNSCOM, 48, 94, 108, 123, 125,
151, 239
United States (US), 6, 9, 13, 15, 20, 189,
204, 205
   and BWC review conferences, 21,
   23, 27, 34-36, 48
   and BWC verification, 48, 214
   and constitutional issues, 131
   and CWC verification, 34, 48
   and declarations, 69, 70, 71, 72, 76,
   77, 80, 82
   and export controls, 145, 148, 213
   and investigations, 120-123, 127,
   129-130, 132, 214
   and OPBW, 191
   and peaceful co-operation, 169, 170,
   171
   and post-2001 BWC policy, 233,
   and rejection of Protocol, 209, 212-
   215
   and special conference, 54, 56
   and VEREX,
   and visits, 90, 95, 97-100, 101, 103,
   106, 108, 109, 111, 112

vaccines
Venezuela, 17
VEREX, 4, 5, 35, 37, 47-54, 93, 166
   Measures, 49, 107, 132,
   Report, 51-54, 58
Verification, 35, 48-50, 53, 54, 56, 214,
226

Wassenaar arrangement, 234, 238
World Health Organization (WHO), 174
World Organization for Animal Health
(OIE), 174

Yellow rain, 19, 27
Yugoslavia, 17

Zimbabwe, 55

UNIVERSITY OF WARWICK LIBRARY